Dimensions of Trade Policy

World Scientific Studies in International Economics
(ISSN: 1793-3641)

World Scientific Studies in International Economics includes works dealing with the theory, empirical analysis, and evaluation of international economic policies and institutions, with topics covering international macroeconomics and finance, international trade theory and policy, as well as international legal and political economy. Monographs and edited volumes will comprise the core of the publications.

Vol. 63 *Dimensions of Trade Policy*
by Martin Richardson (Australian National University, Australia)

Vol. 62 *International Trade and Labor Markets: Welfare, Inequality and Unemployment*
by Udo Kreickemeier (TU Dresden, Germany)

Vol. 61 *Achieving Financial Stability: Challenges to Prudential Regulation*
edited by Douglas D. Evanoff (Federal Reserve Bank of Chicago, USA), George G. Kaufman (formerly Loyola University Chicago, USA), Agnese Leonello (European Central Bank, Germany) & Simone Manganelli (European Central Bank, Germany)

Vol. 60 *International Macroeconomic Interdependence*
by Paul R. Bergin (UC Davis)

Vol. 59 *Contributions to the Economics of International Labor Standards*
edited by Arnab K. Basu (Cornell) & Nancy H. Chau (Cornell)

Vol. 58 *International Economic Integration and Domestic Performance*
edited by Mary E. Lovely (Syracuse University, USA)

Vol. 57 *Trade Policies for Development and Transition*
by David G. Tarr (The World Bank, USA)

Vol. 56 *Nontariff Measures and International Trade*
edited by John Christopher Beghin (Iowa State University, USA)

Vol. 55 *The Future of Large, Internationally Active Banks*
edited by Asli Demirgüç-Kunt (World Bank, USA), Douglas D. Evanoff (Federal Reserve Bank of Chicago, USA) & George G. Kaufman (Loyola University Chicago, USA)

Vol. 54 *Globalization: The Macroeconomic Implications of Microeconomic Heterogeneity*
by Andrei A. Levchenko (University of Michigan, USA)

The complete list of the published volumes in the series can be found at
http://www.worldscientific.com/series/wssie

63 World Scientific Studies in International Economics

Dimensions of Trade Policy

Martin Richardson
Australian National University, Australia

World Scientific

NEW JERSEY • LONDON • SINGAPORE • BEIJING • SHANGHAI • HONG KONG • TAIPEI • CHENNAI • TOKYO

Published by

World Scientific Publishing Co. Pte. Ltd.
5 Toh Tuck Link, Singapore 596224
USA office: 27 Warren Street, Suite 401-402, Hackensack, NJ 07601
UK office: 57 Shelton Street, Covent Garden, London WC2H 9HE

Library of Congress Cataloging-in-Publication Data
Names: Richardson, Martin, 1960– author.
Title: Dimensions of trade policy / Martin Richardson (Australian National University, Australia).
Description: New Jersey : World Scientific, [2017] | Series: World Scientific studies in international economics ; volume 63 | Includes bibliographical references.
Identifiers: LCCN 2017017759| ISBN 9789813207608 (hardcover) | ISBN 9813207604 (hardcover)
Subjects: LCSH: Commercial policy. | International trade.
Classification: LCC HF1411 .R495 2017 | DDC 382/.3--dc23
LC record available at https://lccn.loc.gov/2017017759

British Library Cataloguing-in-Publication Data
A catalogue record for this book is available from the British Library.

Desk Editor: Alisha Nguyen

Typeset by Stallion Press
Email: enquiries@stallionpress.com

Printed in Singapore

About the Author

Martin Richardson has been at the Australian National University since 2003. Obtaining his PhD in Economics at Princeton University, Martin has taught at Georgetown University in Washington DC and the University of Otago in New Zealand as well as at the ANU. He has published widely in international trade and applied microeconomics and has been an academic visitor at, inter alia, the University of Toronto, the Univérsité de Montréal, the University of Copenhagen Business School, University College Dublin and the University of Tübingen. He has been a Lay Member of the NZ High Court since 2000.

Contents

Acknowledgements

My interest in the economics of international trade was initially triggered by my lecturers as an undergraduate in New Zealand and Australia. Paul Wooding and Ben Smith were the most direct of these influences but, particularly once I had completed my Ph.D., the late Neil Vousden was also a supportive and influential figure. However, it was my exposure to international trade as taught by Avinash Dixit and Gene Grossman at Princeton that really persuaded me that this was a field in which I would like to work. Furthermore, both Avinash and Gene have been supportive and helpful throughout my career–supervision doesn't really stop with graduation! I am, of course, very indebted and deeply grateful to all of these figures, as well as to the many colleagues I have encountered through the years whose ideas have been stimulating and challenging. My assorted international economics co-authors, of course, must be at the inner circle of my acknowledgments, particularly those represented in this volume: Dominique Desruelle, Ryan Fang, Dan Knox, Simon Wilkie and, especially, Frank Stähler. But I have also benefited, as we all do, from extensive comments from discussants, referees, editors, seminar and conference attenders and so on. To identify all of these people would be impossible (and would crowd out too much of the volume) and to identify only a few would be improperly unfair to the others. Nevertheless, you know who you are and I am very grateful for all you have done over the years (or, more accurately, tried to do: I have not always been as responsive to suggestions as I might have been!)One of this diaspora who should be mentioned explicitly, however, is Keith

Maskus. Not only has he been a helpful and insightful colleague in the community of trade economists, but he was the initiative behind this volume. I am grateful to him for his encouragement and to the excellent and efficient editorial team at World Scientific Publishing for their help and assistance in putting this volume together.

Introduction

This collection of papers, published over the last 30 years or so, covers a number of areas in the economics of international trade. What they have in common is that they all have some connection to trade policy, be it explicitly directed at regulating international trade in some fashion, or some other intervention that has either direct or indirect consequences for a country's international trade. When we teach international economics, and in most everyday coverage of the economics of international trade, the traditional focus of market intervention has been on the setting and effects of tariffs. But there are many other dimensions of trade policy, a number of which are canvassed in this volume; hence the title.

In one sense, any government action that affects a nation's international trade can be viewed as a trade policy. From this perspective, of course, almost all interventions are trade policies in a general equilibrium setting. A more useful approach is to confine this appellation only to policies that not only affect a country's international trade but are either designed directly to do so or are chosen in the knowledge that they will do so. For example, a production subsidy to an industry might, in many circumstances, simply be a Pigovian intervention or the consequence of a political motive, but if it were to occur immediately after a negotiated tariff reduction one might suspect that its motivation is to partially undo the effects of the tariff reform; consequently, it looks like a trade policy. A more general view of the context in which explicit trade policies — tariffs, quotas and so forth — are set might argue that trade policy is a subset of other policies, such as competition policy or social welfare policy. Indeed, Evans and Richardson (2002) argue that, in the extensive economic liberalisation in New Zealand in the 1980s, "[u]nilateral reduction of border protection was essential because it was an important part of the broader programme to allow open entry into NZ markets and therefore make possible a regime of only light regulation".[1] That is, trade reforms were driven, at least in part, by a perception that competition policy in a small country must rely on open borders: domestic markets are too small to sustain high firm numbers, in industries with significant fixed costs, so the only discipline on domestic market power can come from foreign competition.

In this volume we consider five broad areas of trade related policy. The papers in this book are ordered, very roughly, in the order in which I first considered the topics they address. The first area is local content protection, even though it includes a paper from 2015, as this was an area I first studied in the late 1980s. The largest section of the book includes six papers on preferential trading agreements. There is a section looking at trade and competition policy and their interrelations explicitly, a small section on parallel imports and, finally, a "not elsewhere specified" section of miscellaneous papers, not easily categorised in terms of the preceding sections.

The first broad topic addressed in this book is local content protection. In its most basic form, this is a requirement that producers who sell goods within a country must use a certain amount (however measured) of domestic inputs in producing those goods in order to avoid some sanction, frequently a tariff on imported components. However, these sorts of schemes have also been applied to what might be considered "cultural goods": requirements that broadcasters must include locally produced content, however defined, to be permitted to broadcast at all. In each case the basic mechanism is the same and, if the scheme is binding, it will distort the input choice of a producer/broadcaster away from that they would choose in the scheme's absence. While the use of local content requirements has, at least in

[1]Evans, L. and M. Richardson (2002). Trade reforms in New Zealand: Unilateralism at work. In J. Bhagwati (ed.), *Going Alone: the Case for Relaxed Reciprocity in Freeing Trade*. Cambridge, MA: MIT Press.

principle, now been prohibited in many contexts under the TRIMs agreement of the WTO, they do live on in practice and have been reincarnated in preferential trading areas. In a free trade area (FTA), in order to prevent trade deflection — the entry of goods into a FTA through the lowest external tariff portal for re-export duty-free within the FTA — considerable practical effort is put into writing rules of origin (ROOs) to define what is and is not eligible for duty-free trade within the FTA. The economic analysis of these schemes looks very much like the analysis of local content schemes: sufficient use of within-FTA inputs is required to avoid a tariff penalty on downstream trade. For that reason, the older literature on content protection is still very relevant today.

The first paper in this section appeared in the *Journal of International Economics* in 1993 and focuses on the impact of a local content scheme when downstream competition is imperfect. In a perfectly competitive setting, a local content scheme will benefit domestic input producers but, by raising the costs of the downstream firms to whom it is applied, will raise downstream prices and hurt consumers. When there is imperfect competition downstream, however, things can be quite different. The paper demonstrates that a local content scheme that binds a foreign downstream firm can actually raise the profits of the foreign firm on whom it is imposed, but still be welfare improving for the domestic economy. The reason is that the model allows for upward sloping input supply curves in the home economy: consequently the increased demand for the local input stimulated by the protection scheme raises the costs for the domestic downstream rival of the constrained firm and this can be good for the foreign firm. Nevertheless, domestic welfare may rise if the profitability of domestic input producers is sufficiently enhanced.

The second paper in this volume was published in *Oxford Economic Papers*, also in 1993, and enrichens the analysis of content protection in a number of ways. First, it acknowledges that these schemes are typically imposed in an industry with downstream protection; indeed, it is the protected downstream market that provides the carrot to foreign producers such that they can absorb the stick of the content requirement. This means, however, that these schemes operate in a second best environment and the paper demonstrates how this typically will mitigate the negative effects of an upstream local content scheme. Second, the paper allows for the possibility of foreign direct investment in the upstream sector. As a result, foreign firms can meet any local content requirement by increasing their own domestically located production of the relevant input, through FDI. Third, the paper constructs a competitive general equilibrium framework in which all of these effects can be analysed.

The final two chapters in this first section both consider the application of local content schemes in what might seem a rather novel context: broadcasting. So-called "cultural goods" have long been granted special treatment in the context of trade agreements and liberalization, although whether this is testimony to some actual difference or to the political power of their lobby groups is not so clear. In 1993 France, in particular, pushed for a cultural exception to the general rules of the GATT to permit the use of quotas (i.e., local content requirements) and subsidies to cultural goods, particularly audiovisual products. Likewise, Canada insisted on a similar clause in the original NAFTA in 1994. The first of the two papers on this topic, which appeared in the *Economic Journal* in 2006, sets up a model of radio broadcasting in which, in line with the assertions of proponents of cultural quotas, there is some discernible difference between domestic and international music. This difference is modelled in a Hotelling framework in which consumers have different preferences for the two types of music. Commercial radio stations choose locations on the spectrum (that is, they choose a mix of local and international music) and a local content requirement is essentially a constraint on the stations' locations on that spectrum. The radio stations profit from selling advertising and the paper demonstrates that, absent a quota, the stations will partially differentiate themselves, a differentiation that is reduced by the quota, which also reduces equilibrium advertising as it requires firms to compete more closely. So the quota may raise consumer welfare in this model but it decreases diversity and lowers overall welfare as a consequence.

In that analysis the supply of "product" — music or other broadcasting content — is taken as exogenous but the next paper takes rather a different perspective. Appearing in the *Review of International Economics* in 2015 and co-authored with Simon Wilkie, this paper suggests that a cultural quota imposed, presumably, to encourage cultural diversity in some fashion may have quite the opposite result. This paper models the entire production process of commercial music, from bands through record companies to radio stations and consumers, and suggests that, if a local content requirement is particularly binding in some genres of music (presumably those dominated by international artists) then it is likely to encourage entry by domestic artists — the beneficiaries of the quota — into those areas. As a consequence, domestic music taken in the aggregate starts to sound more "international": precisely the opposite effect of that typically provided as a rationale for such quotas. Perhaps unfairly, the paper labels this the "Canadian diva" effect, suggesting that the abundance of successful Canadian singers in recent years does not seem to include artists with any particularly distinctive "Canadian" flavour!

The second broad topic addressed in this volume is the most substantial in terms of numbers of chapters and that is the topic of preferential trading agreements (PTAs.) This work was a significant area of interest of mine throughout the 1990s, a time in which the proliferation of PTAs and concerns amongst economists as to their consequences, particularly for the future of multilateralism, were starting to grow. This area has, if anything, only become of more significance since that time and the literature has grown substantially. Nevertheless, a lot of the issues being grappled with today are the same as those being considered in the 1990s. So, for example, questions about the effects of PTAs on non-members, the political economy of tariff-setting in PTAs, whether PTAs can be building blocks or will be stumbling blocks on the road to multilateral liberalisation, in Bhagwati's memorable phrase; these are all still important and largely undecided questions. Indeed, the entire relationship between PTAs and multilateral liberalization is an inenubilable one that will continue to provide grist to economists' mills for a long time to come.

The main focus of my work in this area has been on the endogeneity of tariffs set by the PTA against non-members. While the traditional Vinerian focus on trade creation and trade diversion is very much in the spirit of positive analysis, my own work here has been much more normative in flavor and the questions that come up throughout this section are generally concerned with *optimal* policy choices and responses.

The first paper in this section appeared in the *Journal of International Economics* in 1993 and is the most cited paper in this volume. It analyses a model in which the formation of a free trade area (FTA) leads, through an endogenous political mechanism, to a decrease in a country's external tariff against non-members. As such, the paper invites a fairly benign view of FTAs in that it suggests that they may not lead to increasingly isolated fortresses of trading blocks. The mechanism in the paper is a very simple one — if the price of a good in some sector declines in the face of intra-FTA competition, then cutting an external tariff against a non-member to the point at which non-members are slightly more competitive than the partner country will be politically attractive for a government, having approximately no effect on domestic producers and consumers but generating positive tariff revenue. This general idea — that forming a PTA endogenously leads to a lower tariff against non-members — has been investigated both empirically and theoretically, the latter line of enquiry identifying other mechanisms by which it might occur (and some that offset it) and the former line finding some evidence in its favour and some against. A recent article that canvasses a lot of the now extensive literature is Crivelli (2016).[2]

The next paper in the volume, from *Economics and Politics* in 1994, considers the perhaps under-researched question of why countries prefer FTAs to customs unions (CUs). Economic theory is very clear on this: a direct corollary of the Kemp-Wan theorem (discussed more fully below) is that a CU is at least as good as a FTA for member countries, under the conditions of the theorem. And yet PTAs

[2]Crivelli, P. (2016). Regionalism and falling external protection in high and low tariff members. *Journal of International Economics*, 102, 70–84.

in practice are far more likely to be FTAs than CUs. This paper argues that, under a specific model of lobbying, a FTA might emerge endogenously rather than a CU because domestic firms have less lobbying to do in the former than in the latter: a CU, of course, has a common external tariff (CET) which is set jointly in some fashion by all members. Even though there are presumably more firms involved in lobbying in a CU, with an industry able to team up with its fellows in its partner countries, the familiar free-riding problem of lobby group formation can undermine the attractiveness of a CU to politically active firms.

Why is it that PTA formation has flourished in recent decades? One answer sometimes provided is that negotiations amongst a smaller group of countries than, for example, the entire set of WTO members in multilateral negotiations, are more likely to lead to successful outcomes, at least in part because non-trade issues are more easily dealt with. It is well known that, in the standard competitive setting, an import tariff is essentially equivalent to a production subsidy and a consumption tax at equal rates. Consequently, if a country agreed to reduce a particular tariff, for example, but faced no constraints on its domestic policy setting, then it could simply impose a production subsidy and consumption tax and replicate the tariff it has just liberalised. In a paper that first appeared in the *Canadian Journal of Economics* in 1994, I looked at the extent to which this could also be done in a PTA, the issue being that these instruments are non-discriminatory across import sources whereas tariffs in a PTA are not. The paper shows that these instruments are, indeed, generally imperfect substitutes for trade policy in a CU but that there are specifications in which, nevertheless, even bilateral trade liberalisations such as a CU can be undone *ex post* by the use of these non-discriminatory tax and subsidy instruments. The paper makes a broad case in favour of policy coordination that goes beyond trade policy alone — this is a theme to which we return in the next section of the volume when we consider trade and competition policies jointly.

We have had call already to mention the concept of a ROO: rules of origin that are essential in a FTA to prevent trade deflection. But suppose that ROOs are watertight and set to 100% and consider a 2-country FTA in which one partner country has a slightly lower tariff against a particular good than the other. While imports of this good cannot enter the FTA through the low tariff country for sale in the high tariff partner, it is nevertheless the case that all domestic production in the low tariff country can be sold, duty-free, in the high tariff partner. If this were to happen, consumers in the low tariff country would now import from outside the FTA to replace the domestic production now being sold in the partner country, and tariff revenue earned in the lower tariff country would rise dramatically. In the high tariff partner, however, otherwise tariff-earning imports from outside the FTA are now displaced by duty-free imports from the partner and tariff revenue falls accordingly. In a paper published in the *European Economic Review* in 1995 the consequences of this sort of "internal trade deflection" for the tariff setting of partners was investigated and it was shown that, in the extreme case of identical partners, this competition over tariff revenue can lead to external tariffs being set to zero. This is a special and very extreme case, of course, but the paper argues that the possibility of this internal trade deflection might also contribute to lower external tariffs in a FTA than might otherwise be anticipated — again, this points to FTAs as building blocks towards liberalisation.

One of the earliest "optimistic" views of preferential trading areas stems from the justly celebrated Kemp-Wan theorem. This theorem establishes that any two tariff-ridden countries can, in the presence of lump-sum transfers, form a CU and set a CET such that no one is worse off (including the rest of the world) and, almost always, someone gains. There are at least two very major implications of this theorem. First, as already noted, it implies directly that a CU welfare dominates a FTA: the latter is, after all, just a set of tariff-ridden countries. Second, iterated application of the theorem suggests a route, via PTAs, to global free trade: the theorem applied to, say, countries 1 and 2 yields a Pareto improvement and if we then consider that CU as a single country, the theorem applied to that "country" and country 3 also implies the existence of a Pareto improving CU, and so on, inductively and inexorably, to global free trade. However, the paper itself is very clear that it is essentially an existence result: there *exist* a CU and a particular CET (the so-called Vanek compensating tariff) such that the rest of the world is unaffected by the CU but the member countries are typically better off. Nothing is said of the optimality of that CET and, in a paper published in *Oxford Economic Papers* in 1995, I argued that the theorem had often been misinterpreted to suggest that 2 countries participating in a Kemp-Wan CU could form that CU, set the compensating tariff, and unilaterally be sure of gains. That paper argues that the Kemp-Wan CU, even setting the compensating tariff, will almost always induce a tariff response from the rest of the world, if the latter is acting strategically. The essential point is that the Kemp-Wan CU holds post-union trade with the rest of the world constant and does so by setting the compensating CET that, in the language of offer curves, presents the rest of the world the same offer point after the union as it faced previously. But it is very likely that the infra-marginal offer curves of the union members will be changed by their internal liberalisation and, as a consequence, if the rest of the world is setting its own tariff optimally against this pair that will likely induce a change in the tariff faced by the CU. In a nutshell, this paper casts some doubt on the common misinterpretation of the Kemp-Wan theorem as providing a practical route to global free trade.

The final paper in the volume's section on PTAs again considers the issue of the external tariffs chosen by a PTA. This paper from the *Review of International Economics* in 1997 and co-authored with Dominique Desruelle looks at a political economy model of tariff setting with differentiated products, where tariffs affect domestic costs (and so export prices) and the size of any monopolistic rents. The consequences for the CET of a CU here depend on the interests that drive the political setting of tariffs (capital or labour in this simple analysis) and also on how tariff revenue is distributed, in the general equilibrium. The model demonstrates that it is possible for external tariffs to either rise or fall, depending on the constellation of political interests assumed to hold. One of the key elements in the model is that products are differentiated in what is now a very familiar fashion, with a love of variety captured through a CES utility function.

The paper demonstrates that, absent that feature, the formation of a CU would have no impact on external tariffs in the model's small country setting. The paper generates three broad results. First, in most cases the optimal PTA is, indeed, a CU (but, interestingly, there are permutations in which the CU would prefer to maintain a non-zero *internal* tariff, suggesting that Article XXIV of the GATT can be binding in this respect). Second, when there is no PTA and countries choose Nash equilibrium tariffs, typically tariffs set on a monopolistically competitive good exceed those set on CRS goods, because of rent shifting motives. Third, typically the external tariff of the CU will be higher than the unilaterally chosen tariff prior to the formation of the PTA. A notable exception to that is if tariffs are set to favour labour, in terms of their price effects, but tariff revenues do not redistribute back to workers (a shorthand for the notion that tariff revenues are not an important driver in the setting of tariffs.) In this case the "Jericho" version of Fortress Europe from the paper's title comes about. But this is a special case; more generally, the analysis is pessimistic about trading blocks as stepping stones to greater trade liberalisation.

All in all, this section of the volume suggests a number of reasons why preferential trading agreements can either be good or bad for non-members. Overall, I have probably taken a more optimistic view of PTAs than do some commentators in this area, but the practical rationale for PTAs seems to be changing over time and I think more work in terms of their political economy is likely to be productive in future.

The third section of the book collects three papers that have been written to look explicitly at the interaction between trade policy and competition policy in a country. Perhaps it is because I am a New Zealander that I am very aware of the inextricable links between these two areas of policy-making. As noted earlier, in a small country a liberal trading regime is not a luxury if the country wishes to discipline domestic firms; rather, it is essential. The first chapter in this section of the book, which appeared in *Oxford Economic Papers* in 1999, takes a very simple proxy for competition policy in a country — the number of firms competing in a Cournot oligopoly — and looks at its interaction with explicit trade policy. The central question posed (and answered, at least in part!) by the paper is, "if a country loses the use of trade policy, perhaps through successful multilateral negotiations, to what extent can it recreate the effects of that policy through its competition policy?" The suggestion that within-border policies could simply re-create border restrictions and thereby undermine trade agreements — discussed elsewhere in this volume when looking at customs unions and domestic taxes — has long been a concern of commentators. The paper opens with a quote from the 1960s expressing European concern over American corporations, and it is something that has been discussed in the context of U.S.-Japan relationships and, more recently, in most countries' trade relations with China. The paper considers a simple, linear IO model of Cournot competition between two countries. Governments maximise a weighted sum of consumer surplus, government revenue and total domestic profits and, initially, they do this by choosing a tariffs on imports and the number of domestic firms that operate in the global market. When the governments are unrestricted, their behaviour depends, unsurprisingly, on the weight they place on profits and the paper derives various permutations. Suppose both governments are entirely captured by domestic producer interests: they act to maximise domestic profits alone. The paper shows that, if free trade were to break out, each country would *increase* the number of domestic firms (and both governments would be worse off than before the liberalisation.) That is, rather than choosing to monopolise the domestic market in response to the loss of trade policy, the governments' best responses are to *increase* the degree of competition. The reason for this is straightforward and comes by direct analogy with the divisionalization literature. Baye *et al.* (1996)[3] show that parent companies in a Cournot setting have an incentive to create separate, independent, competing divisions in a two stage game in order to take advantage of a perceived Stackelberg-like incentive to commit to higher output in the game's second stage. Similarly here: it transpires

[3]Baye, M., K. Crocker and J. Ju (1996). Divisionalization, franchising and divestiture incentives in oligopoly. *American Economic Review,* 86, 223–236.

that a bigger share of a slightly smaller pie is always attractive in the Nash equilibrium. Of course, when both governments do it, it is not attractive at all.

The paper then considers the question of harmonisation of competition policy. When the countries are symmetric in terms of policy objectives it is easy to show that a mutual reduction in firm numbers makes both governments better off. But when one government is a profit maximiser and the other a wealth maximiser, it is shown that while mutual reductions in firm numbers raises perceived welfare for both countries, it is possible that mutual welfare might increase even if there is "disharmonisation" in the sense that the *difference* in firm numbers across countries actually rises. Hence the paper's title, referring to harmony in discord. The paper concludes by recording the results of a three country numerical simulation, which gives some interesting outcomes. Typically the formation of a CU alone reduces the welfare of member countries, but coordinating competition policy between members makes them better off — this is a result seen elsewhere suggesting that, to be welfare improving, a PTA might need to coordinate policies other than just with respect to trade. In this analysis, the coordination of competition policy within the CU also leads to an increase in the optimal CET — essentially, the reduction in internal firm numbers shifts profits towards nonmembers' firms and these can be clawed back through the higher CET. Indeed, when members coordinate their competition policy in this analysis, the nonmember is always worse off, regardless of its response; another pessimistic view, as if one were needed, on the role of PTAs as stepping stones to greater liberalisation!

The paper just discussed looks at a fairly abstract question; the next paper in the volume considers a rather more detailed application. Throughout the 1980s, many American commentators expressed concerns that perceived access to Japanese markets through negotiated reductions in trade barriers was somehow being undone by the inability to access retail distribution networks within Japan, these being "locked up" by tight and exclusive arrangements between Japanese producers and retailers. This paper attempts to model exactly this phenomenon, which it refers to as "domestic dealing" — it is not exclusive dealing, as usually understood but, rather, an agreement by a retailer to carry not one but many brands, the restriction being that they are all of domestic origin. The paper asks whether turning a blind eye to such an arrangement is more or less attractive when trade policy is or is not available and comes to a pessimistic conclusion: when trade policy can be used, allowing domestic dealing is never attractive but, if trade policy is removed, it may be welfare improving for the government to permit this kind of activity; in that sense "slack" competition policy can be a substitute for trade policy. The model used in the analysis appends, à la Besanko and Perry (1994),[4] a logit model of consumer demand for differentiated products to a circular city model of retailer location, but enriches that analysis by allowing many goods in which firms may be asymmetric (to distinguish foreign and domestic products.) The paper starts by establishing that, absent the tariff, while the entry of a single foreign firm will be welfare reducing for a country, the entry of two or more will be welfare increasing, no matter the number of domestic firms. A little bit of entry is harmful for profit shifting reasons but, as entry increases, the profits of each domestic firm are falling anyway (so, in a sense, there is less to be shifted) and, for a given number of domestic firms, more of the firms in the market are foreign (so profit shifting to a new foreign entrant is less of a concern for the domestic government as more of it is coming from other foreign firms.) But when tariffs can be chosen optimally and the costs of foreign firms consequently raised it turns out that foreign entry is always welfare improving; the reason is simply that the profit shifting that otherwise plagues foreign entry is now handled by the tariff while the benefits of foreign entry persist.

The analysis just described all occurs in a context in which consumers have no outside option: they must buy the good in question from someone. As a consequence none of these changes in tariffs or competition policy affect the retail equilibrium at all. Introducing an outside option into the model can lead to quite different results. For

[4]Besanko, D. and M. Perry (1994). Exclusive dealing in a spatial model of retail competition. *International Journal of Industrial Organisation*, 12, 297–329.

example, the tariff, by pushing up the price of all goods, will lead some consumers to not buy at all. This makes retailers less profitable and will lead to retail exit and this, in turn will raise transportation costs for consumers overall, which is welfare reducing. The paper then establishes that, when consumers can drop out of the market, it is possible that *any* foreign entry is welfare improving, even with no tariff and regardless of the number of domestic firms. This is a rather more positive conclusion, as it suggests that restricting foreign entry after a tariff reduction may not, in fact, be attractive to a domestic government.

The final paper included in this volume on the broad topic of trade and competition policies is one co-authored with Ryan Fang that first appeared in the *Review of Development Economics* in 2010. This paper, which grew from Ryan's honours thesis at the ANU, is motivated by Chinese concerns that acceding to the WTO would somehow "weaken" the Chinese market and expose it to foreign capital. Accordingly a number of high profile domestic mergers were both proposed and undertaken in China in the belief that this would somehow strengthen Chinese "resistance" to foreign firms. Given this belief that mergers were to improve rather than worsen "competitiveness", one assumes that these mergers were driven by the promise of synergies; in particular lower marginal costs. But the question then arises as to why this should be triggered by trade liberalisation — if these mergers are attractive for cost reduction reasons then why not reap the benefits of these synergies whether there is active trade policy or not? This paper contributes to the extensive literature on public and private incentives for horizontal mergers in an open economy. It takes a very standard linear IO Cournot model and distinguishes between two types of firm depending on their marginal costs. Using a notion termed "quantity equivalents" and developed by Ryan, we analyse the effects of mergers across different efficiency domestic firms, given a number of foreign firms and examine both private and public incentives for such mergers. The first result shown is that increasing foreign entry will, in general, discourage non-synergistic mergers, i.e., those that generate no cost savings. If mergers are what we term "weakly" synergistic and involve savings of fixed costs then mergers may become profitable, depending on the magnitude of the fixed cost savings. If they are attractive at some level of foreign entry, however, then they are certainly attractive at higher levels too. Turning to "strongly" synergistic mergers that reduce marginal costs, we find a similar sort of result: lower levels of foreign entry may discourage domestic mergers but higher levels of foreign entry will almost always encourage them. But the point at which the mergers are attractive to the participating firms, in terms of foreign entry, is generally lower than the point at which they are socially attractive. That is, "merger partners might generally be keener to promote a merger than should be the regulator". All in all, the findings of the paper seem quite consistent with the Chinese approach.

The fourth section of this volume contains a pair of papers related to so-called parallel imports. Sometimes called grey market imports, this refers to legitimate branded goods that are imported into a country without the permission of the intellectual property holder. For example, while many cities are awash with fake Rolex watches — a clear example of a black market — if one were to purchase, in the United States, a genuine Rolex imported from Europe but without the agreement of the US Rolex distributor or trademark holder, this would be a grey market, or parallel, import. The two papers in this section were early contributors to what has since become a significant literature on this topic. The first, from the *Journal of International Economics* in 2002, pays titular tribute to the Kemp-Wan paper already discussed here and makes a fairly straightforward observation. The standard explanation for parallel imports is that they arbitrage international third degree price discrimination. A global distributor facing different demand elasticities in two countries would like to price discriminate, charging a higher price in the country with the less elastic demand. If parallel imports are permitted they will flow from the low-price to the high-price country and may force the distributor to impose uniform pricing. If all markets continue to be served under uniform pricing, then it must be welfare improving from a global perspective as all consumers now face the same price so marginal rates of substitution are equated across all markets. However, it may be that the global monopolist is better off simply dropping the smallest markets and continuing to charge higher prices in its larger customer markets; in such a case it may be that global welfare falls. This paper looks not at global welfare but, rather, at the incentives facing individual countries in a world of price discrimination. It establishes a straightforward but fairly powerful result: in a one-shot policy game when countries simultaneously and non-cooperatively choose their parallel import policy, any Nash equilibrium must be one of uniform pricing to, potentially, a subset of the countries. The reason is simple. The countries that would like to permit parallel imports are those that face high prices in the discriminatory outcome and any potential outcome in which price discrimination prevails will trigger, for example, the highest price country to allow parallel imports. It will then be better off, even if pooled, by the monopolist supplier, with some other subset of countries, and so it will permit parallel imports. But that cannot be an equilibrium either, so long as there is any price discrimination: whichever country now faces the highest price globally has the same incentive to permit parallel imports. And so on and so forth: by induction, the only country that may prohibit parallel imports is the "last" of the countries served under a price discrimination regime but it will do it no good as it will be the source of parallel "exports" to the rest of the world.

This is a very stylised setting, of course, and the paper discusses some extensions. The first is to permit trade policy (discussed below), the second is to adapt policymakers' objectives to the Grossman and Helpman (1994)[5] political economy model, in which case it is shown that the conclusion of the paper may be overturned, and the third is to ask what will happen if countries could prohibit the *exports* of grey market goods. Given the intuition of the model just provided, it is not surprising that in this case third degree price discrimination will survive.

The second and last paper in this little section of the volume is co-authored with Dan Knox, and stems from some work in his Honours thesis at Otago University. Published in the *European*

[5]Grossman, G. and E. Helpman (1994). Protection for sale. *American Economic Review*, 84, 833–850.

Journal of Political Economy, also in 2002, its approach echoes that of other chapters in this volume, focusing on the impacts of trade reforms (the reduction of tariffs) on other policy choices (in this case the parallel importing regime). In a simple two country model we show that, absent tariffs, permitting parallel imports will always be attractive (the reasoning being essentially along the lines of the previous chapter) but it may not be attractive if the country has trade policy available to it and can levy an optimal tariff against the supplying monopoly. It is always the case that the relative attraction, in terms of welfare gains, of allowing parallel imports is greater when tariffs are not available than when they are. The monopolist always benefits from the abolition of any tariff against it, of course, but, interestingly, it may be that this benefit is greater than any loss from parallel imports and so a monopolist can gain from a trade liberalisation, even if it leads to parallel imports being permitted. The chapter concludes with a discussion of political economy concerns along the lines of Grossman and Helpman (1994).

The final section of this volume includes three papers that are not easily categorised and so are lumped together under the residual "Miscellaneous" heading! The first paper in this section was published in the *Journal of Environmental Economics and Management* in 2002 and, formally, looks at a model of vertical differentiation in which foreign and domestic consumers incur congestion costs whilst using a common resource. More particularly, it is an enquiry motivated by a common problem worldwide: with greatly reduced international transport costs, international tourism has grown very rapidly in recent decades and has led to pressure on domestic resources that can significantly downgrade the experience of domestic consumers in using those same resources. Given that international tourism is a valued export for many countries, the question then arises as to how best deal with this increased congestion. The paper is motivated by experience in New Zealand with environmental goods and, as such, models a couple of distinctive features: first, access to these resources cannot be differentially priced (by law) in a discriminatory fashion across local and foreign users; second, indeed prices cannot be levied to control access at all. Consequently, the only instrument available to a regulator is, essentially, a quality dimension, in terms of ease of access and use of the resource. The paper demonstrates that, in the context of a single resource, downgrading the quality of access may, in fact, be an optimal second best response to the increased congestion brought about by international visitors. When there is more than one environmental good available, however, the paper demonstrates that quality differentiation may be an effective policy choice, if foreign users have a generically higher taste for quality than domestic users: in that case quality differentiation through the implicit use of congestion costs can partially separate out consumers. The paper suggests that, at least in the New Zealand setting, this presents an accurate picture of reality, in which the so-called "Great Walks" are dominated by international patronage.

The second in this potpourri of miscellaneous trade-related chapters is a paper from the *Economic Record* of 2014 concerning so-called fair trade and is co-authored with Frank Stähler. The phenomenon of fair trade is something that has grown incredibly rapidly in the last decade or so but it has yet to receive much attention in the formal economics literature; this paper is an early exception. The idea of fair trade is that firms trading in certain goods will guarantee higher payments to the original producers of the goods — typically farmers in developing countries — than they would receive or do receive under existing arrangements. It is not an uncontroversial idea and there is a significant literature in other fields discussing the pros and cons of this sort of trade. One feature of fair trading organisations, however, is that they typically impose a range of obligations on their beneficiary farmers in order for the latter to receive a price premium. This paper, motivated by the international coffee market (perhaps the most prominent market in which fair trade prevails) models a fair trade provider as a vertically integrated firm, as it must be, in essence, if it is to ensure "fair" treatment "from the farm to the cup". It operates against non-vertically integrated profit maximising oligopolists but returns all its own surplus to farmers. Driven by certain features of the fair trade sector, this fair trade firm is plagued by moral hazard problems with its farmers. Consumers of the product are, in principle, willing to pay a premium for the fair trade product (the "warm glow" effect) and the paper analyses the international equilibrium in this setting. We consider a number of comparative statics with respect to trade costs and also consider welfare consequences with and without the warm glow effect.

The final chapter in this section and, indeed, in the volume is another paper co-authored with Frank Stähler that appeared in *The World Economy* in 2016. This chapter had its genesis in the so-called "food miles" debate: the notion that consumers should, in deciding between a locally produced and imported good, take into account the environmental cost of transportation. Essentially, this is an environmental version of much older "buy local" campaigns that has come into prominence in recent years. While it would not be surprising that a local producer would be keen on such a notion, what piqued our interest here is the observation that governments have gotten themselves involved in such campaigns. This led to the broader question of when a government might wish to promote the purchase of local goods rather than imports and the paper sets up a model in which the government can affect the premium that local consumers attach to local goods. The paper can be seen as contributing to a literature we have already discussed in this introduction and that is the idea that border barriers, once removed through trade negotiations, can be replicated through internal domestic policy. In this paper we investigate the incentives that a government has to provide information that affects this premium and how those incentives vary when trade costs fall. We suppose that this premium is drawn from some distribution and that the government can, at some cost, vary both the mean and dispersion of that distribution. We show that in autarky, given the profit maximising behaviour of the local firm, a shift in this distribution that increases consumers' willingness to pay for this domestic good will always raise the firm's profit but may or may not raise welfare. However, when we consider a trading equilibrium with a foreign good as well, so long as imports are positive then, in equilibrium, an upward shift in the distribution will raise both profits and welfare. Interestingly, however, a fall in the foreign price — our proxy for a trade liberalisation — reduces the incentives of a government to shift this distribution, whether the government be welfare maximising or profit maximising for domestic firms.

Part I

Content Protection

Chapter 1

The Effects of a Content Requirement on a Foreign Duopsonist

Martin Richardson

Abstract: This chapter considers the operation of a local content requirement in a duopsony between domestic and foreign firms and demonstrates its consequences for the domestic producer of a final good. It is shown that content protection may have perverse effects on a foreign firm's profits and may be welfare-improving overall, shifting profits from the domestic firm to both the foreign firm and domestic input producers.

1. Introduction

In recent years, there has been considerable interest in the analysis of local content plans (CPs). Such schemes, which seem to be growing in popularity internationally, require that a firm use a certain "amount" of domestically-produced inputs in producing its final output. These schemes seem to be imposed solely on foreign-owned firms (either explicitly, as was lobbied for in the U.S. auto industry in the early 1980s; or de facto, either in the absence of domestic firms or by the

Originally published in *Journal of International Economics*, 31, 143–155.

definition of domestic firms). To induce a foreign firm to produce in the country at all, an incentive such as a protected final-good market is usually offered.

Most existing literature on CPs has concentrated on consequences in the input market (the protection of which is presumably the intention of a CP). As a result, there has been little attention paid to the distinction between domestic and foreign final-good firms. But there will be repercussions for domestic firms of a CP imposed on foreign firms to the extent that both purchase inputs on the same market: contraction of the domestic industry is a likely effect of content protection. The welfare effects of this contraction need not be negative, however.

In this paper, we consider the effects of a CP imposed on a foreign firm that produces some final good in the home country using both domestic and (perfectly substitutable) imported inputs. There is also a domestic firm in the same industry that has access to only domestic inputs — the distinction between domestic and foreign final-good firms is solely in this different access to international inputs. The assumption that domestic and foreign inputs are perfect substitutes clearly is not a realistic description of the world, but it does focus attention on the consequences of content protection purely through repercussions on the component market. We demonstrate that the CP may raise the foreign firm's profits in this duopsony setting by committing it to use more of the domestic input, thus pushing up its price and leading the domestic firm to contract. Nevertheless, domestic welfare may be improved because of the increased profits of domestic input producers. This result is closely related to the idea of raising rivals' costs discussed by Salop and Scheffman (1983), but is a case where this strategy is facilitated by apparently harmful regulation: the foreign firm is required to use more domestic inputs, but this may actually make it better off.

An early analytical contribution to the literature on CPs was Grossman (1981). In that paper Grossman considers a partial equilibrium model of a competitive firm that produces some final output using both an input, which may be purchased domestically or imported, and another factor. The firm is subjected to a CP (and Grossman considers both CPs based on value-added and on physical requirements), and Grossman demonstrates the resource-allocating effects of each CP (their effects on total input use, use of imported inputs, total output and so on). He also considers how the analysis is altered in the presence of monopoly in the domestic input producing sector but throughout the analysis the final-good firm is entirely domestic, contrary to the stylized facts of markets where CPs are usually imposed.

A number of other papers have followed Grossman's, but only one addresses directly the issues targeted here. Mussa (1984) allowed domestic and imported inputs to be less than perfect substitutes, for example. Monopoly has been introduced into Grossman's framework at both the final-good level and the input level [see Mussa (1984) and Vousden (1987)] and the welfare consequences of CPs analysed under the different market structures. Krishna and Itoh (1986) examine the effects of CPs in an oligopolistic environment where a domestic firm and a foreign firm both produce the *input* good, in contrast to our model of oligopoly at the final-good stage. They demonstrate that the effect of a CP on the domestic producer's profits may be markedly different to its effect under perfect competition or monopoly, since it affects the very nature of the interactions between the two firms. More recently, Hollander (1987) has investigated the effects of various CPs imposed on foreign firms, but where there are *no* domestic suppliers — the market is a vertically integrated transnational monopolist with a continuum of production stages.

Davidson *et al.* (1987) do consider a duopoly between a domestic and a foreign firm in the final good market. They assume constant costs of inputs, the domestic component being more expensive than the imported version, and show that a content requirement then reduces sales by the foreign firm, increases sales by the domestic firm and makes the domestic firm better off. However, this ignores any repercussions on the domestic firm through the input market. We contrast their results with ours later in the paper.

Section 2 outlines the basic model we use and describes equilibrium in the absence of any CP. Section 3 then introduces a CP and derives its effects and welfare consequences. A final section concludes.

2. The model

We consider a linear model of two firms, one domestic and one foreign, each producing some homogeneous final good. The good is an importable in the small home country and may or may not be subject to a tariff. The domestic price of this good is constant at the world price plus any tariff; we set this price at unity, without loss of generality. Both firms produce this good using a single input and according to the same strictly concave production function. The input is produced in the home country under competitive conditions and the foreign firm can use either or both the domestically-produced input and/or a perfect substitute imported input. The domestic firm has access to only the domestic input.[1]

Letting M_{f} denote the foreign firm's use of the domestically-produced input and M^* its imports of the input, the CP can be written as

$$M_{\mathrm{f}} \geqq j(M_{\mathrm{f}} + M^*),$$

where j is the regulator's policy parameter. We assume that the domestically produced input is supplied competitively under conditions of increasing costs. To the extent that this is only tenable as a short-run characterization, the following is inherently a short-run analysis. The inverse supply curve[2] is thus $p[M_{\mathrm{d}} + M_{\mathrm{f}}]$, $p' > 0$, $p'' = 0$, where p denotes the price of the component, M_{d} the domestic firm's use of the component and $p'(p'')$ the first (second) derivative of p. Letting Q_i denote the output of the ith firm, i = d,f,

[1]This assumption is not critical to our main results, as discussed in section 4, but seems more realistic a representation of industries in which CPs are prevalent than allowing equal access to imported components. In the case of the auto industry, where these schemes are particularly prevalent, the foreign producer tends to be the subsidiary of a multinational and thereby has access to foreign components not available to domestic producers. (Of course, this makes the perfect substitutes assumption between domestic and foreign components a little less plausible, but perhaps not in the context of a particular model line.) This is also why we consider only physical content plans — to avoid transfer pricing issues that arise under value-added schemes.

[2]Throughout this chapter, square brackets denote functions and parentheses denote products.

we have

$$
\begin{aligned}
&Q_{\mathrm{d}} = Q_{\mathrm{d}}[M_{\mathrm{d}}], \quad Q'_{\mathrm{d}} > 0,\ Q''_{\mathrm{d}} < 0,\ Q_{\mathrm{d}}^{-1}[0] = F > 0,\\
&Q_{\mathrm{f}} = Q_{\mathrm{f}}[M_{\mathrm{f}} + M^*], \quad Q'_{\mathrm{f}} > 0,\ Q''_{\mathrm{f}} < 0,\ Q_{\mathrm{f}}^{-1}[0] = F > 0,\\
&p = p[M_{\mathrm{d}} + M_{\mathrm{f}}], \quad p' > 0.
\end{aligned}
$$

The imported component is available to the foreign firm at a fixed price, $p^* \gg p[0]$. The domestic price of the final good is fixed at 1, the cum-tariff world price.[3] This assumption enables us to concentrate on the effects of CPs on inputs without considering repercussions through the product market. So these firms have no monopoly power in the final-good market, but we assume they are both aware of their duopsony power in the market for the domestic component. In this case there are strategic interactions between the firms, and the CP affects the equilibrium of the game they play on the input market.

We assume that each firm entertains Cournot conjectures regarding its rival's behavior on the input market. The domestic firm chooses M_{d} to maximize profits of $\prod_{\mathrm{d}} = Q_{\mathrm{d}}[M_{\mathrm{d}}] - p[M_{\mathrm{f}} + M_{\mathrm{d}}]M_{\mathrm{d}}$ and the foreign firm chooses M^* and M_{f} to maximize profits of $\prod_{\mathrm{f}} = Q_{\mathrm{f}}[M_{\mathrm{f}} + M^*] - \mathrm{p}[M_{\mathrm{f}} + M_{\mathrm{d}}]M_{\mathrm{f}} - p^*M^*$. (The appendix contains complete calculations for this model.) First-order necessary conditions for each firm for the optimal choice of inputs allow for the effect each firm's demand for M has on its price:

$$Q'_{\mathrm{d}}[M_{\mathrm{d}}] - \{p[M_{\mathrm{d}} + M_{\mathrm{f}}] + p'[M_{\mathrm{d}} + M_{\mathrm{f}}]M_{\mathrm{d}}\} = 0; \tag{D}$$

$$Q'_{\mathrm{f}}[M_{\mathrm{f}} + M^*] - \{p[M_{\mathrm{d}} + M_{\mathrm{f}}] + p'[M_{\mathrm{d}} + M_{\mathrm{f}}]M_{\mathrm{f}}\} \leqq 0,$$
$$M_{\mathrm{f}} > 0 \quad \text{with complementary slack;} \tag{F$_1$}$$

$$Q'_{\mathrm{f}}[M_{\mathrm{f}} + M^*] - p^* \leqq 0, \quad M^* > 0 \quad \text{with complementary slack.} \tag{F$_2$}$$

Given concave production functions and the upward-sloping supply curve of the domestic input, these conditions are also

[3]The analysis would be unaltered if the good was an exportable from this small country — the domestic price would then be the given world price.

sufficient for a maximum. Thus, second-order conditions are always satisfied: $Q''_{\mathrm{d}} - 2p' < 0$, $Q''_{\mathrm{f}} - 2p' < 0$, $Q''_{\mathrm{f}} - 1 < 0$ and $2p'(1 - Q''_{\mathrm{f}}) - Q''_{\mathrm{f}} > 0$.

In the absence of any CP we may not observe an interior equilibrium in which the foreign firm uses both domestic inputs and imports, given Cournot behavior. For some M_{d}, if $p^* < p[M_{\mathrm{d}}]$, then the foreign firm uses only imported inputs. Similarly, if $p^* > p[M_{\mathrm{d}} + M_{\mathrm{f}}] + p'[M_{\mathrm{d}} + M_{\mathrm{f}}]M_{\mathrm{f}}$, where M_{f} solves (F_1) with equality, then the foreign firm uses only the domestic input.

Suppose the foreign firm does use both domestic and imported components. Then it earns profits of $\widetilde{\prod}_{\mathrm{f}} = \widetilde{Q}_{\mathrm{f}}[\widetilde{M}_{\mathrm{f}} + \widetilde{M}^*] - p^*\widetilde{M}^* - p[\widetilde{M}_{\mathrm{f}} + \widetilde{M}_{\mathrm{d}}]M_{\mathrm{f}}$, where a tilde over a variable denotes the value when (D), (F_1) and (F_2) all hold with equality. If p^* is such that the foreign firm uses only the imported component, then it must earn profits of at least $\widetilde{\prod}_{\mathrm{f}}$ by revealed preference.

We wish now to construct each firm's reaction function in domestic component space. Given $p^* \gg p[0]$, the foreign firm will always use some of the domestic input if the domestic firm uses none (and may use imports too if its demand is high enough). But, as the domestic firm expands the foreign firm would use less and less domestic input, either decreasing output initially (if $M^* = 0$) or just increasing its use of the import throughout without changing output. Even if $M^* = 0$ initially, eventually, when $p[M_{\mathrm{d}} + M_{\mathrm{f}}] + M_{\mathrm{f}}p'[\cdot] = p^*$, the foreign firm will begin to import. When $p[M_{\mathrm{d}} + M_{\mathrm{f}}] = p^*$, the firm will only use imports. When $M^* = 0$, (F_1) holds with equality. Differentiating with respect to M_{d} and M_{f} gives a slope of

$$0 > \left.\frac{\mathrm{d}M_{\mathrm{f}}}{\mathrm{d}M_{\mathrm{d}}}\right|_{\substack{(\mathrm{F}_1)\\ M^*=0}} = \frac{p'}{Q''_{\mathrm{f}} - 2p'} > -(1/2).$$

When $M^* > 0$, (F_2) implies that $\mathrm{d}M_{\mathrm{f}} = -\mathrm{d}M^*$, so differentiating ($\mathrm{F}_1$) with respect to M_{f}, M_{d} and M^* gives a slope of

$$\left.\frac{\mathrm{d}M_{\mathrm{f}}}{\mathrm{d}M_{\mathrm{d}}}\right|_{(\mathrm{F}_1)} = -\frac{p'}{2p'} = -(1/2).$$

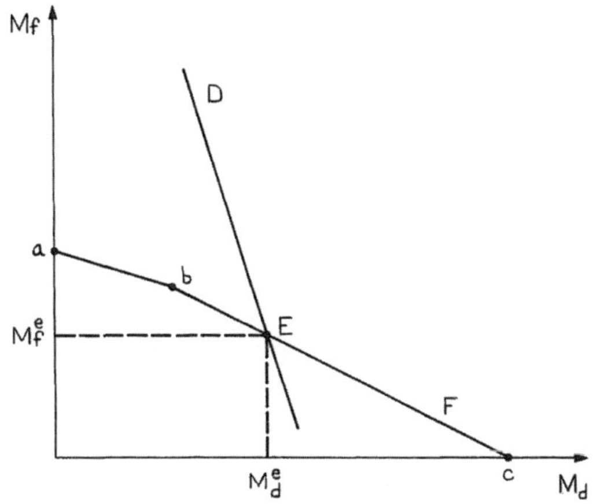

Fig. 1.

The foreign firm's reaction function for its M_f choice is thus downward-sloping against M_d: line F in Fig. 1. The firm uses no imports along the segment $\overline{ab}$ (so output is falling from a to b) but replaces imports for the domestic input one-for-one along $\overline{bc}$.

Similarly for the domestic firm, differentiating (D) yields

$$\left.\frac{\mathrm{d}M_\mathrm{f}}{\mathrm{d}M_\mathrm{d}}\right|_{(\mathrm{D})} = \frac{Q''_\mathrm{d} - 2p'}{p'} < -2.$$

We shall assume that $M^* > 0$ in the unconstrained equilibrium, but M_f may be zero. Figure 1 illustrates the case where both M^* and M_f are positive. The unconstrained Cournot equilibrium is at point E, the foreign firm using M_f^e of the domestic component, the domestic firm M_d^e. Given the identical technologies, this equilibrium entails a greater level of output by the foreign firm than by the domestic one, but with the latter using more of the domestically-produced input than the former.

3. Content protection

Suppose we now impose a CP on the foreign firm. Suppose the CP is set at epsilon above exactly the ratio of M_f to M^* that the firm chooses when unconstrained. This may be almost zero, depending on p^*. The foreign firm now chooses M^* and M_f to maximize profits subject to the CP above. The Lagrangian is

$$\max_{\{M^*,M_\mathrm{f}\}} \mathscr{L} = Q_\mathrm{f}[M_\mathrm{f}+M^*]-p[M_\mathrm{f}+M_\mathrm{d}]M_\mathrm{f}-p^*M^*+\lambda(1-j)M_\mathrm{f}-jM^*).$$

A binding constraint means $\lambda > 0$ and $j > 0$ means $M_\mathrm{f} > 0$. Also, when the constraint is just binding, we know $M^* > 0$ by our assumption that $M^* > 0$ in the unconstrained equilibrium. Hence, all first-order conditions hold with equality and equilibrium is described by

$$Q'\mathrm{d}[M_\mathrm{d}] - \{p[M_\mathrm{d} + M_\mathrm{f}] + p'[M_\mathrm{d} + M_\mathrm{f}]M_\mathrm{d}\} = 0; \tag{D}$$

$$Q'_\mathrm{f}[M_\mathrm{f} + M^*] - j\{p[M_\mathrm{d} + M_\mathrm{f}] + p'[M_\mathrm{d} + M_\mathrm{f}]M_\mathrm{f}\} - (1-j)p^* = 0; \tag{F}$$

$$(1-j)M_\mathrm{f} - jM^* = 0. \tag{CP}$$

Differentiating these conditions and evaluating at the initial level of j it is simple to show (see the appendix) that a small tightening of the CP will raise the foreign firm's use of the domestic input and decrease its use of the import, decrease the domestic firm's output, increase overall demand for the domestic input and either decrease the foreign firm's output or, if it only uses imports in the initial equilibrium, leave its total output unaffected.

All of this may *raise* the foreign firm's profits, depending on the magnitude of the CP requirement. Take the case of an interior equilibrium initially and consider a CP that exactly binds. For all M_f greater than the initial level, the CP has no effect — these satisfy the requirement so the foreign reaction function is unchanged above point E. But at any M_f below M_f^e the CP is violated, given the level of M^*. Now (CP) describes the change in M^* consequent on any change in M_f satisfying the CP, so differentiating (F) with respect to M^*, M_f and M_d solves for the slope of the foreign firm's reaction to a change in M_d when constrained by the CP and allowing for changes in imports

$$0 > \left.\frac{\mathrm{d}M_\mathrm{f}}{\mathrm{d}M_\mathrm{d}}\right|_{\substack{(\mathrm{F})\\(\mathrm{CP})}} = \frac{2j^2p'}{Q''_\mathrm{f} - 2j^2p'} > -1,$$

which is uniformly flatter than in the absence of the CP (as $j < 1$). Thus, the foreign reaction function swivels out around the initial equilibrium point. (It is easily shown that this is true even if

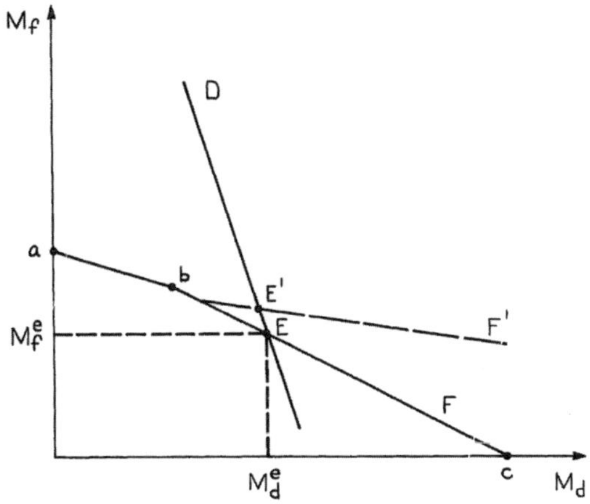

Fig. 2.

equilibrium was initially on the section $\overline{ab}$ in Fig. 1.) Tightening the constraint a little then flattens the reaction function more and shifts it up: more $M_{\rm f}$ is used at each level of $M_{\rm d}$. Figure 2 illustrates this case — the new foreign reaction function is F' yielding a new equilibrium of E'.

A small CP in this setting will make the domestic final-good firm worse off, the foreign firm better off, and the domestic input firm better off. If $M^* = 0$ initially, then the only difference is that foreign profits may be reduced by the CP. It may also raise domestic welfare overall. This all contrasts with the results of Davidson *et al.* (1987) where a CP imposed on foreign firms reduces their final sales, thus increasing those of their Cournot domestic-firm competitor, raising the latter's profits. This, however, may reduce domestic welfare as total sales fall and consumer surplus is decreased (as imports are prohibited in their model).

The intuition of our results is that, in the absence of any scheme, the Nash equilibrium in M quantities entails too much use of M from the firms' collective viewpoint, as each ignores the impact its use of M has on the other (through the price). From society's point of view, however, M is underused, as the firms equate their marginal revenue product with the marginal cost of M, not the price. A small

CP is then equivalent to a credible commitment by the foreign firm to use more of the domestically-produced input, and it induces a contraction in demand by the domestic firm. In this respect the CP moves the foreign firm towards the Stackelberg leader position in the game on the input market. From society's viewpoint the CP yields a gain in that it induces greater total use of M, but this is at least partially offset by the transfer of rents from the domestic final-good firm to the foreign one. It is more likely that there will be a net gain if (1) the input supply curve is flat, as then a given increase in M_{f} has less of an impact on p; and (2) the domestic production function is highly concave, as then a given increase in p has less of an impact on Q_{d}.

It may seem counterintuitive that the foreign firm's profits rise even though its output (and revenue) falls and it uses more domestic inputs. The intuition is that, for a small, just-binding CP, the adjustments in input use have approximately no effect on the firm's profits, by the envelope theorem, leaving the decreased use of the domestic input by the domestic firm as the sole effect on foreign profits. This latter effect is positive. A large CP requirement, on the other hand, could reduce foreign firm profits as the input adjustments become more costly.

It should be pointed out that this effect is not unique to a CP. In fact, a small tariff on the imported input would have similar effects, except that one can show that it will unambiguously raise domestic welfare because of its revenue effects. It should also be clear that allowing the price of the output to vary would not affect the basic intuition, but would complicate the analysis somewhat, as the firms' rents would stem from monopoly power in both the input *and* output markets.

4. Conclusion

One of the most common types of performance requirement imposed on foreign firms by host governments is a requirement that some minimum 'amount' of domestic inputs be used by the firm. Most analyses of such content requirements have concentrated on their consequences for input producers, ignoring the effects on domestic final-good producers who also use these protected inputs. This paper has attempted to remedy this omission.

As mentioned in Section 1, Davidson *et al.* (1987) also consider the case of two final-good producers, but playing against each other in the output market. They assume that production costs of the final good are constant (and the foreign firm has to be forced to use any domestic inputs at all, as they are more costly than inputs in the foreign country). They also have a prohibitive tariff on the final good. It is clear that this will be necessary for the model to work at all: otherwise the foreign firm would continue to export the finished good to the domestic country and would produce nothing domestically. If there was any foreign production domestically *and* imports of the final good, then the final-good price would be fixed and the duopoly would be impotent: it would consist of two firms with no market power. Accordingly, it seems perhaps more reasonable for final-good firms to extract their duopoly power on the input market rather than the output market. The effects of content protection are then markedly different, as shown above.

Our results are not sensitive to the assumption that we start with an interior equilibrium, as explained in the text. Nor is it critical, for the qualitative results, that the domestic firm not have access to the imported component. An increase in the use of the domestic component by the foreign firm will still induce a reduction in use by the domestic firm, which benefits the foreign firm in exactly the same way as above. Also, the assumption that the product price is fixed is not critical: relaxing it gives additional monopoly power to these duopsonists and the CP will have repercussions in the product market. This adds greatly to the algebra without illuminating our basic argument. Finally, it should also be apparent that the results do not depend on there being only two firms here — the same effects will be present in any model with Nash behavior on input markets, regardless of the number of firms. In a competitive framework, our results regarding profitability would be similar (but represented by an increase in the number of foreign firms and a decrease in the number of domestic firms as free entry and exit occurs in response to profits and losses) so long as the domestic supply curve of the input is upward-sloping. However, a CP would always have negative consequences for domestic welfare (aside from any second-best effects on final-good tariff revenue) as there would be no rents to shift on the input market.

References

Davidson, C., S.J. Matusz and M.E. Kreinen (1987). Analysis of performance standards for direct foreign investments. *Canadian Journal of Economics*, 18(4), 876–890.

Dixit, A.K. and V. Norman (1980). *Theory of International Trade.* Cambridge, UK: University Press.

Grossman, G.M. (1981). The theory of domestic content protection and content preference. *Quarterly Journal of Economics*, 96, 583–603.

Hollander, A. (1987). Content protection and transnational monopoly. *Journal of International Economics*, 23, 283–297.

Krishna, K. and M. Itoh (1986). Content protection and oligopolistic interactions. NBER Working paper no. 1843.

Mussa, M. (1984). The economics of content protection. NBER Working paper no. 1457.

Richardson, M. (1989). *Local Content Protection and Foreign Investment.* Mimeo: Georgetown University.

Salop, S. and D. Scheffman (1983). Raising rival's costs. *American Economic Review*, 73(2), 267–271.

Subcommittee on Trade, House Ways and Means Committee (1982). Survey of automotive trade restrictions maintained by selected nations, in: Hearings on Fair Practices in Automotive Products Act, March 2 (Serial no. 97–147) 111–123.

UNIDO (1986). Industrial policy in the developing countries: An analysis of local content regulations (UNIDO/IS.606, 3 February).

Vousden, N. (1987). Content protection and tariffs under monopoly and competition. *Journal of International Economics*, 23(3/4), 263–282.

Appendix

In the absence of a CP, the domestic firm chooses M_{d} to maximize

$$\prod_{\mathrm{d}} = Q_{\mathrm{d}}[M_{\mathrm{d}}] - p[M_{\mathrm{f}} + M_{\mathrm{d}}]M_{\mathrm{d}}.$$

The first-order condition for this problem is listed as (D) in the text. For the foreign firm, the problem is to choose M_{f} and M^* to maximize

$$\prod_{\mathrm{f}} = Q_{\mathrm{f}}[M_{\mathrm{f}} + M^*] - p[M_{\mathrm{f}} + M_{\mathrm{d}}]M_{\mathrm{f}} - p^* M^*.$$

The first-order conditions for this problem are listed as (F_1) and (F_2) in the text.

When a CP is imposed, the domestic firm's problem is unchanged. But the foreign firm now must choose M_{f} and M^* to maximize the following Lagrangian:

$$\mathscr{L} - Q_{\mathrm{f}}[M_{\mathrm{f}} + M^*] - p[M_{\mathrm{f}} + M_{\mathrm{d}}]M_{\mathrm{f}} - p^* M^* + \lambda((1-j)M_{\mathrm{f}} - jM^*).$$

First-order conditions for this problem are rewritten as (CP) and (F) in the text.

Differentiating (D), (F) and (CP), we can write

$$\begin{bmatrix} Q_{\mathrm{d}}'' - 2p' & -p' & 0 \\ -jp' & Q_{\mathrm{f}}'' - 2jp' & Q_{\mathrm{f}}'' \\ 0 & 1-j & -j \end{bmatrix} \begin{bmatrix} \mathrm{d}M_{\mathrm{d}} \\ \mathrm{d}M_{\mathrm{f}} \\ \mathrm{d}M^* \end{bmatrix} = \begin{bmatrix} 0 \\ (p + M_{\mathrm{f}}p' - p^*) \\ M_{\mathrm{f}} + M^* \end{bmatrix} \mathrm{d}_j.$$

Defining the determinant of the coefficient matrix as σ, one can show that

$$\sigma = j^2 p'(2Q_{\mathrm{d}}'' - 3p') - Q_{\mathrm{f}}''(Q_{\mathrm{d}}'' - 2p') < 0$$

(by second-order conditions).

Denoting the ratio of M_{f} to $(M_{\mathrm{f}} + M^*)$ when unconstrained as j^*, note that at j^* we have $p + p'M_{\mathrm{f}} - p^* = 0$. We can now invert the system above to derive the following results discussed in the text:

$$\left.\frac{\mathrm{d}M_{\mathrm{d}}}{\mathrm{d}j}\right|_{j^*} = -\frac{1}{\sigma}(M_{\mathrm{f}} + M^*)Q_{\mathrm{f}}''p' < 0;$$

$$\left.\frac{\mathrm{d}M_{\mathrm{f}}}{\mathrm{d}j}\right|_{j^*} = -\frac{1}{\sigma}(M_{\mathrm{f}} + M^*)Q_{\mathrm{f}}''(Q_{\mathrm{d}}'' - 2p') > 0;$$

$$\left.\frac{\mathrm{d}M^*}{\mathrm{d}j}\right|_{j^*} = -\frac{1}{\sigma}(M_\mathrm{f} + M^*)\{(Q''_\mathrm{f} - 2jp')$$

$$\times (Q''_\mathrm{d} - 2p') - j(p')^2\} < 0;$$

$$\left.\frac{\mathrm{d}(M_\mathrm{d} + M_\mathrm{f})}{\mathrm{d}j}\right|_{j^*} = -\frac{1}{\sigma}(M_\mathrm{f} + M^*)Q''_\mathrm{f}(Q''_\mathrm{d} - p') > 0;$$

$$\left.\frac{\mathrm{d}(M^* + M_\mathrm{f})}{\mathrm{d}j}\right|_{j^*} = -jp'\frac{1}{\sigma}(M_\mathrm{f} + M^*)\{2Q''_\mathrm{d} - 3p'\} < 0.$$

Note that even if M_f is zero initially, so that $j^* = 0$, all the qualitative results above are unchanged. To see the consequences for the foreign firm's profits, $\prod_\mathrm{f}$, note that

$$\left.\frac{\mathrm{d}\prod_\mathrm{f}}{\mathrm{d}j}\right|_{j^*} = \frac{\partial \prod_\mathrm{f}}{\partial M_\mathrm{f}}\frac{\mathrm{d}M_\mathrm{f}}{\mathrm{d}j} + \frac{\partial \prod_\mathrm{f}}{\partial M^*}\frac{\mathrm{d}M^*}{\mathrm{d}j} + \frac{\partial \prod_\mathrm{f}}{\partial M_\mathrm{d}}\frac{\mathrm{d}M_\mathrm{d}}{\mathrm{d}j}$$

$$= \frac{\partial \prod_\mathrm{f}}{\partial M_\mathrm{d}}\frac{\mathrm{d}M_\mathrm{d}}{\mathrm{d}j} \text{ by first-order conditions at } j^*$$

$$= -M_\mathrm{f}p'\frac{\mathrm{d}M_\mathrm{d}}{\mathrm{d}j} > 0.$$

Similarly,

$$\left.\frac{\mathrm{d}\prod_\mathrm{d}}{\mathrm{d}j}\right|_{j^*} = -M_\mathrm{d}p'\frac{\mathrm{d}M_\mathrm{f}}{\mathrm{d}j} < 0.$$

We can define domestic welfare as the sum of consumer surplus, the domestic final-good firm's profits, the domestic input-producing firm's profits and, in the case where the final good is an importable, any tariff revenues. (In the case where the good is an exportable, the following is correct with t set to zero.) Thus, where CS denotes consumer surplus, $\bar{p}$ the world price of the final good, t the specific tariff on imports, $\prod_m$ the profits of the domestic component industry, I imports and W welfare

$$W = CS + \prod_\mathrm{d} + \prod_m + tI$$

$$= CS + (\bar{p} + t)Q_\mathrm{d} + p[M_\mathrm{f} + M_\mathrm{d}]M_\mathrm{f} - C[M_\mathrm{f} + M_\mathrm{d}] + tI$$

after cancellations, where $C[\cdot]$ is the total cost of producing the input. Because the domestic price of the final good is unchanged from unity

$(= \bar{p}+t)$ as j varies, so total demand and CS are unchanged as the CP is varied. Furthermore, the change in imports is just the negative of any change in output by domestic and foreign firms, and competitive supply of the domestic input implies $C' = p$, so

$$\begin{aligned} \mathrm{d}W &= (Q_\mathrm{d}' + M_\mathrm{f}p' - C')\mathrm{d}M_\mathrm{d} + (p + M_\mathrm{f}p' - C')\mathrm{d}M_\mathrm{f} \\ &\quad - t\{Q_\mathrm{d}'\mathrm{d}M_\mathrm{d} + Q_\mathrm{f}'(dM_\mathrm{f} + dM^*)\} \\ &= (Q_\mathrm{d}' - p + M_\mathrm{f}p')\mathrm{d}M_\mathrm{d} + M_\mathrm{f}p'\mathrm{d}M_\mathrm{f} \\ &\quad - t\{Q_\mathrm{d}'\mathrm{d}M_\mathrm{d} + Q_\mathrm{f}'(\mathrm{d}M_\mathrm{f} + \mathrm{d}M^*)\} \\ &= p'(M_\mathrm{d}\mathrm{d}M_\mathrm{d} + M_\mathrm{f}(\mathrm{d}M_\mathrm{f} + \mathrm{d}M_\mathrm{d})) \\ &\quad - t\{Q_\mathrm{d}'\mathrm{d}M_\mathrm{d} + Q_\mathrm{f}'(\mathrm{d}M_\mathrm{f} + \mathrm{d}M^*)\} \end{aligned}$$

by the first-order condition (D). Substituting in for the expressions calculated above and rearranging gives

$$\begin{aligned} \left.\frac{\mathrm{d}W}{\mathrm{d}j}\right|_{j^*} &= A\{Q_\mathrm{f}''(M_\mathrm{d} + M_\mathrm{f})p' + (p'M_\mathrm{f}Q_\mathrm{f}''Q_\mathrm{d}'') \\ &\quad - t[Q_\mathrm{d}'Q_\mathrm{f}'' + jQ_\mathrm{f}'(2Q_\mathrm{d}'' - 3p')]\}, \end{aligned}$$

where $A = -p'(M_\mathrm{f} + M^*)/\sigma > 0$. If the two firms' technologies are identical, then the first-order conditions evaluated at j^* imply $M_\mathrm{d} > M_\mathrm{f}$ and $Q_\mathrm{d}' > Q_\mathrm{f}'$. Thus the first term in the curly brackets above is negative, the second is positive and the third is negative. Thus $\mathrm{d}W/\mathrm{d}j|_{j^*}$ is indeterminate in sign, but more likely to be positive the smaller is p' and the greater is $|Q_\mathrm{d}''|$, as discussed in the text.

Chapter 2

Content Protection with Foreign Capital

Martin Richardson

1. Introduction

In recent years, there has been considerable interest in the analysis of local content plans (CPs henceforth). Such schemes, which seem to be growing in popularity internationally,[1] require that a firm use a certain "amount" of domestically produced inputs in producing its final output. Whilst CPs have long been popular in LDCs as performance requirements on direct foreign investment,[2] they are increasingly required in defining "local" production in a world of trade restrictions and increasing direct foreign investment. A recent spat within the European Community illustrates this well: Japanese

Originally published in *Oxford Economic Papers*, 45, 103–117.

[1]cf. UNIDO (1986, p. 1). Other recent empirical work on CPs and their effects includes OECD (1987) and Guisinger (1986). Greenaway (1990) and Moran and Pearson (1988) provide useful non-technical surveys of some of the issues involved in CPs and other investment related performance requirements.

[2]Not only in LDCs. Herander and Thomas (1986) write, regarding export-related performance requirements, that, "[t]he automobile industries of Australia, Uruguay and Yugoslavia are subject to [these] schemes ... Trade performance policies, however, are not limited to the developing nations". Whilst Australians may not relish this categorization, Australia has imposed CPs on its automobile industry since 1965.

auto manufacturers assembling autos within the UK were accused by the French of using insufficient EC content for the autos to qualify as EC cars and to thereby be exempt from quantitative restrictions on auto imports.

The basic intuition underlying a CP, as articulated in Grossman's (1981) seminal piece, is that a CP will raise the price of domestic inputs, by requiring firms to use more of them, thus benefiting input suppliers and harming the final-good firms subject to the CP. The present paper addresses three aspects of CPs that have not been discussed to date. The first is that, to induce a foreign firm to produce in the country at all, an incentive such as a protected final-good market is invariably offered[3] and so CPs operate in a second-best environment. The European example cited above is a good illustration of this, as EC trade restrictions on imported autos are explicitly source-specific and the stimulus to Japanese auto investment is quite clear. This second-best setting of CPs has not been explicitly considered in the literature but is clearly an important element in any welfare analysis of a CP; we demonstrate that it tends to mitigate the negative effects of a CP.

A stylized fact of content protection is that it tends to induce foreign capital flows: when CPs were imposed on the auto industries of Mexico, Argentina, and Brazil, "[t]he immediate consequence ... was the proliferation of firms in all three countries ... Argentina alone attracted 21 ... there were 11 in Brazil and 8 in Mexico" (UNIDO, 1986, p. 40). This is the second focus of the present paper and, again, has not been dealt with in the literature. However, it is clear that it may well subvert the common intuition regarding CPs: if foreign

[3]This is an empirical point rather than an essential aspect of CPs. Clearly, to the extent that any inputs are cheaper in the host country than the source, foreign firms may still choose to produce domestically rather than exporting, in the presence of a CP. That is, it is at least conceivable that domestic cost advantages are sufficiently great that a CP, in the absence of a protected domestic market, does not drive out all foreign production leaving the market to be serviced by imports. In such a case, of course, it is hard to imagine why a CP would be imposed and, as a practical matter, CPs are inevitably imposed on firms that operate in protected markets: in a survey of the auto markets of 40 countries in 1980 every one of the 27 countries that imposed local content requirements also had some form of import restriction (Subcommittee on Trade, 1982).

capital flows into the input-producing sector this will tend to mitigate the price-increasing effects of the CP as the increased demand for domestic factors will be lessened.

Third, most existing literature on CPs has concentrated on consequences in the input market and there has been little attention paid to the distinction between domestic and foreign final-good firms. Yet these schemes seem to be imposed solely on foreign-owned firms (either explicitly, as was lobbied for in the US auto industry in the early 1980s; or *de facto* in the absence, or by the very definition, of domestic firms). This distinction may also mitigate the intuitive effects of a CP — if foreign firms subject to a CP can simply displace domestic firms (so that inputs previously produced for domestic firms' use are now purchased by foreign firms) the price effects of the CP are again reduced. We investigate these consequences for domestic firms and demonstrate that they may be quite dramatic.

As the analysis of international capital flows is best handled in a general equilibrium (GE henceforth) setting, a further contribution of the paper is a preliminary analysis of content protection in a traditional GE framework. We derive a simple expression identifying the sources of welfare gain and loss from a CP in a competitive constant returns to scale environment with international capital mobility and distinguishing between domestic and foreign firms. The consequences for capital flows and the second-best welfare effects of CPs are then clear. We show that a CP imposed on foreign firms has strong consequences for domestic final-good producers that do exist initially in this setting — any increased use of domestic components by foreign firms induced by the CP causes equal contraction of domestic firms. While the extremity of this result stems from constant returns to scale technologies, the basic idea is more general.[4] Once only foreign firms remain in the industry, further tightening of the CP affects capital and component imports, factor prices, and the output mix of the economy. We isolate the sources of welfare change due to the CP and show that welfare need not fall in this second-best environment.

[4]See Richardson (1991) for an analysis of this effect in a strategic duopsony setting.

An early analytical contribution to the literature on CPs was Grossman (1981). He considers a partial equilibrium model of a competitive firm which produces some final output using both an input which may be purchased domestically or imported and another factor. The firm is subjected to a CP enforced by a penalty tariff on imported inputs in the case of noncompliance. Grossman demonstrates the resource-allocation effects of the CP and also considers the effect of monopoly in the domestic input producing sector. No distinction is made between foreign and domestic final-good firms, however, contrary to the stylized facts of markets where CPs are usually imposed. A number of other papers have followed Grossman's (Hollander, 1987; Krishna and Itoh, 1986; and Vousden, 1987; for example), but none address the issues targeted here. The paper most directly relevant to the present one is that by Rodrik (1987) in which he considers the operation of another form of performance requirement often imposed on foreign capital: an export requirement. In many ways, the analysis of the present paper is closer to Rodrik's work than to the existing literature on CPs and can be thought of as complementary to it, extending it to content protection, a more common form of trade related investment measure.[5]

The remainder of the paper is organized as follows. In the next section, the resource-allocation effects of content protection are analysed in a GE framework with some sector-specific factors (Ricardo–Viner) to determine the effects on domestic final-good producers. In Section 3, we analyse the welfare effects of a CP in order to isolate the means of welfare change through which a CP operates in general and the actual welfare consequences of the CP here. Results are summarized in Section 4.

[5]Moran and Pearson (1988) report that the relative prevalence of different types of performance requirement varies across industries, but, "[i]n automobiles and chemicals... local-content requirements were generally more frequent than export minimums [sic]" (p. 126). As the automobile industry is one in which such requirements are prominent, this is a strong motivation for the study of content protection.

2. Resource allocation

In this chapter, we distinguish between domestic and foreign final-good firms in a simple model by assuming different access to international inputs. Furthermore, we assume that domestic and foreign inputs are perfect substitutes. While unrealistic, this assumption focuses attention on the consequences of content protection through repercussions on the component market. We discuss later some consequences of relaxing this assumption. The structure of the GE model involves production of a final good using both a primary factor and a produced component. We allow for both domestic and foreign firms, the distinction being that the latter can import the component as well as purchase it domestically,[6] and also has access to foreign component-industry capital. Only one sort of CP is considered, a physical content plan (in Grossman's terminology).

In specifying a GE model appropriately, a number of considerations are relevant. First, we suppose that all production activities display constant returns to scale. This is an obvious specification as we wish to consider a perfectly competitive benchmark case with zero profits in every activity. Second, we have not chosen a model of perfect intersectoral capital mobility *à la* Heckscher–Ohlin as it renders incomplete specialization unlikely in the absence of a CP here: we would have three productive activities with three fixed output prices (as the domestic component must sell for the (fixed) imported component's price) to determine only two factor prices. Accordingly, we have chosen a Ricardo–Viner fixed factors specification.

Thus, consider a GE model of two final goods and two primary factors. Both goods, X and Y, trade at world prices normalized to

[6]The justification for this is that in the case of the auto industry, where these schemes are particularly prevalent, the foreign producer tends to be the subsidiary of a multinational who would thereby have access to foreign components not available to domestic producers. (Of course, this makes the perfect substitutes assumption between domestic and foreign components a little less plausible, but perhaps not in the context of a particular model line.) This is also why we consider only physical content plans: to avoid transfer pricing issues which arise under value-added CPs.

unity, but the domestic price of the importable, X, is $p = 1 + t$ due to a domestic tariff. Regarding production, numeraire good Y is produced using labour and sector-specific capital which are available domestically in total amounts $\overline{L}$ and $\overline{K}_{\mathrm{y}}$ respectively, where a bar over a variable indicates that it takes a constant value. Production of X requires inputs of sector-specific capital, available domestically in amount $\overline{K}_{\mathrm{x}}$, and some intermediate good, M. This component is itself produced from primary factors: labour and sector-specific capital available in amount $\overline{K}_{\mathrm{m}}$. We allow for both foreign and domestic producers, the former employing foreign X-sector capital, K_{x}^{*}, and having access to foreign capital of the M-specific kind, K_{m}^{*}, in infinitely elastic supply at a price $\overline{r_{\mathrm{m}}^{*}}$, and imported components, where asterisks are used to indicate foreign quantities and prices.[7] Foreign producers import M^{*} of the component at a constant price $\overline{P_{\mathrm{m}}^{*}}$; domestic firms do not have access to foreign inputs. Thus any CP on component use will clearly only bind foreign firms. Letting X_{f} and X_{d} denote X production by foreign and domestic firms respectively, we can represent the model's structure schematically as in Fig. 1. Note that foreign firms can import the component, purchase it domestically or produce it domestically themselves. It is the possibility of purchasing the component domestically that establishes a major link in this model between the CP and domestic final-good producing firms. The possibility of producing the good domestically is the source of capital inflows into the domestic component-producing industry.

We now suppose that producers are subject to a physical content requirement. Letting M_{f} denote the foreign producer's use of domestically produced M and j the regulator's policy parameter, the CP

[7]Note that equilibrium conditions for capital flows can be interpreted either as specifying the determination of the rental rates for the two kinds of foreign capital, when the quantities are fixed, or the amount of foreign capital used when the world interest rates are given. Henceforth we consider only the latter interpretation for M-specific capital, in which the quantity K_{m}^{*} is chosen, and the former for X-specific capital in which the quantity is given at $\overline{K_{\mathrm{x}}^{*}}$. The reason for this is that we are thinking of X-sector capital as a managerial input. Such inputs are transferable — a manager may work for a foreign or a domestic firm — but are fixed in total supply.

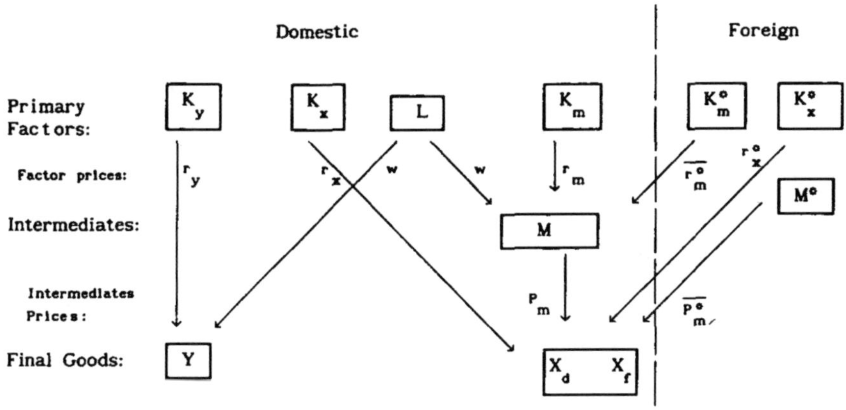

Fig. 1. The Structure of Production.

can be written as:

$$\frac{M_{\mathrm{f}}}{M^{*}+M_{\mathrm{f}}} \geqslant j \tag{CP}$$

We suppose henceforth that either the CP is mandatory or that the penalty for noncompliance is prohibitive. For the CP to be at all interesting here it must bind the producer, so we shall suppose henceforth that the CP holds with equality. Denoting the price of the domestically produced input by P_{m}, the content plan dictates the mix of M and M* that foreign firms will use, and the effective price of a representative unit of the component to the firm is thus $P_{\mathrm{a}} \equiv jP_{\mathrm{m}} + (1-j)\overline{P_{\mathrm{m}}^{*}}$.

Let $\gamma(w, r_{\mathrm{y}})$ represent the unit cost function of the Y industry — this numeraire good is produced under constant returns to scale (CRS henceforth) using labour (at wage w) and specific capital (with rate of return r_{y}). Let $\delta(r_{\mathrm{x}}, P_{\mathrm{a}})$ represent the unit cost function for the X industry where X is produced under CRS using specific capital (with rate of return r_{x}) and the produced input. In the absence of a CP, and assuming the foreign firm uses both domestic and imported components in equilibrium, P_{a}, the average price of a unit of this input, would equal $\overline{P_{\mathrm{m}}^{*}}$. However, as discussed above, a CP makes $P_{\mathrm{a}} = jP_{\mathrm{m}} + (1-j)\overline{P_{\mathrm{m}}^{*}}$ for foreign firms. Let $\mu(w, r_{\mathrm{m}})$ represent the unit cost function of the domestic M producing industry (using both labour and specific capital (with rate of return r_{m}) in a CRS technology) — identical for both foreign and domestic firms.

In the absence of a CP, domestic firms produce all three goods and foreign firms both the final good X and the component M in the domestic country. With domestic firms producing both X and Y, goods market equilibrium requires:

$$1 = \gamma(w, r_{\mathrm{y}}) \quad \text{and} \quad 1 + t = \delta(r_{\mathrm{x}}, P_{\mathrm{m}}) \quad \text{and}$$

$$P_{\mathrm{m}} = \mu(w, r_{\mathrm{m}}) \text{ for domestic firms}$$

$$1 + t = \delta(r^*_{\mathrm{x}}, \overline{P^*_{\mathrm{m}}}) \quad \text{and} \quad \overline{P^*_{\mathrm{m}}} = \mu(w, \overline{r^*_{\mathrm{m}}}) \text{ for foreign firms}$$

where r^*_{m} is the rate of return to foreign X-specific capital. Also, if foreign firms both purchase domestic components and produce components in the domestic country themselves then $P_{\mathrm{m}} = \mu(w, \overline{r^*_{\mathrm{m}}})$. Hence $r_{\mathrm{m}} = \overline{r^*_{\mathrm{m}}}$ so $P_{\mathrm{m}} = \overline{P^*_{\mathrm{m}}}$ initially and the domestic firms' three equilibrium conditions solve for the three factor prices w, r_{y}, and r_{x}. Thus incomplete specialization is innocuous here: while we have three price-cost conditions for domestic firms and two for foreign firms, in the absence of a CP both face the same input prices for components and X-capital and equilibrium requires that r_{m} equals $\overline{r^*_{\mathrm{m}}}$. Thus price-cost conditions in the X and M industries are identical for both firms and we have three independent equations in three unknowns.

Now imposing a content requirement (which will only bind the foreign firm, as the domestic firms uses only domestic inputs) can have no effect on the domestic component price, so long as domestic firms still produce both final goods. To see this, note that production of X implies, for domestic and foreign firms respectively:

$$1 + t = \delta(r_{\mathrm{x}}, P_{\mathrm{m}}) \quad \text{and} \quad 1 + t = \delta(r_{\mathrm{x}}, P_{\mathrm{a}})$$

But the returns to X-sector capital must still be equalized between foreign and domestic firms; if not, the users of the highest-earning capital can simply purchase the services of the lower-earning capital. That is, if $r^*_{\mathrm{x}} > r_{\mathrm{x}}$, for instance, the marginal value of X-capital to foreign firms exceeds that to domestic firms and capital will flow to foreign firms. Thus, $P_{\mathrm{m}} = P_{\mathrm{a}}$, from the equations above, so $P_{\mathrm{m}} = \overline{P^*_{\mathrm{m}}}$ still. But domestic production of the component by foreign firms implies $\overline{P_{\mathrm{m}}^*} = \mu(w, \overline{r_{\mathrm{m}}^*})$, so the domestic wage rate is unchanged. Thus, both r_{m} and r_{y} are unchanged too.

So the only equilibrium consistent with both a binding CP and the continued existence of domestic final-good producing firms is one in which all total quantities and prices are unchanged, but the foreign firm displaces enough of the domestic firms' production of X to satisfy the content requirement. With CRS production, as we have here, firm size is indeterminate, so an expansion of foreign firms and a corresponding contraction of domestic firms in X production is a matter of indifference. Clearly, since there has been no change in any prices or quantities, the CP has no welfare effect at this point. While this result is extreme, it highlights two points raised in the introduction: the repercussions for domestic producers of a CP imposed only on foreign producers and the possibility that foreign firms may satisfy the CP at no cost through the displacement of domestic firms.

What is going on here is that the foreign firm simply "buys out" the domestic firm so M_{f} rises, satisfying the CP, but M_{d} falls and overall use of both the domestic and imported components is unaffected. Components previously produced for and used by domestic producers are now produced for and used by foreign producers. In the auto context, for instance, a British Leyland plant becomes a Toyota plant with no other effects.

Eventually, however, the CP will drive domestic firms completely out of X production and any further tightening of the requirement will mean that less M* and/or more domestic component in total must be used so the CP will have real effects. The appendix explains the derivation of various results as the CP is tightened further. To summarize those of interest for welfare analysis, a small increase in the content requirement will increase the average price of the component thus reducing the return to X-sector capital, decrease output of X and decrease imports of the component. The effects on labour use by domestic firms in the Y sector are ambiguous; however, denoting the level of the CP at which domestic firms are just driven from the market as j°, one can demonstrate that a small increase in the CP beyond j° will initially reduce domestic firms' labour employment.

It should also be noted that the initial effects of increasing the CP beyond j° include an inflow of foreign capital into the component-producing sector. As noted earlier, this result accords with evidence on the effects of content requirements in practice.

3. Welfare analysis

In the setting of the model exposited above, we can represent domestic consumers by an expenditure function[8] $E(1, 1+t, u)$, where u represents consumer welfare. Production activities of producers are then summarized by the revenue functions:

$$R(1, 1+t, \overline{K_{\mathrm{y}}}, \overline{K_{\mathrm{m}}}, \overline{K_{\mathrm{x}}}, L) \quad \text{for domestic firms}$$

$$R^*(1-t, K^*_{\mathrm{m}}, K^*_{\mathrm{x}}, \overline{L} - L, \mathrm{M}^*) \quad \text{for foreign firms}$$

where L denotes total labour used by domestic producers, $\overline{L} - L \equiv L^*_{\mathrm{m}}$, and L^*_{m} denotes total use of labour in the production of good M by the foreign producer. While the underlying structure of the model is one of several price-taking firms, treating this as one price-taking firm is quite legitimate as long as there are no distortions in the production sector, as Dixit and Norman (1980, p. 29) point out. Labour, for example, will be allocated so that the value of its marginal product is identical in every use, so a small reallocation has no effect on the firm's revenue. Thus intermediate stages net out and the revenue function is defined over primary factors only. This is valid here for domestic capital but there is a distortion for foreign capital in the form of the CP and so its revenue does depend on the allocation of its primary factors across all uses. The effect of the CP is to change the price of components to P_{a} and the foreign producer's revenue function is the solution to

$$\max_{\{x\}}(1+t)X \text{ s.t. } (X, \overline{L} - L, M^*, K^*_{\mathrm{m}}, K^*_{\mathrm{x}}) \text{ being feasible.}$$

The crucial element here is that the feasible production set now is that constrained by the CP. Defining the revenue function in such a way retains all its usual properties.[9] Changing the content

[8]See Dixit and Norman (1980) for details on duality analysis.

requirement will now affect the production set, but that is captured in the analysis (in much the same way a change in a factor endowment, which also affects the production set, is captured in the standard approach.) Treating the firms as single price-takers is quite valid for the domestic sector, clearly, but also for foreign firms so long as each is small. It may be easier to think of the foreign sector as being just one firm, however, so long as it is a price-taker. Also, M^*, K^*_{m} and K^*_{m} are obviously endogenous — the revenue function formulation subject to the levels of these is just a convenient description of equilibrium and is to be thought of as being evaluated at the optimal levels.

We can now describe the equilibrium of this system. Requiring that national income equal national expenditure yields

$$E(.) = R(.) + R^*(.) - \overline{P^*_{\mathrm{m}}} M^* - r^*_{\mathrm{m}} K^*_{\mathrm{m}} - r^*_{\mathrm{x}} K^*_{\mathrm{x}} + tI_{\mathrm{x}} \tag{1}$$

where imports of X are denoted I_{x} and r^*_{m} (r^*_{x}) denotes the rate of return to K^*_{m} (K^*_{x}). Equation (1) states that national expenditure equals producers' revenues less returns to foreign capital and the costs of imported inputs, plus any tariff revenues from imports of X. From the properties of the $R(.)$, $R^*(.)$, and $E(.)$ functions,

$$I_{\mathrm{x}} = \frac{\partial E}{\partial p} - \frac{\partial R}{\partial p} - \frac{\partial R^*}{\partial p} \tag{2}$$

where function arguments are suppressed for clarity. For factor market equilibrium:

$$r^*_{\mathrm{m}} = \frac{\partial R^*}{\partial K_{\mathrm{m}}} \tag{3a}$$

$$r^*_{\mathrm{x}} = \frac{\partial R^*}{\partial K^*_{\mathrm{x}}} \tag{3b}$$

$$w = \frac{\partial R}{\partial L} \tag{3c}$$

[9]This would not be the case with a value-added content plan, however. As Färe *et al.* (1988) demonstrate, in such a case constraint parameters enter the objective function and the dual optimisation is complicated somewhat.

where (3c) is a consequence of domestic labour mobility. Again, (3a) and (3b) can be interpreted as specifying either the determination of the rental rates for the two kinds of foreign capital, when the quantities are fixed, or the amounts of foreign capital used when world interest rates are given. As before, we consider only the latter interpretation for M-specific capital, in which the quantity K^*_{m} is chosen, and the former for X-specific capital in which the quantity is given at $\overline{K^*_{\mathrm{x}}}$. Finally, determination of this system requires that the foreign firm take as given the import price of the component: this seems realistic for a small subsidiary of a large MNC.

Now, the content plan specified above causes the effective price of a representative unit of the component to the foreign producer to be $P_{\mathrm{a}} = jP_{\mathrm{m}} + (1-j)\overline{P^*_{\mathrm{m}}}$. This is the marginal cost of another unit of component so the profit maximizing firm will equate this to its marginal revenue product (equals value of the marginal product (VMP)), $\frac{\partial R^*}{\partial M^*}$. Rewriting this condition, we can express the effect of the CP as

$$\frac{\partial R^*}{\partial M^*} - \overline{P^*_{\mathrm{m}}} = j(P_{\mathrm{m}} - \overline{P^*_{\mathrm{m}}}) \tag{4}$$

Similarly, the CP distorts the decisions regarding the allocation of labour to M production. In the absence of a CP the firm uses labour in M production until the value of the marginal product equals the wage, i.e.

$$w = \frac{\partial R^*}{\partial L^*_{\mathrm{m}}} = \overline{P^*_{\mathrm{m}}}\frac{\partial M}{\partial L^*_{\mathrm{m}}}$$

But with a CP the shadow value of another unit of component is P_{a}, so:

$$\frac{\partial R^*}{\partial L^*_{\mathrm{m}}} = \mathrm{VMP}_{L_{\mathrm{m}}} = P_{\mathrm{a}}\frac{\partial M}{\partial L^*_{\mathrm{m}}} = (jP_{\mathrm{m}} + (1-j)\overline{P^*_{\mathrm{m}}})\frac{\partial M}{\partial L^*_{\mathrm{m}}}$$

Hence:

$$\begin{aligned}\frac{\partial \mathrm{R}^*}{\partial \mathrm{L}^*_{\mathrm{m}}} - \frac{\partial R}{\partial L} = \frac{\partial R^*}{\partial L^*_{\mathrm{m}}} - w &= \frac{\partial R^*}{\partial L^*_{\mathrm{m}}} - P_{\mathrm{m}}\frac{\partial M}{\partial L^*_{\mathrm{m}}}\\ &= (jP_{\mathrm{m}} + (1-j)\overline{P^*_{\mathrm{m}}})\frac{\partial M}{\partial L^*_{\mathrm{m}}} - P_{\mathrm{m}}\frac{\partial M}{\partial L^*_{\mathrm{m}}}\end{aligned}$$

where the first equality follows from (3c) and the second from the fact that competitive production of M ensures that the wage, w, equals the value of the marginal product in production of the domestic component, $P_{\mathrm{m}}\frac{\partial M}{\partial L_{\mathrm{m}}^*}$. Thus:

$$\frac{\partial R^*}{\partial L_{\mathrm{m}}^*} - \frac{\partial R}{\partial L} = -(1-j)(P_{\mathrm{m}} - \overline{P_{\mathrm{m}}^*})\frac{\partial M}{\partial L_{\mathrm{m}}^*} \tag{3d}$$

Substituting (2) into (1), totally differentiating, and using (3) and (4) gives (5):[10]

$$\left(\frac{\partial E}{\partial u} - t\frac{\partial^2 E}{\partial p \partial u}\right)\frac{\mathrm{d}u}{\mathrm{d}j} = j(P_{\mathrm{m}} - \overline{P_{\mathrm{m}}^*})\frac{\mathrm{d}M^*}{\mathrm{d}j} + (1-j)(P_{\mathrm{m}} - \overline{P_{\mathrm{m}}^*}) \times \frac{\partial M}{\partial L_{\mathrm{m}}^*}\frac{\mathrm{d}L}{\mathrm{d}j} - \overline{K_{\mathrm{x}}^*}\frac{\mathrm{d}r_{\mathrm{x}}^*}{\mathrm{d}j} - t\frac{\mathrm{d}X}{\mathrm{d}j} \tag{5}$$

Assuming, for stability, that the term $((\partial E/\partial u) - t(\partial^2 E/\partial p\partial u))$ is positive,[11] equation (5) identifies the channels through which a change in the CP will affect overall welfare and is easily interpreted. The first two terms on the right hand side capture the direct effects of factor reallocations due to the CP, the third term any affects on payments to foreign X-sector capital, and the last term captures the effects of the CP on domestic production of the final good and thus on imports and tariff revenues.

A decrease in use of M* alone, for example, would reduce welfare (from the first term) because it is already being underused, given the content requirement, to the extent that $\overline{P_{\mathrm{m}}^*}$ is less than P_{m}. But this would raise welfare (from the last term) in that it decreases output of the importable which increases imports and thus tariff revenues. (Note that consumption of the final good is unchanged in the face of changes in the content requirement alone.) Similarly, any increased use of labour in the domestic production of the component by the foreign firm will lead to a fall in welfare (from the second term) to the extent that labour's marginal product is less than the wage (as is likely under a CP as the firm is induced to produce "too much" of the

[10]Details of these calculations are provided in the appendix.

[11]See Dixit and Norman (1980, p. 187, and references therein).

domestic component). Also, the corresponding increase in production of the final good would reduce tariff revenues and further reduce welfare.

While this analysis is at a fair level of generality, we can now substitute in the resource allocation effects of a CP in this model calculated earlier in order to sign these derivatives explicitly so as to determine welfare effects more directly once the CP has reached the level at which domestic producers no longer participate in the market.[12] It is clear from equation (5) and our comparative statics results that nothing certain can be said about this for just any level of the CP. A small increase in the CP requirement reduces welfare by reducing imports of the component and this effect, by the first term on the right-hand side of (5), is worse the greater the CP and thus the greater the $(P_{\mathrm{m}} - \overline{P_{\mathrm{m}}^*})$ distortion. It will also lower welfare, for levels of the CP close to j°, by reducing the use of labour by domestic firms: the second term in (5). This is because such a reduction corresponds to increased labour use in domestic production of the component and this is welfare-reducing to the extent that the domestic component is already overused in the presence of a CP. Finally, the CP raises welfare by reducing payments to foreign owners of X sector capital and by reducing output of good X, thus increasing imports (underused due to the tariff) and corresponding tariff revenues. Hence the larger is the foreign X-sector capital stock and the greater the response of X output to changes in the CP, *ceteris paribus*, the more likely is a CP to raise welfare.

While it is not possible to weigh up these conflicting effects unambiguously in general, it is clear that a very small CP just above j° will raise welfare overall. This is because the $(P_{\mathrm{m}} - \overline{P_{\mathrm{m}}^*})$ margin distortion is of second-order significance when $j \cong j^\circ$ and we are left with only the beneficial tariff revenue effect of the CP and the beneficial effect of reduced payments to foreign X-sector capital.

[12]At the earlier stage of the CP, when foreign firms 'buy out' domestic final-good producers, expression (5) remains unchanged because they are simply employing factors previously employed by domestic firms. Payments to factors still accrue to domestic sources and national income is unchanged.

4. Summary and conclusion

This chapter has attempted to remedy several perceived omissions in the literature on content protection by stressing the distinction between foreign and domestic final-good firms and by allowing for the effects of final-good tariffs and direct foreign investment in the domestic component-producing industry in mitigating a CP's effects. We have discussed the effect of content protection in a two-stage general equilibrium (GE) production model with foreign capital flows and shown that the second-best welfare consequences of such a plan depend, *inter alia*, upon its effects on imported inputs (both primary and produced). These effects were explicitly worked out in a simple GE model. It was also shown that, once a content requirement "bites" (in a sense made clear in the paper), it will induce foreign firms to increase their own domestic production of the component input and so will induce capital flows, a result that accords with empirical observations of the effects of content protection.

Some concluding remarks are in order regarding the robustness of our results. The expression we derived for the welfare consequences of a CP (Equation 5) is, in fact, quite general and applies in any competitive model where foreign firms have access to imported components and domestic firms do not. The trade-off between inefficient resource allocation effects and changes in tariff revenues is, of course, a feature of the second-best setting but, as argued earlier, this is the correct context for the analysis of a CP. The specific interpretation of (5) stems from the particular resource allocation effects derived in Section 2.

Regarding these effects, we have stressed a particular motivation for a CP in this chapter: the protection of a domestic component industry whose output is not more heavily used in the absence of a CP because of increasing costs (given the domestic capital stock). This is the basic model of a CP as developed by Grossman (1981). An alternative reason that domestic components may be "underused" in the absence of a CP is that they are not perfect substitutes for the foreign counterpart.[13] One possible specification of this is as in Mussa (1984), wherein a final good is produced according to a neoclassical CRS technology treating foreign and domestic inputs as separate factors. While allowing concentration on incentives for factor substitution induced by a CP, this approach is problematic in that it not only suggests that both inputs are necessary in production but also precludes the empirically compelling distinction between domestic and foreign firms on the basis of input use.

An alternative notion of imperfect substitutability is that the two inputs are simply of different qualities. Indeed, this may often be the motivation for a CP in the first place — foreign producers do not use domestic inputs as they are perceived to be of inferior quality. To capture such a difference, consider a specification in which superficially identical inputs differ in efficiency in production of the final good. For instance, a production function $X = F(M^* + aM)$ where $a \in (0, 1)$ captures this notion wherein a measures the degree of inferiority of the domestic input M.

In either of the specifications above, the general flavour of our results will still obtain (but with less force in some cases) so long as domestic and foreign firms are differentiated by access to imported inputs. With capital mobility, the initial impact of a CP will still be displacement of domestic firms by foreign firms, with no overall consequences: so long as both domestic and foreign firms are producing in the X sector using some domestic component, the price of the domestic component must equal that of the import (adjusted for efficiency differences) and, with the same production functions across firms, zero profit conditions then require that factor prices are unaffected by the CP. Only if the foreign firm would choose to use no domestic components at all *sans* CP would the latter have any effect initially (but in such a case the effects of a CP in driving up domestic factor prices would be mitigated somewhat by the inflow of M-specific foreign capital).[14]

---

[13]I am grateful to an anonymous referee for raising this alternative approach.

[14]This suggests an interesting extension of the present paper. Consider a model in which capital in the source country produces according to some more efficient technology than that in the host. If the technology is not transferable — the implicit assumption in

We conclude with a final note of clarification concerning capital flows and content protection. We have stressed that capital flows into the component (M) industry because of a CP — thereby reducing the upward pressure on domestic component prices through increased factor demands — but another form of capital flow also tends to accompany CPs in practice. This is the initial setting-up of domestic final-good (X) production facilities by foreign producers. However, this is a consequence of the final-good protection that invariably accompanies content protection and not of the CP itself. As in the EC example cited earlier it is protection of the X sector that induces 'tariff-jumping' foreign investment in that sector and a CP is a response to stimulate demand for domestic components, M.[15] We have not modelled this here, taking both X protection and the level of foreign investment in the X industry as given.

References

Davidson, C., S.J. Matusz and M.E. Kreinen (1987). Analysis of performance standards for direct foreign investments. *Canadian Journal of Economics*, 18(4), 876–990.

Dixit, A.K. and V. Norman (1980). *Theory of International Trade.* Cambridge, UK: Cambridge University Press.

Davidson *et al.* (1987) wherein domestic production is simply more costly than that abroad — then tightening the CP simply has the effects we noted above, albeit reduced somewhat. Foreign capital inflows are increased as they flow into production of the component domestically (according to the same domestic technology) but the domestic component is still more costly than the import. However, suppose that the technology is transferable. Then the foreign firm will produce components domestically according to its more efficient foreign technology and this will represent an additional source of efficiency gain for other domestic factors employed in the component industry. Of course, this raises the question of why the technology was not licensed out to domestic firms originally but, in the context of many LDCs, limited protection of intellectual property rights is a fact of life that may prohibit any such technology sharing. In this setting, a CP becomes a way of inducing technology flows as it is in the interests of the foreign firm to produce in the most efficient way when it is forced to produce domestically.

[15]As a referee has pointed out, this can be perceived as a means of recapturing, for domestic input producers, some of the tariff rents associated with the original protection but lost due to the tariff-jumping investment. To the extent that domestic inputs are priced greater than their imported counterparts, payments from foreign assemblers to domestic input producers contain a rent component.

Fare, R., J. Logan and C.A. Knox Lovell (1988). *The Economics of Content Protection: A Dual Approach.* Mimeo: Southern Illinois University.

Greenaway, D. (1990). Trade related investment measures: Political economy aspects and issues for GATT. *The World Economy*, 13(3), 367–85.

Grossman, G.M. (1981). The theory of domestic content protection and content preference. *Quarterly Journal of Economics*, **96**, 583–603.

Guisinger, S. (1986). Do performance requirements and investment incentives really work? *The World Economy*, 9, 79–95.

Herander, M. and C. Thomas (1986). Export performance and export-import linkage requirements. *Quarterly Journal of Economics*, **101**, 591–607.

Hollander, A. (1987). Content protection and transnational monopoly. *Journal of International Economics*, 23, 283–97.

Krishna, K. and M. Itoh (1986). Content protection and oligopolistic interactions. NBER Working Paper No. 1843, February.

Moran, T.H. and C.S. Pearson (1988). Tread carefully in the field of TRIP measures. *The World Economy*, 11(1), 119–34.

Mussa, M. (1984). The economics of content protection. NBER Working Paper No. 1457.

Oecd (1987). Trade related investment measures: An overview of characteristics. Incidence and Effects, TC/WP (87) 78.

Richardson, M. (1991). The effects of a content requirement on a foreign duopsonist. *Journal of International Economics*, 31, 143–55.

Rodrik, D. (1987). The economics of export-performance requirements. *Quarterly Journal of Economics*, **102**, 633–650.

Subcommmittee on Trade, House Ways and Means Committee (1982). Survey of automotive trade restrictions maintained by selected nations. In hearings on *Fair Practices in Automotive Products Act*, March 2, Serial No. 97–147, 111–23.

Unido (1986). Industrial Policy in the Developing Countries: An Analysis of Local Content Regulations, UNIDO/IS.606, 3 February.

Vousden, N. (1987). Content protection and tariffs under monopoly and competition. *Journal of International Economics*, 23(3/4), 263.

Appendix

1. Derivation of Equation (5)

Substituting Equation (2) into Equation (1) yields

$$
\begin{aligned}
E(1,1+t,u) = {} & R(1,1+t,\overline{K_{\mathrm{x}}},\overline{K_{\mathrm{m}}},\overline{K_{\mathrm{y}}},L) \\
& + R^*(1+t,K^*_{\mathrm{m}},\overline{K^*_{\mathrm{x}}},\overline{L}-L,M^*) \\
& -\overline{P^*_{\mathrm{m}}}M^* - r^*_{\mathrm{m}}K^*_{\mathrm{m}} - r^*_{\mathrm{x}}\overline{K^*_{\mathrm{x}}} + t\left(\frac{\partial E}{\partial p} - \frac{\partial R}{\partial p} - \frac{\partial R^*}{\partial p}\right)
\end{aligned}
$$

Differentiating and rearranging terms:

$$\left(\frac{\partial E}{\partial u} - t\frac{\partial^2 E}{\partial p \partial u}\right) \mathrm{d}u = \left(\frac{\partial R^*}{\partial M^*} - \overline{P_{\mathrm{m}}^*} - t\frac{\partial^2 R^*}{\partial p \partial M^*}\right) \mathrm{d}M^* - r_{\mathrm{m}}^* \mathrm{d}K_{\mathrm{m}}^*$$

$$+ \frac{\partial R^*}{\partial K_{\mathrm{m}}^*} \mathrm{d}K_m^* - \overline{K_{\mathrm{x}}^*} \mathrm{d}r_{\mathrm{x}}^*$$

$$+ \left[\frac{\partial R}{\partial L} - \frac{\partial R^*}{\partial L_{\mathrm{m}}^*} - t\left(\frac{\partial^2 R}{\partial p \partial L} - \frac{\partial^2 R^*}{\partial p \partial L_{\mathrm{m}}^*}\right)\right] \mathrm{dL}$$

By Equations (3a), (3d), and (4), this expression becomes:

$$\left(\frac{\partial E}{\partial u} - t\frac{\partial^2 E}{\partial p \partial u}\right) \mathrm{d}u = j(P_m - \overline{P_{\mathrm{m}}^*}) \mathrm{d}M^* - \overline{K_{\mathrm{x}}^*} \mathrm{d}r_{\mathrm{x}}^*$$

$$-(1-j)(\overline{P_{\mathrm{m}}^*} - P_{\mathrm{m}}) \frac{\partial M}{\partial L_{\mathrm{m}}^*} \mathrm{d}L - t\{.\}$$

where

$$\{.\} = \left\{\frac{\partial^2 R^*}{\partial p \partial M^*} \mathrm{d}M^* + \left(\frac{\partial^2 R}{\partial p \partial L} - \frac{\partial^2 R}{\partial p \partial L_{\mathrm{m}}^*}\right) \mathrm{d}L\right\}$$

Finally, $(\partial R/\partial p) = X_{\mathrm{d}}$ and $(\partial R^*/\partial p) = X_{\mathrm{f}}$, by the properties of revenue functions, so

$$\frac{\partial^2 R^*}{\partial p \partial M^*} = \frac{\partial X_{\mathrm{f}}}{\partial M^*}, \quad \frac{\partial^2 R^*}{\partial p \partial L_{\mathrm{m}}^*} = \frac{\partial X_{\mathrm{f}}}{\partial L_{\mathrm{m}}^*}$$

and

$$\frac{\partial^2 R}{\partial p \partial L} = \frac{\partial X_{\mathrm{d}}}{\partial L}$$

Thus $\{.\} = \mathrm{d}(X_{\mathrm{d}} + X_t) = \mathrm{d}X$ and we have Equation (5) of the text.

2. General equilibrium comparative statics

Equilibrium in the final goods markets requires that price equals cost for each good. For the Y industry this is just $\gamma(w, r_y) = 1$. When the CP binds, only the foreign firm produces X. The unit cost of X production is $\delta(r_{\mathrm{x}}, P_{\mathrm{a}}) = \delta(r_{\mathrm{x}}, jP_{\mathrm{m}} + (1-j)\overline{P_{\mathrm{m}}^*})$ where $P_{\mathrm{m}} = \mu(w, r_{\mathrm{m}})$. We also require factor markets to clear and, using the standard derivative properties of unit cost functions, we can derive factor demands and equate these to factor supplies. Finally, our equilibrium also requires that the CP is satisfied. Thus equilibrium is now described by the following eight equations:

$$1 = \gamma(w, r_{\mathrm{y}}) \tag{A.1}$$

$$1 + t = \delta(r_{\mathrm{x}}, P_{\mathrm{a}}) \tag{A.2}$$

$$P_{\mathrm{a}} = j\mu(w, \overline{r^*_{\mathrm{m}}}) + (1 - j)\overline{P^*_{\mathrm{m}}} \tag{A.3}$$

$$\frac{\partial\gamma(w, r_{\mathrm{y}})}{\partial w} \cdot Y + j\frac{\partial\delta(r_{\mathrm{x}}, P_{\mathrm{a}})}{\partial P_{\mathrm{a}}} \cdot \frac{\partial\mu(w, \overline{r^*_{\mathrm{m}}})}{\partial w} \cdot X = \overline{L} \tag{A.4}$$

$$\frac{\partial\gamma(w, r_{\mathrm{y}})}{\partial r} \cdot Y = \overline{K_{\mathrm{y}}} \tag{A.5}$$

$$\frac{\partial\delta(r_{\mathrm{x}}, P_{\mathrm{a}})}{\partial P_{\mathrm{a}}} j \frac{\partial\mu(w, \overline{r_{\mathrm{m}}})}{\partial r^*_{\mathrm{m}}} \cdot X = \overline{K_{\mathrm{m}}} + K^*_{\mathrm{m}} \tag{A.6}$$

$$\frac{\partial\delta(r_{\mathrm{x}}, P_{\mathrm{a}})}{\partial P_{\mathrm{a}}}(1 - j) \cdot X = M^* \tag{A.7}$$

$$\frac{\partial\delta(r_{\mathrm{x}}, P_{\mathrm{a}})}{\partial r_{\mathrm{x}}} X = (\overline{K_{\mathrm{x}}} + \overline{K^*_{\mathrm{x}}}) \tag{A.8}$$

These equations determine $w, r_{\mathrm{y}}, r_{\mathrm{x}}, P_{\mathrm{a}} X, Y, K^*_{\mathrm{m}}$, and M^*. We assume that all inputs are substitutes in all goods.

Differentiating these equations and solving for the various comparative static effects, only a few clear results are available.[16] A small increase in the local content requirement causes the average price of the component, P_{a}, to rise, the return to X-capital, r_{x}, to fall, imports of the component, M^*, to decrease, and production of final good X to decrease. These results hold for any level of the CP. The effects on other variables are dependant on the level of the CP, however. Denoting the level of the CP at which domestic firms are just driven from the market as j°, one can demonstrate that a small increase in the CP beyond j° will drive wages up and the return to

[16]Full derivation of these results is available from the author on request.

Y-capital, r_{y}, down, will decrease output of final good Y, and will yield an inflow of foreign capital into the M sector, K_{m}^{*}.

The fact that these results do not necessarily hold at all levels of the CP corresponds to Grossman's (1981) findings in a similar but partial equilibrium model and for similar reasons. The initial impact of the CP is to increase demand for the domestic component in lieu of the imported version. Increased foreign M-capital is combined with increased labour, driving up the wage rate. Given the fixed quantity of X-capital, substitution into capital is not possible and the reaction to the increasing component price is a fall in X output. This effect tends to dominate as the CP is raised and demand for the domestic component may begin to fall. Accordingly, the wage rate may begin to fall as the CP is tightened; hence the ambiguity also in r_{y}, Y, and K_{m}^{*}.

Chapter 3

Commercial Broadcasting and Local Content: Cultural Quotas, Advertising and Public Stations

Martin Richardson

Abstract: This chapter considers two radio stations choosing combinations of local and international content to broadcast to consumers with preferences over those combinations. Station revenue derives from sales of advertising time, the demand for which depends negatively on its price and positively on the station's market share and consumers get disutility from advertising. This chapter derives the laissez-faire solution to this model and considers the consequences of a local content quota, an advertising cap and a non-commercial public station for broadcasting diversity and welfare with and without an externality attached to local content.

Many countries have expressed concerns that local culture is threatened by an international cultural hegemon (i.e., the US), be it in film, television or radio broadcasting. Consequently, elaborate and long-lasting local content requirements — or cultural quotas — have been implemented all over the world. For example, the first regular Canadian radio station went to air in 1919; only 13 years later the Canadian Radio Broadcasting Commission was established to regulate broadcasting, setting the number, location and power of

Originally published in *The Economic Journal*, 116, 605–625.

radio stations as well as the time that should be devoted to national and local programming. Numerous rationales have been provided for cultural quotas — national prestige, merit goods, production externalities — but most hinge on another externality argument: that such schemes preserve local culture (by increasing the demand for its outputs — although, as Jacobsen (2000) notes, local content requirements affect supply only and cannot ensure that increased local programming is actually consumed, a feature we see in our model) thus generating some intangible spin-off. (Or, indeed, *tangible* spin-off — such schemes are generally viewed favourably by domestic artists as they are seen to increase payments to such artists by increasing the demand for their outputs. We do not consider this explicitly; effectively, we suppose there is free entry into music production so artists earn competitive returns. Nevertheless, any supernormal returns are easily handled in our framework as a part of the externality that accrues from an increased audience for local content.)

One might anticipate a number of consequences of a cultural quota. Presumably it is perceived that, in its absence, consumers listen to "too little" local content.[1] A quota might simply induce entry by local artists, as demand for their output increases and, to the extent that their entry was unprofitable before the quota, this must represent a welfare loss from reduced quality. Or programming might simply concentrate on domestic artists that are very similar in style to those already played (although this, of course, is exactly the opposite of the quota's desired effect, encouraging domestic artists to become more like international ones rather than preserving any perceived cultural distinctiveness. In fact, some schemes do not count such artists as local: see Footnote 1.)

[1]Defined in whatever way. The Canadian MAPL system generally requires that Canadian content satisfy two of the following requirements: M (music)–composed entirely by a Canadian; A (artist) — performed principally by a Canadian; P (production)–a live performance that is (*i*) recorded wholly in Canada, or (*ii*) performed wholly in Canada and broadcast live in Canada; L (lyrics) — written entirely by a Canadian. See http://www.crtc.gc.ca/eng/INFO_SHT/R1.htm. See also Krattenmaker and Powe (1994) for a comprehensive discussion of the philosophy and practice of the regulation of broadcasting.

In this chapter, our focus is not on the *production* of local content (the artists) but on the medium of its dissemination; we consider the impact of a cultural quota on commercial radio stations. Taking the proponents of such quotas at face value, we suppose that there *is* something about local content that is unique and that is not a quality difference: we suppose that there is horizontal differentiation between local and international content and take this as given. Preferences over the two types of content vary across consumers and radio stations choose their broadcast mix of content types in an effort to maximise revenue from advertisers who attempt to reach the largest audience possible amongst the consumers who dislike advertising. A cultural quota here is effectively a "locational" constraint on radio stations.

We allow that the hearing of local content might yield some external benefit to policy makers, perhaps reflecting the cultural arguments that the proponents of quotas claim. In this setting the social optimum, *sans* externality, is maximal differentiation between the stations but the laissez-faire solution involves less than maximal differentiation and a cultural quota further reduces that differentiation. While a quota may raise consumer welfare it lowers overall welfare — again in the absence of any externality — by decreasing diversity (and thus advertising.) We consider two other policies — a limit on advertising and a publicly provided non-commercial station and show that neither is as effective as a quota, even allowing for an externality, in achieving greater airplay for local content at least welfare cost, unless the fixed costs of the latter are sufficiently low. Interestingly, both policies reduce the diversity of content played.

While it appears that competition between stations here is between characteristics of the stations themselves, rather than the programming they offer, in fact locational choice is a *programming* decision. Our assumption that local and international content are different in kind can be interpreted as either being independent of programming genre (applying to similar-format stations) or as applying across genres: if local content correlates with genres (being more concentrated in rock music than classical, say) then a cultural quota can be interpreted as a constraint on the genre formats of radio stations. Indeed, jurisdictions such as Australia have different content requirements across different formats to reflect this.

Our analysis is most closely related to Gabszewicz, Laussel and Sonnac (2000); (GLS henceforth). They model television broadcasting in much the same way as in this chapter. But their only policy concern is with the impact of advertising limits and they also model advertising very differently which leads to quite different results. Another closely related paper is that of Gal-Or and Dukes (2003) who also consider a spatial model of broadcasting location with broadcasters funded by informative — but nuisance advertising, as in this chapter. They take a very different model of advertising, however, in which broadcasters and advertisers bargain over their joint surplus (which leads to a result of minimal differentiation across the broadcasters) and they explore no policy instruments. While a number of economists have looked at radio broadcasting, informally discussing general issues or formally modelling econometric analyses of specific aspects of the market (Berry and Waldfogel, 1999a,b; Anderson and Coate, 2000), none address the issues we analyse here.

There is a substantial policy-oriented literature discussing cultural quotas and related issues at an informal level — see, for example, Acheson and Maule (1990) and Jacobsen (2000) — but we are aware of only two recent papers that construct formal models of cultural protection. Francois and van Ypersele (2002) present a model in which cultural goods are produced in different countries under increasing returns and in which protection of a domestic market may raise welfare in both countries. However, their model is very different from — and largely unrelated to — our work and our policy instrument is a restriction on those media rather than on the underlying goods themselves. Crampes and Hollander (1999) look at a number of regulatory schemes for broadcasting, including content requirements, but in a model of subscriber-supported media, so they do not deal with advertising at all. Finally, Owen and Wildman (1992) provide a survey of much of the literature on the economics of TV broadcasting but without directly discussing the issues addressed here.

In the next section we set up the model before turning to an examination of some benchmark comparisons. Section 3 then considers the laissez-faire market solution and in Section 4, we consider three alternative policies for a cultural regulator concerned with the amount of local content played: a quota, an advertising ceiling and a public non-commercial station playing only local content. A final Section concludes.

1. A model

Suppose there are two types of content, Local and that of the Rest of the world. There are two radio stations and each makes a 'locational' choice in terms of the mix that it plays of these two kinds of content (for concreteness we shall henceforth talk only of music as the content). We shall denote a choice of only Local content as being at a location 0 on the interval [0,1], *à la* Hotelling (1929), and a choice of only Rest of the world content as being at the other end of this interval at point 1. The two stations, L and R, are then described by their location along this interval and we also use the notation L and R to denote their locations where, without loss of generality, $L \leq R$.

1.1. *Demand*

Consumers are distributed uniformly along this unit interval in terms of their preferences for mixes of the two kinds of music and have one unit of time to devote to listening to the radio. Note that the types of content are different in a horizontal rather than a vertical sense: local music is not thought by all listeners to be inferior to the international product, or superior, but, rather, it is a matter of taste. An insight of GLS is that this set-up mirrors the 'combinable products' of Anderson and Neven (1989): each consumer located between the stations can 'roll their own' optimal mix of the two kinds of content by taking an appropriate combination of the two stations.[2]

[2] We assume that there are no switching costs involved in changing channels. Introducing such costs would greatly complicate the analysis for little payoff in terms of qualitative results. One might interpret the observed format heterogeneity of commercial stations as

Every consumer gets utility of v from listening only to their ideal mix of music and we suppose this is always sufficiently high that all consumers listen to the radio: the market is covered. As in GLS, we assume that a consumer's disutility from a less-than-ideal mix of content types is increasing and quadratic in the 'distance' from their ideal mix to the mix they consume. So a consumer located at point s consuming a bundle $\Gamma_s = \lambda L + (1-\lambda)R$ gets disutility associated with a less-than-ideal product mix of $t(\Gamma_s - s)^2$ where t measures the utility cost of having a less-than-ideal mix.

Why would a consumer between L and R ever choose a less-than-ideal product mix? While the radio stations are free to listeners, we suppose that consumers also get disutility from advertising interrupting their programming. If station $j = L, R$ chooses to fill a fraction a_j of its broadcast time with advertising then the advertising disutility associated with bundle Γ_s is $\tau[\lambda a_L + (1-\lambda)a_R]$. This disutility is linear in advertising and there is no difference between advertising heard at one station or the other. In this respect we have not only horizontal differentiation (in the location-specific disutility of a less-than-ideal mix) but vertical (in the non-location-specific advertising disutility). Thus a consumer at location s gets total utility of $u(s, \lambda, L, R, a_L, a_R) = \underline{v} - t[\lambda L + (1-\lambda)R - s]^2 - [\lambda a_L + (1-\lambda)a_R]$ and choosing λ to minimise this yields[3] the *optimal* λ_s from which the optimal bundle Γ_s follows:

$$\lambda_s = \frac{2_t(R-s)(R-L) + (a_R - a_L)}{2t(R-L)^2}$$

$$= \frac{(R-s)}{(R-L)} + \frac{(a_R - a_L)}{2t(R-L)^2} \tag{1}$$

$$\Gamma_s = s - \frac{(a_R - a_L)}{2t(R-L)}. \tag{2}$$

evidence that such costs *are* significant in practice; nevertheless, we do not model them here.

[3]All omitted derivations are provided in a Technical Appendix available from the journal's website, http://www.res.org.uk/economic/to/tahome.asp

This differs from the consumer's ideal mix only to the extent that advertising differs across the two stations. Also, from (1),

$$\lambda_s \geq 1 \,\text{as}\, s \leq L + \frac{(a_R - a_L)}{2t(R-L)} \equiv s_L$$
$$\lambda_s \leq 0 \,\text{as}\, s \geq R + \frac{(a_R - a_L)}{2t(R-L)} \equiv s_R \tag{3}$$

where s_L and s_R are critical locations such that all consumers at $s \leq s_L (\geq s_R)$ listen only to station $L(R.)$ So a consumer's mix depends on location:

$$\left.\begin{matrix} s \leq s_L \\ s \in [s_L, s_R] \\ s \geq s_R \end{matrix}\right\} \Rightarrow \lambda_s = \begin{cases} 1 \\ \dfrac{(R-s)}{(R-L)} + \dfrac{(a_R - a_L)}{2t(R-L)^2} \\ 0 \end{cases} \tag{4}$$

where, to minimise notation, we let λ_s denote the optimal λ subject to the constraint $\lambda \in [0,1]$. Note that the interval $s_R - s_L = R - L$.

We can now calculate the total audience, X_j, listening to each station $j = L, R$:

$$x_L = \int_0^{s_L} f(s)\mathrm{d}s + \int_{s_L}^{s_R} \lambda_s f(s)\mathrm{d}s. \tag{5}$$

But $s \sim U[0,1], \lambda_s(s_L) = 1$ and $\lambda_s(s_R) = 0$ so, where x_R also follows from $x_R = 1 - x_L$:

$$\begin{aligned} x_L(L,R,a_L,a_R) &= \frac{1}{2}\left[\frac{(a_R - a_L)}{t(R-L)} + (R+L)\right] \\ &= s_L + \frac{1}{2}(R-L) \\ x_R(L,R,a_L,a_R) &= \frac{1}{2}\left[2 - (R+L) - \frac{(a_R - a_L)}{t(R-L)}\right] \\ &= 1 - s_R + \frac{1}{2}(R-L). \end{aligned} \tag{6}$$

1.2. *Advertising*

The role of advertising in the broadcasting literature is a controversial one; Anderson and Coate (2000) provide a more complete discussion of alternative views of the role of advertising in economic models. At one extreme it might be seen as purely a nuisance on aggregate: while it determines which products consumers favour, it has no effect on overall expenditure so advertising costs are a deadweight social loss resulting from a Prisoners' Dilemma amongst competing advertisers. At the other extreme it provides information to otherwise ignorant consumers. As in all models of broadcasting, the exact welfare results of our analysis will be sensitive to the view taken on the rationale for advertising. The model we use here represents a reduced form of a model developed by Anderson and Coate (2000), who consider broadcasters airing one of two programmes. In their model, a continuum of producers indexed by $\sigma \in [0, \underline{\sigma}]$ (where $\underline{\sigma} < 1$) sells new goods that must be advertised to make consumers aware of them. When a consumer sees an advertisement for a particular product they are willing, with probability σ, to pay their reservation price ω for it and, with probability $1-\sigma$, to pay 0; this compares to paying 0 with probability 1 if they do not see the advertisement. So producers all rationally set a price of ω and, while advertising is socially useful (advertisers sell nothing in its absence but get positive expected surplus from it) it nevertheless yields no net benefit to consumers. This model of advertising, embedded in a particular model of commercial broadcasting, results in a demand curve for advertising at a station that is decreasing in the price of advertising and increasing in the station's market share.

We think that these comparative statics seem very compelling in the context of free-to-air broadcasting. Other features of the Anderson and Coate (2000) model, however, do not; in particular their result that demand for advertising at one station is independent of whether or not the producer has advertised at the other station. Similarly, the GLS model results in demands for advertising at each station that do *not* depend at all on the rival's advertising price. So our approach is simply to capture these desirable comparative statics in the simplest possible formulation of the advertisers' problem. We suppose that each radio station simply faces a competitive demand for advertising time from advertisers who seek to maximise some monotonic increasing function of total advertising exposure, $f(a_j x_j), j = L, R$. This affects advertisers' sales of output, which has price $\underline{p}$. So advertising is potentially socially useful here ("potentially" only, because the gain to advertisers must be set off against the nuisance cost of advertising to consumers) although it yields no net gain to consumers. Each advertising minute costs p_j so, given this price, advertisers solve the following programme:

$$\underset{\{a_j\}}{\text{Max}}\, \underline{p}f(a_j x_j) - p_j a_j \Rightarrow p_j = \underline{p}f' \frac{\mathrm{d}(a_j x_j)}{\mathrm{d}a_j}. \tag{7}$$

While advertisers at one station do not advertise at the other, we show below that they are still affected by prices at the other station (as these affect advertising there and thus, through market share, the efficacy of their own advertising.) The main rationale for this assumption is that it mirrors the reality of radio advertising where advertisers are very genre- and therefore station-specific and it can be formalised in a very simple way.[4] Suppose that the likelihood of a consumer responding to an advert for a particular product correlates with their preferences over music content. That is, exposure to adverts for L-type (r-type) products is more effective in persuading a consumer the stronger is the consumer's preference for L-type (R-type) programming. For example, a heavy metal enthusiast may be more (less) likely than a fan of easy listening music to respond to an advertisement for ear studs (golf clubs). If there is some fixed cost to advertisers in constructing an advertising campaign at a station then, even if the degree of consumer susceptibility to adverts for different types of product varies continuously with preference for music type (i.e., location), an advertiser may choose to run a campaign at only one station. The chosen station will be the one at which advertising for that product is more effective in terms of appealing to consumer

[4] I thank the Editor for suggesting more detailed discussion of this aspect of the model. The formalisation is available in the Technical Appendix.

types. As noted, casual empiricism supports the notion that radio advertisers target specific stations and do not tend to diversify their campaigns. This seems less true of television advertising, at least in the context of network broadcasters, but this is consistent with the model outlined above: TV networks tend to be more homogeneous in their programming (compared to niche radio broadcasters) but it is the relative specialisation of content that attracts advertisers in our story.[5]

1.3. *Welfare*

Welfare, W, is radio stations' profits plus consumer utility, U, plus the total surplus of advertisers at each station, S_L and S_R, where $S_j = pf(a_j x_j) - p_j a_j$. For consumers,

$$U = \int_0^{s_L} [\underline{v} - a_L - t(L-s)^2]\mathrm{d}s + \int_{s_L}^{s_R} \{\underline{v} - [\lambda_s a_L + (1-\lambda_s a_R)]$$

$$-t(\Gamma_s - s)^2\}\mathrm{d}s + \int_{s_R}^{1} [\underline{v} - a_R - t(s-R)^2]\mathrm{d}s. \tag{8}$$

Let A denote total advertising heard i.e.

$$A \equiv a_L x_L + a_R x_R. \tag{9}$$

Then, substituting in for the optimal λ_s, we can rewrite utility:

$$U = \underline{v} - A - \frac{t}{3}[L^3 + (1-R)^3] - \frac{4t}{81}(R-L)[1-(R+L)]^2. \tag{10}$$

Now, defining Y as (broadly) producers' surplus,

$$\begin{aligned} Y \equiv \pi_L + \pi_R + S_L + S_R &= (p_L a_L - F) + (p_R a_R - F) \\ &\quad + [pf(a_L x_L) - p_L a_L] + [pf(a_R x_R) - p_R a_R] \\ &= pf(a_L x_L) + pf(a_R x_R) - 2F, \end{aligned}$$

[5]Note that I do not carry this formal model through the rest of the chapter as it would complicate matters excessively. In particular, policy interventions that lead the radio stations to become more similar, while not reducing the incentive to advertise at only one station, would lessen the attraction of advertising at any particular station.

where each radio station incurs a fixed operating cost of F. Thus,

$$W = \underline{v} - 2F - \frac{t}{3}[L^3 + (1-R)^3] - \frac{4t}{81}(R-L)[1-(R+L)]^2 + \sum_{j=L,R} [a_j x_j - pf(a_j x_j)]. \quad (11)$$

1.4. *A restriction*

We assume henceforth a particular form of the $f(\cdot)$ function such that $f'(\cdot) = a_j x_j$ and we normalise $\underline{p}$ to unity. Hence producers' surplus becomes $Y = A - 2F$ and so welfare is:

$$W = \underline{v} - 2F - \frac{t}{3}[L^3 + (1-R)^3] - \frac{4t}{81}(R-L)[1-(R+L)]^2. \quad (12)$$

While the normalisation of $\underline{p}$ to unity is innocuous, assuming that the marginal product for advertisers, in terms of goods sales, of another unit of audience is always unity (i.e., that $f'(\cdot) = 1$) is not so innocent. Indeed, it is the source of our later result that advertising has no welfare effects in this model. As a consequence advertising here serves a role isomorphic to that of prices in the more usual Hotelling model: it is purely a transfer between consumers and firms. The rationale for this assumption is tractability: it enables the model to be solved in closed-form. Nevertheless, it should be recognised that it does determine the specific nature of our welfare results; we provide some conjecture on their robustness in the paper's conclusion.

Given this restriction, from (6) we can solve the first-order conditions in (7):

$$a_L(L, R, p_L, p_R) = \frac{1}{3}t(R-L)[2 + (R+L) - 2(2p_L + p_R)]$$

$$a_R(L, R, p_L, p_R) = \frac{1}{3}t(R-L)[4 - (R+L) - 2(2p_R + p_L)]. \quad (13)$$

Note that advertising with station $j = L, R$ decreases both with its own price and the price of advertising at the other station: advertising prices are strategic substitutes for the radio stations — in contrast to both the Anderson and Coate (2000) and GLS models, as noted earlier. The reason for this is that an increased price at one station discourages advertising thus increasing consumer demand and so making advertising at the rival station less attractive to advertisers.

2. Some benchmarks

2.1. *The subscription case*

First, to isolate the role played in our subsequent analysis by our advertising model, suppose the radio stations were funded purely by subscription.[6] While this is currently more of a reality for television than radio, nevertheless it provides a useful benchmark. We consider two versions of a subscription channel. One involves solely a fixed fee for subscription, independent of the amount of listening/viewing undertaken. The other involves a price charged directly to consumers per minute of broadcasting time consumed (pay-per-view in the context of television). In reality, TV subscriptions typically involve a bundled subset of channels, many of which carry advertising but, in the context of our two-station model, a bundle with a subscription fee is isomorphic to the non-subscription case, except that consumers also pay a fixed fee. One might argue that the existence of advertising within a subscription package indicates that advertising is, on net, a social benefit (otherwise the provider could eliminate it and charge a fee that more than compensates for the lost revenue). But this co-existence is consistent with our model where it is a matter of indifference to consumers whether they face higher advertising or a higher subscription fee that leaves the provider unaffected.

In the first of these, a consumer must pay a fixed fee, P_j, to station $j = L, R$ in order to receive its programming. If the market is covered (i.e., all consumers receive at least one station), we again have three types of consumer: those who listen to only one station and those that listen to both. For the latter, utility is given by $u(s, \lambda, L, R, a_L, a_R) = \underline{v} - t[\lambda L + (1 - \lambda)R - s]^2 - (P_L + P_R)$ and there is now no reason to

[6] I am grateful to a referee for suggesting this exercise.

ever choose an optimal mix that differs from s: the optimal λ is just $\lambda = (R-s)/(R-L)$ yielding utility of $\underline{v}-(P_L+P_R)$. This compares to $\underline{v}-t(s-j)^2-P_j$ when consuming only $j=L,R$ so we can again categorise consumers by their location and listening pattern:

$$\left.\begin{array}{r}\text{only to L}\\ \text{Listen to both}\\ \text{only to R}\end{array}\right\} \text{ as } \begin{cases} s < s_L \equiv L + (\sqrt{P_R}/t)\\ s \in (s_L, s_R)\\ s > s_R \equiv R - (\sqrt{P_L}/t).\end{cases}$$

Suppose there exists a range of consumers subscribing to both stations. Then the total number of listeners at each station is $X_L = s_R$ and $X_R = 1 - s_L$ and profits of the two stations are simply $\pi_L = P_L x_L = P_L s_R$ and $\pi_R = P_R x_R = P_R(1-s_L)$. Maximising these over the relevant price yields stations' optimal prices and evaluating s_j at these prices yields $s_L^* = \frac{1}{3}(2-L)$ and $s_R^* = \frac{1}{3}R$. But for consumers to subscribe to both requires that $s_L^* < s_R^*$ or $R+L>2$ which is inconsistent with $L \leq R \leq 1$. So, regardless of locations, it is always optimal for prices to be raised until consumers choose to subscribe only to one station.

Consequently, our results for this case are exactly as in a standard Hotelling model with non-combinable products. There is a marginal consumer and we can solve for optimal prices, which then yield profit functions for the firms. Choosing locations to maximise profits then yields maximal differentiation: $L=0$ and $R=1$. In this setting, as in Hotelling, maximal differentiation of the stations is not socially optimal: the subscription fees are a transfer and social welfare is consumer utility less the stations' fixed costs so the socially optimal locations are those that minimise aggregate transport costs: $L=1/4$ and $R=3/4$.

An alternative form of subscription station is one in which the stations charge by the extent of a listener's usage — the analogue of pay-per-view television. In this set-up the prices charged by the stations serve exactly the role played by advertising levels in our model. Consequently, consumer demands here are exact analogues of those in Section 1.1 but with prices replacing advertising levels: p_j instead of a_j. Station $j=L,R$ then chooses p_j to maximise $\pi_j = p_j x_j - F$ which yields price reaction functions and these can be solved for equilibrium prices in terms of locations alone yielding, in turn, market shares and profits, all as functions of locations. Choosing locations simultaneously to maximise these profit functions yields the principle of maximal differentiation: the radio stations choose locations $L = 0$ and $R = 1$. Again this is not socially optimal for the same reasons as in the previous subscription model.

2.2. *The first-best solution*

Second, returning to the model laid out in Section 1, suppose a benevolent social planner could choose all quantities and locations.[7] As noted, the level of advertising is irrelevant to social welfare — it washes out of (12) as it is purely a transfer from consumers to radio stations and advertisers. This also implies that even if the planner could *only* choose locations the first-best could still be attained. The first-best choice of locations, then, seeks solely to minimise the disutility to consumers of getting a less than ideal music mix and involves maximal differentiation $-L = 0$ and $R = 1$ – and yields $W = \underline{v} - 2F$. Maximal differentiation means every consumer can construct his or her own ideal mix of content so there are no disutility costs at all. What sort of music is played in equilibrium? Clearly a half of all music *played* is local and a half is from the rest of the world. This is also true of the music *heard*, which we denote M_L: all listeners get a mix of L and R for, on average, 50% local content. So in the first-best we get $M_L = 1/2$. We summarise this all in Proposition 1.

Proposition 1. *In the absence of any externality attached to local music, first best locations involve maximal differentiation:* $L = 0$ *and* $R = 1$*, whether or not advertising levels can also be chosen: the level of advertising is irrelevant to welfare in the first best. Half of all music heard in equilibrium is of local origin.*

---

[7]One might also consider a second-best solution in which the planner is subject to a non-negative profit constraint on the radio stations. We ignore this constraint throughout (because it is effectively a condition on F that is uninteresting unless one is concerned with the pattern of entry, which is not the focus of this chapter — implicitly we assume that any losses are covered by the regulator.)

3. The laissez-faire solution

Now suppose the planner delegates all choices of locations and prices to the radio stations i.e., we look for the laissez-faire market solution.

3.1. *The stations' problem*

We seek a subgame perfect equilibrium to a 2-stage game in which radio stations first choose their locations simultaneously and then simultaneously set advertising prices, given the advertising demand of advertisers, as already discussed. In the second stage, each station chooses the price to charge for advertising, knowing the advertisers' consequent demands as given in (13). So station L, for example, chooses p_L to maximise $\pi_L = a_L p_L$ given locations and given (13). That is,

$$\underset{\{p_L\}}{\text{Max}}\, \pi_L = a_L p_L - F = \frac{1}{3}t(R-L)[(2+R+L-2p_R)p_L - 4p_L^2] - F$$

$$\Rightarrow p_L = \frac{1}{8}[2+(R+L)-2p_R]. \tag{14}$$

Similarly, R chooses p_R to maximise $\pi_R = a_R p_R$ given locations and (13), which yields:

$$p_R = \frac{1}{8}[4-(R+L)-2p_L]. \tag{15}$$

Solving the reaction functions (14) and (15) yields equilibrium prices and these in turn yield equilibrium advertising levels as functions of locations only. We can then use these to get profits as functions of locations only. To summarise:

$$p_L(L,R) = \frac{1}{30}[4+5(R+L)]$$

$$p_R(L,R) = \frac{1}{30}[14-5(R+L)]$$

$$a_L(L,R) = \frac{t(R-L)}{45}[8+10(R+L)]$$

$$a_R(L,R) = \frac{t(R-L)}{45}[28-10(R+L)]$$

$$\pi_L(L,R) = \frac{t(R-L)}{(45)(15)}[4+5(R+L)]^2 - F$$

$$\pi_R(L,R) = \frac{t(R-L)}{(45)(15)}[14-5(R+L)]^2 - F. \tag{16}$$

In the first stage of the game, then, the stations choose these locations simultaneously knowing the subsequent prices and advertising levels that will result. Solving for the equilibrium locations yields closed-form expressions for equilibrium prices, advertising levels and profits, denoting laissez-faire values with asterisks:

$$\begin{aligned} &L^* = 0.05 \quad R^* = 0.95 \\ &p_L^* = p_R^* = \frac{3}{10} \quad a_L^* = a_R^* = \frac{9}{25}t \\ &\pi_L^* = \pi_R^* = \frac{27}{250}t - F \quad x_L^* = x_R^* = \frac{1}{2}. \end{aligned} \tag{17}$$

Note that, in contrast to both GLS who demonstrate maximal differentiation and Gal-Or and Dukes (2003) who obtain minimal differentiation, we get incomplete differentiation. As with similar models (d'Aspremont *et al.*, 1979) there is an incentive here for forward-looking stations to locate away from each other in order to lessen subsequent competition which shows up here in advertising levels; these serve the role of prices to consumers. The difference between this model and a standard Hotelling model, however, is in the relationship between market share and profits. In the usual Hotelling setting an increase in market share, at given prices, feeds directly into higher profits as the firm's maximand is the product of price and market share. But here the effect of market share is mediated through the price of advertising: given the level of advertising, increased market share enables the firm to charge more for its advertising time. So whereas a Hotelling firm in the direct analogue of this model would choose location to maximise a_jx_j directly (a_j serving the role of prices), our firm seeks to maximise a_jp_j where $p_j = d(a_jx_j)/da_j$ from the first-order condition for advertisers. As a consequence the losses to a firm from moving away from its rival in this model are greater than those from the same exercise in the more usual Hotelling setup and we get less than complete differentiation. This does not stem from the combinable products aspect of the model (as it does not hold in the subscription version of the model, as noted) but, rather, from our modelling of advertising. What matters here is the marginal viewing minute of every consumer, not the marginal consumer as in standard Hotelling (which is also why our earlier subscription model with a fixed fee (standard Hotelling) differs from that with a usage fee).

What sort of music is played in equilibrium? Again a half of all music *played* is local and a half is international. This is also true of music *heard*: 5% of listeners listen only to station L and get 95% local content, 5% listen only to station R and get only 5% local content, and the remainder get a mix of L and R for, on average, 50% local content. So in the no-intervention case, as in any symmetric outcome, $M_L = 1/2$.

3.2. *Welfare*

In the laissez-faire solution, from (16), we can evaluate consumers' utility and social welfare directly as $U^* = \underline{v} - (4,321t/12,000)$ and $W^* = \underline{v} - (t/12,000) - 2F$ respectively. Diagrammatically we can portray utility as in Figure 1. All consumers suffer some disutility from advertising (equal at both stations). Welfare is highest for consumers between s_L and s_R who mix both stations to get their ideal personal mixes. Consumers closer to 0 (respectively 1) than $L(R)$ listen only to $L(R)$ but incur increasing quadratic disutility costs the more (less) local content they prefer.

It is straightforward to show that the optimal symmetric locations are $L = 0$ and $R = 1$. If the planner were to impose this maximal differentiation but let the stations determine the advertising equilibrium, we would get higher profits for the stations and greater surplus for advertisers than in the laissez-faire solution. But total consumer welfare is actually lower: even though this would yield $U = \underline{v} - a$ (so the only disutility is from advertising) we would have greater advertising in equilibrium than in the laissez-faire solution.

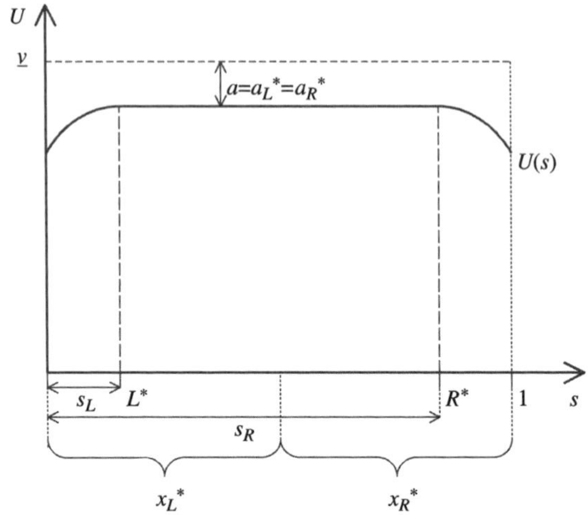

Fig. 1. Consumer welfare in Laissez-faire

Indeed, consumer utility is maximised at $L = R = 1/2$ when market equilibrium advertising is considered — *less* differentiation than in the laissez-faire solution. Interestingly, if the radio stations were to collude on their locations we would also get maximal differentiation: the socially optimal solution.

In contrast to the standard Hotelling model in which the laissez-faire solution gives more differentiation than is socially optimal, in our model we get less. This is both because our social optimum is more differentiated than in Hotelling and because our laissez-faire outcome is less differentiated. The former is due to the combinable goods: in a standard Hotelling model prices are a pure transfer and optimal locations are simply those that minimise total transport costs whereas with combinable products transport costs play less of a role in determining the social optimum. The latter effect is because, as discussed, the incentive to move apart is lessened by the way in which market share feeds, through the demand for advertising, into the stations' profits.

We summarise this discussion in Proposition 2.

Proposition 2. *The laissez-faire solution yields less than maximal differentiation. Compared to the maximal differentiation outcome* *with endogenous advertising — also the outcome if firms were to collude on location choices — the laissez-faire solution yields lower advertising, higher consumer surplus and lower profits to both radio stations and advertisers. Half of all music heard is local.*

4. A cultural regulator

Now suppose we have a cultural regulator. As noted earlier, we wish to allow that there may be something to the arguments made by proponents of local content requirements that hearing local music generates some "cultural" external benefit. In the partial equilibrium setting we have here, we propose simply that the regulator's objective function considers not just social welfare but the amount of local content heard: they seek to maximise $v^R = W + \rho M_L$ where ρ measures the value of this external benefit that is linear in the amount of local content heard. This is a very terse means of capturing the elaborate and emotional arguments that are frequently made in defence of cultural protection but, in the context of a fairly simple model, it seems the most accurate way in which to give some power to these arguments. Thus,

$$\begin{aligned} v^R &= \underline{v} + \rho M_L - 2F - \frac{t}{3}[L^3 + (1-R)^3] \\ &\quad - \frac{4t}{81}(R-L)[1-(R+L)]^2. \end{aligned} \tag{18}$$

But total local content heard, from (6), is:

$$\begin{aligned} M_L &= x_L(1-L) + x_R(1-R) = M_L \\ &= \frac{1}{2}\left[\frac{1}{t}(a_R - a_L) + (R-L)(R+L) + 2(1-R)\right]. \end{aligned} \tag{19}$$

Consider the first-best choices of locations and advertising such a regulator would make. With $\rho > 0$ the optimal choice of L is still zero: if local music heard has value in itself then the regulator would not wish to move station L from playing only local music. Furthermore, it would choose zero advertising at that station to increase its audience. The optimal location of R is now a complicated function of ρ and t with the property that an interior solution is decreasing in ρ: the more valuable is local music the more the planner would choose the second station to play, trading that off against the desirability of spanning the distribution of consumers. Welfare is everywhere increasing in the level of advertising at station R (as it increases the audience of L) and is effectively constrained by the demand curve from advertisers. Thus:

Proposition 3. *With an externality* (ρ) *attached to local music, first best locations still involve one station playing only local content* ($L = 0$), *but the other station also plays some local content* ($R \leq 1$), *the amount increasing in* ρ. *Advertising at the local music station is zero with advertising at the other station maximised.*

4.1. *A cultural quota*

Consider now the imposition of a local content requirement — a cultural quota — requiring that both stations play a minimum percentage — at least $c\%$ — local content. Station R has no incentive to more than satisfy the constraint so it will bind exactly on the station. As the quota is a locational constraint it is cleaner to deal with $\gamma \equiv 1-c$: the maximum permitted fraction of non-local content. So a greater local content requirement — a tighter quota — corresponds to a lower y.

Before looking at the optimal quota we first derive the comparative static effects of changes in the quota. Inspection of L's best response function reveals that there are two qualitatively different quota levels here: if $\gamma \leq 0.8$—*a restrictive* quota — then L's best response is to locate at the end of the segment i.e., $L = 0$, whereas for $\gamma \in (0.8, 0.95]$ — a *mild* quota — L will not completely specialise in local content.

4.1.1. *Effects on local content audience*

Consider first the case of a restrictive quota ($\gamma \leq 0.8$). Consequently $R = \gamma$ and L's best response is $L = 0$. We can then recalculate the values of all variables of interest. Our first result is that the profits of both stations are increasing in γ so tightening a restrictive content requirement (a *lower* γ) makes both stations worse off. (As noted earlier, there is a non-negative profit constraint on the regulator, which we ignore, implicitly assuming any losses are covered by the regulator.) As the quota is tightened, the price of advertising at L decreases and that at R increases but, nevertheless, advertising at both stations falls: L's market share is falling while R's is rising. With a restrictive quota, clearly more local content is *played* $-L$ is now playing only local content and R is playing more than before — indeed, total local content aired is now $\frac{1}{2}(2-\gamma)$. But we may have fewer people listening only to station L and we certainly have a greater fraction listening only to R. For the rest, we need to integrate over the consumers listening to both stations. Doing so, we can show that tightening the quota always leads to more local content being heard overall.

If we consider instead the case of a mild quota (in which $\gamma \in (0.8, 0.95)$) then, as with a restrictive quota, both the price and level of advertising at L decrease as the quota is tightened, as its market share falls, while R's price rises with its market share and advertising at R also increases. While station L's profits increase in γ, R's profits are decreasing so R gains from a tighter quota while L is harmed by it. The observation that a constraint can benefit the constrained firm is a familiar one from the literature; see Crampes and Hollander (1995). As with a restrictive quota, total local content heard here exceeds 50% and tightening a mild quota always leads to more local content being heard.

Putting these two quota regimes together, we can plot the amount of local content played and heard as in Figure 2 (not to scale). The quota has two effects on the amount of local content being listened to — it changes the mix played by each station (an effect that always works to increase the amount of local content) but it also changes the audience each station faces. As it is tightened, both stations move down the spectrum. While R's market increases, the audience shifting effect — more people listening to the less local content intensive station — never outweighs the mix effect.

In summary,

Comparative statics of a cultural quota:

Tightening a local-music quota

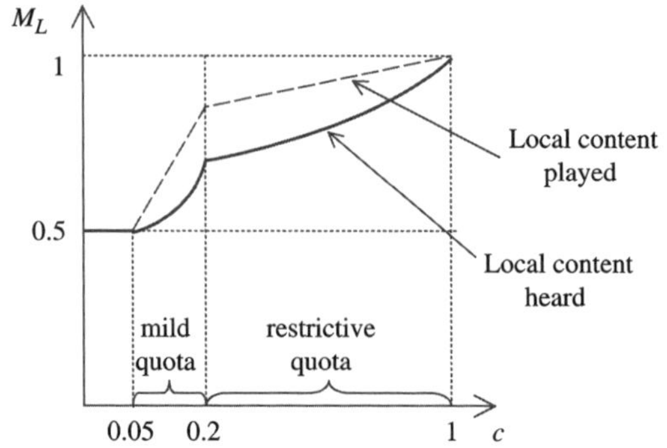

Fig. 2. Local content shares with quota

(i) *monotonically reduces both R and L, the latter reaching zero at a quota of 20%, increasing R's market share at L's expense;*
(ii) *reduces the profits of L and initially raises then decreases those of R;*
(iii) *reduces both the price and level of advertising at L but increases both the price and level of advertising at R;*
(iv) *increases the amount of local music heard, but by less than the increase in the amount played.*

In our earlier subscription benchmark, a content requirement intuitively acts just like a restrictive quota above: as the laissez-faire solution is maximal differentiation so a quota on R elicits no locational response from L. As it is tightened, local music heard increases, both firms' profits decline and both utility and welfare decline.

4.1.2. *Welfare*

Again, consider first a restrictive quota. For consumers listening only to L disutility is $a_{L\gamma} + ts^2$ where a gamma subscript indicates values taken under a restrictive quota. These consumers gain as the quota is tightened because the only effect on them, at the margin, is the decrease in $a_{L\gamma}$ as γ falls. For consumers listening only to R disutility is $a_{R\gamma} + t(s - \gamma)^2$ and they gain from decreased advertising at R as y falls but lose as R moves down the spectrum and becomes less appealing. Finally, for consumers listening to both stations disutility

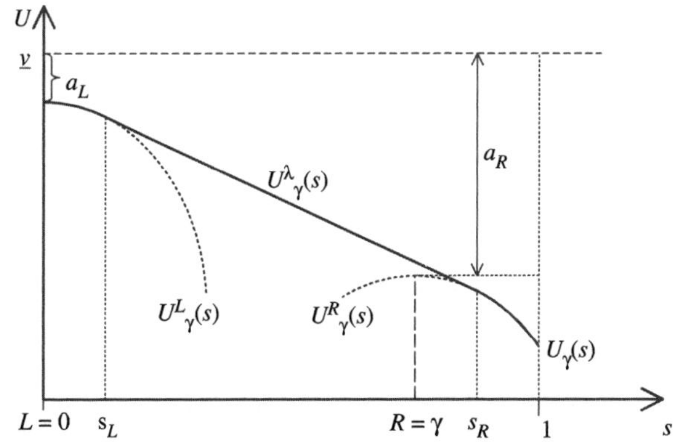

Fig. 3. Consumer welfare with quota

is $t(\Gamma_s - s)^2 + a_{R\gamma} - \lambda_s(a_{R\gamma} - a_{L\gamma})$. All up:

$$v_\gamma^R = \underline{v} - 2F + \frac{\rho}{18}(5\gamma^2 - 14\gamma + 18) - \frac{t}{81}(27 - 77\gamma + 73\gamma^2 - 23\gamma^3). \tag{20}$$

Without the externality ($\rho = 0$) welfare is everywhere increasing in γ so the quota is always harmful. Figure 3 illustrates the effects of this quota on consumers.

Utility is highest for a consumer at 0 who listens only to L, her ideal station (which also has the lowest advertising.) Other consumers at $s \leq s_L$ also consuming only L because of the low advertising incur increasing disutility the less local content they prefer. Consumers between s_L and s_R mix both stations but get lower utility as their preferred mix of R rises (because of its higher advertising.) Consumers listening only to R are the worst off. Note that a consumer located at R gets utility of $\underline{v} - a_R$ if they consume only R but can do better by listening to some lower-advertising L as well.

With a mild quota, in the absence of any externality, welfare is increasing in γ over the entire range of $\gamma \in [0.8, 0.95]$. So welfare again falls as the quota is tightened (and falls more steeply than for the more restrictive quota). If we look at the various components of welfare, consumers actually gain from a small quota: their welfare initially rises as the local content requirement is increased from the no-quota level of 5% and then increases more rapidly as it rises beyond $c = 20\%$. It is maximised at around $c_2 \cong 62\%$ and then falls. What is driving this is that, as the quota is tightened, the stations become less differentiated and total advertising heard falls. This raises the welfare of consumers who dislike advertising, but with further increases in the quota the welfare gains from reduced advertising are more than offset by the disutility losses of less ideal station content mixes. Looking at the other components of welfare, $(\pi_L + \pi_R)$ and $(S_L + S_R)$ are isomorphic. While profits and surplus are monotonically decreasing in the local content requirement, once it exceeds 20% and station L plays only local content, profits and surplus decline more steeply in c.

So far we have said little of the externality. Its effects, however, are quite straightforward. While in the absence of any external benefit associated with listening to local content a cultural quota is welfare-reducing, the more significant the externality becomes, the more attractive is a quota. Figure 4 presents a numerical simulation of the model that illustrates this point. With no externality ($\rho = 0$) welfare is declining monotonically in the quota. When the externality

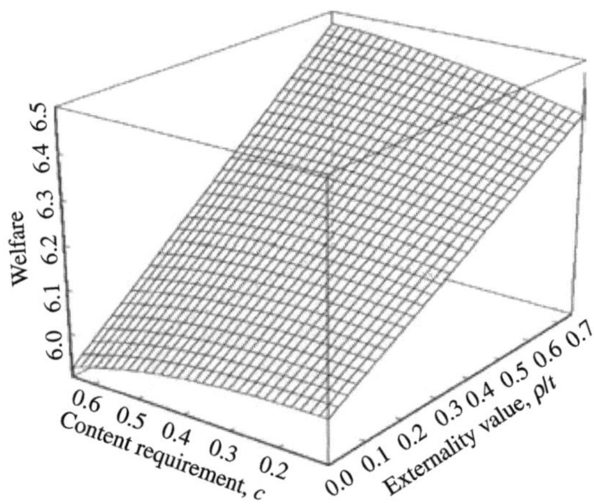

Fig. 4. Welfare with quota and externality

is more significant ($\rho = 0.7t$) welfare is increasing monotonically in the quota. At intermediate values of ρ we find an optimal level of the content requirement that, intuitively, is increasing in ρ.

We summarise the discussion of this section as follows:

Proposition 4. *Tightening a cultural quota*

(i) *Monotonically reduces social welfare;*
(ii) *initially increases consumers' welfare but eventually reduces it;*
(iii) *monotonically reduces stations' and advertisers' total surplus;*
(iv) *increases a regulator's welfare if the value, ρ, placed on local music is sufficiently high — thc regulator's optimal quota is then increasing in ρ.*

4.2. *Advertising limits*

The gains in welfare from imposing a cultural quota come in this model from the decreased advertising such a quota induces by making the radio stations more similar in programming. This suggests that a better policy would be simply to cap the amount of advertising stations can offer. In this section we consider such a policy, which has been proposed for television regulation (see the discussion in GLS).

Suppose the amount of advertising each station can place is limited to $\underline{a}$. If this ceiling is "very low" it will constrain both stations and each will simply choose its price such that the demand from advertisers is exactly $\underline{a}$. (If the limit is not "very low" then equilibrium locations will be those that yield $\underline{a}$ as an optimal choice in the absence of any advertising limit. We focus only on symmetric equilibria: see GSL for a detailed derivation in their model of the constraint binding both stations as an equilibrium property.) Inverting (13) and solving the resulting reaction functions yields prices as functions of locations and $\underline{a}$. In the first stage of the game, then, radio station $j = L, R$ chooses its location to maximise $\pi_j = p_j\underline{a}$. We can then solve for equilibrium locations and hence prices and profits as functions of $\underline{a}$ (available in the Technical Appendix http://www.res.org.uk/economic/ta/tahome.asp)

Turning to welfare, we again have

$$v^R = \pi_L + \pi_R + U + S_L + S_R + \rho M_L$$

where U is given in (10). The Technical Appendix demonstrates that welfare is *everywhere* decreasing as advertising is restricted over the range $\underline{a} \in [0, 0.36t]$. Consumer welfare alone, however, is maximised at $\underline{a} \cong 0.01$ at which point (subject to our earlier caveat concerning zero-profit constraints) we get $U \cong \underline{v} - 0.707t$ which compares favourably to the laissez-faire level of consumer welfare, $(\underline{v} - 0.3601t)$.

So while an advertising ceiling is always welfare-reducing, it does benefit consumers. As in GLS, it leads to both stations locating progressively much nearer to the centre of the spectrum and thus leads to much lower differentiation between them — not surprisingly, as the only rationale for differentiation here is to foster advertising — and exactly half of all music heard being local. But while consumers find that the disutility costs associated with an undesirable product mix are increased, this is more than offset by gains from reduced advertising. Nevertheless, an advertising cap is less successful in achieving the goals of a cultural quota than the quota itself as it reduces welfare by more as well as having no effect on the amount of local music heard.

An interesting implication of this is that the optimal advertising policy is to impose an advertising floor of $\underline{a} = 0.4t$ which gives maximal differentiation and consumer utility of $\underline{v} - \underline{a}$. But, while consumer welfare is lower, total welfare is higher.

We summarise the discussion of this Section in Proposition 5.

Proposition 5. *An advertising ceiling, compared to the laissez-faire solution,*

(i) *decreases diversity by leading L and R to locate closer together;*
(ii) *monotonically reduces the joint surplus of advertisers and radio stations;*
(iii) *initially increases consumer welfare before decreasing it;*
(iv) *monotonically reduces social welfare;*
(v) *has no impact on the amount of local music heard.*

4.3. *A public station*

Suppose the government were to provide a publicly-funded radio station — denote it P — that broadcasts no advertising and plays only local content and so is located at 0 on our spectrum. A consequence of such a policy is that L will move up the spectrum and the Technical Appendix identifies an equilibrium in which $P < L < R$. We show that for any locations $0 = P < L < R$ it must be the case that a_L is such that no consumer mixes P and R. The reason is that if any consumer finds it optimal to combine P and R then all consumers between P and R must do so too, thus leaving no market for L.

Proceeding as before, we solve for L and R :

$$L = \frac{2\sqrt{489} - 10}{87} \cong 0.3934 \quad R = \frac{318 + 6\sqrt{489}}{522} \cong 0.8634. \tag{21}$$

From this we can calculate all the variables of interest. Note that while the existence of the public station drives station L to play less local content, it leads station R to play *more*. So, rather surprisingly, the provision of P induces *less* diversity because of the reaction of L to the new entrant: L is displaced by a non-commercial station leading to a drastic reduction in its advertising to attract listeners. This puts pressure on R so it moves closer to increase its market share and appeal to advertisers. While both stations have substantially lower profits than in the absence of P, if R were to move further up the spectrum it would be followed by L. How much local content is played and heard? Local content *played* is a little over 58.1% of total airtime and local content *heard* is a little under 58.3% of total broadcasting heard.

Turning to welfare, we find that a non-commercial public radio station playing only local content yields surplus to the regulator of v_P^R:

$$\begin{aligned} v_p^R &= U + \pi_p + \pi_L + \pi_R + S_L + S_R + \rho M_L \\ &\cong \underline{v} + 0.5830\rho - 0.0071t - 3F. \end{aligned} \tag{22}$$

How effective is a publicly-provided station? If the regulator's objective is to increase the amount of local content heard, we have seen that this policy achieves that. If we chose the local content requirement that yielded the same amount of local content we would need a requirement of around 28% which would yield welfare of $\underline{v} + 0.5830\rho - 0.0098t - 2F$. This may be greater than that associated with the public station depending on the costs of establishing the latter: if greater than $0.0027t$ then a publicly provided station is not an attractive option.

Fixed costs aside, however, the public station is preferred to the local content- equivalent quota (but not necessarily to the regulator's optimal quota) for a couple of reasons. As total advertising washes out of the welfare calculus, the only sources of welfare differences can be disutility costs from less than ideal mixes for consumers. But market 'coverage' is greater with the public station than under the local content- equivalent quota. Furthermore, the differences in advertising levels across the stations distort the listening choices of inframarginal consumers away from their ideals less dramatically with the public station than the equivalent quota: with the public station, the difference in advertising levels between the commercial stations is only $0.0801t$ whereas under the equivalent quota it is $0.0896t$.

We summarise this discussion in Proposition 6.[8]

Proposition 6. *A publicly-provided non-commercial radio station (no advertising) playing only local music, compared to the laissez-faire solution,*

(i) *induces L to play less local music but R to play more;*
(ii) *reduces profits at both commercial stations;*
(iii) *increases local music heard above the level played;*
(iv) *increases consumers' welfare;*

[8] I have also looked at the impact of a public firm competing with a single commercial broadcaster *à la* "mixed oligopoly" models. In such a case we assume the public firm, with no advertising, chooses its location to maximise welfare. Its equilibrium location turns out to be at around $L = 0.112$ which induces the commercial station to locate at around $R = 0.704$. Advertising at R is around 0.175 at a price of 0.296, local music heard is around 62.5% of total listening time and welfare, for $\rho = 0$, becomes $W \cong \underline{v} - 2F - 0.0101t$. This compares favourably to welfare under the local content-equivalent quota (of $\gamma \cong 0.173$) of $W \cong \underline{v} - 2F - 0.1943t$. I am grateful to a referee for suggesting this exercise.

(v) *can increase a regulator's welfare above that of the local music-equivalent quota if the fixed cost of establishing the public station is sufficiently low.*

5. Conclusion

This chapter has developed a model in which radio stations choose a mix of local and international content to play to consumers with diverse preferences, driven by the ability to sell advertising to advertisers seeking maximum market coverage. We consider a number of benchmarks and look at three policy options for a regulator that wishes to increase the exposure of local content. A local content requirement — a cultural quota — will indeed increase the amount of local content heard and can even increase utility for consumers. However, it harms advertisers and the radio stations (eventually — a mild quota, we have seen, benefits the constrained station, R) by reducing the differentiation between the stations and overall is welfare reducing in the absence of any externality associated with an increased local content audience.

A cap on advertising and a publicly-funded non-commercial station playing only local content are also analysed and we find that the quota can welfare-dominate, with or without an externality. The advertising cap also decreases diversity but it does so by leading the stations to locate closer together in the centre of the spectrum. While consumers gain from the lower advertising, more are harmed by the decreased diversity of the stations available. The problem with the publicly provided station is that it competes most directly with the more local content oriented station, L. So the latter must cut its advertising which induces the other commercial station to move in closer rather than to move further away. Note that when advertising is endogenous, closer locations lead to greater aggression in the form of lower advertising, which is why laissez-faire locations are well apart as the firms, in anticipation of that competition, locate away from each other. When advertising is limited exogenously, as here, a firm is drawn closer to its rival: the incentive to move in is the higher market share and the incentive to move out — to lessen advertising competition — has been stifled by the regulation. So, again, diversity is reduced. Indeed, the optimal advertising policy here is to require that stations advertise *more:* the laissez-faire solution has too little diversity (as critics often suggest) and if stations are required to sell *more* advertising each would move away from the other.

While our exact results are, of course, special to the exact assumptions we have made, the overall thrust of them seems more general. In particular, the analysis in this chapter highlights the fact that a cultural quota decreases the diversity of radio stations and stresses the ramifications of this for advertising. The general tenor of our comparative statics results also seems quite robust as they stem from the model's Hotelling construction in which horizontally differentiated firms who are forced closer together will tend to compete more fiercely. Our welfare conclusions, however, are likely more fragile. We have maintained a restriction on the advertising side of the model resulting in the level of advertising having no effects on aggregate welfare, the gains to advertisers exactly offsetting the losses to consumers. If, instead, it were assumed that advertising has a net positive (negative) effect then one might expect a cultural quota to be less (more) attractive than in our model because, in reducing diversity, it also decreases the amount of advertising heard.

In terms of future work that might be pursued here, we have assumed in our analysis that the market is always covered — all consumers listen to radio stations. If we allow that consumers will not listen if the combined disutility of the content mix and advertising level is 'too high' then an extra welfare-reducing effect of a cultural quota will arise: some consumers with a strong preference for international content will drop out of the market in the face of the quota. Further, our model has the testable empirical implications that a local content scheme will increase the local content of all radio stations, whether the scheme is directly binding on them or not and that it will reduce advertising, *ceteris paribus.*

References

Acheson, K. and C. Maule (1990). Canadian content rules: A time for reconsideration. *Canadian Public Policy*, 16(3), 284–97.

Anderson, S. and S. Coate (2000). Market provision of public goods: The case of broadcasting. Cambridge, MA: NBER Working Paper 7513.

Anderson, S. and D. Neven (1989). Market efficiency with combinable products. *European Economic Review*, 33, 707–19.

Berry, S. and J. Waldfogel (1999a). Free entry and social inefficiency in radio broadcasting. *RAND Journal of Economics*, 30(3), 397–420.

Berry, S. and J. Waldfogel (1999b). Public radio in the United States: Does it correct market failure or cannibalize commercial stations? *Journal of Public Economics*, 71, 189–211.

Crampes, C. and A. Hollander (1995). Duopoly and quality standards. *European Economic Review*, 39(1), 71–82.

Crampes, C. and A. Hollander (1999). The regulation of audiovisual content: Quotas and conflicting objectives. Mimeo: University of Montreal.

d'Aspremont, C., J. Gabszewicz and J.-F. Thisse (1979). On Hotelling's stability in competition. *Econometrica*, 47(5), 1145–50.

Francois, P. and T. van Ypersele (2002). On the protection of cultural goods. *Journal of International Economics*, 56, 359–69.

Gabszewicz, J., D. Laussel and N. Sonnac (2000). TV broadcasting competition and advertising. CORE Discussion Paper No. 2000/6.

Gal-Or, E. and A. Dukes (2003). Minimum differentiation in commercial media markets. *Journal of Economics and Management Strategy*, 12(3), 291–325.

Hotelling, H. (1929). Stability in competition. *Economic Journal*, 39(153), 41–57.

Jacobsen, V. (2000). *Local Content Regulation of New Zealand Television.* Wellington, NZ: Arthur Andersen.

Krattenmaker, T. and L. Powe (1994). *Regulating Broadcast Programming.* Cambridge, MA: The MIT Press and Washington DC: The AEI Press.

Owen, B. and S. Wildman (1992). *Video Economics.* Cambridge, MA: Harvard University Press.

Chapter 4

Faddists, Enthusiasts and Canadian Divas: Broadcasting Quotas and the Supply Response

Martin Richardson and Simon Wilkie

Abstract: This chapter constructs a model of the recorded music market to investigate the consequences of local content requirements in broadcasting for the "internationalization" of domestic music. It models the entry decisions of bands, the contracting decisions of record companies, the airplay decisions of radio stations and the radio listening and recording purchasing decisions of consumers. The chapter shows that a local content quota leads, perversely, to the increased internationalization of domestic music. A quota that also requires increased broadcasting of "new" music yields an additional welfare loss but does nothing to a record company's incentives to sign up new bands.

1. Introduction

Many countries prevent domestic broadcasters from freely choosing the proportions of international and "domestic" content that they broadcast. Why is this done? Mas-Colell (1999) draws a useful distinction between "protection of national cultural production" and "protection of the production of national culture." The former is protection designed to maintain the existence of a particular industry, be it sound recording or movie-making and, as Mas-Collel suggests, it is difficult to see why the case for such protection is much different

Originally published in *Review of International Economics*, 23(2), 404–424.

to the case for preserving shoe-making, car assembly or any other sector of the economy. The second term, however, refers to policies designed to, "promote the availability and consumption of [cultural goods] transmitting "Spanish," "French" or "Catalan" content: language, historical episodes, costumes, traditions, and the like." While the former is certainly cited by proponents of cultural protection, their principal arguments are of this latter sort: that cultural industries[1] should be protected to save unique aspects of the local culture and identity and to foster global cultural "diversity".[2]

The primary way in which broadcasting quotas might be used to achieve these goals is that being exposed to domestic music on the radio leads consumers to buy more such recordings, but a local content requirement constrains radio stations from choosing the airplay mix they prefer and so might impact on welfare through distorting this mix. Furthermore, the requirement may not bind on all genres. It will be particularly relevant where there is a greater preference for international content and one might anticipate that it will induce a shift in airplay away from international providers of those genres towards domestic artists in the same genre. Finally, a positive link between airtime and recording sales means a binding quota will induce entry by content providers into these constrained genres. Thus a local content quota might lead to the increased

[1]The scope of industries that might be considered "cultural" is vast, including food industries, protected under geographical indications legislation as well as more directly. Gordon and Meunier (2001, p. 30) cite the following position of one French commentator: "McDonald's ··· commercial hegemony threatens our agriculture and its cultural hegemony insidiously ruins alimentary behaviour — both sacred reflections of the French identity."

[2]This is by no means an uncontroversial proposition. It finds an extravagant expression in the words of ex-French President Mitterand, cited at p. 1147 of Acheson and Maule (2006): "Creations of the spirit are not just commodities··· What is at stake is the cultural identity of all our nations.··· A society which abandons to others the way of showing itself, that is to say the way of presenting itself to itself, is a society enslaved." By contrast, Revel (2003) perceives the French position as being essentially one of anti-Americanism and writes, "The idea that a culture can preserve its originality by barricading itself against foreign influences is an old illusion that has always produced the opposite of the desired result. Isolation breeds sterility."

"internationalization" of domestic music: Celine Dion, Shania Twain, Avril Lavigne and other Canadian singers might be considered essentially indistinguishable from US artists.[3]

To model this policy instrument fully requires a setting in which listening to radio airplay affects record purchasing decisions and in which both the entry decisions of artists and the contracting decisions of record companies are considered. There is an extensive literature on the economic analysis of broadcasting, discussed more fully in Richardson and Wilkie (2013), but few authors address the issues focused upon here. In particular, we are not aware of any literature that formally models the artist/record company/radio station/consumer interaction. This paper analyzes the consequences of a local content requirement in radio broadcasting when entry decisions of artists are endogenous. To do so, it constructs a model of the market for recorded music, integrating consumers (as both radio listeners and purchasers of recordings), radio stations, record companies and content providers ("bands"). In any genre there is an endogenous set of new domestic bands that could be contracted by a record company and some (endogenous) subset is, in fact, so contracted. Record companies extract record sales revenues and rents (from activities like concerts) from contracted bands for up to two periods; surviving bands then go off-contract and retain such income themselves. Genre-specific radio stations choose the airplay mix between new and established bands to maximize the listening time of their audience (in order to sell advertising time[4]) and consumers only buy the recordings of bands aired on the radio.

---

[3]Hence our titular reference. Our first encounter with the term "Canadian divas" was in an online opinion piece of Paul Krugman's suggesting that, "Boston residents who indulge their taste for Canadian divas do undermine the prospects of local singer-songwriters and might be collectively better off if local radio stations had some kind of cultural content rule" Krugman (1999). He goes on to note that, "there is a very fine line between such arguments for collective action and supercilious paternalism, especially when cultural matters are concerned".

[4]Mangani (2003) considers a model of broadcasting in which programs differ along both a vertical and a horizontal dimension and in which profit maximization and audience maximization are different things. This is not the case here.

We then consider the imposition of a local content quota in broadcasting — one that just specifies an upper limit on the share of airtime devoted to international music — in this setting and derive its steady state effects on entry decisions and welfare. Such quotas are typically justified on the grounds of thwarting the "internationalization" of music, but we show that they can have exactly the opposite effect by inducing a shift in the pattern of band entry into "international" genres. Nevertheless, we show that a mild quota[5] will be welfare-improving in this model, for (*inter alia*) a novel reason: it raises the profitability of successful domestic bands and thus encourages entry by new domestic entrants, the increased diversity of which appeals to some consumers. In practice, some countries have refined their quotas to remedy a perceived problem with the simple quota: the latter can be (and is, in our model) met by just increasing the airplay of established domestic bands and thus appears to do little for new talent.[6] We discuss the consequences of such a modification and show that, while the addition of a "new" band component decreases the total amount of radio listening time by consumers (yielding a welfare loss), it does nothing to incentives to sign up new bands.

A number of economists have looked at radio broadcasting (e.g. Coase, 1966; Berry and Waldfogel, 1999a,b; Anderson and Coate, 2005; Rogers and Woodbury, 1996). There is a long literature addressing the question of optimal program diversity and its relationship to market structure (see, for example, Doyle, 1998; Richardson, 2006) but in the context of models in which a broadcaster chooses its programming mix from some spectrum. There is a substantial policy-oriented literature discussing cultural quotas and related issues at an informal level (see, by way of example, Acheson and Maule, 1990; Jacobsen, 2000) but only a few recent papers (such as Francois and van Ypersele, 2002; Bala and Long, 2005) construct

[5]We use "mild" to describe a quota that is just binding in a genre.

[6]France and Australia, for example, require that a specified fraction of the local content quota must be met by the playing of "recent" recordings. "French music radio stations must broadcast a minimum of 40% French music (50% of which must be dedicated to 'new' French artists)." American University ICT Database (2001). For more on the prevalence of local content requirements in broadcasting see the Appendix to this paper, available online or upon request.

formal models of cultural protection. These are "big picture" models of cultural goods, considering whether there might be something distinctive about the production (Francois and van Ypersele, 2002) or the consumption (both papers) of such goods that gives rise to novel arguments for protection. Our paper focuses more specifically on a particular sector and a particular policy instrument.

Some papers have looked explicitly at broadcasting quotas (Crampes and Hollander, 1999; Owen and Wildman, 1992; Richardson, 2006) but none share our focus. Perona (2010) articulates explicitly the suggestion made above that a simple quota can be met just by putting established domestic artists on higher rotation in a model focused on the decisions of radio stations regarding which set of *genres* to broadcast. He does not consider the decisions of bands and record companies, in contrast to this paper, but models radio stations' decisions more thoroughly than we do. Our scope is rather different, looking primarily at the decisions of suppliers of content — bands and recording companies and, while Perona's "loss of diversity" result is from the broadcasting of fewer genres by radio stations, ours is from changes in the induced pattern of entry into genres.

Section 2 lays out our model, Section 3 explains the timing of actions and Section 4 exposits the laissez-faire, no-quota equilibrium of the model. Section 5 analyzes the impacts of local content quotas, a further section considers the robustness of the analysis and a final section concludes.

2. The model

We consider a model with four sets of actors: bands, record companies, radio stations, and consumers. The model is effectively an overlapping three-period model. We consider each set of actors in turn.

Bands

We make a small country assumption: there is a fixed number of foreign bands all of which are, by definition, "successful" and may be either on- or off-contract with foreign record companies — all revenues and rents earned by foreign bands accrue offshore. There is a large number of potential new domestic bands indexed by $j = 1, 2, \ldots$ that might enter into genre g; an endogenous subset M_g actually does so.

New bands incur a fixed cost F_B to enter a genre $g \in G = \{1, 2, \ldots, G\}$ and may be approached by record companies and contracted. In their first period bands make record sales that depend positively on their radio airtime but earn nothing from this, as they are under contract to a record company. In any genre, some new entrants will fail and exit while others will succeed and survive into the next period.[7] Successful bands not only sell records but generate a rent each period, representing surplus from concert revenues, T-shirt sales and so forth. In a band's first period of success this, too, accrues to the record company. There is some probability $1 - h$ of exit for a band after one period of success (under contract) so with probability h a successful band in its second period goes on to become a successful band in its third (and final) period, when any rents accrue to the now "off-contract"[8] band. So in any genre g there will be n_g^* successful foreign bands, n_{g2} (n_{g3}) successful domestic bands on- (off-) contract and n_{g1} new domestic entrants, for a total of $N_g \equiv N_{gs} + n_{g1} \equiv (n_g^* + n_{g2} + n_{g3}) + n_{g1}$ bands.

---

[7]The online Appendix discusses the nature of band "success" in more detail (and note that our model does not capture degrees of success — superstars vs regular stars) but, briefly, one can endogenize the choice of bands that are retained by record companies (i.e., are "successful") in a number of ways that still preserve the flavor of the analysis here. In the model here we assume no innate differences between new bands. Introducing an exogenous quality differential across new entrants (which is, presumably, imperfectly observable by record companies) would complicate matters but it is not clear that it would impact much upon our results. In particular, recognizing that music is, to some extent, an experience good, the Appendix notes that one can model a record company's decision to re-sign a band as depending on some inference drawn regarding the latter's quality from its first-period sales.

[8]By "off-contract" we simply mean that bands themselves capture a larger share of the surplus they generate, normalized to one for convenience. Successful bands still remain with record companies in practice and this simplification is intended just to capture the idea that the financial rewards to bands are postponed until after they are demonstrated successes. Note, too, that if bands were to get some surplus in earlier periods, this would not affect the analysis unless there were some bargaining process that was itself affected by a quota.

Record companies

We focus only on domestic record companies (or autonomous domestic affiliates of international companies).[9] Each of an exogenous number of risk-neutral record companies incurs a fixed cost in period one, F_1, for managing a new band (which covers recording and promotion expenditures) and a fixed cost in period two, F_2, for managing a successful band that is still on-contract. Each record company specializes in a particular genre (so our record companies can alternatively be thought of as independent units within record companies): there is a one-to-one mapping between the set of record companies and the set of genres.[10]

A record company will consider the set of new entrant bands in its genre (M_g), choose a number of them to sign up (n_{g1}) and offer them a contract that involves a payment to the band in return for the record company being entitled to all revenues from the band for its first two periods: record sales less F_1 in the band's first period and the band's second period record sales and rents (if successful) less F_2. Because bands commit to a genre before a contract is signed and because each genre has a single record company in it, so all surplus from the relationship can be extracted by the record company. We assume bands have an outside option valued at zero; hence the equilibrium contract offer to a band is zero.[11] Nevertheless, every new band costs the record company F_1 to record and promote and it will seek to make money particularly on those bands that subsequently succeed. A record company then records its new artists and presents and promotes these bands to radio stations.

[9]In practice the surplus generated by foreign artists will be a factor in determining record company attitudes towards broadcasting quotas, but here we focus solely on their positions *visa-vis* their domestic artists.

[10]This is a significant assumption needed to make the model tractable and its impact is discussed in section 6 (first sub-section).

[11]One might consider that a band could be offered less than this. It could self-fund some of F_t either directly or through borrowing, but the unobservability of a band's quality makes the latter infeasible (in the case where bands differ in quality) and, if bands have zero assets, the former is also infeasible. We take the two-period contract as exogenous to capture an observed feature of reality.

Radio Stations

As our focus in this analysis is on the responsiveness of producers — bands and record companies — to cultural quotas, we do not model the decision-making of radio stations completely. Each of K_g (endogenous) radio stations incurs an entry cost F_s and specializes in genre g. Each station's effective objective is to maximize the time its listeners devote to listening to it — enabling it to sell more (unmodeled) advertising — and this entails maximizing the welfare of its audience, insofar as it can. The station has a fixed endowment of airtime, normalized to one, to allocate to bands and we assume it faces a two-stage problem in this decision: first it chooses the allocation of airtime between successful, established bands and new entrants and then it decides how much of each of these allocations to devote to each relevant band. We assume that each station receives α in advertising revenue per unit of listener time it attracts to its programming.[12]

Consumers

Two types of consumer derive utility from a particular genre[13] of music from two sources: listening to it on the radio and buying a recording. Each of the L consumers, normalized to one henceforth, has lexicographic preferences over the genres so that they are divided across the genres that are aired and a fraction λ_g listen to genre g (so $\sum_g \lambda_g = 1$). All consumers consider new music and established music to be differentiated generically, insofar as purchasing recordings is concerned. Within genre g some consumers — an exogenous fraction μ_g — are "enthusiasts" or "purists": they value diversity within their preferred genre and derive utility both from hearing music on the

[12]So a radio station broadcasts throughout the day — one unit of time — and splits that between new and established bands. A consumer listens to the radio for some period of time and it is assumed implicitly that that is randomized across the day so that a consumer will hear new and established bands in the same ratio in which they are played by the radio station.

[13]Berry and Waldfogel (1999b) note that there is a positive and significant relationship between the number of different formats offered in radio broadcasting — our genres — and the share of the population that actually listens to the radio, suggesting that consumers do, indeed, have genre preferences.

radio and from purchasing the recordings of their favorite new artist. The remaining fraction $1 - \mu_g$ of a genre's consumers are "faddists": they derive utility from being part of the latest trend and buying the recordings only of successful artists, domestic and foreign. Both kinds of consumers' problems boil down to which recording to buy and how much time to devote to radio listening.

We assume that all consumers in any genre are equally split across the (identical) radio stations in the genre and, purely for reasons of tractability, have identical Cobb-Douglas preferences with respect to radio listening — as opposed to recording purchases, where faddists and enthusiasts differ — defined over the mix of airtime devoted to new entrant bands in the genre and to established, successful artists. In particular, the utility derived by a consumer in genre g from listening to the radio depends on A_g (the airtime devoted in genre g to new bands), A_{gs} (the airtime devoted to successful, established bands, whether domestic or foreign), t_g (the consumer's choice of time to devote to radio listening) and w (the consumer's opportunity cost of time spent listening to the radio), all in the fashion expressed in (3) below.[14]

But the consumer also chooses to purchase the recordings of their favorite band and derives additional utility from that. We model this as a discrete choice in the following way: a consumer places a value v_{gj} on purchasing the recording of band j in genre g and this value depends on the band's share of radio airtime a_{gj}, the (common) price of the recording p,[15] and a random idiosyncratic component ε_{gj}. Thus $v_{gj} = a_{gj} + \varepsilon_{gj} - p$ and we assume the idiosyncratic values are independently and identically distributed according to the double-exponential distribution function:

$$F(\varepsilon) = \exp\{-e^{-\varepsilon}\}. \tag{1}$$

[14]A referee has noted that it is a little peculiar that faddists and enthusiasts get identical utility from hearing broadcast music, given their different tastes when purchasing music. As we discuss in section 6 (second sub-section), one could remove the entire faddist/enthusiast distinction and this, of course, would also address this point.

[15]We do not model the setting of uniform prices in this sector, but take it as a longstanding feature of the industry (if puzzling to economists: see Shiller and Waldfogel (2011); however, see Richardson and Stahler (2013) for one possible asymmetric information based explanation).

We can then calculate the probability, denoted x_{gj}, that a particular new band j yields the maximum utility across all new bands in the genre for an enthusiast consumer:

$$x_{gj} = \frac{\exp\{a_{gj}\}}{\sum_{k=1}^{n_{g1}} \exp\{a_{gk}\}}. \tag{2}$$

Note from this that, if all bands had the same airtime, each would be equally likely to be a consumer's favorite band (with probability $1/n_{g1}$).

The expression for x_{gj} indicates a consumer's likelihood of purchasing the recording of band j in genre g, but consumers also derive utility from hearing music on the radio, as discussed, so the problem facing the consumer who buys the recording of artist j is to choose t_g to maximize their total consumer utility given by:

$$U_g = \ln(t_g)(A_g^{\beta} A_{gs}^{l-\beta}) + (1 - t_g)w + v_{gj} \tag{3}$$

For radio stations, the only choice variable is the airtime devoted to each band and we assume that they give each new (established) band an equal share of the total airtime the station itself chooses to devote to new (established) bands. So the radio station's choice — *sans* quota — is how much of its airtime to devote to new music and how much to devote to established music; within each of these allotments it simply divides up the time available equally across all relevant bands.[16]

Figure 1 presents a summary of these relationships within a genre.

3. Timing

We assume that before each period t the government imposes any domestic music quota; all potential new bands then choose their

[16]If consumers have any preference for diversity within the A and A_s allocations (so would prefer to hear each of 20 songs once rather than hear the same song 20 times), as in Perona (2010), then it would be optimal for the radio stations to behave as supposed here. We do not explicitly model this, however: the actual sub-allocation here is strictly a matter of indifference to radio stations.

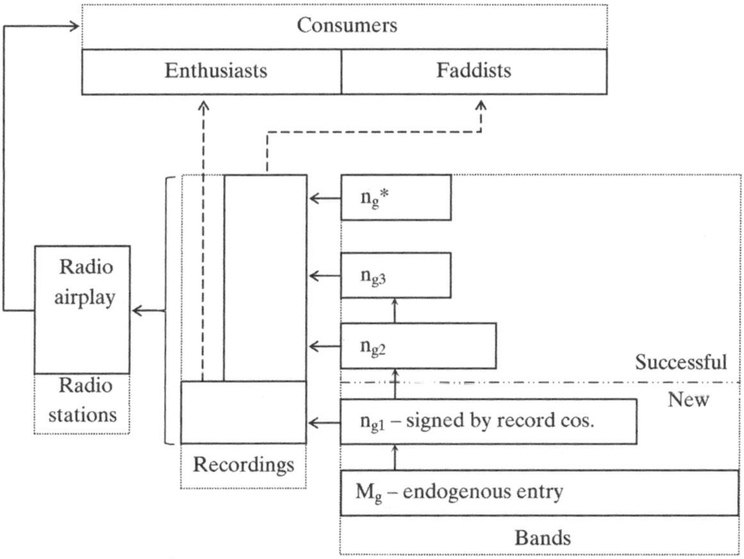

Fig. 1. Schematic representation of model structure

genre; they present to the genre-specific record company and are either contracted or not; contracted bands are recorded and presented by the record companies, along with established, successful bands, both domestic and international, to radio stations who choose how to allocate airtime to these recordings; consumers devote time to listening to a radio station, given these allocations, and purchase recordings of either new or established artists. Then some bands "succeed" and become established, earning rents for periods $t+1$ and (with survival probability h) $t+2$ before disappearing, while unsuccessful new bands from t fail and disappear before $t+1$. We consider only steady-state equilibria.

4. No quota

Agents' choices

Consider first the decisions of radio stations. A genre-specific station in g knows that a fraction μ_g of its $\lambda_g L/K_g$ consumers choose t_g to maximize (3) and the rest choose $t_g F$ to maximize an analogous expression and so choose their listening times so that:

$$\begin{aligned} A_g^{\beta} A_{gs}^{1-\beta} &= t_g w \\ A_g^{\beta} A_{gs}^{1-\beta} &= t_{gF} w. \end{aligned} \tag{4}$$

To maximize t_g and t_{gF}, the times consumers spend listening to the radio, the station should thus choose its mix to maximize the left-hand side of each equation in (4), subject to the constraint that the overall airtime shares sum to one. So, in equilibrium, $t_g = t_{gF}$.

The profitability of a radio station depends directly on its audience size. So radio stations choose their genre such that, given the distribution of other stations, no alternative genre is more profitable. In genre g there are $\mu_g \lambda_g$ enthusiast consumers each devoting time t_g to listening to the radio and $(1 - \mu_g)\lambda_g$ faddists devoting time t_{gF} to radio listening so that the total listening time of fans in genre g is $\{\mu_g t_g + (1 - \mu_g) t_{gF}\}\lambda_g$. Supposing that genre g attracts K_g stations, the profit of each is:

$$\pi_{sg}\left(\frac{\lambda_g}{K_g}\right) = \frac{\alpha\lambda_g}{K_g}\{\mu_g t_g + (1 - \mu_g) t_{gF}\} - F_s = \alpha\frac{\lambda_g t_g}{K_g} - F_s \tag{5}$$

where the second equality follows in equilibrium, wherein $t_g = t_{gf}$.

Rolling back to the decisions of the record companies, they take the number of radio stations in their genre as given. All recordings sell for a price p and the record company retains all such earnings for new bands, by virtue of its contract with each band. Expected recording sales revenue from a typical new band in genre g is:

$$S_{gj} = p x_{gj} \mu_g \lambda_g \tag{6}$$

where x_{gj} is given in (2).

On top of new band record sales revenues, record companies also receive record sales and a genre-specific rent of φR_g from a successful band in genre g for one period — where φ, discussed below, is less than one — and this is all discounted by the common discount factor δ. In steady state, new entrant band numbers and successful band numbers (in expectation) are constant so the record company's maximand is:

$$\pi_g = p\lambda_g \left[\mu_g \sum_{k=1}^{n_{g1}} x_{gk} + (1-\mu_g) \sum_{k=1}^{n_{g2}} x_{gsk} \right]$$
$$+ n_{g2}\varphi R_g - n_{g1}F_1 - n_{g2}F_2. \tag{7}$$

Finally, we turn to the entry decisions of bands. The essential choice for them is whether or not to enter (i.e. to form a band that seeks a record contract). In genre g there are M_g bands vying for recording contracts, which are granted only to $n_{g1} \leq M_g$ of the bands. All bands are *ex ante* identical so a band's probability of an initial contract is simply n_{g1}/M_g. If $f(n_{g1})$ new entrants succeed (discussed more fully below) then the probability of success, conditional on being contracted, is $f(n_{g1})/n_{g1}$. With the probability of surviving from period 2 to period 3 being h, the overall *ex ante* probability of an entrant making it to period 3 (and so going off-contract) is then $(n_{g1}/M_g)(f(n_{g1})/n_{g1})h$ or $(f(n_{g1})/M_g)h$. An entrant incurs a fixed cost of F_B initially and, if it turns out to be unsuccessful, it will then receive zero (its losses being borne by the record company), so its decision is driven solely by its payoff in the case of success. If a band enters it anticipates that it will, if it survives to period 3, receive φR_g plus record sales revenues (of $[p\lambda_g(1-\mu_g)]x_{g2j}$) in that period. In equilibrium, then, a band will be indifferent about entry only if its expected return is zero. Denoting by $G*$ the set of genres profitable for radio stations, our equilibrium condition is:

$$\frac{f(n_{g1})}{M_g} h(p\lambda_g(1-\mu_g)E(x_{g3}) + \varphi R_g)\delta^2 = F_B \forall_g \in G^*. \tag{8}$$

We now say a little more about the per-band rent in a genre, R_g. We assume that this is an increasing function of the faddist consumer demand for that genre, $\lambda_g(1-\mu_g)$, and a decreasing function of the number of successful bands in that genre, $N_{gs} = n_{g2}+n_{g3}+n_g^*$. To be specific, we suppose that the aggregate rent in g is a linear function of consumer numbers, $c_g\lambda_g(1-\mu_g)$ for some constant c_g, and that the per-band rent is then simply their record-sales weighted share of this. So we assume, using x_{gs} to denote the expected record sales of a successful domestic band, that

$$R_g = x_{gs}\lambda_g(1-\mu_g)c_g \forall g \in G^*. \tag{9}$$

This rent is a transfer from faddist consumers buying T-shirts, for example, or attending concerts, and represents the aggregate value placed by such consumers on these services. It costs the bands real resources to provide these services and we suppose simply that this cost is some fraction of the consumer valuation. Consequently, if consumers pay R_g for services they value at that price, only a fraction $\varphi \in [0,1]$ accrues to bands as rent. Then equilibrium condition (8) becomes:

$$\frac{f(n_{g1})}{M_g} h\lambda_g(1-\mu_g)E(x_{g3})(p+\varphi c_g)\delta^2 = F_B \forall g \in G^*. \tag{10}$$

Welfare

Free entry by bands and radio stations ensures zero expected profits for them,[17] leaving record company profit and consumer surplus as the components of national welfare. For record companies we have profit as described in (7) in any period. Following Anderson and de Palma (1992), consumer surplus in genre g is:

$$\begin{aligned} CS_{ge} &= \mu_g\lambda_g \ln\left(\sum_{j=i}^{n_{g1}} \exp(a_j + T - p)\right) \\ &= \mu_g\lambda_g(T-p)\ln\left(\sum_{j=1}^{n_{g1}} \exp(a_j)\right) \end{aligned} \tag{11}$$

[17] As noted previously, we do not model the advertising side of the radio stations' problem explicitly. In terms of welfare, we assume that the advertising market is competitive and that advertisers extract no surplus from advertising.

for enthusiast consumers and, for faddists for all successful bands:[18]

$$CS_{gf} = (1-\mu_g)\lambda_g(T^f - p)\ln\left(\sum_{j=1}^{N_{gs}} \exp(a_j)\right) \tag{12}$$

with $T = [\ln t_g(A_g^{\beta} A_{gs}^{1-\beta}) + (1-t_g)w]$ and T^f defined isomorphically. So aggregate consumer surplus in genre g can be written:

$$\begin{aligned} CS_g &= CS_{ge} + CS_{gf} \\ &= \lambda_g \left[\mu_g(T-p)\ln\left(\sum_{j=i}^{n_{g1}} \exp(a_j)\right) \right. \\ &\qquad \left. +(1-\mu_g)(T_f - p)\ln\left(\sum_{j=i}^{N_{gs}} \exp(a_j)\right)\right]. \end{aligned} \tag{13}$$

In sum, in any period in steady state we have welfare generated by genre g, W_g, as:

$$\begin{aligned} W_g = \lambda_g &\left[p\mu_g \sum_{k=1}^{n_{g1}} x_{gsk} + (1-\mu_g)(p+\varphi c_g)\sum_{k=1}^{n_{g2}} x_{gk}\right] - n_{g1}F_1 - n_{g2}F_2 \\ + \lambda_g &\left[\mu_g(T-p)\ln\left(\sum_{j=i}^{n_{g1}} \exp(a_j)\right) \right. \\ &\left. +(1-\mu_g)(T^f - p)\ln\left(\sum_{j=1}^{N_{gs}} \exp(a_j)\right)\right]. \end{aligned} \tag{14}$$

Note that if each successful band gets the same airtime, a, then CS_{gf} simplifies down to $(1-\mu_g)\lambda_g(T^t - p)[\ln(N_{gs}) + a]$.

[18]Note that the rent transfer does not enter into consumer welfare as it represents the valuation consumers place on the non-recording services received from successful bands and so washes out.

The Nature of Band "Success"

We have assumed that at the end of a period only some fraction of new entrants in genre g will survive. The Appendix[19] discusses a number of alternative ways in which this success might be modeled. For the remainder of the paper we take the case in which success is entirely exogenous: the number of successful bands is a known, deterministic function of the number of new entrants:

$$n_{g2} = f(n_{g1}), \quad f(0) = 0, \quad f' \in (0,1), \quad f'' \leq 0. \tag{15}$$

As only a fraction h of period 2 successful bands go on to be successful bands off-contract in period 3, we have $n_{g3} = hn_{g2} = hf(n_{g1})$ so that the total number of successful bands in genre g in any period is given in steady state by $N_{gs} = (1+h)f(n_{g1}) + n_g^*$.

In period one the record company in genre g signs up n_{g1} bands, but, because all new bands in a genre sign with the same record company, so all revenues from new band sales accrue to the same company. As record sales are expressed in terms of market shares, so the record company's share of new band sales is always one. Of course, $n_{g2} = f(n_{g1})$ of these bands then succeed and go onto period two, and this is where the choice of n_{g1} impacts potential record company profits. With n_{g2} deterministic, so too is per-band airtime and the record company's profit is:

$$\pi_g = k_1 + k_2 E(n_{g2}x_{g2}) - n_{g1}F_1 - n_{g2}F_2 \tag{16}$$

where $k_1 = p\mu_g\lambda_g$ and $k_2 = (1-\mu_g)(p+\varphi c_g)\lambda_g$ are positive constants. That is, denoting by a_{gs} the airtime devoted to a successful band in genre g,

$$\begin{aligned}\pi_g(n_{g1}) = k_1 + k_2 f(n_{g1}) &\frac{\exp(a_{gs})}{(1+h)f(n_{g1})\exp(a_{gs}) + n_g^* \exp(a_g^*)} \\ &- n_{g1}F_1 - f(n_{g1})F_2. \end{aligned} \tag{17}$$

[19]The Appendix to this paper is available online as "Richardson & Wilkie — Faddists enthusiasts & Canadian divas — Appendix.pdf" at https://sites.google.com/site/martin richardsonanu/patents-in-channel.

Equilibrium

Solving a radio station's problem yields:

$$A_{gs} = 1 - \beta, \quad A_g = \beta. \tag{18}$$

Deviations from this ratio will reduce consumer welfare and therefore reduce their listening time devoted to the radio.

As $t_g = t_g F$ in equilibrium so expressions (4) and (18) imply that $t_g = \beta^{\beta}(1-\beta)^{1-\beta/w}$ so total listening time is $\beta^{\beta}(1-\beta)^{1-\beta}\lambda_g/w$, earning the station total advertising revenues of $\alpha\beta^{\beta}(1-\beta)^{1-\beta}\lambda_g/w$ Thus (5) becomes:

$$\pi_{sg}\left(\frac{\lambda_g}{K_g}\right) = \alpha\frac{\lambda_g}{K_g}t_g - F_s = \frac{\alpha}{w}\frac{\lambda_g}{K_g}(\beta^{\beta}(1-\beta)^{1-\beta}) - F_s. \tag{19}$$

We ignore the integer constraint on the number of radio stations and treat it as a continuous variable. Consequently our free entry condition for radio stations becomes, denoting by G^* the set of weakly profitable genres,

$$\alpha\frac{\lambda_g}{K_g}t_g = F_s \Rightarrow K_g = \alpha\frac{\lambda_g}{F_s}t_g = \frac{\alpha}{w}\frac{\lambda_g}{F_s}(\beta^{\beta}(1-\beta)^{1-\beta})\forall g \in G^*. \tag{20}$$

From this, note that the more popular the genre,*ceteris paribus,* the larger will be the number of radio stations operating in that genre: K_g is increasing in λ_g.

The problem facing a record company in genre g is,

$$\max_{\{n_{g1}\}} \pi_g(n_{g1}) = k_1 + k_2\frac{f(n_{g1})}{\{(1+h)f(n_{g1}) + ng^*\}} - n_{g1}F_1 - f(n_{g1})F_2. \tag{21}$$

This yields a FOC and SOC as follows:

$$\begin{aligned}\frac{dE(\pi_g)}{dn_{g1}} &= k_2\frac{f'(n_{g1})n_g^*}{\{.\}^2} - (F_1 + f'(n_{g1})F_2) = 0\\ \frac{d^2E(\pi_g)}{(dn_{g1})^2} &= k_2 n_g^*\frac{f''(n_{g1})\{.\} - 2(f'(n_{g1}))^2(1+h)}{\{.\}}f''(n_{g1})F_2 \leq 0.\end{aligned} \tag{22}$$

The online Appendix (see note 19) demonstrates that the SOC holds and that the solution to the record company's problem yields an optimal choice of n_{g1} where the signs of partial derivatives are as shown:

$$n_{g1} = n_{g1}\left(\underbrace{p, \lambda_g, \phi C_g,}_{(+)} \underbrace{\mu_g, h, F_1, F_2,}_{(-)} \underbrace{n_g^*}_{(+/-)}\right). \tag{23}$$

For bands, with no quota $\mathrm{E}(x_{gS}) = 1/N_{gS}$ so (10) solves for M_g as follows:

$$\frac{f(n_{g1})\lambda_g(1-\mu_g)}{F_B N_{gs}}(p + \phi c_g)\delta^2 h = M_g$$

$$\Rightarrow M_g = M_s\left(\underbrace{n_{g1}, \lambda_g, \phi c_g, \delta, h, p,}_{(+)} \underbrace{\mu_g, F_b, n_g^*}_{(-)}\right). \tag{24}$$

In many models of entry behind a fixed cost we observe that the laissez-faire solution leads to over-entry from a social perspective owing to the well-known business- stealing effect. In this model, however, the "entry" decision for new bands (in terms of being contracted, etc.) is made by a record company for *all* the potential entrants. Any business stealing by a new band is pure cannibalization and so it will be taken into account when entry is determined. For this reason, there is no presumption in this model that there will be over-entry.

On the contrary, we can see that the laissez-faire solution in this model involves *too few* new domestic (and, consequently, subsequently successful domestic) bands. The record company chooses n_{g1} to maximize its own profits but welfare is the sum of profits and the consumer surplus of both faddist and enthusiast consumers. From (11) and (12):

$$CS_{ge} = \mu_g\lambda_g(T-p)\left(\ln(n_{g1}) + \frac{A_g}{n_{g1}}\right)$$

$$\Rightarrow \frac{dCS_{ge}}{dn_{g1}} = \frac{\mu_g\lambda_g(T-p)}{n_{g1}}\left(1 - \frac{A_s}{n_{g1}}\right) > 0$$

$$CS_{gf} = (1-\mu_g)\lambda_g(T^f - p)\left(\ln[n_g^* + (1+h)f(n_{g1})] + \frac{A_{gs}}{\{.\}}\right)$$

$$\Rightarrow \frac{dCS_{gf}}{dn_{g1}} = \frac{(1-\mu_g)\lambda_g(T^f-p)(1+h)f'(n_{g1})}{\{n_g^* + (1+h)f(n_{g1})\}}\left(1 - \frac{A_{gs}}{\{.\}}\right) > 0 \tag{25}$$

So, unsurprisingly, consumer surplus for all consumers is increasing in n_{g1} and the implication is that the laissez-faire solution involves too few bands from a social welfare perspective, as the record company ignores the impact on CS of its contracting decisions. Clearly, however, this is not a first-best intervention, as an optimal intervention to correct this would be one that directly targets n_{g1}; that is, a subsidy to F_1, the fixed cost of contracting new bands.

We summarize these results in the following proposition:

Proposition 1. *The laissez-faire equilibrium of this model involves*

(i) *The radio broadcasting of new and established music in the proportion $\beta/(1-\beta)$ in every genre;*
(ii) *Entry of radio stations into a genre in direct proportion to λ_g, the popularity of the genre in the listening public;*
(iii) *The choice by a record company in a genre of the number of new bands to sign to contracts, where this number is increasing in the price of recordings, the popularity of the genre in the population, and the rents that accrue to bands in the genre; is decreasing in the proportion of the genre's consumers that are enthusiasts, the survival rate of successful bands and the record company's fixed cost of contracting bands, and is non-monotonic in the number of foreign bands in the genre;*
(iv) *The entry into the genre of a number of bands seeking contracts where that number is increasing in the price of recordings, the popularity of the genre in the population, the rents that accrue to bands in the genre, the number of new bands signed up by the record company, the band's discount factor and the survival rate of successful bands; and is decreasing in the proportion of*

the genre's consumers that are enthusiasts, the number of foreign bands in the genre and the fixed cost of entry by bands;

(v) *Too few contracted bands from an aggregate welfare perspective.*

5. A local content quota

A simple[20] local content requirement imposed on a genre g will require stations in that genre to play domestic music in a certain proportion — equivalently, airtime devoted to foreign music must be less than some proportion of total airtime. Thus the quota is a constraint that $\sum_{m=1}^{n_g^*} a_{gm}^* \leq Q$ for some airtime level Q.

As is shown more formally in the online Appendix, a just-binding simple quota on foreign bands' airtime will, in the short run,[21] lead to an increase in the airtime devoted to successful domestic bands, with no consequences for the aggregate airtime split between new and established bands. As a consequence, nothing disturbs the free-entry condition governing radio stations in each genre. However, the increased airtime for successful domestic bands means higher expected record sales for such bands and thus higher expected profits for new bands in the affected genre. This induces immediate entry by new bands into that genre. In the medium run this entry of new bands will lead to an increased number of successful domestic bands in the genre who are on-contract to record companies and, in the long run, this will flow through to the number of successful domestic bands off-contract.

Turning to welfare, there is clearly a profit-increasing effect of a tighter quota. This occurs for standard profit-shifting reasons: given the fixed recording price, the quota shifts airtime to successful domestic bands and so increases domestic record sales and profits therefrom. As noted, there is no distortion of the optimal airtime mix but both n_{g1} and N_g are increased by the quota.

[20]By which we mean a quota that draws no distinction between new and established domestic artists.

[21]Immediately the policy is imposed and before "successful" band numbers can respond. That is, in the first period following the policy's imposition.

Our expression for consumer surplus is now, noting that $T = T^f$ in equilibrium and that each new band gets the same airtime $1/n_{g1}$,

$$CS_g = \lambda_g(T - P)\left[\mu_g\left(\ln(n_{g1}) + \frac{1}{n_{g1}}\right) + (1-\mu_g)\ln\left(n_g^*\exp\left(\frac{Q}{n_g^*}\right)\right.\right.$$
$$\left.\left. +(1+h)f(n_{g1}\exp)\left(\frac{A_{gs}-Q}{(1+h)f(n_{g1})}\right)\right)\right]. \qquad (26)$$

Consequently there are conflicting effects on consumers of a tightening of the quota. Enthusiast consumers are strictly better off: the quota induces entry of new bands and enthusiasts' welfare is increasing in the number of bands, n_{g1}, an effect that more than offsets their losses from lower airtime per band. These bands are signed up because the profitability of successful bands has increased. In many contexts, this kind of entry — induced at an earlier stage by the prospect of subsequent profits — will simply dissipate any subsequent rents and so is welfare-neutral, at best, but in this model enthusiast consumers benefit from an increased diversity of new bands, whether they subsequently succeed or not. For some faddist consumers, however, there is a welfare loss from the reduced airtime for foreign bands: consumers who purchase the recordings of foreign bands now get lower gains from such purchases, but that reduced airtime is now devoted to successful domestic bands, the number of which has increased and this benefits faddist consumers. The online Appendix demonstrates that any simple quota that induces entry must raise the consumer surplus of faddist consumers overall; this is certainly the case for a mild (i.e. just-binding) quota.

Turning to other players, the quota has no effects on radio stations' entry decisions, but for bands a quota gives an incentive for entry into a constrained genre as a result of both the increase in expected third-period record sales — the proceeds of which accrue to the band — and the increase in the number of bands signed in the genre. So there is an increase in the number of bands in the genre seeking contracts.

Now suppose that the economy as a whole is characterized by a variety of genres differing by foreign band concentration. Suppose that a common quota is imposed across all genres.[22] The relative impact on one genre versus another will depend ultimately on the relative impact of the quota on expected record sales for successful bands across genres — while it is the third-period manifestation of this that is of interests to bands in their entry decisions, it is the second-period occurrence that induces record companies to sign up more new entrant bands. A given quota will be more profitable in terms of raising domestic record sales the more binding it is on foreign acts, i.e. the greater is the proportion of airtime devoted to foreign bands in the absence of a quota. Hence we see our "Canadian divas" effect: a sector-wide common quota induces greater entry of domestic bands seeking contracts in genres where foreign music is more concentrated.

We summarize these results in the following proposition:

Proposition 2. *A simple local content quota in steady state in this model,*

(i) *Will leave the radio airplay mix between new and established bands unaffected but will increase the share of airplay devoted to successful domestic bands;*
(ii) *Will leave entry decisions by radio stations unaffected;*
(iii) *Will increase both entry and contracting of domestic bands and thus the number of both new and successful domestic bands;*
(iv) *Will lead to greater "internationalization" of domestic music: a greater share of domestic music (both played by entrants and contracted bands and heard on the radio) is produced by bands in genres where international music is most prevalent;*
(v) *Is welfare-improving if the quota is mild: just binding.*

[22] Australia, however, has genre-specific quotas, with higher local content requirements in more popular genres. There are five categories of music and local content requirements range from 25% in the contemporary popular music format (and at least 25% of the local content must be "new": released in the previous 12 months) to 5% in niche formats, such as jazz, with no "new" constraint.

A new-music quota

As noted in the Introduction, a number of countries have introduced rather more complicated quotas that require not only that domestic music receive a greater share of radio airtime but that some proportion of this be allocated to "new" domestic music. This is to prevent exactly the behavior just described: that a radio station meets the quota simply by playing more established domestic artists, rather than airing new ones. Such a quota has two components: a "simple" quota as analyzed above combined with a requirement that more new music be played.[23] In this subsection we focus on the second of these two effects and, as all new entrant music in our model is generated by domestic bands, we consider a policy that requires an increase in A_g/A_{gs}.

If a policy is imposed that requires an increase in A_g at the expense of A_{gs} then this will reduce the overall time devoted to listening to the radio, by (4). Ignoring this change in t_g for the moment, for given band numbers, the increase in A_g has no effect on record company profits: the increase in airtime each band receives has no impact on their record sales as it is common to all bands in the genre and overall record sales are unchanged (at $\mu_g\lambda_g$.) The decrease in A_{gs} will be shared across all successful bands, foreign and domestic, so every successful band will get reduced airtime, but the overall domestic share of record sales and rents will be unaffected by this and, again, total record sales are unaffected so the domestic record company is not impacted by this policy at all. Hence it signs no additional bands and there are no entry/exit consequences of the policy.

Welfare is impacted through the distortion induced in the radio airtime mix and the consequent reduction in airtime devoted to radio

---

[23]In fact, the requirement can be met by playing new releases from established bands. Our model does not permit this possibility: implicitly bands here issue a single recording at the start of their lives and sell it for, potentially, three periods.

listening by consumers.[24] This distortion reduces the overall time devoted to listening to the radio so consumer surplus for all consumers falls. For a just-binding quota this effect is second-order, of course, but the reduction in listening time is reflected in exit by radio stations. If the quota affects some genres more than others then we will observe in this case an *increase* in the relative amount of domestic music broadcast: all stations broadcast more domestic content *and* exiting stations are those in genres where the quota binds most tightly, i.e. those with a greater concentration of foreign artists.

Now, this quota involves the packaging of the policy just described with a simple quota, analyzed previously. Consequently, this quota when just-binding will be welfare-improving under the same circumstances and for the same reasons that a just- binding simple quota is welfare-improving. However, a non-marginal new-music quota will yield lower overall welfare than the equivalent simple quota.

We summarize these results in the following proposition:

Proposition 3. *In this model, a new-music quota in steady state will, beyond the effects of the simple quota,*

(i) *Alter the radio airplay mix in favor of new (domestic) bands;*
(ii) *Lead to lower airtime for every successful band, domestic or foreign, and increased airtime per new domestic band, both for each remaining radio station and in aggregate;*
(iii) *Have no consequences for record sales;*
(iv) *Lead to the exit of some radio stations;*
(v) *Have no consequences for entry or the contracting of new domestic bands and thus for the number of both new and successful domestic bands;*

[24] In a richer model of advertising, this reduction in t_g would also impact on the advertising market. In this model we will see a decrease in the number of radio stations in genre g following the quota, as t_g falls in (19). This is a feature of our model: consumers have no preferences across radio stations in a particular genre, as they are all identical, so when less time is devoted to listening to a genre it is reflected not in the listening time per station but in the total number of stations. This exit of stations has no welfare consequences of its own, owing to the zero profit condition for station equilibrium.

(vi) *Lead to greater "internationalization" of domestic music to the extent that it drives out radio stations in the most heavily affected genres: those that are most "international";*
(vii) *Reduce welfare at a greater rate than a simple quota when it becomes increasingly binding.*

6. Modeling choices and robustness

Multiple record companies in each genre

The assumption that each genre is characterized by a single record company buys us a great deal in terms of the tractability of the analysis by reducing the company's choice of the number of new entrants to sign down to a decision that depends only on later period profits and not those in the first period. With competition among record companies in a genre the optimal choice of n_{g1} would also consider its impact on business- stealing from other competing record companies (see online Appendix.) This is likely to lead to greater numbers of bands throughout the market and so to lessen, or even completely offset, the under-entry problem discussed. Consequently, the welfare consequences of local content requirements are likely to be more negative than in our analysis. At the other extreme one could imagine that every band has its own record company, but erring on the side of less competition, as we do, seems more justifiable than the other extreme as an empirical matter: in 2006, for example, the four major record companies in the USA had an 88% share of the total US album market.[25]

Consumers as faddists and enthusiasts

An alternative to our faddist/enthusiast distinction would be simply to posit a single type of consumer who draws their favorite band from the entire set of alternatives. Under the discrete choice model of record buying used here, the probability of a consumer buying the

[25]See Elberse and Ofek (2007) Exhibit 1b as discussed in the online Appendix to the present paper.

recording of band j in genre g would become:

$$x_{gi} = \frac{\exp\{a_{gi}\}}{\sum_{k=1}^{n_{g1}} \exp\{a_{gk}\} + \sum_{i=1}^{ngs} \exp\{a_{gi}\}}. \tag{27}$$

We suspect that such a change would make little difference to the qualitative results of our analysis, but would complicate the algebra significantly. Under our current separation, if all bands of one type receive the same airplay (e.g. absent any quota) then each has an equal market share. With this more general specification that is still the case, but the denominator of these market share expressions for each type of band depends on the airtimes of *all* the bands in the genre, domestic or foreign, new or successful. So an increase in the airtime devoted to successful domestic bands (the novel component of the new-music quota discussed above) will now directly impact the record sales of new domestic bands, independent of any effect on entry.

A further extension would be to allow consumers to listen to and consume more than one genre of music. One feasible way to handle such an extension is to consider a nested logit model in which the top nest is defined over genres and the sub-nests as we have here. This would yield equilibrium behaviour as we have here — each consumer buying a single band in a single genre — but would essentially endogenize consumers' preferences over genres. It would also imply that record companies compete with each other across genres, with the implications discussed above in the previous sub-section.

Technological change

Our model is motivated by an industry structure that has prevailed for some decades in the commercial music business. With high fixed costs of recording and promoting artists, record companies fill an essential role of funding start-ups (new entrants), radio plays an essential role in bringing new recordings to consumers' attention and successful bands and record companies share, in some fashion, in both the proceeds from record sales and any other rents that might be generated by successful bands. Since the 1990s, many things have changed in the way that music is commercialized and here we reflect briefly on how these changes might impact on our model. See Richardson and Wilkie (2013) for a more complete discussion. Our conclusion is that the quota analysis is robust to these changes wrought, particularly, by the internet.

This millennium has seen at least four significant and related developments in the music industry. First is a substantial reduction in the costs of recording and disseminating music. Second is the growth of electronic music downloading, both legal and otherwise. Third is a dramatic decrease in the importance of recording sales revenues for bands, compared with concert and related revenues. Fourth is the rise of internet radio and the role of internet services in the dissemination of new music.

The development of cheap software and hardware has made it easier for artists to run home studios and the use of social media is often perceived as reducing the costs of disseminating music.[26] Simply reducing the fixed cost of recording and promotion, so long as artists cannot sidestep the record companies completely, has straightforward effects in our model, through the comparative statics of a change in F, and does nothing to affect the qualitative analysis of a quota. Note, too, that the empirical incidence of artists bypassing the record company model successfully is vanishingly small: because of the marketing services a record company provides, the vast majority of commercially successful artists still transact with record companies along the lines modeled here.[27]

The existence of new online distribution structures also has little impact on our qualitative analysis of the effects of a quota: it does not matter if distribution is through buying physical CDs at a shop

[26]A referee notes that this is essentially equivalent to a band "vertically integrating" with a record company.

[27]See Table 1 at p. 671 of Connolly and Krueger (2006), which identifies the top earning 35 artists who toured the US in 2002. All of these are affiliated with recording companies and most with the then major labels (Sony, Warner, BMG, EMI and Universal, or subsidiaries thereof). More recently, Businesswire.com (2012) reports that in Nielsen Soundscan's 2011 Music Industry Report the four large record companies — Sony and BMG merged in 2004 — had a combined market share of 90% of sales of physical album sales in 2011, 86% of sales of digital albums and 87% of sales of digital tracks. The residual shares are likely to be dominated by smaller record companies.

(either online or not) or downloading an MP3.[28] The explosion of illegal downloading could be significant insofar as it undermines the record company business model, but the structure of record companies has not much changed in the internet era and our analysis seems to apply equally to the current situation.[29]

Connolly and Krueger (2006) provide a thorough description of the economics of popular music and one of their main observations is that, for most modern artists, non-recording related income is much more significant than income derived from the sales of recorded music.[30] This has little impact on our analysis; it is an observation regarding the relative size of recording revenues and what we model as rents, a ratio that does not affect our results, so long as they are complementary[31] in the sense that record sales are a necessary prerequisite to success as a touring artist.

In the abstract, the rise of internet radio means little for our analysis: whether a recording is heard on AM/FM radio, a digital radio or streamed over the internet, so long as it feeds into the likely success of an artist then our analysis still applies.[32] More significantly, though, internet radio threatens the very feasibility of the policy instrument we have analyzed here: the local content quota. The technology of

---

[28]Cowen (2008) notes that, in 2008, the most significant retailer of music in the USA was still Wal-Mart, although Apple's iTunes was second.

[29]Record companies have experienced declining revenues from the increase in downloading since 2000 and we have seen a concomitant increase in so-called "360 degree" contracts, in which record companies take shares of profit from non-record sale related activities of their artists. This is essentially built in to our analysis already, as we assume that all revenues generated by a band on-contract, whether from record sales or not, accrue to its record company at first.

[30]They note that in 2003 recording sales in the USA earned US$11.8 billion vs US$2.1 billion for concert ticket sales. They quote one band manager as saying that the top 10% of artists make money selling records, but the rest go on tour (p. 673.)

[31]See Connolly and Krueger (2006, p. 687). Note, too, that the US Billboard pop charts that document the "top" recordings of the week are constructed to reflect explicitly both the highest selling albums of the week and which tracks from those albums are aired most regularly on radio broadcasting.

[32]There is some evidence that radio airplay was, relatively recently, still a significant factor in the music purchasing decisions of consumers. French Music Bureau (2003) at p. 67 notes that the two most significant factors influencing the decision to buy a new album in the UK in 2002 were "hearing tracks from it on the radio" and "already know hit from hit single".

radio broadcasts means that, for most national regulators, controlling the broadcasts of all stations within one's sovereign territory means controlling the lion's share of radio broadcasts heard by denizens of that country.[33] For example, the ability of a Canadian regulator to control the content of a Californian internet radio station is effectively zero, unless the station is simply blocked completely. The rise of new media for the circulation of music is, in our judgment, the most serious threat to the use of local content requirements in broadcasting, from a regulator's perspective.

Finally, our analysis supposes that consumers hear new music only through their radio listening (which is why radio airtime is critical for bands' success) and we have cited survey data that supports the importance of radio listening in this fashion (see note 31). The development of internet radio services such as Pandora (www.pandora.com) changes this nexus, as they provide individualized playlists based on a consumer's listening patterns. Nevertheless, so long as consumers continue to have preferences over music listening as we have modeled here, a commercial provider still has the same incentive as radio stations in our model to provide playlists in that same ratio.[34]

7. Conclusion

This chapter has presented a model of the recorded music industry, integrating the demand and supply sides through the modeling of

[33]This clearly varies from country to country. It is far easier for Australia, for instance, to regulate what its citizens hear on the radio than for France, although language barriers reduce the temptation of French consumers to listen to, for example, German radio broadcasts. Outside of land-based radio broadcasts, it is unclear what a regulator can do. In Australia, Vizard (1999) expresses this pithily: "Do we have jurisdiction over offshore suppliers who beam in by Internet, phone and satellite? How do we force the Los Angeles news Internet provider to include content relevant to us? How do we mandate that the BBC international news service include Australian weather reports? Or that the Discovery Channel include a pack of Tasmanian Devils savaging a sparrow?"

[34]The main way in which services such as Pandora.com change the music market is in catering to preference heterogeneity across individual consumers. Our model has no heterogeneity *within* a genre.

consumers, radio stations, record companies and artists. The model has then been used to analyze the supply-side consequences of local music quotas imposed on broadcasters. We show that a mild (just binding) quota will be welfare-improving in this model, as it induces a domestic record company to sign up more new bands and this is welfare-improving for consumers who gain from diversity. Nevertheless, the quota will induce an "internationalization" of domestic music — what we dub the "Canadian divas effect" — by inducing domestic entry primarily into genres most dominated by international artists. If the quota also requires that some increased proportion of new domestic music be played, we identify an additional welfare loss owing to the distorted programming choices it induces from affected radio stations.

While the online Appendix does discuss this matter, for tractability in this model we finesse the potentially significant issue of band quality: all bands here have the same probability of success (for a given amount of radio airtime). So one possible negative welfare effect of a quota — quality downgrading as record companies sign up lower-quality bands in response to the quota on foreign music — is not a feature here.

We consider the central contributions of the paper to be, first, its identification of the "Canadian diva" effect — the internationalization of domestic music in response to a quota — and, second, its development of an integrated model of this sector. We identify a new channel by which such a quota might raise welfare but also illustrate its possibly perverse effects on the diversity of domestic music.

We conclude by noting that, while much of our analysis defies empirical testing, as it relies on broadly ineffable notions such as the internationalization of music, the model's central result — the Canadian Divas effect — is testable, at least indirectly. Whatever it means for a country's music to become more internationalized, it surely must imply that it becomes more popular on the world stage. Consequently, the analysis implies that a domestic local content quota should be reflected in increased sales of domestic music abroad: import protection as export promotion. This remains a topic for further analysis.

References

Acheson, K. and C. Maule (1990). Canadian content rules: A time for reconsideration. *Canadian Public Policy*, 16, 284–97.

——— (2001). Culture in International Trade. In V.A. Ginsburgh and D. Throsby (eds.), *Handbook of the Economics of Art and Culture*, Amsterdam: Elsevier.

Anderson, S. and S. Coate (2005). Market provision of public goods: A welfare analysis. *Review of Economic Studies*, 72, 947–72.

Anderson, S. and A. de Palma (1992). The logit as a model of product differentiation. *Oxford Economic Papers*, 44, 51–67.

Bala, V. and N.V. Long (2005). International trade and cultural diversity with preference selection. *European Journal of Political Economy*, 21, 143–62.

Berry, S. and J. Waldfogel (1999a). Free entry and social inefficiency in radio broadcasting. *RAND Journal of Economics*, 30, 397–420.

——— (1999b). Public radio in the United States: Does it correct market failure or cannibalize commercial stations? *Journal of Public Economics*, 71, 189–211.

Businesswire.com, The Nielsen Company & Billboard's 2011 Music Industry Report, available at http://www.businesswire.com/news/home/20120105005547/en/Nielsen-Company -Billboard%E2%80%99s-2011-Music-Industry-Report (2012).

Coase, R. (1966), The economics of broadcasting and government policy. *American Economic Review*, 56, 440–47.

Connolly, M. and A. B. Krueger (2006). Rockonomics: The economics of popular music. In V. A. Ginsburgh and D. Throsby (eds.), *Handbook of the Economics of Art and Culture*, Amsterdam: Elsevier.

Cowen, T. (2008). Why everything has changed: The recent revolution in cultural economics. *Journal of Cultural Economics*, 32, 261–73.

Crampes, C. and A. Hollander (1999). The Regulation of Audiovisual Content: Quotas and Conflicting Objectives. *Centre de Recherche sur les Transports.* Montreal, Canada: University of Montreal.

Doyle, C. (1998). Programming in a competitive broadcasting market: Entry, welfare and regulation. *Information Economics and Policy*, 10, 23–39.

Elberse, A. and E. Ofek (2007). Octone Records, Harvard Business Review Case Study 9-507-082 (revised 2011). Boston MA: Harvard Business School.

Francois, P. and T. van Ypersele (2002). On the protection of cultural goods. *Journal of International Economics*, 56, 359–69.

French Music Bureau (2003). *The British Music Market in Comparison with the French Music Industry.* London: Insitut-Francais.

Gordon, P. and S. Meunier (2001). Globalization and french cultural identity. *French Politics, Culture, & Society*, 19, 22–41.

Jacobsen, V. (2000). *Local Content Regulation of New Zealand Television.* Wellington, NZ: Arthur Andersen.

Krugman, P. (1999). Enemies of the WTO: Bogus Arguments against the World Trade Organization, *Slate*, available at http://www.slate.com/articles/business/the_dismal_science/1999/11/enemies_of_the_wto.html.

Mangani, A. (2003). Profit and audience maximization in broadcasting markets. *Information Economics and Policy*, 15, 305–15.

Mas-Colell, A. (1999). Should cultural goods be treated differently? *Journal of Cultural Economics*, 23, 87–93.

Owen, B. and S. Wildman (1992). *Video Economics*. Cambridge, MA: Harvard University Press.

Perona, M. (2010). How Broadcasting Quotas Harm Program Diversity. MPRA, Munich.

Revel, J.-F. (2003). The anti-American obsession. *The New Criterion*, Foundation for Cultural Reviews, Inc., New York.

Richardson, M. (2006). Commercial broadcasting and local content: Cultural quotas, advertising and public stations. *Economic Journal*, 116, 605–25.

Richardson, M. and F. Stahler (2013). On the 'Uniform Pricing Puzzle' in Recorded Music. *ANU working papers in Economics and Econometrics*, 612, Australian National University.

Richardson, M. and S. Wilkie (2013). Faddists, enthusiasts and Canadian divas: A model of the recorded music market. *ANU working papers in Economics and Econometrics*, 600, Australian National University.

Rogers, R. and J. Woodbury (1996). Market structure, program diversity and radio audience size. *Contemporary Economic Policy*, 14, 81–91.

Shiller, B. and J. Waldfogel (2011). Music for a song: An empirical look at uniform pricing and its alternatives. *The Journal of Industrial Economics*, 59, 630–60.

Vizard, S. (1999). Andrew olle media lecture. Sydney, Australia: Australian Broadcasting Corporation.

Part II

Preferential Trading Agreements

Chapter 5

Endogenous Protection and Trade Diversion

Martin Richardson

Abstract: Traditional positive analysis of preferential trading areas has focused on the trade-offs between (beneficial) trade creation and (potentially harmful) trade diversion. We consider the latter phenomenon in the formation of a free-trade area (FTA) between countries where tariffs against non-members are set endogenously. We show that such tariffs will fall consequent to the formation of FTAs and trade diversion is likely to become trade creation. This is illustrated in a model in which tariffs are levied to maximize a political support function. We conclude with some comments on the generality of this result and directions for future research.

1. Introduction

Preferential trading arrangements (PTAs henceforth) can take the form of free-trade areas (FTAs), customs unions (CUs) or more integrated arrangements such as the post-1992 European Community. In the United States, in particular, the formation of FTAs with Israel in 1985 (basically implemented in 1989, scheduled to be fully implemented by 1995) and with Canada (to be completed by 1999) have prompted interest in further FTAs.[1]

Originally published in *Journal of International Economics*, 34, 309–324.

[1]See, for example, the discussion in Schott (1989) regarding potential FTAs of the United States with Mexico, ASEAN, Taiwan and even Australia.

The focal point of traditional analyses of PTAs is the distinction between trade creation and trade diversion. Trade creation arises when the arrangement induces a country to increase imports of a good from a more efficient supplier, trade diversion when imports increase from a less efficient source. In the latter case it is possible that net surplus gains to domestic consumers (net of losses to domestic producers) are more than offset by decreased tariff revenue and that the arrangement makes the country *worse* off.[2] Accordingly, the net effects of forming a PTA are ambiguous and depend on the pattern of external tariffs applied to non-members of the PTA.

In investigating these potential tradeoffs, the literature has not always distinguished between a CU (in which members' external tariffs are equal) and a FTA (where external tariffs are determined separately by each member). In general the presumption has been that it is a CU that is being formed. The present paper applies the theory of the political economy of protection[3] to demonstrate that, in a setting where protection arises endogenously, the welfare-reducing effects associated with trade diversion in the formation of a CU are diminished in the case of a FTA. The reason is that the country in a FTA with a comparative disadvantage in a good (relative to its partner) will not maintain protection against imports from the rest of the world — protection will decrease as the political influence of the declining domestic industry decreases. The consequence is a distinction between FTAs and CUs which suggests that the second-best problems that pervade CUs do not apply equivalently to FTAs.

The approach to PTAs emphasizing that net gains depend on the outcome of trade creation and diversion (amongst a number of other potential effects that have been identified) has been complemented by the observation that the external tariff need not be taken as exogenously fixed, but can be *chosen*, by the member country itself (in a FTA) or jointly by members of a CU. A theorem due to Kemp and Wan (1976) and extended by Dixit and Norman (1980) notes that two tariff-ridden countries forming a CU can choose a common

[2]See Lipsey (1970) for an excellent summary.
[3]See Hillman (1989b) for a review of this literature.

external tariff and internal production and consumption taxes in such a way as to make each country (weakly) better off.[4] Endogeneity of the external tariff has also appeared in the unilateral tariff reduction critique: that is, the observation [see Wonnacott and Wonnacott (1981) and the references therein] that one member of a PTA can generally do better with a unilateral reduction of tariffs against all sources of imports.

I shall assume, as substantiated by considerable evidence,[5] that protectionist policies are *politically* endogenous. When determined through the political system, protection in a FTA will decline endogenously, reducing the potential for welfare loss via trade diversion. A caveat regarding the limitations of the paper is in order at this point. The theorem of Kemp and Wan (1976) and its extension by Dixit and Norman (1980) has the clear implication that not only does a CU dominate a FTA [see Richardson (1991)] but, by repeated iteration of the argument, that a CU can be extended, in a Pareto-improving fashion, to include *all* countries. From this perspective, then, it is a mystery why FTAs form rather than CUs and, indeed, why exclusive PTAs exist at all; most analysis of them is subject to this meta-criticism. We argue later that the framework used in the present paper may not be susceptible to this criticism but our arguments are not stated formally. Furthermore, in general one could cite a number of reasons why bilateral trading arrangements form in preference to multilateralism based on monitoring costs and verifiability of agreements[6] but, again, these are not explicitly dealt with in this paper. We do, however, address the issue of why a FTA forms at all.

---

[4]This is also true for a FTA, as a CU is just a FTA where partners have identical external tariffs.

[5]See the survey of empirical evidence in Hillman (1989b, ch. 11).

[6]One of the main factors in the successful ratification of the U.S.–Canada FTA that came into operation in 1989, in fact, was the establishment of well-defined dispute settlement procedures which, "go well beyond the past or prospective achievements of GATT" [Hufbauer (1989, p. 147)]. These procedures, involving joint negotiations on acceptable rules for contingent protection and the establishment of bilateral review panels are much more manageable on a bilateral level than they would be at the GATT level, for example.

An illustration

The following provides an illustration. Suppose a smaller country A (e.g., New Zealand) is to form a FTA with a larger country B (Australia) that excludes country C (the rest of the world). Suppose also that in each of the partners there exists a horribly inefficient industry (auto production) which is slightly less hopeless in country B than in country A. The industry only exists in country A and country B because of high protection secured by the lobbying activities of domestic producers. Consequent to the FTA, the industry in country A contracts as trade diversion occurs and country A switches the source of imports from country C to country B. In Fig. 1, ED_{A} represents (partial equilibrium) excess demand for imports in country A. The good is subject to a non-discriminatory specific tariff of t^0. As illustrated, country C is the most efficient supplier and country A would initially import only from country C, at price $p^{\mathrm{C}} + t^0$, gaining tariff revenue of areas 1+2. With the FTA, however, country A would now switch suppliers, buying only from country B at a price p^{B}, gaining areas $1 + 3$ in net surplus but losing all tariff revenues. The net effect then is a gain of $3 - 2$ which may be positive or negative. So trade diversion can be welfare-reducing if country C is a sufficiently cheaper source of supply than country B.[7,8]

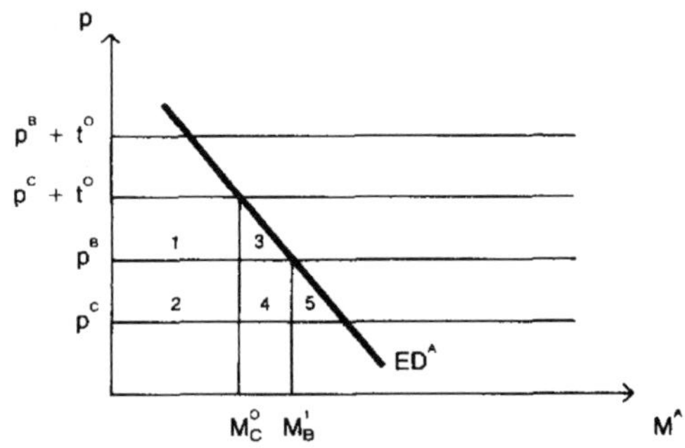

Fig. 1.

[7]Hillman (1989a) presents an alternative exposition of trade diversion and a prisoners' dilemma explanation, *given* the external tariff.

[8]The unilateral tariff reduction critique, in this context, observes that country A can do better than joining the FTA by simply abolishing all tariffs unilaterally, for a net gain of 3 + 4 + 5.

The model that I shall set out notes (i) that *within* the context of a FTA all losses associated with trade diversion can be avoided by reducing the tariff on imports from country C to (slightly less than) $p^{\mathrm{B}} - p^{\mathrm{C}}$, so the net surplus gain is area $1+3$ and tariff losses are area 1, yielding an overall gain of area 3, and (ii) such tariff reduction can be expected to occur endogenously in a more complete model of tariff-setting. A fall in the tariff against country C to $p^{\mathrm{B}} - p^{\mathrm{C}}$ has no consequences for domestic firms, but yields tariff revenue. Accordingly, no domestic group benefits from maintaining the tariff above $p^{\mathrm{B}} - p^{\mathrm{C}}$. Similarly, there are no domestic employment effects from reducing the tariff, nor any other consequence that motivates maintaining the tariff above $p^{\mathrm{B}} - p^{\mathrm{C}}$. In the extreme case in which country A's industry vanishes altogether, there is no reason at all to maintain a tariff since there are only losers within A from what is equivalent to a discriminatory consumption tax. With protection endogenously determined, trade diversion becomes trade creation as A's tariff against country C is ultimately dropped. That is, as the FTA leads the New Zealand auto industry to contract in the face of less inefficient Australian competition, there is less political reason to maintain protection of the New Zealand industry against competitors in the rest of the world.[9] I now formalize these arguments.

2. The model

As an analytical framework, we require a model in which protection is determined endogenously. There are a number of variants of such models. Here I adopt a multi-sector generalization of the model of Long and Vousden (1991) (L&V henceforth). The basic model is Hillman's (1982) reduced-form Stigler–Peltzman political support function augmented by considering the allocation of tariff revenues. The tariff-setting authority is concerned with both the profitability

[9]The example of Australia and New Zealand is fictional in at least one important respect: the auto industry has generally been afforded special treatment within the Closer Economic Relations FTA pact between the two countries.

of the protected industry and the wellbeing of consumers. It achieves its goals through setting domestic prices via tariffs; L&V enrich this specification by also considering the allocation of tariff revenues.

In the L&V version, the government maximizes a weighted sum of utilities through the choice of domestic prices via tariffs. We employ a multi-sector version of their Ricardo–Viner production model. Country A produces $n+1$ goods: an untaxed numeraire X^0 and n other goods indexed X^i, $i = 1, \ldots, n$. The production functions $X^i = F^i[\bar{K}^i, L^i]$ exhibit constant returns to scale (CRS), where L^i and $\bar{K}^i$ denote employment of labor and (fixed) capital, respectively, in sector $i = 1, \ldots, n$. In the numeraire sector, production is also CRS but in labor alone: $X^0 = F^0[L^0] = wL^0$ for some constant w. So long as this good is produced in equilibrium, as we shall assume throughout, this fixes the competitive wage at w. All firms are competitive. All goods are tradeable. The domestic price of X^i, p^i, is equal to the world price, p^{*i}, plus a specific trade tax (tariff if i is imported, export tax if exported), t^i, determined in accordance with the specification below. We denote by $\boldsymbol{t}, \boldsymbol{p}$ and $\boldsymbol{p}^*$ the $1 \times n$ vectors of trade taxes, domestic prices and world prices, respectively. Henceforth we shall simply refer to $\boldsymbol{t}$ as a vector of tariffs which should be taken to be export taxes if the good in question is an export.

Letting M^i denote imports of good i (exports if negative), $\boldsymbol{M}$ is then the $n \times 1$ vector of non-numeraire imports. The scalar R then denotes net tariff revenues where

$$R = \boldsymbol{tM} = (\boldsymbol{p} - \boldsymbol{p}^*)\boldsymbol{M}. \tag{1}$$

If β^i is the exogenously determined share of revenues that are allocated to capital-owners in sector i,[10] then firms choose L^i to maximize profits denoted I^i:

$$I^i = p^i F^i[\bar{K}^i, L^i] - wL^i + \beta^i R. \tag{2}$$

[10] As Long and Vousden (1991) observe, the parameters β^i must be exogenous to the government in a more general setting or else the political problem becomes inessential: Free trade will be chosen and all redistributive goals achieved through lump-sum transfers.

The government's objective is to maximize a weighted sum of the utilities of capital-owners and workers. Where workers receive a share β^w of tariff revenues, we denote workers' welfare as $V^w[\boldsymbol{p}, I^w]$, where $I^w = \text{income} = w\bar{L} + \beta^w R$ and $\bar{L}$ denotes the total labor supply in the economy. Full employment implies $\sum_{j=0}^{n} L^j = \bar{L}$. Letting $V^i[\boldsymbol{p}, I^i]$ represent the indirect utility of X^i-sector capital-owners, the government's objective is to choose $\boldsymbol{p}$, given world prices $\boldsymbol{p}^*$, to maximize

$$G[\boldsymbol{p}, \boldsymbol{p}^*] = \sum_{i=1}^{n} a^i V^i[\boldsymbol{p}, I^i] + a^w V^w[\boldsymbol{p}, I^w], \tag{3}$$

where a^i and a^w are positive constants. Note that $\beta^w + \sum_{i=1}^{n} \beta^i = 1$.

Demands are assumed to be homothetic. Thus, where C^{ij} denotes consumption of good i by group $j, i = 0, 1, \ldots, n, j = w, 1, \ldots, n$, $C^i = \sum_j C^{ij}$ and $I = \sum_j I^j$, we have

$$C^{ij}[\boldsymbol{p}, I^j] = \phi^i[\boldsymbol{p}]I^j, \quad C^i[\boldsymbol{p}, I] = \phi^i[\boldsymbol{p}]I \tag{4}$$

for some function $\phi^i[\boldsymbol{p}]$. Total imports are therefore

$$M^i = \phi^i[\boldsymbol{p}]I - F^i[\bar{K}^i, L^i]. \tag{5}$$

Finally, aggregate income is given by

$$I = wL^0 + \sum_{i=1}^{n} p^i F^i[\bar{K}^i, L^i] + R. \tag{6}$$

Substitution of (5) and (1) into (6) yields (7), following some manipulation:

$$I = (1/\Delta)\left\{wL^0 + \sum_{i=1}^{n} p^{*i} F^i[\bar{K}^i, L^i]\right\} \tag{7}$$

where

$$\Delta = \left(1 - \sum_{i=1}^{n} t^i \phi^i[\boldsymbol{p}]\right) = 1 - \sum_{i=1}^{n} (p^i - p^{*i})\phi^i$$
$$> 1 - \sum_{i=1}^{n} p^i \phi^i = 1 - \sum_{i=1}^{n} (p^i C^i)/I = C^0/I > 0.$$

From the definition of I^j, $j = w, 1, \ldots, n$, note that

$$\left.\frac{\partial I^j}{\partial p^{*i}}\right|_p = \beta^j \left.\frac{\partial R}{\partial p^{*i}}\right|_p. \tag{8}$$

So, because $\beta^w + \sum_{i=1}^n \beta^i = 1$,

$$\left.\frac{\partial I}{\partial p^{*i}}\right|_p = \left.\frac{\partial R}{\partial p^{*i}}\right|_p = -M^i/\Delta < 0, \tag{9}$$

where the first equality also follows directly from (6) and the second from (7) and the definition of Δ.

We wish to consider the effects of country A forming a FTA with country B against country C. The main thrust of our argument concerns incentives to reduce tariffs in an import-competing industry wherein trade diversion occurs; we shall henceforth concentrate on a single sector X^1, without loss of generality. The final aspect of the model to be specified is the relative size of each of the three countries. The argument is seen most clearly in Fig. 1 where country A is small relative to both of its trading partners. We consider only this case in the paper since it isolates welfare effects of the FTA by removing terms-of-trade reasons for tariffs.

In a model in which policy is endogenously determined, the issue of how a FTA comes to form in the first place cannot be ignored.[11] However, since my main focus is on the determination of external tariffs *within* a FTA I shall deal with this issue first, turning to the formation of the FTA in the next section of the paper.

---

[11]This is in stark contrast to much of the early literature on preferential trading areas (PTAs) which was motivated simply by asking what the effects of a PTA would be, were it to form. A subsequent literature, which falls under the umbrella title of the unilateral tariff reduction critique (UTR), has noted that, in many cases, a country could do better than joining a PTA by unilaterally reducing its own tariffs. While our analysis is immune to the UTR critique, as nonzero tariffs emerge in a unilateral tariff-setting equilibrium for a small country here, taking the formation of the FTA as given is nevertheless even harder to justify here than in the earlier literature on PTAs because of the endogeneity of policy.

2.1. *The pre-FTA equilibrium*

Before the formation of the FTA, all tariffs are non-discriminatory, all imports come from country C and the political equilibrium tariff is characterized implicitly by the first-order conditions for maximization of the political support function. We shall argue later that a FTA can only come about from an underlying shift in this function: we shall denote the pre-FTA utility weights by $\tilde{a}^i$ and the support function as $\tilde{G}[\boldsymbol{p}, \boldsymbol{p}^*]$. To keep the analysis of interest, we assume that the $\tilde{G}$ function achieves a global maximum[12] at a price for good 1, our focus, greater than $p^{\mathrm{B1}} > p^{\mathrm{C1}}$ but less than the autarkic price in country A. Thus the equilibrium tariff on good 1 is positive but not prohibitive.

2.2. *The post-FTA equilibrium*

After the FTA is formed the domestic X^1 industry is no longer protected against imports from country B. This heralds the industry's decline via the FTA which, through the political endogeneity of protection, leads the tariff against country C to fall. We maintain the assumption that the political support function, $G[\boldsymbol{p}, \boldsymbol{p}^*]$, achieves a global maximum at a price $p^1 > p^{\mathrm{B1}}$ in order to keep the analysis from being trivial; if the change in the political support function was such that the optimum domestic price, unconstrained by the FTA, was now *less* than p^{B1}, then no trade diversion would occur at all. We now show that the new equilibrium level of the tariff, t^1, must be such that $p^{\mathrm{B1}} \geqq p^{\mathrm{C1}} - t^1$.

Suppose not. That is, suppose $p^{\mathrm{B1}} < p^{\mathrm{C1}} + t^1$: this is where there is water in the tariff. In such a case all imports come from B, there is no tariff revenue and the domestic price of good 1 is p^{B1}. Denoting by $\boldsymbol{p}_{-1}$ the $(n-1) \times 1$ domestic price vector $(p^2, p^3, \ldots, p^n)$, and by $\boldsymbol{p}^*_{-1}$ the corresponding vector of 'world' prices, $G[\boldsymbol{p}, \boldsymbol{p}^*] =$

[12]The G function need not be everywhere concave in $\boldsymbol{p}$. However, if more than one local maximum exists, we assume that the equilibrium is at the global maximum.

$G[(p^{\text{B1}}, \boldsymbol{p}_{-1}), (p^{\text{B1}}, \boldsymbol{p}^*_{-1}]$.[13] But, from (3),

$$\left.\frac{\partial G}{\partial \boldsymbol{p}^{*1}}\right|_p = \left(\sum_{k=1}^{n} a^k V_I^k \beta^k + a^w V_I^w \beta^w\right) \left.\frac{\partial R}{\partial p^{*i}}\right|_p, \tag{10}$$

where $V_I = \partial V/\partial I$. As $V_I^j > 0$, $j = w, 1, \ldots, n$ so, from (9), $\partial G/\partial p^{*1}|_p < 0$ at all domestic prices for which $M^1 > 0$. Thus $G[(p^{\text{B1}}, \boldsymbol{p}_{-1}), (p^{\text{B1}}, \boldsymbol{p}^*_{-1})] < G[(p^{\text{B1}}, \boldsymbol{p}_{-1}), (p^{\text{C1}}, \boldsymbol{p}^*_{-1})]$ because $p^{\text{B1}} > p^{\text{C1}}$ by assumption: the tariff-setting authority can do better by trading with country C with a tariff of $p^{\text{B1}} - p^{\text{C1}}$ and hence a domestic price of p^{B1}.

For the reasons noted, a reduction in the tariff against country C to $p^{\text{B1}} - p^{\text{C1}}$ meets no domestic political opposition but yields positive tariff revenue. The source of imports is a matter of indifference to the domestic industry and individuals as consumers but whatever imports come from country C yield tariff revenue. Figure 2(a) shows the relationship between the government's objective and the discriminatory tariff against C in this case. If the tariff exceeds the price differential between country B and country C, then all trade is with the partner and $G = G[(p^{\text{B1}}, \boldsymbol{p}_{-1}), (p^{\text{B1}}, \boldsymbol{p}^*_{-1})]$. When the tariff equals the price differential, trade with either country can lie anywhere between zero and all of country A's imports, yielding the same domestic price, tariff revenues between zero and $R[(p^{\text{B1}}, \boldsymbol{p}_{-1}), (p^{\text{C1}}, \boldsymbol{p}^*_{-1})]$ inclusive and any value of $G[\boldsymbol{p}, \boldsymbol{p}^*]$ between $G[(p^{\text{B1}}, \boldsymbol{p}_{-1}), (p^{\text{B1}}, \boldsymbol{p}^*_{-1})]$ and $G[(p^{\text{B1}}, \boldsymbol{p}_{-1}), (p^{\text{C1}}, \boldsymbol{p}^*_{-1})]$. As the tariff is reduced below the price differential, all trade is with country C and G declines continuously, in the case shown in Fig. 2(a), from $G[(p^{\text{B1}}, \boldsymbol{p}_{-1}), [(p^{\text{C1}}, \boldsymbol{p}^*_{-1})]$ to $G[(p^{\text{C1}}, \boldsymbol{p}_{-1}), (p^{\text{C1}}, \boldsymbol{p}^*_{-1})]$ at full free trade.

[13]Within a FTA it need not be the case that $\boldsymbol{p}_{-1} = \boldsymbol{p}^*_{-1}$ except insofar as trade in a particular good occurs between the FTA members. If a good is imported by both from C, for example, then different external tariffs would yield different domestic consumer prices. Also, the vector of world prices faced within the FTA, $\boldsymbol{p}^*$, will not, in general, be the same as that faced when setting tariffs unilaterally since country B must drop tariffs on A's exports within the FTA. To avoid notational clutter, I do not denote these vectors differently where no confusion will result.

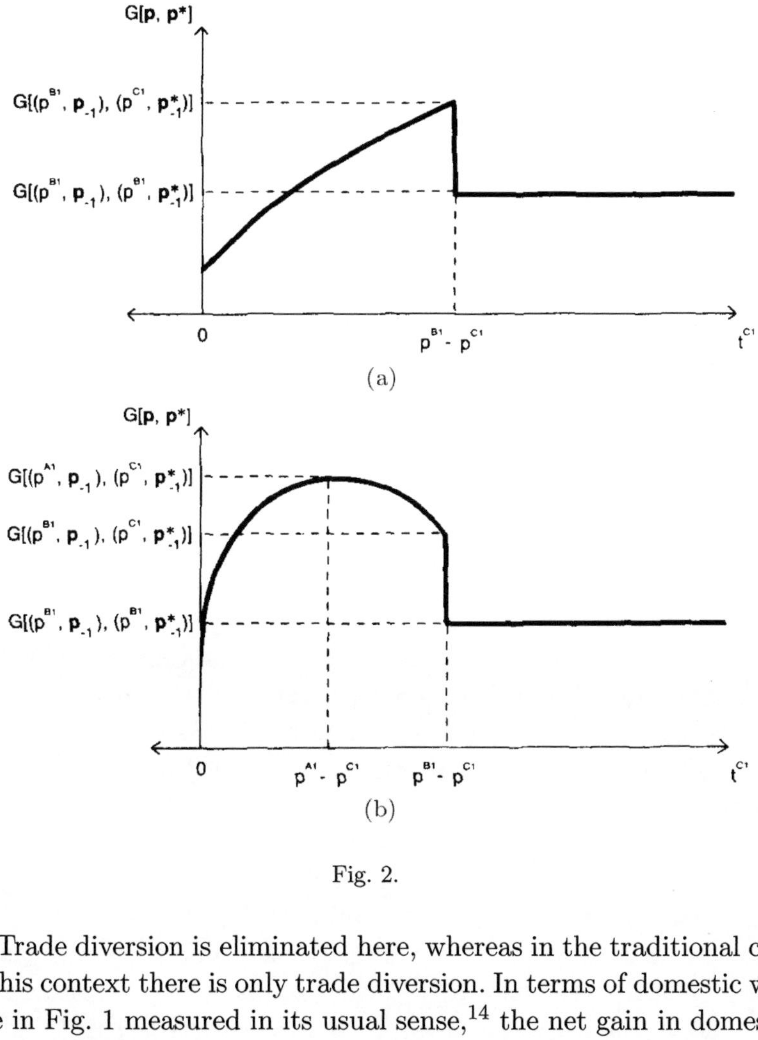

Fig. 2.

Trade diversion is eliminated here, whereas in the traditional case in this context there is only trade diversion. In terms of domestic welfare in Fig. 1 measured in its usual sense,[14] the net gain in domestic welfare is 3+4.

In fact, it is possible that the tariff may fall well below $(p^{\mathrm{B1}} - p^{\mathrm{C1}})$ yielding greater gains, depending on the shape of the $G[\boldsymbol{p}, \boldsymbol{p}^*]$ function at $p^1 = p^{\mathrm{B1}}$. Although the global maximum occurs at some

[14]In a model of endogenous policy, this measure is not easily interpreted. The usual potential compensation justification for aggregating surplus and revenue gains is invalid where the government's objectives are explicitly modelled, as here. See Rodrik (1986) for a discussion of this issue.

$p^1 > p^{B1}$, it is possible that other local maxima exist. Figure 2(b) illustrates a case in which a local maximum occurs at p^{A1}, where $p^{C1} < p^{A1} < p^{B1}$. In such a case the government can do even better by reducing the tariff against C to $p^{A1} - p^{C1}$. This is the case implicit in the earlier example: the FTA merely begins the domestic industry's decline and it is continued by reductions in tariffs against C.

3. The formation of the FTA

So far we have said little about how the FTA comes into being in the first place. This seems particularly important in light of the example provided in the first part of the paper: if the FTA will lead to an extensive decline in the New Zealand auto industry, would the industry not be a vocal opponent of its formation?

For a FTA to arise in this context it must be the case that there be overall gains, in the sense of increasing the government's political support function, despite any particular sectoral losses. It is easy to see how this might occur: gains to exporters from reduced tariffs in B can easily outweigh losses to importers from reduced tariffs against B (and C, following the arguments of this paper.) In the model used here where A is small relative to B, such aggregate gains are likely in the sense that B's tariffs have terms of trade effects on A and are likely to be higher than A's tariffs on B.

Formally, let $\boldsymbol{p}^{\text{FTA}}$ denote the optimally chosen vector of domestic prices in A given a FTA with B (where not all prices can be chosen freely, note) and $\boldsymbol{p}^{*\text{FTA}}$ the vector of world prices faced by A in a FTA with B, so $\boldsymbol{p}^{\text{FTA}} \in \operatorname{argmax} G[\boldsymbol{p}, \boldsymbol{p}^{*\text{FTA}}]$. Similarly, denote by $\boldsymbol{p}^{\text{opt}}$ the optimally chosen vector of domestic prices if the same government in A sets tariffs unilaterally facing world prices $\boldsymbol{p}^*$, so $\boldsymbol{p}^{\text{opt}} \in \operatorname{argmax} G[\boldsymbol{p}, \boldsymbol{p}^*]$. A FTA will be chosen if $G[\boldsymbol{p}^{\text{FTA}}, \boldsymbol{p}^{*\text{FTA}}] \geqq G[\boldsymbol{p}^{\text{opt}}, \boldsymbol{p}^*]$. It is clear that this condition can hold even if $p^i, \text{FTA} < p^{i,\text{opt}}$ for some $i = 1, \ldots, n$ (in particular, for $i = 1$ in our earlier analysis) depending on the nature of $\boldsymbol{p}^*, \boldsymbol{p}^{*\text{FTA}}$ and $\boldsymbol{p}^{\text{FTA}}$. The appendix provides a simple example of this possibility.

This argument that a FTA 'packages' tariff reductions that, whilst harming some sectors, are beneficial on aggregate, still leaves a number of questions unanswered. First, how do FTAs *arise*? What stimulates the movement from an initial situation of unilateral tariff setting to a FTA? Second, why do FTAs arise rather than multilateral tariff reductions through the GATT, for example?[15]

The second of these points we addressed briefly in the introduction, arguing that a number of reasons stemming from informational imperfections might explain the formation of small trading clubs in preference to large multilateral organizations, but the endogeneity of tariff-setting also mitigates this meta-criticism of PTAs somewhat. The Kemp–Wan proposition is predicated upon the existence of lump-sum transfers; the Dixit–Norman extension on comprehensive commodity and factor taxation. However, the L&V model implicitly rules out both powers: if lump-sum grants were available the entire problem would collapse (see L&V, p. 95) and if comprehensive commodity taxation were available the government's choice problem should explicitly allow for their setting.[16]

Furthermore, there is no presumption that Pareto-improving multilateral changes in tariffs alone exist in this context. In a standard tariff-setting model, Turunen-Red and Woodland (1990) derive certain (admittedly weak) conditions that must hold for there to exist Pareto-improving multilateral reductions in tariffs for any pattern of tariffs in the presence of both domestic and international transfers. But, as noted above, the structure of the model employed in the

[15]I am grateful to a referee for raising this point and also for noting that, while multilateral tariff reductions (MTRs) and FTAs both act to constrain lobby groups in the present setting, they differ in the manner in which they do so. A FTA is essentially discriminatory, leaving considerable latitude for external tariff-setting while a MTR leaves no such leeway. Accordingly, MTR is likely to be far more difficult to achieve.

[16]While L&V argue (fn. 9) that the β parameters can be thought of as representing the outcome of the government's redistribution efforts through such taxation, this interpretation seems less than compelling as the levels of such instruments would not be invariant to the levels of tariffs chosen. The L&V specification is more usefully seen as a highly constrained optimal tax problem with an explicit social welfare function where policy instruments are limited to tariffs. In such a setting there is no presumption that the trading club can always be expanded to include another member a la Kemp/Wan and Dixit/Norman.

present paper necessarily precludes such transfers and these earlier results are not applicable. Nor are the more specific results of Mayer (1981) which concern mutually beneficial bilateral tariff reductions from a starting point of a Nash equilibrium in tariffs. As Mayer notes (section V) the introduction of interest groups into his analysis raises the possibility that positive tariffs in both countries may be a Pareto-optimal outcome (this is not true in the standard case). Accordingly, there may be no multilateral reductions in tariffs which are agreeable to all countries.

There is still a question here of how a FTA arises in the first place: What triggers its formation? In fact, the model of endogenous policy used here is better able to answer this question than is the traditional economic framework. The entry of countries into new bilateral or multilateral trade agreements is very often triggered by underlying shifts in political power or support.[17,18] In the present model, this is easily captured through L&V's interpretation of the a^i parameters in the support function as utility weights which are determined in some earlier political contest and are taken as fixed for the time period of L&V's analysis. They suggest that in an interpretation of their model in which there are no explicit lobby groups, simply voting groups defined by factor ownership, these weights, 'might simply reflect such things as the balance of powers in the constitution and the delineation of electoral boundaries ... ' (L&V, fn. 7). Similarly, they might reflect election of political parties where the formation of the FTA occurs within a term but the election itself is the event that brings the pro-FTA party to power, or they might reflect increased organization and consequent political power of some factor owners.

[17]In communications in 1990 with government officials in New Zealand, it was suggested to me that the recent expansion of a FTA with Australia (signed in 1983 but gathering most momentum in 1988 when it was agreed that it would be fully implemented by 1990, five years ahead of the original schedule) was one facet of a greater commitment to trade policy reform attributable to the newly elected Labour government. Similarly, Hufbauer (1989, p. 143) suggests that ratification of the U.S.–Canada FTA of 1989 was only cemented by Canadian elections of 1988 in which it was the central, if not sole, issue.

[18]I am grateful to a referee for suggesting this explanation for the formation of a FTA in this context.

Formally, taking this interpretation of the model, let $\tilde{G}[\boldsymbol{p}, \boldsymbol{p}^*] = \sum_{i=1}^n \tilde{a}^i V^i[\boldsymbol{p}, I^i] + \tilde{a}^w V^w[\boldsymbol{p}, I^w]$ again represent the initial political support function (of the government where tariffs are set unilaterally) and $G[\boldsymbol{p}, \boldsymbol{p}^*] = \sum_{i=1}^n a^i V^i[\boldsymbol{p}, I^i] + a^w V^w[\boldsymbol{p}, I^w]$ the subsequent support function (e.g. of the new government). It is clear that changes in the a^i terms can alter these functions so that $G[\boldsymbol{p}^{\text{FTA}}, \boldsymbol{p}^{*\text{FTA}}] \geqq G[\boldsymbol{p}^{\text{opt}}, \boldsymbol{p}^*]$ but $\tilde{G}[\boldsymbol{p}^{\text{FTA}}, \boldsymbol{p}^{*\text{FTA}}] \leqq \tilde{G}[\boldsymbol{p}^{\text{opt}}, \boldsymbol{p}^*]$, in terms of our earlier notation and, additionally, letting $\tilde{p}^{\text{opt}} \in \operatorname{argmax} \tilde{G}[\boldsymbol{p}, \boldsymbol{p}^*]$. The first inequality, discussed earlier, suggests that the new government will choose a FTA over unilateral tariff-setting while the second states that the initial government chooses the opposite. The appendix provides a simple example to illustrate these possibilities.

4. Further remarks

In this paper we have argued that the consequences for trade protection of a FTA may be more extreme than they at first appear — not only are trade barriers with the partner removed, but protection against non-member countries will fall. This is a potentially important distinction between a FTA, in which a country sets its own external tariff, and a CU, where external tariffs are determined jointly. We have cast this argument in the context of a particular model of tariff-setting, due to Long and Vousden (1991), but the general principles apply to a much wider range of tariff-setting situations. First, in the traditional analysis of PTAs, our results highlight a role for unilateral tariff reduction within a FTA (as opposed to the usual arguments for UTR in lieu of a PTA).

Second, we have shown elsewhere (Richardson, 1990a) that the exact same analysis of this paper can be applied where tariffs are the outcome of explicitly modelled lobbying by interested firms. As an industry contracts in the face of increased competition from the FTA partner so its lobbying activities decrease and the level of protection from non-members granted it by policy-makers also decreases. It is never in the interests of firms to expend real resources on a tariff with water in it so, again, trade diversion is reduced. However, one important additional issue arises in the lobbying context. While the domestic industry is indifferent about the source of imports (and the domestic government prefers imports from non-members) the industry in the FTA partner country strictly prefers that it is the source of imports. Foreign surplus is increased when they are granted preferential access to the home market.[19] Accordingly, they would seek to maintain that preferential access and would oppose any reduction in the external tariff levied by the home country against non-members of the FTA. In the model of the paper, where the tariff was granted solely for reasons of political support from domestic voters, there is no explicit channel by which foreign interests can be represented in the political process. Hillman and Ursprung (1988) have developed a lobbying model in which foreign firms make campaign contributions to domestic politicians in order to sway outcomes in their favor. A useful line of future research would be the incorporation of such considerations into a more complete model of endogenous policy formation. There are reasons to suspect, however, that the model of the present paper is robust to this modification. In particular, political participation by interested industries from *non*-member countries will help offset the efforts of firms in the partner country.

Three final points are of interest. The flavor of the analysis above suggests that a country might be more favorably disposed towards a FTA than towards a CU, especially if the potential partner country or bloc is large. In such a case the common external tariff against non-members of a CU can more reasonably be treated as exogenous and is more likely to sustain trade diversion than in a FTA. Richardson (1990b) considers one aspect of this issue, stressing the externalities involved in lobbying efforts.

[19]This does not occur in the model of the paper as the home country is small relative to both trading partners. The only impact of the FTA on the partner country, then, would be the loss of tariff revenues levied against the home country's exports — while we take the membership decision of country B as exogenous, import subsidies would presumably be required to induce B to join such a FTA. An interesting extension of the current analysis would be to countries of similar sizes in which this 'rationality' constraint is imposed on both members of the FTA.

Second, another implication of the present model is that trade between member countries of a FTA may not expand following a FTA, even when "trade creation" occurs. The reason is that the trade creation we have considered occurs as one member expands trade with *non*-members (in contrast to the usual case of trade creation *intra*-FTA).

Finally, the empirical implications of our results are clear. While the essential mechanism operating in our analysis — the declining political support of declining industries — has been well established empirically [see Cassing and Hillman (1986) and the references therein] our main implication is that external tariffs of a country joining a FTA should fall in those industries in which imports from the partner country initially increase. The intertemporal nature of this argument means that it is too early to judge it on the basis of the most obvious candidates — the FTAs between the US and Canada, between the US and Israel and between Australia and New Zealand. Such an investigation would be a useful line of future study.

Appendix

In this appendix, we report the results of a simple numerical model (full details of the simulations are available from the author on request) calculated to demonstrate some of the assertions of the text. We consider a three-good case with numeraire Z produced according to $Z = \bar{w}L_z$, where $\bar{w}$ is a constant, and goods X and Y both produced according to a CRS technology $F^i[\bar{K}^i, L^i] = (\bar{K}^i L^i)^{1/2}$. Assuming Z is produced, the wage rate is fixed at $\bar{w}$.

Domestic prices of X and Y are p_x and p_y, respectively. The government's maximand, G, is the weighted sum of utilities of workers, V^w, and the utilities of owners of the two sector-specific fixed factors, V^x and V^y. The weight on each component is a^w, a^x and a^y, respectively and we assume that $a^w + a^x + a^y = 1$. So $G = (1 - a^x - a^y)V^w + a^x V^x + a^y V^y$. Each group has identical Cobb–Douglas preferences represented by the indirect utility function $V^i(p_x, p_y, I^i) = \ln(I^i) - b_x \ln(p_x) - b_y \ln(p_y)$ for expenditure shares b_x and b_y. Finally, we shall suppose that all tariff revenues go to workers: $\beta^w = 1$. Thus,

$$G = (1 - a^x - a^y)\ln(I^w) + a^x \ln(I^x) + a^y \ln(I^y) - b_x \ln(p_x) - b_y \ln(p_y).$$

This analysis will only hold, note, so long as $L^x + L^y < \bar{L}$ or else the Z industry will close down and the wage will not stay at $\bar{w}$. Also, as p_i, $i = X, Y$, is controlled by trade taxes and subsidies, each can neither exceed the level at which imports are zero and the tariff no longer affects domestic price nor fall below the level at which exports are zero and an export tax does not affect domestic price. Thus the government's optimization is constrained in that the domestic price of a good and the world price of the good must both lie above (below) the zero-trade price if the good is an export (import). The government's problem is to choose p_x and p_y to maximize G, subject to these constraints. (For the analysis to be accurate we must check that the solution also satisfies $L^x + L^y < \bar{L}$.)

Numerically, we suppose that $\bar{K}^x = \bar{K}^y = 4$, $b_x = b_y = 1/3$, $\bar{w} = 2$ and $\bar{L} = 400$. We suppose that country C is willing to import Y at a price of 20 and export X at a price of 2. Country B, on the other hand, initially exports X, free of taxes or subsidies, at a price of 3 and imports Y at a price of 25. The domestic price of Y within B, however, is 35 as Y is subject to a tariff in B. In the absence of a FTA, then, country A faces world prices of $p_x = 2$ and $p_y = 25$, exporting Y to B and importing X from C. Once the FTA with B is formed, however, the 'world' price of Y for country A becomes 35 as B's tariff no longer applies. We suppose also that A trades only with B in good X post-FTA: at the pre-FTA tariffs in each case this would be true and we would have trade diversion in good X but the FTA will nevertheless be shown to be beneficial for one government. Our point, recall, is that A can do even better by reducing its tariff on C: we demonstrate this also.

The initial government has utility weights $\tilde{a}^x = 0.4$ and $\tilde{a}^y = 0.2$, putting more weight on the welfare of importers; the subsequent government has $a^x = 0.1$ and $a^y = 0.6$, putting more weight on the welfare of exporters. (There is nothing particularly sacred about any of these numbers — this argument applies in

Table 1.

				Domestic prices	Trades	Maximum value of G
Initial	$\tilde{a}^y = 0.2$	$p_y^* = 25$	pre-	$\tilde{p}_y = 26.62$	$E^y = 9.3$	$\tilde{G}_1 = 3.898$
government	$\tilde{a}^x = 0.4$	$p_x^* = 2$	FTA	$\tilde{p}_x = 20.81$	$M^x = 1.3$	
		$p_y^* = 35$	post-	$p_y = p_y^* = 35$	$E^y = 21.5$	$\tilde{G}_2 = 3.008$
		$p_x^* = 3$	FTA	$p_x = p_x^* = 3$	$M^x = 154.4$	
Subsequent	$\tilde{a} = 0.6$	$p_y^* = 25$	pre-	$p_y = 39.23$	$E^y = 27$	$G_1 = 4.450$
government	$\tilde{a} = 0.1$	$p_x^* = 2$	FTA	$\tilde{p}_x = 4.21$	$M^x = 109.5$	
		$p_y^* = 35$	post-	$p_y = p_y^* = 35$	$E^y = 21.5$	$G_2 = 4.455$
		$p_x^* = 3$	FTA	$p_x = p_x^* = 3$	$M^x = 154.4$	

many parameterizations.) The model was simulated numerically via grid search techniques run in GAUSS. Table 1 reports our results.

The initial government, which favors importers, imposes a very large tariff on imports in unilateral tariff setting (UTS) (raising p_x from 2 to 20.81 and only importing 1.3 units of X). It also offers a small export subsidy on Y, raising the domestic price to 26.62; exports are then 9.3 units. The government's objective function is maximized at $\tilde{G}[\tilde{\boldsymbol{p}}^{\text{opt}}, \boldsymbol{p}^*] = \tilde{G}[(20.81, 26.62); (2, 25)] \equiv \tilde{G}_1 = 3.898$. But if the FTA is joined and A operates at B's internal prices, exports and imports both increase and G falls to $\tilde{G}[\boldsymbol{p}^{\text{FTA}}, \boldsymbol{p}^{*\text{FTA}}] = \tilde{G}[(3, 35); (3, 35)] = \tilde{G}_2 = 3.008$. So this government would not choose to join the FTA.

For the government which favors exporters, however, the UTS optimum is to levy a very small tariff on X, raising the domestic price to 4.21 and importing 109.5 units and to offer a much larger subsidy to exporters, raising their price to 39.23 and inducing exports of 27 units. The government's objective function is then maximized at $G[\boldsymbol{p}^{\text{opt}}, \boldsymbol{p}^*] = G[(4.21, 39.23); (2, 25)] \equiv G_1 = 4.450$. But joining the FTA gives $G[\boldsymbol{p}^{\text{FTA}}, \boldsymbol{p}^{*\text{FTA}}] = G[(3, 35); (3, 35)] = G_2 = 4.455$. So this government *would* join the FTA.

This case, then, provides an example in which $\tilde{G}[\boldsymbol{p}^{\text{FTA}}, \boldsymbol{p}^{*\text{FTA}}] < \tilde{G}[\tilde{\boldsymbol{p}}^{\text{opt}}, \boldsymbol{p}^*]$ and $G[\boldsymbol{p}^{\text{FTA}}, \boldsymbol{p}^{*\text{FTA}}] \geq G[\boldsymbol{p}^{\text{opt}}, \boldsymbol{p}^*]$, the latter even if $p^{i,\text{FTA}} < p^{i,\text{opt}}$: for good X the price in the FTA is 3, whereas both governments would choose a higher domestic price if setting tariffs unilaterally. The intuition for these outcomes is straightforward: the initial government, which favors import-competers, is made worse off by joining the FTA because, even though exporters gain, the loss to import-competers from lower prices is greater. The reverse is true for the exporter-oriented government.

A final exercise is to demonstrate that the second government could do even better than joining the FTA and leaving external tariffs untouched by reducing its tariff against C to (epsilon less than) 1. In simulating this case, country A faces $p_y = p_y^* = 35$ and $p_x = 3$, $p_x^* = 2$. Now all imports of X come from C, raising revenue of 173.75 and the income effect of this revenue cuts exports of Y to 19.85 and increases imports of X, compared with the benchmark of the FTA. The government's payoff increases from $G_2 = 4.455$ to 4.514.

References

Cassing, J. and A. Hillman (1986). Shifting comparative advantage and senescent industry collapse. *American Economic Review*, 76(3), 516–523.

Dixit, A. and V. Norman (1980). *Theory of international trade* (Nisbet and CUP, Cambridge).

Hillman, A. (1982). Declining industries and political-support protectionist motives. *American Economic Review*, 72(5), 1180–1187.

Hillman, A. (1989a). Resolving the puzzle of welfare-reducing trade diversion: A prisoners' dilemma interpretation. *Oxford Economic Papers*, 41, 452–455.

Hillman, A. (1989b). The political economy of protection (Harwood, Chur, Switzerland).

Hillman, A. and H. Ursprung (1988). Domestic politics, foreign interests and international trade policy. *American Economic Review*, 78(4), 729–745.

Hufbauer, G.C. (1989). The free trade debate, Background paper for reports of The Twentieth Century Fund Task Force on the Future of American Trade Policy (Priority Press Publications, New York).

Kemp, M. and H. Wan Jr. (1976). An elementary proposition concerning the formation of customs unions. In M. Kemp, (ed.) *Three topics in the theory of international trade: Distribution, welfare and uncertainty*. Amsterdam: North-Holland.

Lipsey, R.G. (1970). *The theory of customs unions* (Weidenfeld and Nicolson, London).

Long, N.V. and N. Vousden (1991). Protectionist responses and declining industries. *Journal of International Economics*, 30, 87–103.

Mayer, W. (1981). Theoretical considerations on negotiated tariff adjustments. *Oxford Economic Papers*, 33, 135–153.

Richardson, M. (1990a). Trade diversion and endogenous tariff formation. Working paper 90-2, Department of Economics, Georgetown University.

Richardson, M. (1990b). Why a free trade area? The tariff also rises. Working paper 90-14, Department of Economics, Georgetown University.

Richardson, M. (1991). *The Dominance of a Customs Union Over a Free Trade Area.* Mimeo: Georgetown University.

Rodrik, D. (1986). Tariffs, subsidies and welfare with endogenous policy, *Journal of International Economics*, 21, 285–299.

Schott, J., ed. (1989). Free trade areas and U.S. trade policy (Institute for International Economics, Washington, DC).

Turunen-Red, A.H. and A.D. Woodland (1990). *Strict Pareto-Improving Multilateral Reforms of Tariffs.* Mimeo: University of Texas at Austin.

Wonnacott, P. and R. Wonnacott (1981). Is unilateral tariff reduction preferable to a customs union? The curious case of the missing foreign tariffs. *American Economic Review*, 71, 704–714.

Chapter 6

Why a Free Trade Area? The Tariff also Rises

Martin Richardson

Abstract: This chapter considers the choice between a customs union (wherein partners share a common external tariff) and a free trade area (wherein each partner chooses its own tariff against non-members). Following the result that a customs union dominates a free trade area, with coordination of domestic tax policies, we show that a free trade area may nevertheless be chosen if tariffs are determined endogenously through industry lobbying. This is so even when the free trade area equates producer prices within its borders and induces tariff revenue competition and whether or not there is domestic free-riding in lobbying.

1. Introduction

WHY WOULD TWO countries ever form a free trade area (FTA)? Woodland (1982, pp. 348-350) demonstrates that the optimal form of preferential trading agreement amongst countries, when international transfers exist, is one with a common external tariff; i.e., a customs union (CU). By a simple application of the results of Dixit and Norman (1980, pp. 191–194). this is also true if member countries have only commodity and factor taxation available and coordinate these taxes (see Richardson, 1992). One reason tree trade areas are the preferential trading agreement of choice for many countries may

Originally published in *Economics and Politics*, 6(1), 79–96.

be that this degree of coordination is lacking. This paper highlights another reason: we demonstrate that a country may choose a FTA rather than a CU if tariffs are set endogenously through the lobbying efforts of interested industries. In a FTA a domestic industry need lobby only the domestic government for a particular external tariff whereas, in a CU, a given tariff requires that a larger legislative group be courted. Of course, there are also more firms involved in lobbying as those in the partner country also seek protection but there is correspondingly a greater degree of free-riding in the lobbying process within a CU than within a FTA; this lessens the attractiveness of the former to firms.[1,2]

This approach also bears upon the merits of preferential trading arrangements (PTAs) versus unilateral tariff reductions. In our analysis we consider two small countries combining in some agreement excluding a large third country (the rest of the world) which trades in every commodity. Accordingly, there are no terms of trade gains associated with the union and, if governments were traditional aggregate welfare maximizers, the question would arise as to why there is any external tariff at all. This problem plagues many traditional analyses of CUs[3] but in our set-up a non-zero tariff occurs as an equilibrium lobbying outcome.

[1]Dani Rodrik has noted that this argument is similar to one in the Federalist Papers concerning the benefits of a large republic. One such benefit is that, *ceteris paribus,* a faction is likely to have less power in a large than a small republic due to the increased likelihood of opposing cartels. So policies in a large republic are less likely to be hostage to the interests of any particular faction.

[2]A referee has pointed out that the criteria of choice between a CU and a FTA are rather different in our setup and those of Dixit and Norman (1980) and Woodland (1982). They consider a country's welfare as traditionally defined in terms of a representative agent, whereas the choice in our model is implicitly determined by the profitability of firms. We argue that trade policy is effectively set by the lobbying activities of interested firms and demonstrate that a FTA may be more profitable to firms than a CU; accordingly firms will lobby for the former.

[3]Wonnacott and Wonnacott (1981), however, provide an example in which a union of two small countries with "traditional" welfare-maximizing governments may be mutually beneficial in the presence of either transport costs or *non*-members tariffs.

One question not dealt with here is why a PTA is entered into at all. Richardson (1993a) discusses a number of reasons why the formation of a PTA may be more likely, in general models of endogenous policy, than either small tariff changes or multilateral reforms. In brief: regarding the latter, there is no presumption that Pareto-improving multilateral changes in tariffs even exist in models of endogenous policy. Also, in such models, bilateral agreements might prevail where unilateral tariff reductions would not as they bring more interested producer groups (namely exporters) into the process by virtue of the reciprocal nature of tariff reductions. Essentially, PTAs "package" tariff reductions that might individually be rejected as harmful to an interested sector but which are, on aggregate, welfare improving. Finally, a political equilibrium might be disturbed by large bilateral changes in tariffs when small changes would be rejected if there are costs of participation in the political process — large changes then might yield welfare gains that exceed the participation "threshold".

Further, the political determination of the *form* of PTA is easily introduced as the outcome of an earlier lobbying process in which the industry group, anticipating the effects of a FTA and a CU as described in this paper, lobbies for one form of PTA or the other. Adding this stage of lobbying explicitly serves only to obscure our central point and is therefore omitted.

The remainder of the paper is organized as follows. In the next Section we turn to an analysis of tariff-setting in a FTA and a CU where internal producer prices are equated in the FTA. Firms lobby for tariff protection and we show that free-riding problems amongst lobbying firms may lead them to favor a FTA over a CU. We show that the same results hold in a more standard model of a FTA and we also show that they hold regardless of whether or not there is free-riding amongst lobbying firms *within* a country. We demonstrate that the traditional welfare consequences of CU formation are positive, however. A final Section summarizes and concludes.

2. A political economy model of tariff-setting

2.1. *The model*

The results of Dixit and Norman (1980) and Richardson (1992)[4] suggest that formation of a FTA is suboptimal for members compared to a CU and yet preferential trading arrangements in the world are very commonly FTAs One explanation for this is that either commodity taxes themselves, or the degree of cooperation in tax-setting needed to guarantee gains from a CU, are not present in most PTAs. The former possibility is irrelevant for any moderately developed country and the latter, while perhaps explaining why countries pursue completely independent trade policies rather than forming PTAs of any sort, seems to be less credible in explaining why countries that *do* cooperate to the extent of forming a FTA do not go the extra yard to a CU.

In this Section we argue that one potential reason for this apparently mysterious behavior is that tariffs are not chosen in the national interest but rather are the outcome of lobbying by interested parties. We consider two countries starting in a FTA and deciding whether to move to a CU, and we suppose that firms in an industry lobby their government for protection, if the good is an importable, or for export subsidies if an exportable.[5] The issue of the formation of a FTA in a model of endogenous policy is discussed in Richardson (1993a) and we do not pursue it here, taking the FTA as a starting point and considering the decision to form a CU instead. We consider two countries, A and B, in a FTA excluding the rest of the world, C. A and B are small relative to C and so face fixed trading prices

[4]Dixit and Norman (1980) show that any two tariff-ridden countries can form a CU and arrange internal taxes in such a fashion that neither is worse off (and each is strictly better off if there is any smooth transformation on the production possibility surface). That any FTA can be weakly dominated by an appropriately chosen CU is a direct consequence of this result; Richardson (1992) demonstrates that internal free trade in a FTA equalizes producer prices so that the result is weakened to equivalence between any FTA and some CU. However, the equivalent CU is unlikely to be optimal so, in general, the dominance result will still hold strictly.

[5]We refer to "the tariff" henceforth but this is meant to include export subsidies.

with C. This highlights the role of lobbying in determining the tariff — the traditional optimal tariff for each country is zero, given internal free trade, but in our model each country chooses a non-zero external tariff in FTA equilibrium.

We consider a simple two-good general equilibrium model involving lobbying by firms. The model we use is similar to that of Rodrik (1986) but we suppress internal free-riding within a country and our tariff-setting function is a little different in order to capture the effects on lobbying of creating a CU. As Lloyd (1982) has argued, a truly satisfactory analysis of preferential trading arrangements must include at least three goods to avoid either asymmetrics or a lack of trade between member countries. Our purpose here, however, is not to establish the generality of particular results but rather to provide an illustration of a particular intuition. Accordingly, we consider a model in which there is no trade between the member countries[6] but each trades the same goods with the rest of the world. As demonstrated in Richardson (1992) these are the only categories of goods in which the two partners might face different internal prices in a FTA.

Consider typical member country A. The country produces numeraire good Y according to a constant returns to scale production function in labor alone. It also produces good X according to a constant returns to scale production function in labor and sector-specific capital. Labor is intersectorally mobile and the country exports Y to country C from which it imports X. We assume that A is incompletely specialized at all relevant prices. The domestic consumer price of X is $p = p^* + t^A$ where p^* is the world price which is given and t^A is a specific tariff set according to the lobbying activity of the specific factor in the X sector. Without loss of generality, we normalize p^* to unity henceforth. The X industry consists of n identical owners (firms) of the X-specific total capital stock, K, each with $k = K/n$.

[6] In fact, we shall subsequently assume each country is identical in order to isolate the lobbying externality on which our argument focuses so even in a more general setting there would be no trade between member countries. The question then arises as to why these countries wish to form a FTA in the first place but this is a question that plagues any model of preferential trading arrangements between small countries, albeit for different reasons than in the present setting.

The main challenge in modeling the FTA/CU choice here is in specifying the mechanism by which tariffs are set in such a way that comparisons can be made between tariff-setting in an individual country and tariff-setting for a pair of countries in a CU. We adopt a model of representative democracy in which the political system is assumed to be identical in both member countries, yielding a reduced-form tariff-setting function which applies both at a country level and at the CU level.

We suppose that firms devote real resources to lobbying the tariff-setting authority. The latter is modeled, according to a very simplistic (and somewhat cynical) view of representative democracy, as a collection of automata. The level of tariff protection is determined by the votes of political representatives, each of whom can be "bought off" through lobbying activities.[7] All representatives are identical, each representing an identical constituency, and each has an identical, positive monotonic "cost" function mapping per-representative lobbying expenditures into the level of the tariff they will support. That is, each representative resists protection, in the interests of the consumers she represents, but lobbying can overcome that resistance according to a deterministic function wherein a given amount of lobbying will persuade a representative to support a certain tariff. This can be thought of as a reduced-form political-support function á la Hillman (1982) except that the relative weight placed on producers versus consumers is endogenous. All other things being equal, greater lobbying yields greater protection.[8] However, the greater the number of voters in the economy the more representatives there are and thus the more lobbying the industry will need to undertake in order to secure a given level of protection. This interpretation provides a solid foundation for the intuitive proposition that a million dollars spent on lobbying will secure a higher level of protection for an industry in a

[7]This activity is not bribery — we assume that resources devoted to lobbying represent a welfare loss to the economy as a whole and are not simply a transfer.

[8]We take lobbying expenditures to be equal across these symmetric representatives but it does not matter if, instead, efforts are concentrated on only a few of them. With majority voting, lobbyists would be best to concentrate their efforts on only a fraction ((1/2)+1) of the representatives but this does not affect our analysis.

small economy than the same sum spent in a much larger economy.[9] Also, this specification enables the direct comparison of FTA and CU equilibria as the form of the tariff-setting function is unchanged when countries form a CU; however, the number of representatives to be lobbied increases.

For concreteness, letting L be the total labor force of the economy (and, for neatness, the total electorate)[10] and L^S the total amount of resources put into lobbying by interested producers, we suppose that the domestic consumer price $p = 1+t$ is determined by some function $p[L^S,L]$.[11] We make the following assumptions about this function: where numerical subscripts denote appropriate partial derivatives of a function, $p[0, L] = 1$, $p_2 < 0$, $p_{22} > 0$, $p_1 > 0$, $p_{11} < 0$ and $p_{12} < 0$. That is, with no lobbying, no protection is granted. The greater the number of representatives (the greater the size of the electorate), the lower is the tariff, *ceteris paribus.* The impact of a greater number of representatives on the tariff decreases, in absolute magnitude, as the number rises. The greater the amount of lobbying, the higher is the tariff but this also has a decreasing effect and, finally, an increase in lobbying reduces the marginal effect of an increase in L on the tariff. Further, we suppose that to obtain any given tariff in a larger economy requires greater lobbying effort in equal proportion — this captures the idea that it is the number of representatives that must be lobbied that is critical in determining the effectiveness of lobbying and embodies the fact that all representatives have identical preferences and represent identical electorates. Thus p[.] is homogeneous of degree zero in L^S and L.

[9]This model of the political process can be formalized as the choice of prices p by policy-makers to maximize a payoff function $G[\mathscr{L}^S,V[p,I]]$ where $\mathscr{L}^S$ denotes per-representative industry lobbying, V[.] is the typical voter's indirect utility function defined over prices and income, $\partial G/\partial \mathscr{L}^S > 0$ and $\partial G/\partial V > 0$. The number of representatives is assumed to be linear in L, the number of voters, so this problem determines a policy-maker's optimal tariff as a function of both L and L^S, total lobbying. We suppose that policy-makers care only about their own consumers, even when a CU is formed. Were they to care about the partner country's consumers too then resistance to a tariff in a CU would be greater, reinforcing our results.

[10]This assumption is easily modified to include the n capital owners as voters also in which case the electorate is $L + n$. This change has no impact on our analysis.

[11]Throughout this paper, square brackets contain function arguments.

As we wish to concentrate on the effect of forming a CU, we suppose initially that the X industry within each country is perfectly cohesive. So lobbying efforts are coordinated and there is no domestic free-riding problem. This simplification of Rodrik's model is not essential (and is relaxed later) but makes our notation tidier.

One final aspect of our model deserves some attention as we differ from the usual approach taken in the literature on FTAs. It is usually supposed that if two members of a FTA have different external tariffs on an imported good then their internal prices will differ. This stems from the enforcement of rules-of-origin to prevent the erosion of any such price differences through re-exporting (or trade "deflection".) However, Richardson (1992) and (1993b) points out that such rules can only maintain differences in consumer prices: while re-exporting of external goods can be prohibited, the export of goods produced within a FTA partner cannot. Thus, producer prices within a FTA must be equalized regardless of tariff (and consumer price) differences. This simple observation has a number of serious consequences for the analysis of FTAs; in particular it will affect the equilibrium level of external tariffs, possibly quite dramatically as the following example shows.

If one partner has a higher domestic price, *all* intra-FTA production will be sold in that country. For instance, suppose that $t^B < t^A$. To keep matters simple, suppose that total production of X in A and B combined is less than demand in one of the countries at all relevant prices;[12] in such a case all production of X is sold in A at a price $1 + t^A$ (recalling the normalization of the world price to unity) and all of B's consumption (at $p^B = 1 + t^B$) is imported from C. In this model of endogenous tariff-setting there is no incentive to expend *any* resources on lobbying in B in such a case as the tariff is completely redundant in protecting the industry in B so long as the partner's tariff is higher. However, the free-riding by B's producers has no consequences for the industry in A (even though it costs country A in terms of tariff revenues foregone) as the price faced by

[12]While this is not critical to the argument that producer prices will be equalized, it does determine the *level* at which such equalization occurs.

producers in A is still $1 + t^A$. Note that a CU is *not* affected by this problem as both partners' tariffs are then equal.

To complete the description of the model, we specify the problem facing the X industry. In the Y sector, production occurs according to $Y = wL_Y$ where w is a positive constant and L_Y denotes total labor employed in the Y sector. So long as the country is incompletely specialized, as assumed above, this guarantees that the wage rate in the economy is constant at w. Denoting industry values with upper-case letters and firm values with lower-case letters, the typical X-sector firm in country A (suppressing A superscripts for clarity) has a profit function given by π^i:

$$\pi^i = p^{max} f[1^{xi,k}] - w(l^{xi} + 1^{si}) \quad \text{where}$$
$$p^{max} \equiv \max\{p[L^{S,-i} + 1^{Si}, L], 1 + t^B\}(\pi^i)$$

where 1^{Si} and 1^{xi} denote labor devoted to lobbying and production respectively, $L^{S,-i} = \sum_{k \neq i}^{n} 1^{sk}$ and f[.] is the firm's linear homogeneous production function. Given the assumed cohesion of the industry lobby, the aggregate amount of labor to devote to lobbying, L^S, and the amount to employ in production, L^X, are chosen in order to maximize profits given by $\prod^* = n\pi^i$. We seek a Nash equilibrium in lobbying expenditures so that each country's lobby group takes the level of lobbying in the other country as given. The industry's problem is then described in (1):

$$\underset{\{L^S, L^X\}}{\text{Max}} \prod^{*} = p^{max} F[L^X, K] - w(L^S + L^X) \tag{1}$$

where $p^{max} = \max\{p[L^S, L], 1 + t^B\}$ and $F[.] = nf[.]$.

Suppose first that $t^B = 0$ so that $p^{max} = p[L^S, L]$. First-order conditions (FOCs) for problem (1), assuming an interior solution, are then given in (2) and (3) where subscripts denote partial derivatives and asterisks denote optimal levels of L^X and L^S in the FTA regime. Each firm then sets $1^{xi} = L^{X*}/n$ and $1^{si} = L^{S*}/n$.

$$p[L^S*, L]F_1[L^{X*}, K] - w = 0 \tag{2}$$

$$p_1[L^S*, L]F[L^{X*}, K] - w = 0 \tag{3}$$

Second-order conditions (SOCs) for a maximum require, dropping function arguments for clarity, that $F_{11}^* < 0, p_{11}^* < 0$ and $p^* F_{11}^* p_{11}^* F^* - (p_1^* F_1^*)^2 > 0$. We also assume $p_{111} = F_{111} = 0$.

However, suppose instead that $1 + t^B \geq p[L^{S*}, L]$. In this case $p^{max} = 1 + t^B$ and the industry in A would be better served by free-riding on B's tariff, selling all its output in B, doing no lobbying and so saving on lobbying expenses.

2.2. *FTA or CU?*

The effect of a lobbying externality on the choice between a CU and a FTA is most clearly seen when A and B are identical. We start with a FTA between the two, with the external tariff in each set by optimal lobbying by firms in that country alone. The Appendix shows that a FTA in this context may be characterized by one of three Nash equilibria: two asymmetric outcomes in which one partner sets a zero tariff and free-rides on the other's lobbying and one mixed strategy equilibrium in which each industry sometimes lobbies and sometimes does not, attempting to free-ride.[13] In all cases, when an industry does lobby its optimal level is determined by (2) and (3).

Consider now the formation of a CU. While the level of protection depends on the resources devoted to lobbying by both countries, production still depends on resource allocation at the *national* level. In lobbying for protection in a CU the firm is faced with a larger anti-protection group, modeled here as the innate resistance to protection of a greater number of policy-makers representing a larger number of voters, than in the single-country case. On the other hand, there is also a greater number of firms lobbying for protection as the CU

[13]It is this mixed strategy equilibrium that complicates the analysis if lobbying were plagued by a free-rider problem at the *national* level. If firms' lobbying were not coordinated then any mixed- strategy behavior by n firms between, say, $l^s = 0$ and l^{s*} would yield a total lobbying (and so tariff) distribution with n+1 mass points ($L^S = 0, 1^{s*}, 2l^{s*}, \ldots, L^{S*}$). Equilibrium would require that each firms strategy be an individually optimal response to the others' given this profile in both the home here and partner countries. As this wrinkle seems to add nothing to the analysis, we have concentrated here on the simpler case of coordinated domestic lobby groups.

tariff affects firms in *both* countries. Were a CU to be formed, the tariff would be set according to $p[L^{SA} + L^{SB}, L^{A} + L^{B}]$ where L^{Sj} and L^{j}) denote the total amount of labor used in lobbying and the total size of the electorate respectively in country $j, j = A, B$. In this case, the industry in A, for example, faces problem (4), where tildes denote the CU regime:

$$\text{Max}\,\{L^{SA}, L^{XA}\}\widetilde{\prod} = p[L^{SB}+L^{SA}, 2L]F[L^{XA}, K]-w(L^{SA}+L^{XA}) \tag{4}$$

FOCs for an interior solution to this problem are given in (5) and (6) where tildes denote optimal levels of L^X and L^S in the CU. Each firm sets $\tilde{l}^{xi} = \tilde{L}^X/n$ and $\tilde{l}^{si} = \tilde{L}^S/n$.

$$P[L^{SB} + \tilde{L}^S, 2L]F_1[2\tilde{L}^X, 2K] - w = 0 \tag{5}$$

$$P_1[L^{SB} + \tilde{L}^S, 2L]F[2\tilde{L}^X, 2K] - 2w = 0 \tag{6}$$

In writing (5) and (6) we have used the fact that both A and B are identical and so have aggregated the FOCs over 2n firms. While total lobbying may rise from the FTA to the CU (as one industry does no lobbying at all in the pure strategy FTA equilibrium) *effective* lobbying — in the sense of determining the producer price — will fall in the CU. There will be free-riding between the two countries' industries and so a lower level of lobbying by an active firm and thus a lower level of protection than is jointly optimal for the industry, but the free-riding is of a different nature to, and is not as extreme as, that in the FTA case.

We now show that the price received by producers in the CU is less than that received in the FTA pure strategy equilibria.[14] In the latter, firms in both A and B receive a price $p[L^{S*}, L]$, regardless of which country is actively lobbying. This price will only emerge in the CU if both industries expend L^{S*} on lobbying. It is clear that (5) and (6) cannot be solved by $\tilde{L}^S$ equal to L^{S*} and $\tilde{L}^X$ equal to L^{X*}: if this were the case then $F_1[\tilde{L}^X, K]$ would equal

[14]I am grateful to an anonymous referee for suggesting the following approach instead of my earlier rather clumsy proof.

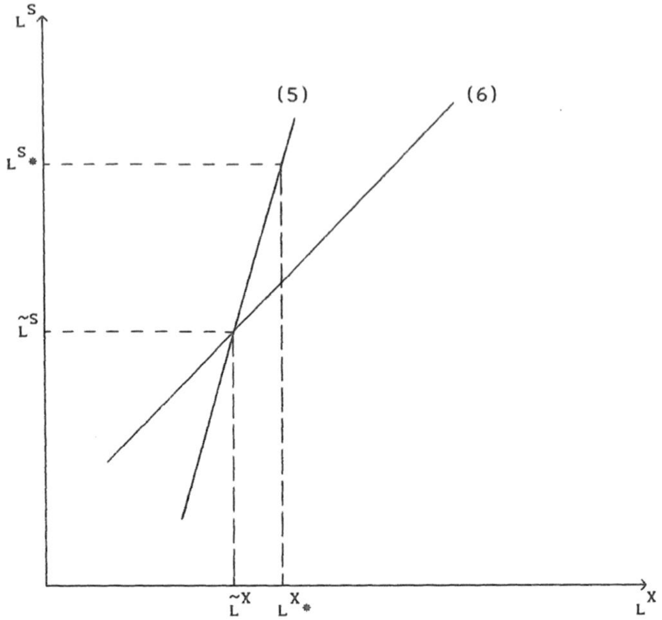

Fig. 1.

$F_1[\tilde{L}^{X*}, K]$ so that $p[L^{SB} + \tilde{L}^S, 2L]$ equals $p[L^{S*}, L]$ also, by (5). But then (6) and (3) would be inconsistent: $p_1[2\tilde{L}^S, 2L]F[\tilde{L}^X, K]$ equals $(1/2)p_1[L^{S*}, L]F[L^{X*}, K]$ by the homogeneity properties of p[.].

To see that L^S and L^X would both fall were a CU to be formed note that, for (5) to hold, L^S and L^X must both either rise or fall $((dL^S/dL^X)|_{(5)} = -(pF_{11}/p_1F_1)>0)$. This is shown as an upward-sloping locus (5) in L^S/L^X space in Figure 1. Equation (6) also defines a locus of L^S and L^X which is upward-sloping: $((dL^S/dL^X)|_{(6)} = -(p_1F_1/p_1F_1) > 0)$. By SOCs, (5) is steeper than (6). While (5) is satisfied at $L^S = L^{S*}$ and $L^X = L^{X*}$, the LHS of (6) is less than the RHS at this point. The value of the LHS of (6) is increasing in L^X, given L^S, thus the FTA point L^{S*}, L^{X*} must lie to the left of the locus satisfying (6), as drawn. So the values of L^S and L^X that jointly satisfy (5) and (6) must both be less than the FTA values.

Hence firms in the X industry would be less profitable under a CU than under the FTA. This is true for both the industry not lobbying in the FTA (as it now incurs lobbying expenditures *and* receives a lower price than in the FTA) and for that which is lobbying.[15] In the mixed strategy FTA equilibrium the results are similar: the Appendix shows that expected profits are equal to those of the industries when *both* lobby in an amount L^{S*}. Again, this exceeds the profit that would ensue in a CU.

In the model exposited here we have established that firms in the import-competing sector would prefer a FTA to a CU (in fact, in this model with no trade between partners, our model implies that firms prefer independent external tariff-setting in general to a CU). We have not specified either how the choice between a CU and FTA is actually made or, indeed, how a preferential trading agreement gets onto the political agenda at all. In a model of endogenous policy, however, these are important issues. As noted in the Introduction, I have argued elsewhere (Richardson (1993a)) that there are a number of reasons that a preferential trading arrangement may succeed where marginal tariff reductions will not in models of endogenous tariffs. As far as the *form* of that arrangement is concerned, however, just as firms lobby for tariff levels, presumably they also lobby for their preferred arrangement. Our results above suggest firms would have a preference for a FTA in which the equilibrium external tariff will be higher.

Beyond the case of identical countries, it is clear that the externality effect will be more of a disincentive to forming a CU for a small country than for a large one. This is particularly true if internal lobby groups are *not* cohesive: a large country will then have a lower tariff in a FTA than a small country, as the externality problem is more extreme. Upon formation of a CU, the common external tariff will then be lower for *both* countries, thus the smaller partner will favor a FTA over a CU even more than the larger partner.

2.3. *Some modifications*

Our results have been framed in a model with two prominent features. First, we assumed that lobbying firms were cohesive within a country

[15]The fall in profitability for the industry that lobbies follows from the fact that lobbying was optimal in the FTA equilibrium, from the industry point of view.

but not within a CU and it might seem that the results follow from the presence of free-riding at the international level but not intranationally. Second, we have cast our analysis in a model in which producer prices are always equated within a FTA. While we argue that this is the correct context for analysis of a FTA, it might also seem that our results are a consequence of this framework in that, for example, only one industry lobbies in the pure strategy FTA equilibrium. This Section demonstrates that our conclusions are robust to both of these features of the model. Briefly, the presence of internal free-riding does not change the qualitative results as the free-riding problem is still exacerbated by the formation of a CU (with 2n firms lobbying as opposed to n.) Nor is the equality of producer prices in a FTA qualitatively significant here: in the standard approach we have *both* industries lobbying in the amount L^{S*} in the FTA as opposed to just one in the pure strategy equilibrium above.

In this set-up, each of n firms lobbies independently, taking the efforts of the others as given, and the producer price in the FTA is simply the outcome of domestic lobbying, regardless of the partner country's efforts. Typical firm i chooses l^{si} and l^{xi} to maximize $\pi^i = p[L^{S,-i} + l^{si}, L]f[l^{xi}, k] - w(l^{xi} + l^{si})$. FOCs are (7) and (8):

$$p_1[.]f[.] - w = 0 \tag{7}$$

$$p[.]f_1[.] - w = 0 \tag{8}$$

As f[.] is hom(1) (and so $f_1[.]$ is hom(0)) so adding (7) and (8) up over n symmetric firms gives (9) and (10), where double asterisks denote FTA equilibrium values[16]:

$$p_1[.]f[nl^{xi}, nk] - nw = 0 \quad \text{or} \quad p_1[L^{S**}, L]F[L^{X**}, K] = nw \tag{9}$$

$$p[.]f_1[nl^{xi}, nk] - w = 0 \quad \text{or} \quad p[L^{S**}, L]F_1[L^{X**}, K] = w \tag{10}$$

[16]Comparing (7) and (8) with (2) and (3), the latter two in the case where $p^{max} = p[L^{S*}, L]$, one can see the added free-rider effect here: the value of the marginal product of labor devoted to lobbying is equated to nw in the present case but w in our former specification. Clearly, per-firm lobbying is lower here.

For a CU, L is doubled and each of the 2n firms lobbies the same tariff-setting agent. Deriving FOCs as before, using carets to denote optimal aggregate levels in one country, aggregating over 2n firms and invoking symmetry, we get (11) and (12):

$$p_1[2\hat{L}^S, 2L]F[2\hat{L}^X, 2K] = 2nw \tag{11}$$

$$p[2\hat{L}^S, 2L]F_1[2\hat{L}^X, 2K] = w \tag{12}$$

If the CU were to leave optimal labor employment in each use unchanged, so that $\hat{L}^S = L^{S**}$ and, $\hat{L}^S = L^{S**}$, then (12) would hold as both p [.] and F_1[.] are hom(0) in their arguments. However, while the RHS of (11) is twice that of (9), the LHS is the same, from the homogeneity properties of F[.] and p1[.]. Inspection of (11) and (12), as earlier, demonstrates that both L^S and L^X must fall when the CU is formed.[17] Further, it is clear that firms' profits must fall when the CU is formed-the internal free-riding which leads to lobbying and output both being too low already in the FTA is worsened by international free-riding in the CU which leads output and lobbying to fall even further. To see this formally, note first that per-firm profits are simply $\pi^i = \prod/n$ so if $\prod$ falls so too does π^i. Then,

$$\begin{aligned} d\prod &= (p_1[.]F[.] - w)dL^S + (p[.]F_1[.] - w)dL^X \\ &= (n-1)wdL^S > 0 \end{aligned}$$

when evaluated at the FTA outcome L^{x**}, L^{S**}: (9) implies that $P_1[L^{S**}, L]F[L^{x**}, K]$ equals nw and (10) that $p[L^{S**}, L]F_1[L^{X**}, K] - w$ equals 0. That is, aggregate profits would rise if L^S were increased (and L^X too: as we go from a FTA to a CU, L^X continues to be chosen optimally, for each L^S, so (10) gives L^X as an implicit function of L^S and implies that $dL^X/dL^S = -(p_1[.]F_1[.])/(p[.]F_{11}[.]) > 0$.) Thus the *decrease* in L^S and L^X that the CU induces only serves to lower profits further.

[17]In the manner of Section 2.2, (11) and (12) define upward-sloping locii of L^S and L^X and, by SOCs, (12) is steeper than (11). While (12) is satisfied at $L^S = L^{S**}$ and $L^X = L^{X**}$, the LHS of (11) is less than the RHS at this point. The value of the LHS of (11) is increasing in L^X, given L^S, thus the FTA point L^{S**}, L^{X**} must lie to the left of the locus satisfying (11): the values of L^S and L^X that jointly satisfy (11) and (12) must both be less than the FTA values.

2.4. *Welfare*

We turn now to analysis of the welfare consequences of changes in the external tariff. As these are small countries it is clear that consumers must lose from any tariff. However, tariff reductions yield additional gains here in that they occur as a consequence of decreased lobbying, an activity that uses real resources. As Rodrik (1986) notes, it is not clear exactly what interpretation can be placed upon the standard welfare calculus in this sort of model as policy-makers are automata who do not attempt to maximize any particular measure of social welfare. Furthermore, policy-makers may themselves derive some welfare from lobbying activities and this is not considered in the following analysis. Nevertheless, it is instructive to examine the effects on the representative consumer of any change in lobbying here, using the model of Section 2.3 above.[18]

Intuitively, the ideal is to have free trade and waste no resources in lobbying. With a positive tariff too much of the importable is produced from the point of view of an efficient allocation of resources *and* there is wasteful lobbying. The CU, in reducing the level of lobbying, improves welfare on both these fronts.

Letting u denote the utility level of the aggregate consumer we can describe consumers' behavior by an aggregate expenditure function E[l,p,u] which has all of the usual properties (see Dixit and Norman (1980)). National income in this economy is the sum of the values of output of X and Y plus any tariff revenue earned on imports of X. Thus the economy's budget constraint is given by:

$$E[l, p, u] = p[L^S, L]F[L^X, K] + w(L - L^S - L^X) + (p - p^*)m^X \quad (13)$$

[18]Welfare analysis is rather more complex in the model of Section 2.1 for the following reasons. Consider the FTA equilibrium in which country A does no lobbying at all but country B does so A sells all its domestic production in B at a price $1 + t^B$. National income in A thus includes tariff revenue on total *consumption.* Formation of a CU now is definitely welfare-improving in the traditional manner in B: not only does the tariff fall but lobbying resources are saved *and* tariff revenue is earned on imports now sourced from outside the union rather than tariff-free from A. In country A, however, things are not so rosy. The consumer price will rise (in the FTA there is no tariff, recall) and lobbying expenses increase.

where m^X denotes imports of X. We use the following tacts to totally differentiate (13) and rearrange to get (14) which measures welfare effects of any small changes in L^S or L^X. First, the partial derivative of E [.] with respect to p, E_p, gives the compensated demand for X. Second, imports are consumption minus production, so $m^X = E_p[.] - F[.]$. Third, $t = p - p^*, dp^* = 0$ (small country) and $dp = p_1 dL^S$.

$$(E_u - tE_{pu})du = (tE_{pp}p_1 - w)dL^S - tF_1 dL^X \quad (14)$$

We make the usual stability assumption that the Hatta term, $(E_u - tE_{pu})$, is positive. Expression (14) identifies three channels through which an increase in L^S or L^X will affect welfare. The coefficient on dL^S on the right hand side is comprised of two effects. As E_{pp} is negative (E[.] is concave in prices) so the term $tE_{pp}p_1 dL^S$ represents lost tariff revenue on decreased imports of X resulting from a higher consumer price as increased lobbying raises the tariff. An extra unit of labor devoted to lobbying decreases Y production by w, hence the second term — wdL^S is a welfare loss due to this lost output and represents the real resource cost of lobbying. The final term in (14) captures the loss of tariff revenues from increased output of the importable at home if more labor is devoted to its production.

We demonstrated in 2.3 above that $dL^S < 0$ and $dL^X < 0$ as we go from a FTA to a CU. From (14), therefore, these changes are unambiguously welfare-improving.[19]

[19] In considering the transition from a FTA to a CU we wish to deal with large, discrete changes in L^S and L^X. Furthermore, as a CU is formed so the number of representatives to be lobbied increases; that is, the second argument of p[.] also rises. Nevertheless, the expression above can be used directly in the case of two identical countries forming a CU. The reason we can ignore the increase in L is that in the symmetric equilibrium the effect of doubling the number of voters is exactly offset by the effect of doubling the number of firms, insofar as per-firm lobbying is unchanged, due to the homogeneity of p [.]. So the only net effect on the tariff is from changes in L^S and even though the magnitude of the tariff response for some dL^S is lessened in the CU, as $p_{12} < 0$, the qualitative effect is unchanged. The discrete changes in L^S and L^X leave the welfare conclusions unaltered because utility is monotonic in L^S and L^X where changes in L^s and L^X are related by FOCs (2) and (3).

3. Summary and conclusion

In this paper we have argued that, when policy is set for reasons other than traditional welfare considerations — specifically, when it is the outcome of a particular endogenous political process — there may be reasons a FTA is preferred to a CU. In particular, in our model of lobbying, a CU entails a lobbying externality and leads to lower tariffs and decreased profitability of firms. We have shown that this conclusion holds whether or not producer prices are equated in a FTA and whether or not lobbying is plagued by free-riding at the national level.

One final comment on the model used here is in order. We have taken a very simple two-good framework in which to exposit our main result. As noted, a more satisfactory treatment of preferential trading arrangements requires at least three goods in order to motivate the formation of a FTA with internal trade whilst also featuring goods traded by both partners with the non-partner. Adding another good, however, greatly complicates the analysis of the political market — another fixed factor, for example, would also indulge in lobbying against the tariff on X and results on the desirability of a CU would hinge critically upon which industry is more plagued by the free-riding externality. Nevertheless, the basic results of this paper should carry over to more sophisticated models with appropriate modifications.

References

Dixit, A. and V. Norman (1980). *Theory of International Trade.* Cambridge, UK: Cambridge University Press.

Hillman, A. (1982). Declining industries and political-support protectionist motives. *American Economic Review*, 72(5), 1180–1187.

Lloyd, P. J. (1982). 3 × 3 theory of customs unions. *Journal of International Economics*, 12, 41–64.

Richardson, M. (1992). Some implications of internal trade in a free-trade area. *Working paper* No. 92–01, Department of Economics, Georgetown University.

Richardson, M. (1993a). Endogenous protection and trade diversion. *Journal of International Economics*, 34, 309–324.

Richardson, M. (1993b). *Tariff Revenue Competition in a Free Trade Area.* Mimeo: Department of Economics, Georgetown University.

Rodrik, D. (1986). Tariffs, subsidies and welfare with endogenous policy. *Journal of International Economics*, 21, 285–299.
Wonnacott, P. and R. Wonnacott (1981). Is unilateral tariff reduction preferable to a customs union? The curious case of the missing foreign tariffs. *American Economic Review*, 71, 704–714.
Woodland, A.D. (1982). *International Trade and Resource Allocation.* Amsterdam: North Holland.

Appendix

This Appendix works through the analysis of Section 2.1 when producer prices are equated within a FTA even if external tariffs differ. We confine our attention to the case wherein total demand for X in A and B exceeds total intra-FTA supply at all relevant prices; thus the free-riding effect has no impact on consumer prices.

As a FTA cannot restrict the location of sales of firms from either member country, so producers in both countries face the same price as each other even if external tariffs (and thus consumers' prices) differ. Accordingly, given a world price 1, if consumer prices in country $i = A, B$ are denoted $p^i = 1 + t^i$ then producers in i face a price $p^i_p = p^m \equiv \max\{p^A, p^B\}$. Let the tariff that results from the solution to the industry's problem in Section 2 of the paper be denoted t^*. That is, t^* is the tariff that results when each industry lobbies for its own protection — this is not only the FTA equilibrium in the analysis of Section 2.3 (and the pure strategy equilibrium level of FTA tariff in the country that lobbies in the model of 2.1) but, in this model of identical countries, is also the tariff that would result if A and B were to have no FTA but were to set tariffs unilaterally instead. As a last piece of notation, let $\prod^i[t^A, t^B]$ now denote the derived profit function of the industry in country i = A, B in a FTA, written as a function of external tariffs. Profits depend directly on the choice of L^S and L^X but the former maps monotonically into a tariff rate. Let $L^{Xi}[L^{Si}]$ denote the solution to the following partial maximization problem, *given* L^{Si}:

$$\underset{|L^{Xi}|}{\mathrm{Max}}\, p[L^{Si}, L^i]F[L^{Xi}, K] - w(L^{Si} + L^{Xi})$$

Then, where $t^i[L^{Si}]$ is the tariff that results from lobbying of L^{Si}, we define:

$$\prod^A[t^A, t^B] \equiv \prod^A[t^A[L^{SA}], t^B[L^{SB}]]$$
$$= p^{max}F[L^{XA}[L^{SA}], K] - w(L^{SA} + L^{XA}[L^{SA}])$$

where $p^{max} = 1 + \max\{t^A[L^{SA}], t^B[L^{SB}]\}$. The industry's problem is then to choose L^{SA} to maximize $\prod^A$ but, as $p_1 < 0$ and L^i is fixed, each level of L^{Si} is associated with a unique t^i; thus we can write profits in terms of tariffs rather than the more fundamental lobbying levels.

A useful way to view this problem is to consider $\prod^A$ as a composite function[20]:

$$\prod^A[t^A, t^B] = \max\left\{\prod^{A1}[t^A], \prod^{A2}[t^B]\right\}$$

$$\text{where}\begin{cases}\prod^{A1} = (1 + t^A[L^{SA}])F[.] - (wL^{SA} + L^{XA}[L^{SA}])\\ \prod^{A2} = (1 + t^B)F[L^{XA}, K] - wL^{XA}\end{cases}$$

This is generically illustrated in Figure 2 for some $t^B = t''$ where profits from doing no lobbying and free-riding on B's tariff are shown as $\prod^{A2}[t'']$, profits from lobbying for one's own tariff are shown as $\prod^{A1}[t^A]$ and the composite upper envelope of the two is shown as the heavy continuous line $\prod^A[t^A, t'']$. L^{XA} is chosen optimally in all cases. Note that (i) when $t^A = t''$ it is more profitable to free-ride ($\prod^{A2}[t''] > \prod^{A1}[t^A]$) as lobbying expenses of $wL^{S''}$ are saved (where $L^{S''}$ is the amount of lobbying needed to generate $t^A = t''$), and (ii) $\prod^A[t^A, t'']$ itself is continuous in t^A.

Returning to our earlier notation, we also note for later use that:

$$\prod^A[0, t^*] > \prod^A[t^*, t^*] = \prod^A[t^*, 0] > \prod^A[0, 0].$$

[20] I am grateful to a referee for suggesting this approach.

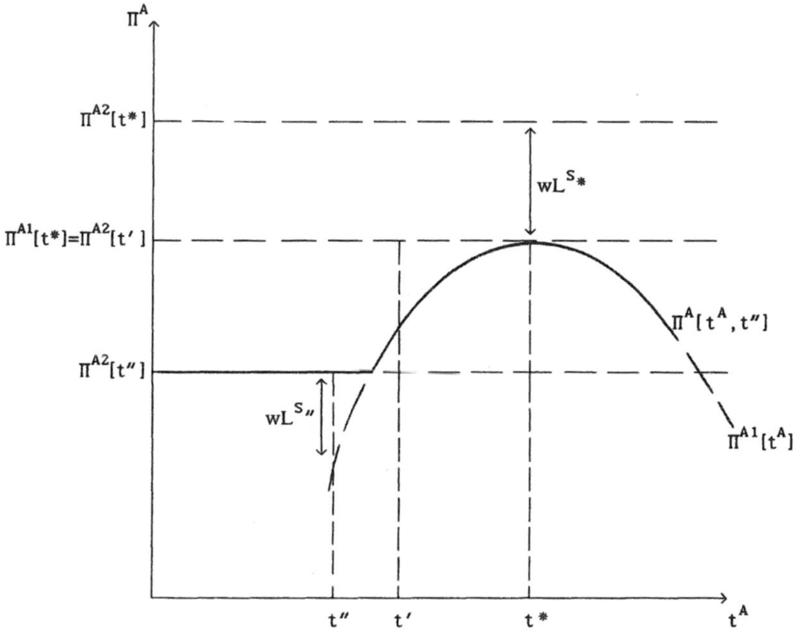

Fig. 2.

The first inequality follows from the fact that, while the price faced by A's producers is the same in each case, in the first case it does no lobbying and, by revealed preference arguments, must be better off. The equality stems from our assumption regarding the relative magnitudes of demand and supplies — if B's producers free-ride on A's tariff it has no effect on A's producers. The second inequality follows from the optimality of t^* in a unilateral tariff setting context.

We consider the problem facing the industry in country A (by symmetry, that facing the industry in country B is identical.) We wish to construct a reaction function describing A's optimal tariff in response to each t^B, taking the latter as given. Note that the industry's direct choice is of lobbying efforts but this maps directly into the tariff that we are considering. Bearing in mind that if producers in B sell in country A this has no effect on A's producers, for very "low" levels of t^B (described more precisely below) the problem facing the industry in A is just that described in program (1) of Section 2 of the paper, leading to $t^A = t^*$.

However, as t^B increases, the prospect of doing no lobbying and free-riding on B becomes more attractive. Certainly if $t^B \geq t^*$ the industry in A will do no lobbying. However, there is also a range of tariff levels less than t^* for which this strategy is more profitable for the industry in A than is lobbying for its own tariff. The reason is simply that it saves on lobbying expenses. By continuity of the industry profit function in (1), even though it is less profitable to sell at a price below $1 + t^*$, the loss in profits when t^B is only slightly less than t^* is more than offset by the discrete gain in saved lobbying resources. This will be true for all levels of the tariff in the partner above some critical minimum t' where $t' < t^*$. Formally, t' is defined by the following equality: $\prod^A[0, t'] = \prod^A[t^*, t']$ where the latter also equals $\prod^A[t^*, 0]$. We can illustrate this critical point in Figure 2. If $t^B = t^*$ then $\prod^{A2}[t^*] = \prod^{A1}[t^*] + wL^{S*}$ (that is, free-riding is more profitable than lobbying to the extent that lobbying expenditures are saved.) The critical $t^B = t'$ occurs where the saved expenditures are exactly offset by foregone profits from a lower price.

Thus Figure 3 illustrates the discontinuous reaction function for country A as the two horizontal double lines labeled R^A and the symmetric function for B as the heavy vertical lines labeled R^B. Accordingly, there are two pure strategy equilibria to this game at points E and E′ in the Figure corresponding to $\{t^A, t^B\} = \{t^*, 0\}$ and $\{0, t^*\}$ respectively. In the former, country B is a free-rider, $\prod^A = \prod^A[t^*, 0] = \prod^A[t^*, t^*]$ and $\prod^B = \prod^B[t^*, 0] > \prod^B[t^*, t^*]$; in the latter the roles are reversed, country A free-rides, $\prod^A = \prod^A[0, t^*] > \prod^A[t^*, t^*]$ and $\prod^B = \prod^B[0, t^*] = \prod^B[t^*, t^*]$. These contrast to the unilateral tariff setting equilibrium (and FTA equilibrium of the analysis of section 2.3) at E^*.

However, there is also an equilibrium in mixed strategies in which each industry lobbies for a tariff of t^* with probability and does no lobbying with probability $(1 - \alpha)$. In this equilibrium, expected profit to each industry is $\prod^i[t^*, t^*], i = A, B$. To establish this as an equilibrium we need to show both that the profitability of each element of the strategy is the same in response to the strategy of the

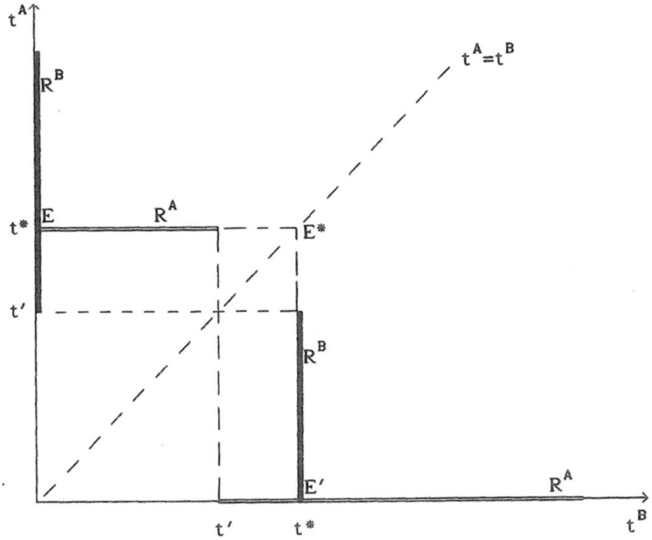

Fig. 3.

rival and that the industry can do no better in response to the rival's strategy. Suppose $t^A = 0$. Then, as B mixes over 0 and t^*, expected profits in A are $E\prod^A = \alpha\prod^A[0, t^*] + (1-\alpha)\prod^A[0,0] \equiv \overline{\prod}^A$. But if $t^A = t^*$ then $E\prod^A = \alpha\prod^A[t^*, t^*] + (1-\alpha)\prod^A[t^*, 0] = \prod^A[t^*, t^*]$ by the equivalences listed earlier. But $\prod^A[0, t^*] > \prod^A[t^*, t^*] > \prod^A[0, 0]$ so there exists some $\alpha \in (0,1)$ such that $\overline{\prod}^A = \prod^A[t^*, t^*]$.[21] Overall expected profit from this strategy is $\prod^A[t^*, t^*]$, as claimed. To see that the industry can do no better than this strategy, in response to the same strategy of the rival, note that L^{S*}, the optimal level of lobbying in the pure strategy equilibrium in which the industry in A lobbies, solves:

$$\frac{\partial E(\prod^A[L^{SA}])}{\partial L^{SA}} = \prod_1^A [t^A, 0]\frac{dt^A}{dL^{SA}} - w = 0$$

[21]With risk-neutral firms this is all we need. With risk-aversion the equilibrium survives with the mixing proportions on the two elements of the strategy altered such that the certainty equivalent of profits when setting $t^A = 0$ equals $\prod^A(t^*, t^*)$.

In the mixed strategy equilibrium, the industry lobbies with only probability α. In these instances, the optimal level of lobbying solves:

$$\frac{\partial \mathrm{E}(\prod^{\mathrm{A}}[\mathrm{L}^{\mathrm{SA}}])}{\partial \mathrm{L}^{\mathrm{SA}}} = \alpha\left\{\frac{\mathrm{dt}^{\mathrm{A}}}{\mathrm{dL}^{\mathrm{SA}}}\left[\alpha\prod_{1}^{\mathrm{A}}[\mathrm{t}^{\mathrm{A}},\mathrm{t}^{\mathrm{B}}] + (1-\alpha)\prod_{1}^{\mathrm{A}}[\mathrm{t}^{\mathrm{A}},0]\right] - \mathrm{w}\right\}$$
$$= \alpha\left\{\frac{\mathrm{dt}^{\mathrm{A}}}{\mathrm{dL}^{\mathrm{SA}}}\prod_{1}^{\mathrm{A}}[\mathrm{t}^{\mathrm{A}},0] - \mathrm{w}\right\} = 0$$

where the equality follows from the equivalence of $\prod^{\mathrm{A}}[\mathrm{t}^{\mathrm{A}},0]$ and $\prod^{\mathrm{A}}[\mathrm{t}^{\mathrm{A}},\mathrm{t}^{\mathrm{B}}]$ for $\mathrm{t}^{\mathrm{A}} \geq \mathrm{t}^{\mathrm{B}}$. Thus the optimal degree of lobbying is $\mathrm{L}^{\mathrm{S}*}$, as claimed.

Chapter 7

Customs Unions and Domestic Taxes

Martin Richardson

Abstract: It is well known that non-discriminatory domestic taxes and subsidies are perfect substitutes for non-discriminatory trade policies and would render useless international agreements restricting trade policy alone. We show that these instruments generally are imperfect substitutes for trade policy in a customs union. However, in one popular specification of trading patterns, access to such tax powers nevertheless renders a customs union useless. Furthermore, numerical simulations demonstrate that a union may be ineffective in many other cases, severely curtailing the potential unions that are attractive to both members. We illustrate the restrictive conditions under which a union will then form.

1. Introduction

Perhaps the most significant example of a customs union in practice — and certainly the example most often cited by economists — is that of the European Community (EC).[1] The EC, however, has gone well beyond the degree of cooperation that makes a group of

Originally published in *The Canadian Journal of Economics*, 27(3), 537–550.

[1] The other major historical example of a customs union is the *Zollverein* of 1834 to 1870 among German states. It is difficult to assess this union's effects on its members, however, since it coincided with the rapid expansion of German railways, which stimulated internal demand and unified many markets. Furthermore, it appears that the external tariff of the *Zollverein* was perhaps more a political instrument than a purely economic one; see Mathias and Pollard (1989, pp. 762–769).

countries a customs union. While there are many obvious reasons for this fact, both economic and political, the present paper suggests that a union that coordinates tariffs alone may not be a particularly tenable organization.

The "pure" customs union (CU) of economics textbooks entails full free trade among member countries and the joint choice of a common external tariff (CET). Thus, while a member's direct *trade* policies are controlled, a CU does not inherently involve restrictions on non-discriminatory domestic taxes or subsidies. Accordingly, a country can, at least in part, "undo" a binding restriction on explicit trade taxes (a CU) by use of domestic taxes: it is well known that in a competitive environment a consumption tax and a production subsidy at equal rates are perfectly equivalent to an import tax at that same rate. This paper examines the consequences for CU formation of permitting such domestic tax powers in a simple but popular model and in a number of simulations. We demonstrate that such powers may render a CU empty in the sense that nothing is to be gained from joining it; we argue that greater cooperation, then, may be a means of ensuring that the CU's potential gains from tariff harmonization are realized.

That consequences for CU formation might be important is clear from the general equivalence of these policies with trade policies. The degree to which domestic policies can undermine the CU trade agreement, however, is curtailed by the CET's discriminatory nature. A CU enables a member country to generate two tariffs: the CET against outsiders alone and a domestically constructed tariff that applies to partners and outsiders alike. Thus the extent to which domestic policy can fully undo preferential trade liberalization, which we investigate in this paper, is rather more complicated than it might at first seem.

In related work, Copeland (1990) has analysed the general case of bilateral negotiations over trade policy when there exist non-negotiable domestic policy instruments. He demonstrates, among other things, that the existence of domestic policies that are perfect substitutes for the negotiated trade policies renders tariff reduction meaningless — in the two-country world that he considers this includes the tax/subsidy package discussed above. In our case, however, we are considering bilateral negotiations in a three-country world, and the tariff policy is inherently discriminatory while the domestic policy "equivalent" is not. That is, a policy that is a perfect substitute for trade policy in a two-country world may be only an imperfect substitute for trade policy in a three-country world.[2] We show that in one simple but popular model the CU is completely ineffective precisely because domestic and trade policies are perfect substitutes. We show via numerical simulations, however, that this strong result also holds in a model in which a country's imports of a good come from both within and outside of the CU and domestic and trade policies are *not* perfect substitutes.

One light in which to consider the approach of this paper stems from a result (due to Dixit and Norman, 1980 building on Kemp and Wan, 1976) that any two tariff-ridden countries can form a CU, set a CET, and *coordinate* domestic tax policies, with no lump-sum transfers, in such a way that no individual is worse off and, in general, some can be made better off.[3] We examine the following, perhaps more realistic, scenario: two countries form a CU, cooperatively choose a CET, and then set their domestic tax policies independently. In this context we seek an equilibrium in which the setting of the CET accounts for the subsequent effects on each country's tax policies, in order to ask under what circumstances a mutually beneficial CU can arise and whether they are more or less restrictive than in the absence of such policies.

The rest of the chapter is organized as follows. In the next section, we consider a popular specification of trading arrangements and show that allowing independent tax setting subsequent to agreement on a CET destroys the dominance of a CU over unilateral tariff setting. Section 3 then discusses a more general setting, noting the various trade-offs involved. A final section summarizes and concludes.

---

[2] I am a grateful to an anonymous referee for suggesting this wording.

[3] This argument is articulated fully in Appendix A of Richardson (1992).

2. Independent tax setting

2.1. *The general framework*

The formal structure of the problem we wish to address is as follows. We consider two countries both of which are large, in the sense of being able to affect their terms of trade. Initially each sets its own external tariff — the unilateral tariff-setting case, or UTS — which is non-discriminatory: it applies whether the source of imports is the partner country or the rest of the world. This tariff yields a Nash equilibrium that we assume is stable and unique.[4] We then consider the consequences of forming a CU with a jointly agreed CET but independent domestic tax policies, the latter also being determined as a Nash equilibrium, unique for each CET. As the setting of the CET is assumed to precede that of domestic tax policies, we seek a subgame perfect equilibrium wherein the CET is set, knowing its consequences for the pursuant domestic policy subgame. Throughout the analysis, the behaviour of non-members is optimal. For a precise analysis of equilibrium, the bargaining procedure by which the CET is determined must be specified.[5] Our main interest, however, is in the *existence* of mutually welfare-improving CUs (compared with the UTS case), so we do not model the bargaining explicitly but consider rather the extreme cases in which one or other of the member countries chooses the CET to maximize its own welfare subject to the partner's doing as least as well as it would in the UTS case. We compare these outcomes with those occurring when the final stage of tax setting is absent, this being the only scenario considered in the literature to the best of our knowledge.

This general structure is similar in flavour to the model of Copeland (1990), which considers restrictions on negotiable instruments and the consequent subgame perfect Nash equilibrium in non-negotiable instruments. But, while the intuition he develops provides

[4]The uniqueness assumption is made to demonstrate the neutrality of the CU below. If it is relaxed, then obviously neutrality is a possibility only.

[5]There is a growing literature that addresses this important issue. See Gatsios and Karp (1991) for a particularly interesting discussion of one aspect.

insights into our case, his formal analysis of two countries and two goods does not generalize easily to encompass the issues we seek to address. Any search for very general results in this setting is doomed by two unavoidable features. First, the analytical determination of optimal tariffs in a world of more than two goods is notoriously difficult in any but the simplest models, even given a pattern of trade. Second, as CUs involve discrete changes in tariff rates, a fully general equilibrium treatment of CU formation should allow for changes in trade patterns as a consequence of a CU. Hence the determination of optimal tariffs in a CU context is even more difficult in any moderately sophisticated model.

Clear results *are* available in a model that has been extensively used in the literature on CU formation, however, which illustrates the possibility of quite dramatic consequences for CUs of independent tax setting.[6]

2.2. *A three-good example*

A recent paper by Kennan and Riezman (1990) (**KR** henceforth) describes the formation of CUs and free trade areas by way of simulations of a tractable endowment model. This model enables the calculation of expressions defining optimal tariffs (and all other variables of interest) in terms of endowments and preference parameters alone. **KR** then generate a number of 3×3 examples which they simulate for explicit welfare solutions. In these examples the pattern of trade involves each country's exporting one good and importing two. Letting the potential CU partner countries be A and B and the rest of the world C, this trade pattern is represented in Fig. 1.[7]

[6]The results in the following example may be formalized along the lines of Copeland (1990); the procedure is set out in a technical appendix available from the author on request.

[7]This pattern has been very popular in the literature for the analysis of CUS. Corden (1984) calls it the Meade Model after its use in Meade's (1955) pioneering work. The popularity of this trading pattern stems from its symmetry and the fact that all countries trade with each other — both features cannot hold in two-good models. The model exposited here differs from Meade's formulation in permitting production of all three goods in each country and in giving A and B market power against C.

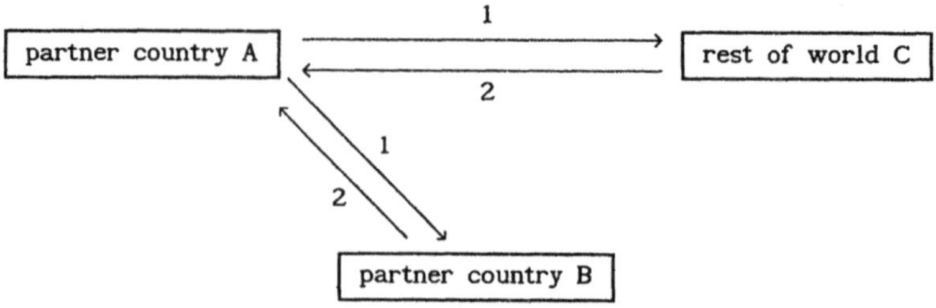

Country A exports good 1, imports 2
Country B exports good 2, imports 1
Country C exports good 2, imports 1

Fig. 1. The Meade (1955) trade pattern

KR consider a variety of scenarios in which countries' endowments differ, and they illustrate that, in every case, the welfare of CU members is increased over its UTS level.[8] In this trade pattern each country imports a different good from each of its partners. Thus a tariff levied by country A on imports of good 2, for example, affects only country B. If it is reduced to zero by the CU agreement but A then institutes an equivalent domestic subsidy/tax package, then the net effect is identical. Thus the CET is non-discriminatory here and the analysis of Copeland (1990) holds exactly: tariffs and domestic policies *are* perfect substitutes, so restrictions imposed on only one set of instruments have no equilibrium consequences.

This equivalence of the CU equilibrium and the UTS equilibrium applies in any model in which each good is exported by only one country, regardless of preferences, number of goods, or whether or not there is production; the critical element is that countries can exactly replicate tariffs through domestic instruments. Given the

[8]**KR** note that CU formation should properly be modelled as a two-stage game where the first stage involves the choice of partners; their model focuses on the second stage of choice of tariffs. That welfare rises in the CU versus UTS might seem a minimum requirement for countries voluntarily to join a CU, but in a complete model of partner choice a country might join a CU even if welfare falls relative to global UTS, if the alternative is not UTS but rather formation of a CU by the other two countries. The **KR** result, then, is not trivial in this setting.

popularity of this model in the literature, the result seems significant. It also has the broader implication that, aside from any issues of CU formation, negotiated tariff reductions in such a world are meaningless.[9]

3. The general case

3.1. *A two-good model*

While the example of the previous section is of some interest, since it is a commonly used specification of trading patterns in the analysis of preferential trading arrangements, it would be useful to have some sense of the impact of such policies in a more general setting. As suggested earlier, an analytical description of such effects is not possible in a many-good, many-country world in which there is more than one source of imports for any particular good; in this subsection, however, we consider such a model in which explicit solutions can be obtained for optimal tariffs and subsidies, and in the next we report results from numerical simulations.

To illustrate the significance of discriminatory tariffs and the extent to which they constrain subsequent domestic policies, it is clear that we need a model in which a country's imports derive from more than one source. The simplest possible scenario is the two-good case illustrated in Fig. 2, where one member country (B) has no trade with the rest of the world (C).

We commence with a UTS equilibrium in which countries A, B, and C levy Nash equilibrium tariffs. Note that there is no incentive to employ domestic instruments when tariffs are available — the only source of gain from policy here is from the terms-of-trade effect of trade restrictions, all of which is captured by the tariff. If A and B now form a CU, they levy a common tariff on imports of good 2, but each can then institute domestic policies as it wishes. In this case, the reasoning of the previous section no longer applies

[9] Almost trivially, this result applies in any two-country model, regardless of the number of goods. In particular, were domestic policies such as those we consider permitted in Copeland's (1990) model, all tariff negotiations would be meaningless.

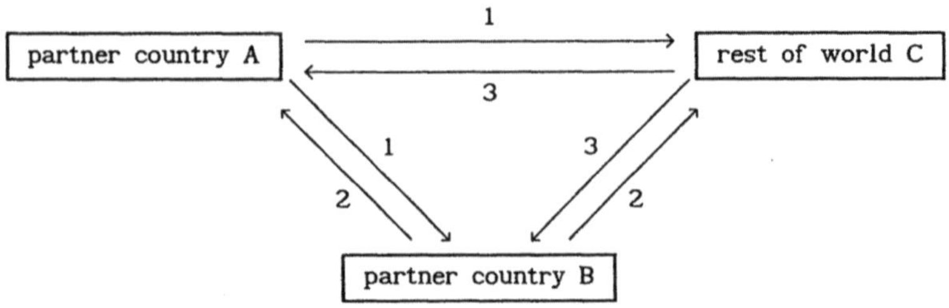

Country A exports good 1, imports 2 and 3
Country B exports good 2, imports 1 and 3
Country C exports good 3, imports 1 and 2

Fig. 2. An asymmetric two-good trade pattern

directly — A cannot exactly replicate its UTS tariff through domestic policies, for any given level of the external tariff, since they apply to imports from both sources but the tariff applies only to imports from C.

Nor will the UTS outcome generally be the best that A can achieve, even allowing for B's domestic policy powers. In fact, the CU *with* domestic policies may enable A to discriminate more effectively between its suppliers. This is not possible at all in the UTS case nor is effective discrimination possible in a traditional CU analysis, since in both of these cases the internal price of the import in A must be the same, whether it is sourced from C or B, by virtue of simple consumer arbitrage. Thus, in the UTS context, A cannot levy discriminatory tariffs, because potential arbitrage between B and C prevents them from facing different prices from A. Similarly, in a CU without domestic policies, country B always receives A's internal price for the import.[10] But in the CU under consideration A can construct an *implicit* tariff against B through domestic tax/subsidy policy, but this stricture applies *as well as* the explicit tariff to C, so effectively A can levy a different tariff against B and C.

[10]Discrimination is possible in the sense of levying the CET against C and a zero tariff against B. Indeed, in the simulations in table 2b this situation occurs — A wishes to favour C and, when choosing a CET in a traditional CU, does so with a *negative* CET.

In the simulations that follow, we adopt a two-good version of the general equilibrium model exposited by **KR,** and the reader is referred to that paper for a full and clear exposition of the approach.[11] Each country is endowed with each good and seeks to maximize a utility function that generates a linear expenditure system.

3.2. *Simulation results*

We consider three arrays of endowments, one in which countries B and C are identical (the symmetric case) and two others in which either B or C has a greater endowment of their export good, good 2. In each case, the UTS equilibrium is calculated and four CU cases are presented — the outcomes when domestic policies are not considered (the standard case) and those where they are permitted and, in each alternative, the outcomes in which either A or B chooses the CET. In each case we find the CET that maximizes the chooser's welfare subject to the other partner's obtaining a welfare level no less than in the UTS case. We also calculate and report welfare levels for global free trade, by way of a benchmark. All policies are set optimally, in the Nash sense. Results are shown in Tables 1 and 2.

In the symmetric case of Table 1 note that the CU is attractive to both members in the absence of domestic policies, for the usual reasons. However, the strong results of the previous section carry over when domestic policies are considered: the CU can do no better than UTS (at least for A; therefore no non-trivial CU can form, since A would join no CU with a non-zero CET.) The intuition for this result is most easily seen by noting that there are two features of a CU that make it potentially of interest to A.[12] First, the CU allows discriminatory treatment of imports in A — a situation not possible in UTS. Such discriminatory treatment may be desirable if B and C present different export supply curves to A. But the symmetry here between B and C means A's optimal tariff is non-discriminatory, so

[11]A formal description of this model is available from the author on request.

[12]There is no gain from internalizing a tariff externality with this trade pattern.

Table 1. Symmetric case with B and C identical

$U = \frac{\ln(C_1)+\ln(C_2)+20}{2}$		Country A (tariffs and taxes on good 2)	Country B (taxes and UTS on good 1, CU tariffs on good 2)	Country C (tariffs on good 1)
Endowments	1	0.8	0.1	0.1
of good	2	0.0	0.5	0.5
Global free trade	Welfare	9.0837	8.7960	8.7960
UTS	Tariff	1.7290	0.6335	0.6335
	Welfare	9.0200	8.7289	8.7289
CU, no taxes	Tariff	0.8380	0.8380	0.3905
A chooses CET	Welfare	9.0440	8.8864	8.6748
CU, no taxes	Tariff	2.1010	2.1010	0.2630
B chooses CET	Welfare	9.0200	8.9221	8.5795
CU, with taxes	Tariff	0	0	0.6335
A chooses CET	Tax	1.7290	0.6335	—
	Welfare	9.0200	8.7289	8.7289
CU, with taxes	Tariff	0	0	0.6335
B chooses CET	Tax	1.7290	0.6335	—
	Welfare	9.0200	8.7289	8.7289

this first element is absent. All that A can gain from granting a tariff preference to B is the second potential benefit of the CU: B's abolition of its tariff on A's export. But, with domestic policies available, B cannot commit to this action, since it can exactly replicate its tariff.[13]

[13]It is not the case that B would choose its UTS tariff for *any* level of the CET; rather, that choice is still a best response *if* the CET is set at zero. Determining B's off-equilibrium behaviour is what makes simulation necessary here. The intuition that it is B's behaviour that constrains the formation of the CU, however, is borne out by the following reasoning. Consider some Nash tariff of B's given arbitrary tariffs of A and C, in the absence of domestic policies. If A's tariff is replaced by domestic policy (in A), then the same behaviour by B is still a best response, albeit as domestic policy rather than a tariff. But now suppose A and B add a small CET on good 2 *given* A's "domestic" tariff: A's demand for B's exports would now be increased at every price, rendering less elastic, in the "usual" case, the excess demand curve facing B. Then B's optimal tariff against A would be higher than it would be with no CET and A would be worse off. That is, the welfare outcome for A of any particular tariff against B is (weakly) lower when constructed through domestic policy in the CU (given B's optimal response) than

Table 2a. Asymmetric case with C larger than B

$U = \frac{\ln(C_1)+\ln(C_2)+20}{2}$		Country A (tariffs and taxes on good 2)	Country B (taxes and UTS on good 1, CU tariffs on good 2)	Country C (tariffs on good 1)
Endowments	1	0.8	0.1	0.1
of good	2	0.0	0.2	0.8
Global free trade	Welfare	9.0837	8.1029	9.2015
UTS	Tariff	1.7000	0.1935	1.6715
	Welfare	8.9125	8.1177	9.1268
CU, no taxes	Tariff	2.2535	2.2535	1.0565
A chooses CET	Welfare	8.9594	8.2947	8.9922
CU, no taxes	Tariff	5.5890	5.5809	0.7440
B chooses CET	Welfare	8.9125	8.3484	8.8538
CU, with taxes	Tariff	1.2275	1.2275	1.3555
A chooses CET	Tax	1.3625	0.2935	—
	Welfare	8.9387	8.2228	9.0249
CU, with taxes	Tariff	3.8165	3.8165	1.0365
B chooses CET	Tax	−0.0800	0.3925	—
	Welfare	8.9125	8.3517	8.9350

Country B would like, in the traditional case, to set the CET at a level prohibitive of all trade between A and C, but, because A would not join such a CU, B would instead choose the highest CET (2.101) such that A's welfare remains at the UTS level. In the present setting, however, B can set no CET that credibly commits it to an overall level of protection that leaves A no worse off. Given the CET, the determination of domestic policies is the same game regardless of who chose the tariff, with the same outcome for each CET. A's best choice of CET, which leaves it indifferent to the union, is one of zero, so there is no CET that B can choose that can entice A to enter.

is so in the UTS case. But we already know that a CET of zero yields the UTS optimum for A; a non-zero CET can therefore do no better.

Table 2b. Asymmetric case with B larger than C

$U = \frac{\text{In}(C_1)+\text{In}(C_2)+20}{2}$		Country A (tariffs and taxes on good 2)	Country B (taxes and UTS on good 1, CU tariffs on good 2)	Country C (tariffs on good 1)
Endowments	1	0.8	0.1	0.1
of good	2	0.0	0.8	0.2
Global free trade	Welfare	9.0837	9.2015	8.1029
UTS	Tariff	1.7000	1.6715	0.1935
	Welfare	8.9125	9.1268	8.1177
CU, no taxes	Tariff	−0.0790	−0.0790	0.1290
A chooses CET	Welfare	9.0764	9.2033	8.1166
CU, no taxes	Tariff	1.2495	1.2495	0
B chooses CET	Welfare	9.0248	9.2479	8.0440
CU, with taxes	Tariff	0	0	0.1935
A chooses CET	Tax	1.7000	1.6715	—
	Welfare	8.9125	9.1268	8.1177
CU, with taxes	Tariff	0	0	0.1935
B chooses CET	Tax	1.7000	1.6715	—
	Welfare	8.9125	9.1268	8.1177

Turning to the asymmetric case, in the case of Table 2a, where C is the largest supplier of A's import good, there is now a gain to A from levying a higher tariff against C than against B. When domestic policies are permitted, country A can do better in the CU than in UTS because the tariff against B is simply that created through domestic policy alone, while the tariff against C is that *plus* the CET. Country B is playing a similar game, however, and we see that in this example both end up worse off than in the CU without domestic policy when A sets the CET. When B chooses the external tariff, A's welfare is reduced to its UTS level in either case, but B does better when domestic policies are permitted. Note also that in this case when a CU forms, country C does better if domestic policies are available than if they are not. This is the case even though A's effective tariff against C is higher (e.g., when A chooses the tariff, the CET on C's exports with no domestic policy is 2.2535; the CET plus implicit tariff when domestic policy is available is 2.59). The reason is that in the latter case B levies an implicit tariff against A, which benefits C through the traffic externality effect between two countries' importing the same good.

Finally, when B is the larger of A's trading partners, as in Table 2b, more interesting results emerge. In this case A's first-best solution would be to levy a higher tariff on B than on C — which is why, when A chooses the CET in the absence of domestic policy, it chooses an import *subsidy* rather than a tax — this applies only to imports from C and so yields a lower price paid to the partner than to non-members.[14] When domestic policy is permitted, however, we again get the strong results of the previous section: there is no non-trivial CU that is attractive to both A and B! The reason is that the reduction in B's tariffs on A's goods that the CU entails is still not a "credible promise" from B, since it can simply recreate such tariffs through domestic policy. The only attraction to a union for A, then, is the ability to discriminate in its tariffs, but in this case such discrimination is *against* the partner, B. Thus it is now B that will not be willing to join a CU with A; again the CU is meaningless![15] Note also that C does better when excluded from a CU (and, indeed, in UTS) than with global free trade — a small country "wins" a tariff war. The reason is found in the pattern of trade here and the importance of the tariff externality effect — a tariff on good 1 by country B reduces the supply price in A, which benefits fellow importer C.

[14]This does not benefit C, however, because of the intra-CU trade diversion effects of internal free trade. Also, B's choosing the CET does not drive A's welfare back down to the UTS level in this case. The reason is that trade with country C goes to zero (and the tariff becomes redundant as a means of controlling domestic prices before this point is reached), since C is the smaller trading partner here.

[15]Indeed, one can show that if the CET is negative, it is B that loses out from the CU whereas, if it is positive, it is A who does worse than it does in UTS.

4. Summary and further comments

When countries have the power to levy domestic consumption and production taxes and subsidies, they can effectively recreate or undo tariffs. This paper considers the consequences of such domestic policies for the formation of CUs in which partners agree on common external tariffs against non-members but then set their domestic policies independently. We show that if each import good derives from only one source, such policies completely emasculate a CU. We demonstrate in a number of simulations that this strong result also carries over to certain other cases.

Our analysis has implications first, for the *sort* of trade agreements that are likely to form between countries and, second, for the kinds of *countries* that are likely to join such agreements. Our results make a case for greater policy coordination within a CU than harmonization of trade policy alone. Indeed, the analysis implies that, aside from any direct benefits of increased coordination, it may be needed to allow the realization of gains from jointly setting trade policy. This fact may at least partially explain why the "pure" CU of economics textbooks has been rare historically and why the most prominent of modern CUs, the European Community, has gone well beyond tariff coordination. A corollary of this incentive for increased coordination is that trade agreements involving less harmonization than a CU are completely emasculated by the existence of the sorts of domestic policy discussed in this paper. Indeed, in any free-trade area (FTA) in which intra-FTA trade is tariff free but each member country retains the power to set its own external tariff against non-members, domestic tax and subsidy policies *are* perfect substitutes for trade policies, and the results of Copeland (1990) again apply: an FTA alone can have no equilibrium impact.[16]

[16]This implies that restrictions on non-trade policies are even more critical to the formation of an FTA than they are to that of a CU, which might seem to be at odds with the very formation of the preferential trading area (in that a CU requires greater trade policy cooperation than an FTA). Nevertheless, recent practical experience with FTAs suggests that parties do look beyond the simple reduction of internal trade barriers.

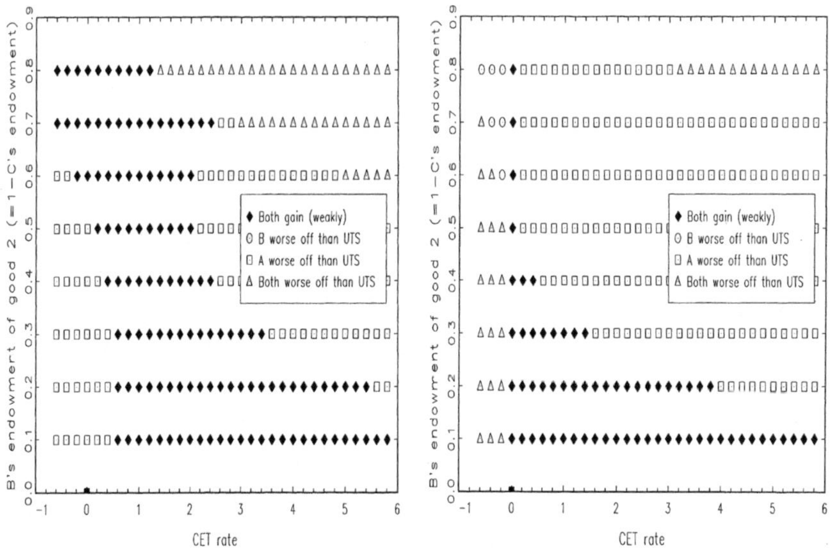

(a) (b)

Fig. 3. (a) Welfare effects of CU at different CETs, with domestic policies, (b) Welfare effects of CU at different CETs, with domestic policies

Regarding the kinds of country that are more likely to form a CU, in the two-good model of the previous section there is an incentive for the "hub" country (country A) to form a CU with the smaller trading partner, in contrast to the usual incentive, in the absence of domestic policies, to form with the larger partner. The reason, as explained earlier, is that A would like to discriminate against a large partner so the latter would not join such a union. Figure 3 makes this point dramatically. Here we simply fix the CET and consider whether or not each member country does better in the CU than in the UTS case. We consider a range of CET values and of endowments of the export good in B and C. Figure 3a shows that in the standard case of a CU with no domestic policies there exists a wide range of external tariffs that yield a mutually beneficial CU for each endowment pattern. Figure 3b shows the case where each member sets internal policies optimally and demonstrates that the range of mutually beneficial gets is reduced. In accordance with our earlier intuition there is no CET that can yield a non-trivial CU if B is no smaller than C.

Our analysis also implies that CUs are more likely to form, ceteris paribus, if domestic tax/subsidy policies are infeasible, for whatever reason. In particular, the imposition of commodity-specific consumption taxes and production subsidies is often politically impossible in many countries. Somewhat perversely, our analysis suggests that this restriction on policy options may be beneficial to a country.

In the light of recent debate over "Fortress Europe" and the liberalizing effects of preferential trading areas, an interesting issue is how close to free trade we can get here. In some simulations the presence of domestic policies constrains the tariff-setting behaviour of the CU, and it is more liberal than it would be without domestic policy: using C's welfare as a metric for the liberalism of a CU, in the case of Tables 1 and 2b a regular CU harms country C relative to the UTS outcome, and so, since a CU with domestic policy simply replicates the UTS outcome, C prefers the CU when domestic policy is available. Our results confirm the idea that CU formation harms non-members,[17] because *any* sort of CU here leaves C no better off than in the UTS case.

References

Copeland, B. (1990). Strategic interaction among nations: Negotiable and non-negotiable trade barriers. *This Journal*, 23, 84–108.

Corden, W.M. (1984). The normative theory of international trade. In R.W. Jones and P.B. Kenen (eds.), *Handbook of International Economics*, Vol. 1. Amsterdam: North-Holland.

Desruelle, D. and M. Richardson (1992). Fortress Europe: Jericho or Château d'If?' Department of Economics Working Paper No. 92-11, Georgetown University.

Dixit, A. and V. Norman (1980). *Theory of International Trade*. Cambridge, UK: Cambridge University Press.

Gatsios, K. and L. Karp (1991). Delegation games in customs unions. *Review of Economic Studies*, 58, 391–7.

Kemp, M. and H. Wan, Jr. (1976). An elementary proposition concerning the formation of customs unions. In M. Kemp (ed.), *Three Topics in the Theory*

[17]But see Desruelle and Richardson (1992) for a political economy model of intra-industry trade in which this conclusion does not apply.

of International Trade: Distribution, Welfare and Uncertainty. Amsterdam: North Holland.

Kennan, J. and R. Riezman (1990). Optimal tariff equilibria with customs unions. *This Journal*, 23, 70–83.

Mathias, P. and S. Pollard, eds. (1989). *The Cambridge Economic History of Europe*, vol. 8. Cambridge, UK: Cambridge University Press.

Meade, J. (1955). *The Theory of Customs Unions*. Amsterdam: North-Holland.

Richardson, M. (1992). Some implications of internal trade in a free trade area. Department of Economics Working Paper No. 92-01, Georgetown University.

Chapter 8

Tariff Revenue Competition in a Free Trade Area

Martin Richardson

Abstract: This note argues that important consequences for the analysis of free trade areas (FTAs) follow from the observation that, with no transport costs, producer prices must be equalised across member countries of a FTA, even if external tariffs differ. In particular, the well-known tariff externality of a FTA is exacerbated by *internal* trade deflection and competition for external tariff revenues. Consequently, a FTA will involve lower external tariffs than might otherwise be expected. We illustrate an extreme case of a FTA between identical partners wherein equilibrium, if it exists at all, is one of zero external tariffs.

Keywords: Tariff revenue competition; Free trade area; External tariff

1. Introduction

A free trade area (FTA) is a form of preferential trading area which entails full free trade amongst members but in which each country chooses its own external tariffs. It has long been recognised in the literature that, if member countries have different tariffs against non-members on some homogeneous good, restrictions on re-exporting (Lambrinidis, 1965) will be required to maintain any differences in domestic prices that might otherwise be eroded through such trade deflection (Corden, 1984). Where rules-of-origin are effective in preventing such behaviour however, the presumption in the literature

Originally published in *European Economic Review*, 39, 1429–1437.

has been that external tariff differences between members then imply differences in domestic prices, for both producers and consumers.

The central point of the present note stems from the observation that, even when trade deflection and consumer arbitrage are prevented, internal free trade implies that prices at which *producers* can sell are equated across members of a FTA, regardless of external tariff differences. This is because all intra-FTA production of a good can be sold anywhere within the FTA duty-free. While this observation has not previously been made,[1] certain important implications follow from it.

In particular, this producer price equalisation[2] leads to a new source of competition between member countries in the setting of external tariffs. Consider a FTA in which some good is imported by both partners. Assume that total intra-FTA production of the good is less than consumption in either country at all relevant prices. If one partner, say country A, were to levy a slightly higher tariff on the good than the other, country B, then, ignoring any transport costs[3], all of B's production would be sold in A at the higher price: the world price plus A's tariff. All of B's consumption would then be imported from outside of the FTA, raising tariff revenue for the government of B. If A were to reduce its tariff to slightly below that of B then the roles would reverse and the government in A would pick up tariff revenue on all consumption in A. Thus there is some conflict within a FTA over tariff revenues from trade with non-members. This competition implies lower external tariffs in the FTA than would otherwise prevail; indeed, we provide an example in which it leads to either zero tariffs or to the non-existence of equilibrium.

---

[1]While a referee suggests that it has long been known that this might raise problems regarding equilibrium, these problems have not been formally articulated. See Richardson (1994) and Grossman and Helpman (1994) for treatments of endogenous policy that *do* allow for this, both building on Richardson (1992).

[2]Henceforth we use the term 'producer price' in country A, for example, to refer to the price actually received by a producer in A: if she sells in country B then this is B's domestic price. A referee notes that this is *not* the common usage of this term but we maintain the present usage for ease of exposition.

[3]We discuss below the impact of introducing transport costs into the model.

In the next section we show that producer prices can *not* differ within a FTA and, in a partial equilibrium setting, expose our main results. A third section interprets the results and discusses their robustness to extensions of the model.

2. A partial equilibrium analysis

2.1. *Producer price equalisation in a FTA*

Consider two countries, A and B, in a FTA excluding the rest of the world (country C.) We assume no transport costs at this point. By arbitrage and internal free trade, the only goods in which consumer prices in A and B can differ, in the absence of non-trade taxes, are those which both members either import from or export to the rest of the world — consumer prices may then differ to the extent that external tariffs differ. However, prices received by producers must be equalised.

To see this, consider some homogeneous good X which both A and B import from C, subject to different tariffs. Let specific tariffs, domestic prices, supplies and demands in country $i = \mathrm{A}, \mathrm{B}$ be denoted t^i, p^i, $X^i(p^i)$ and $D^i(p^i)$ respectively. Suppose, without loss of generality, that t^{B} exceeds t^{A} so that p^{B} exceeds p^{A}. Now, all of A's production of X can legitimately be sold in B, tariff-free, netting A's suppliers the higher price p^{B}, so long as $X^{\mathrm{A}}(p^{\mathrm{B}})+X^{\mathrm{B}}(p^{\mathrm{B}}) < D^{\mathrm{B}}(p^{\mathrm{B}})$. If this inequality does not hold then B will import no X from C and p^{B} will be driven down until one of the following occurs: either (a) $X^{\mathrm{A}}(p^{\mathrm{B}'})+X^{\mathrm{B}}(p^{\mathrm{B}'}) = D^{\mathrm{B}}(p^{\mathrm{B}'})$ at some $p^{\mathrm{B}'}$ weakly in excess of p^{A}, or (b) if $X^{\mathrm{A}}(p^{\mathrm{A}}) + X^{\mathrm{B}}(p^{\mathrm{A}}) > D^{\mathrm{B}}(p^{\mathrm{A}})$, until p^{B} exactly equals p^{A} and producers in the FTA are indifferent about the destination of their sales. In every case producer prices within the FTA are equalised (as are consumer prices in the last case only.) This occurs not from *trade* deflection but rather from deflection of sales of *domestic* production from the low- to the high-tariff member so it cannot be stopped in a FTA.[4]

[4]It should be stressed that consumer prices need not be equated in a FTA. We have argued that producer arbitrage will lead all intra-FTA production to be sold in only

2.2. *Tariff revenue competition and equilibrium*

It has long been recognized that if FTA partners have external market power then there is a negative externality associated with independent tariff-setting: "if country A raises its tariff on imports from C... this improves not only its own terms of trade, but... will also improve B's terms of trade" for tariffs on goods imported by both partners (Corden, 1984, p. 122). We argue that a pure strategy Nash equilibrium in external tariffs in a FTA, if it exists, will in addition be characterised by competition over tariff revenues as described in the Introduction. So Nash equilibrium tariffs are even lower than the externality argument alone suggests. Indeed, we shall show that if a pure strategy equilibrium exists at all for identical FTA members in this context it is at zero external tariffs. Further, non-existence of a pure strategy equilibrium is possible as a result of this revenue competition.

Using the notation above, welfare in country A is the sum of consumer surplus, $CS(p^{\mathrm{A}})$, producer surplus, *PS*, and tariff revenues, $t^{\mathrm{A}}M_{\mathrm{C}}^{\mathrm{A}}$, where $M_{\mathrm{C}}^{\mathrm{A}}$ denotes imports into A from country C. Country C's inverse excess supply of X is given by an increasing function $p^* = p^*(M_{\mathrm{C}})$ where $M_{\mathrm{C}} \equiv M_{\mathrm{C}}^{\mathrm{A}} + M_{\mathrm{C}}^{\mathrm{B}}$. An assumption maintained throughout this paper, for concreteness, is

Assumption 1. Aggregate intra-FTA supply of X is less than demand in either partner at any relevant prices: $X^i(p^j) + X^j(p^j) < D^j(p^j)$ for $i, j = \mathrm{A}, \mathrm{B}$, $i \neq j$, where $t^i \geq t^i$.

the higher-tariff country so any arbitrage to erode consumer price differentials must require internal cross-border movements of goods that originate *outside* the FTA. This, however, violates rules-of-origin and so contravenes both the principle and the operation of FTAs in practice. FTAs are increasingly common and the evolution into what would effectively be customs unions (CUs), with common external tariffs (CETs), that such consumer arbitrage would imply (as described in Vousden (1990, pp. 234–235)) is not apparent. In Canada, for example, proposals for greater integration with the U.S. (such as a CU) are roundly opposed. Second, trade deflection à la Corden *is* closely monitored and prevented in FTAs so that consumer price differences due to tariff differences are not eroded by re-exporting. Third, travellers within FTAs are restricted in the value of goods they can transship. All in all, the extent of arbitrage that consumers can undertake is highly limited and is unlikely to erode consumer price differences due to different external tariffs.

The ability to trade freely within the FTA renders A's welfare discontinuous in its own tariff. To see this, note that if $t^{\mathrm{A}} < t^{\mathrm{B}}$ then all of A's production will be sold in B at a price $p^{\mathrm{B}} > p^{\mathrm{A}}$ so producer surplus is $PS(p^{\mathrm{B}})$ (which is unaffected by a small change in t^{A}). Further, A will import its entire demand from country C in this case so earning tariff revenue of $t^{\mathrm{A}}D^{\mathrm{A}}(p^{\mathrm{A}})$. Thus $W^{\mathrm{A}} = CS(p^{\mathrm{A}}) + PS(p^{\mathrm{B}}) + t^{\mathrm{A}}D^{\mathrm{A}}(p^{\mathrm{A}})$ if $t^{\mathrm{A}} < t^{\mathrm{B}}$. However, if $t^{\mathrm{A}} = t^{\mathrm{B}}$ then we have the usual case in which domestic production is sold at home and all imports come from country C so $W^{\mathrm{A}} = CS(p^{\mathrm{A}}) + PS(p^{\mathrm{A}}) + t^{\mathrm{A}}[D^{\mathrm{A}}(p^{\mathrm{A}}) - X^{\mathrm{A}}(p^{\mathrm{A}})]$. Finally, in the case in which t^{A} strictly exceeds t^{B} then all of A *and* B's production will be sold in A so $W^{\mathrm{A}} = CS(p^{\mathrm{A}}) + PS(p^{\mathrm{A}}) + t^{\mathrm{A}}[D^{\mathrm{A}}(p^{\mathrm{A}}) - X^{\mathrm{A}}(p^{\mathrm{A}}) - X^{\mathrm{B}}(p^{\mathrm{A}})]$. In sum,

$$W^{\mathrm{A}} = \begin{cases} CS(p^{\mathrm{A}}) + PS(p^{\mathrm{B}}) + t^{\mathrm{A}}D^{\mathrm{A}}(p^{\mathrm{A}}) & \text{if } t^{\mathrm{A}} < t^{\mathrm{B}}, \\ CS(p^{\mathrm{A}}) + PS(p^{\mathrm{A}}) + t^{\mathrm{A}}[D^{\mathrm{A}}(p^{\mathrm{A}}) - X^{\mathrm{A}}(p^{\mathrm{A}})] & \text{if } t^{\mathrm{A}} = t^{\mathrm{B}}, \\ CS(p^{\mathrm{A}}) + PS(p^{\mathrm{A}}) + t^{\mathrm{A}}[D^{\mathrm{A}}(p^{\mathrm{A}}) - X^{\mathrm{A}}(p^{\mathrm{A}}) - X^{\mathrm{B}}(p^{\mathrm{A}})] & \text{if } t^{\mathrm{A}} > t^{\mathrm{B}}. \end{cases}$$

For a given level of t^{B}, then, W^{A} is discontinuous in t^{A} at $t^{\mathrm{A}} = t^{\mathrm{B}}$: a small increase in t^{A} above t^{B} will induce a discrete fall in W^{A} as imports from C, subject to A's tariff, are displaced by duty-free imports from B. Conversely, a small cut in t^{A} when $t^{\mathrm{A}} = t^{\mathrm{B}}$ will induce a discrete increase in W^{A} as consumption previously met by domestic production is now met by imports from C which raise tariff revenues. Note that this production deflection has no effect on the FTA's aggregate position vis-à-vis the rest of the world: if $t^{\mathrm{A}} = t^{\mathrm{B}}$ and then t^{A} is cut slightly, for instance, then B's imports from C will fall by $X^{\mathrm{A}}(p^{\mathrm{B}})$ but A's imports from C will rise by $X^{\mathrm{A}}(p^{\mathrm{A}})$.

This discontinuity in a country's welfare function implies that there can be no Nash equilibrium in which $t^{\mathrm{A}} = t^{\mathrm{B}} > 0$. If tariffs are low enough there is a welfare loss associated with tariff reductions (as terms of trade with C worsen) but this effect can be made arbitrarily small by a sufficiently small tariff cut. The revenue shifting effect noted above is a discrete welfare improvement regardless of the size of the tariff reduction, so a small unilateral tariff cut away from a symmetric outcome will always increase a country's welfare given the partner's positive tariff.

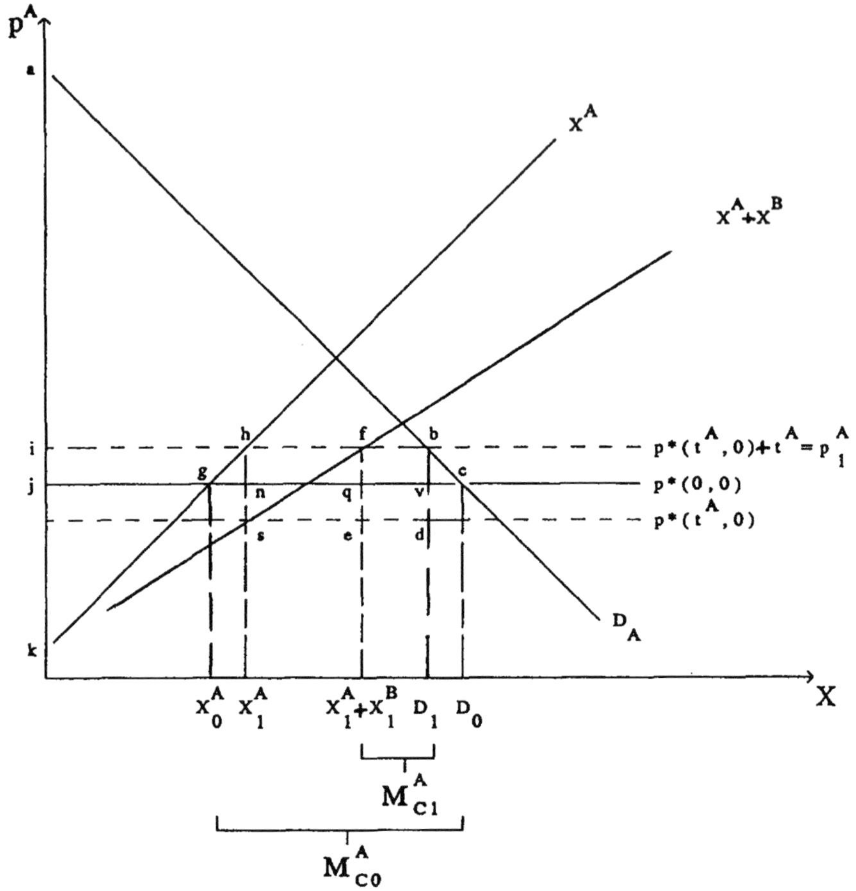

Fig. 1.

At $t^B = 0$, however, there are two possibilities to consider depending on whether or not the terms of trade gains to A from levying a positive tariff against C exceed the discrete losses from B's free-riding. Figure 1 captures the issue here. The world price, p^*, depends on aggregate FTA imports which depend on the external tariffs chosen by A and B. Accordingly, we can write the world price as $p^*(t^A, t^B)$, a declining function of t^A and t^B. Figure 1 shows A's demand curve for X, D^A, A's supply curve, X^A, the FTA's aggregate supply curve, $X^A + X^B$, and the world price when $t^{\mathrm{A}} = t^{\mathrm{B}} = 0\,(p^*(0,0))$. In free trade A's consumption is D_0, its production is X_0^{A} and it imports $M_{C0}^{\mathrm{A}} = D_0 - X_0^{\mathrm{A}}$ all from country C. Welfare is simply consumer surplus (the area labelled *acj* beneath D^A but above $p^*(0,0)$) plus producer surplus (area *kgj*). Suppose that, given $t^{\mathrm{B}} = 0$ and given C's excess supply curve, A's optimal tariff is that shown as t^{A} in the figure and that, consequently, the world price would be $p^*(t^{\mathrm{A}},0)$. The domestic price in A would then rise to $p_1^{\mathrm{A}} = p^*(t^{\mathrm{A}},0) + t^{\mathrm{A}}$ and, in the standard analysis ignoring the effects we have discussed above, consumption and imports would fall to D_1 and $D_1 - X_1^A$ respectively. Thus consumer surplus would fall by *bcji* as the domestic price in A increases and producer surplus would rise by *hgji*. Non-discriminatory tariffs would yield increased tariff revenue of *bdsh* for a net gain of *vdsn* — *hng* — *bcv*, the first term representing the usual terms of trade gain from an optimal tariff and the last two the tariff's production and consumption losses respectively.

However, this tariff would actually induce B to sell in A, duty-free, so revenue of only *bdef* would be earned (on imports from C of $M_{C1}^{\mathrm{A}} = D_1 - (X_1^{\mathrm{A}} + X_1^{\mathrm{B}})$) for a net gain of *vdeq* — *ghfq* — *bcv*. This equals the gain in the non-discriminatory case less *hfes* which, in turn, is $t^{\mathrm{A}}X^{\mathrm{B}}(p_1^{\mathrm{A}})$: the foregone tariff revenue on imports now coming from B. If the net gain from such a tariff is negative then A will choose $t^{\mathrm{A}} = 0$ and full free trade is an equilibrium outcome. If the net gain is positive then A would levy this tariff and suffer B's free-riding. B then would not choose $t^{\mathrm{B}} = 0$ (rather, $t^{\mathrm{B}} = t^{\mathrm{A}} - \epsilon$) and full free trade is not a pure strategy Nash equilibrium either.

We can state more exactly the conditions under which free trade can prevail as an equilibrium. For $t^{\mathrm{B}} = 0$, any $t^{\mathrm{A}} \geq 0$ puts us in the regime in which $t^{\mathrm{A}} \geq t^{\mathrm{B}}$.[5] Given the slopes of the demand and supply functions here, $\partial W^{\mathrm{A}}/\partial t^{\mathrm{A}} > 0$ at $t^{\mathrm{A}} = t^{\mathrm{B}} = 0$ is sufficient to establish that A's optimal tariff is positive. Differentiating W^{A}, holding $t^{\mathrm{B}} = 0$,

$$dW^{\mathrm{A}} = [-D^{\mathrm{A}} + X^{\mathrm{A}}]\mathrm{d}p^{\mathrm{A}} + t^{\mathrm{A}}[\mathrm{d}D^{\mathrm{A}} - \mathrm{d}X^{\mathrm{A}} - \mathrm{d}X^{\mathrm{B}}] + [D^{\mathrm{A}} - X^{\mathrm{A}} - X^{\mathrm{B}}]\mathrm{d}t^{\mathrm{A}}. \quad (1)$$

[5]Note that the only difference between W^{A} when $t^{\mathrm{A}} = t^{\mathrm{B}}$ and W^{A} when $t^{\mathrm{A}} > t^{\mathrm{B}}$ comes from differences in tariff revenues and thus they are equivalent at $t^{\mathrm{A}} = 0$.

But $p^{\mathrm{A}} = p^*(t^{\mathrm{A}}, 0) + t^{\mathrm{A}}$ so $\mathrm{d}p^{\mathrm{A}} = \mathrm{d}p^* + \mathrm{d}t^{\mathrm{A}}$ and, where $\mathrm{d}p^* = (\partial p^*(0,0))/(\partial t^{\mathrm{A}})\mathrm{d}t^{\mathrm{A}}$,

$$\mathrm{d}W^{\mathrm{A}}|_{t^{\mathrm{B}}=t^{\mathrm{A}}=0} = -(D^{\mathrm{A}} - X^{\mathrm{A}})\mathrm{d}p^* - X^{\mathrm{B}}\mathrm{d}t^{\mathrm{A}}. \tag{2}$$

The two terms in this expression correspond to areas $+vdsn$ and — $hfes$ respectively in Fig. 1. Overall, this expression is more likely to be negative, and thus the free trade outcome more likely, ceteris paribus, the larger is the partner country's supply (X^{B}), the larger is domestic supply (X^{A}), the smaller is domestic demand (D^{A}) and the less responsive is the world price to a change in A's tariff ($\partial p^*(0,0)/\partial t^{\mathrm{A}}$). The first three of these effects increase the losses to A from B's free-riding, the last decreases the terms of trade gain from a tariff against C. In all cases B's free-riding is more costly to A, relative to terms of trade gains against C, if $t^{\mathrm{A}} > 0$ is chosen in response to $t^{\mathrm{B}} = 0$. Thus a response of $t^{\mathrm{A}} = 0$ is more likely in each case.

To summarise, under our maintained Assumption 1 we have argued that there is no pure strategy Nash equilibrium in FTA external tariff setting involving equal, positive tariffs in the two member countries.[6] Further, full free trade may or may not be a Nash equilibrium depending on whether (2) is negative or positive for a small increase in t^A which itself depends on a number of factors identified above.

An implication of this analysis is that where the two FTA members are *identical* (so that any equilibrium is symmetric) the only possible pure strategy Nash equilibrium is full free trade; alternatively there is no such equilibrium at all.

[6]If Assumption 1 does *not* hold then the incentive to undercut is lessened but still exists (unless total production exceeds total FTA consumption so the good is not an import in the first place). It is lessened because undercutting reduces the producer price in the high-tariff country rendering that tariff redundant and reducing producers' income for the free-rider. But it still exists because of the increased tariff revenue still associated with any intra-FTA production deflection.

3. Interpretation and robustness

The zero-tariff equilibrium described above is similar to the 'Bertrand paradox' outcome but not exactly analogous. In the latter, two identical firms, producing a homogeneous good and competing in prices, price at marginal cost as each attempts to undercut the other and being undercut yields zero sales. In the FTA game, gains from undercutting are traded off against terms of trade gains against non-members; it may still pay to levy a tariff even if one is undercut so the zero-tariff outcome is a possibility only.[7]

In the case where no equilibrium exists, each country attempts to export its production to the other which contrasts with the pre-FTA case where no trade occurs between A and B. This is trade diversion but of an unusual sort, occurring between net importers of the *same* good, rather than between an exporter and importer.

We conclude with some discussion of the robustness of our results. While the exact results presented above are specific to the case of identical partners, zero transport costs and homogeneous goods, the broad implication that tariff revenue competition in a FTA leads to lower external tariffs than might otherwise be expected seems quite general. First, the partial equilibrium framework employed here is not critical — we have shown elsewhere (Richardson (1992), available on request) that our results also hold in a general equilibrium setting. Second, if domestic and foreign goods were only imperfect substitutes then a country would not serve the entire FTA market by marginally undercutting its partner and a symmetric equilibrium with positive tariffs could obtain. However, an incentive for some undercutting, relative to the tariffs that would prevail if the price equalisation were

[7]Were consumer arbitrage possible within the FTA this Bertrand-like equilibrium of full free trade would *always* prevail: when consumer prices are equalised the higher of the two tariffs is redundant but there are still gains from undercutting. Revenue competition then drives tariffs to zero and, as in Vousden (1990), internal arbitrage turns a FTA into a CU, but one with a zero CET!

ignored, would still remain. Third, increasing the number of FTA members simply exacerbates the effects noted here: each country's pre-FTA Nash tariff is lower (as the tariff externality is worsened) but the gains from undercutting one's partners are unchanged.

Fourth, our exact results do depend on symmetry. If one partner is relatively large then an asymmetric equilibrium with positive tariffs is possible as this country may choose to bear the other's free-riding in order to reap external terms of trade gains. This has the empirical implication that a FTA is more tenable where one member country is large and, indeed, many actual FTAs have this structure.

Finally, the analysis would be affected by internal transport costs within the FTA, as the potential for the trade diversion we have identified is then lessened. If per-unit transport costs were constant at some rate τ, say, then country A's welfare function is still discontinuous in t^{A} but at $t^{\mathrm{A}} = t^{\mathrm{B}} - \tau$ rather than at t^{B}. To disturb the pre-FTA symmetric equilibrium by undercutting B, A must reduce its tariff by a discrete amount thereby incurring a discrete terms of trade loss vis-à-vis C (a loss which is increasing in the size of the tariff cut). So if τ is sufficiently high the pre-FTA equilibrium may remain in the FTA. But if τ is low enough that undercutting is attractive at that equilibrium, a new outcome may obtain in which $t^{\mathrm{A}} = t^{\mathrm{B}} > 0$. Thus, while the extreme nature of our earlier result with identical countries (zero tariffs if there is any pure strategy equilibrium at all) does not hold here, the general tendency for lower external tariffs still does. This is also the case if per-unit transport costs are increasing in the volume of trade and $\tau(0) = 0$. In this case the welfare discontinuity stressed earlier would disappear completely but a small tariff cut would still be attractive at the pre-FTA equilibrium as it would displace some domestic production with revenue-increasing imports. Accordingly, a symmetric equilibrium with positive tariffs can occur but again with lower tariffs than the usual analysis suggests.

References

Corden, W.M. (1984). The normative theory of international trade. In R.W. Jones and P.B. Kenen (eds.), *Handbook of International Economics*, Vol. I, pp. 63–130. Amsterdam: North-Holland.

Grossman, G. and E. Helpman (1994). The politics of free trade agreements. *American Economic Review*, 85(4), 667–690.

Lambrinidis, J.S. (1965). The structure, function and law of a free trade area (Praeger, for The London Institute of World Affairs, New York).

Richardson, M. (1992). On equilibrium in a free trade area, Mimeo. Washington, DC: Georgetown University.

Richardson, M. (1994). Why a free trade area? The tariff also rises. *Economics and Politics*, 6(1), 79–96.

Vousden, N. (1990). *The Economics of Trade Protection.* Cambridge, UK: Cambridge University Press.

Chapter 9

On the Interpretation of the Kemp/Wan Theorem

Martin Richardson

1. Introduction

IN A JUSTLY celebrated paper, Kemp and Wan (1976) (KW henceforth) note that in a competitive world with any pattern of trade taxes where some subset of countries form a customs union (CU), "there exists a common tariff vector and a system of lump-sum compensatory payments involving only members of the union, such that each individual, whether a member of the union or not, is not worse off than before the formation of the union." The common external tariff vector (CET) to which they refer is the so-called Vanek compensating tariff — that tariff which maintains the aggregate trade of the CU members with the rest of the world at its pre-CU levels.[1] In the language of offer curves, because non-members face the same offer point from the union countries after the CU as before it, they can maintain their pre-CU welfare by making the same trades and so be unaffected by the formation of the CU.

Originally published in *Oxford Economic Papers*, 47(4), 696–703.

[1]McMillan (1993) has suggested that the logic of this theorem would provide a better underpinning for GATT criteria concerning the permissible basis for regional trading blocs than does the existing GATT provision in Article XXIV. That is, the criterion for admissibility of such blocs should be that they do not reduce the volume of external trade of the bloc, rather than the existing requirement that tariff levels not exceed pre-union averages.

This powerful result has increasingly been interpreted as suggesting that, with internal side-payments, any subset of countries can form a CU and unilaterally set their CET in such a fashion as to guarantee that no country (member or not) is harmed by the union. The purpose of the present note is to stress that the KW theorem implies no- such thing. In particular, in a world in which countries behave optimally,[2] non-members may choose to set a different tariff post-CU than pre-CU even if the CU's offer point is unchanged by the union. We illustrate this possibility with a numerical example.

2. The basic argument

The essence of the KW argument is very simple: roughly, CU member countries can benefit (on aggregate and therefore individually by virtue of lump-sum transfers) from internal trade liberalisation. So, if trade with non-members is unchanged (by virtue of the compensating tariff) the CU will represent a global Pareto improvement over the previous situation. A critical presumption in this is that the rest of the world will respond to a given price vector with the same net supplies and demands both pre- and post-CU.[3] We can summarise this general area by noting that there are four generic cases of the effects on members of CU formation, depending on whether or not tariffs are set optimally by CU members and non-members, as shown in Table 1.[4] Here we refer to whether a CU can guarantee (weak) gains for its members when internal transfers exist. The CU can set either the Vanek compensating tariff or some optimally chosen tariff

---

[2]A referee has noted that the KW set-up is not itself optimal in that the Vanek compensating tariff generally will not be optimal for the CU. KW's purpose is simply to demonstrate the existence of a Pareto-improving CU. The stress of the present paper is on the case where non-members behave optimally; however, in our simulations we also consider optimal tariff-setting by the CU members both pre- and post-union.

[3]This is implicit in KW's statement that, 'the required vector of common tariffs [that maintains CU trade with non-members at, "the equilibrium pre-union net excess supply of the rest of the world"] may be computed as the difference between the vector of pre-union world prices and the vector of internal union prices.'

[4]I am grateful to an Editor for suggesting this Table.

Table 1. Effect on members' welfare of CU depending on tariff-setting behaviour. A (+) indicates that rhutual improvement can be guaranteed

		Non-members	
		Static	Optimal
CU members	Compensating tariff	(+)	
	Optimal tariff	(+)	

and non-members may either act optimally or not: the "static" case is where the union is presented with the same offer curve as its members faced, jointly, before the union. The case considered directly by KW is the first quadrant where CU members set the compensating tariff and face the same offer curve as before the union. Their result must also apply where the CU behaves "optimally" however, as the union could always choose the compensating tariff. The present paper fills in the remaining two elements of the table showing that, in both, a CU can not guarantee mutual gains.

While Kemp and Wan themselves make clear that they establish only the existence of a Pareto-improving CU contingent on this behaviour in the rest of the world, their theorem is often cited as suggesting that a CU can unilaterally guarantee that it raises the welfare of each of its members. For example, Corden (1984, p. 121) suggests that, "[a]ny group of countries can form a union and improve joint welfare provided the common external tariff is adjusted appropriately. If it is fixed... at the compensating common tariff level some improvement for the union members will be ensured and no loss for outsiders." As a final example, Krugman (1991, p. 11) writes,

> while a customs union with a given external tariff may be harmful to the members, a customs union that adjusts its tariff optimally is always beneficial... The Kamp-Wan [sic] point... is that by adjusting the external tariff, the members of a customs union can always ensure a gain.

The present note argues that these interpretations implicitly must suppose that non-members do not react to the formation of the

CU.[5] That is, it may not be possible for the union members alone to choose any CET which raises their own joint welfare, when the optimal reaction of non-members is taken into account. The basic idea is that, while the CU may present the rest of the world with the same point on its joint offer surface as before the union (i.e. the same vector of prices), intra-CU trade liberalization may change the inframarginal shape of the CU's offer surface. The rest of the world may then choose a different optimal tariff of its own, possibly to the union's overall detriment, compared to the pre-union outcome. Indeed, there may be no CET at all which raises joint CU welfare (allowing for internal transfers) when C reacts optimally. The next section simulates a numerical model to generate offer curves and optimal tariffs that show exactly this outcome.

3. A numerical example

We simulate a 3-good 3-country model in which each country imports and exports only one good.[6] The non-member country behaves optimally throughout. Country A imports good Y from the rest of the world, C, and exports good Z to potential partner B who, in turn, exports good X to C: good Z is traded only within the union countries. This pattern of trade is shown in Fig. 1.

Preferences in countries A and B are given in (1) and (2) respectively,[7]

$$U^A(D_y^A, D_z^A) = \gamma \text{ In}\,(D_y^A - \overline{D_y^A}) + \beta \text{ In}\,(D_z^A) \tag{1}$$

$$U^B(D_x^B, D_z^B) = D_x^B + \beta \text{ In}\,(D_z^B) \tag{2}$$

where D_j^i denotes consumption of good $j = X, Y, Z$ in country $i = A, B, \beta$, and γ are constants and $\overline{D_y^A}$ is a consumption minimum of

[5] Even if the CU is small, in the usual sense, non-members would adjust their tariff as the union CET changed. Non-reaction by non-members implies that they are behaving non-optimally in the aggregate.

[6] This contrasts to other three-good models where trade is symmetric, e.g. McMillan and McCann (1981).

[7] These preferences differ so that the effects of CU trade liberalization do not offset each other via symmetric income effects.

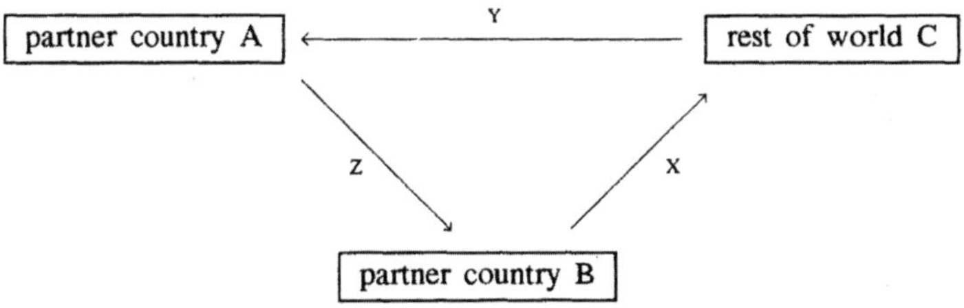

Country A exports good Z, imports Y
Country B exports good X, imports Z
Country C exports good Y, imports X

Fig. 1. The pattern of trade

good Y in country A. Each country i has an endowment ω_j^i of good j. Country C is assumed to be large relative to A and B so that its internal prices are unaffected by trade. We denote these prices as p_x^C and p_y^C and normalize the latter to unity. The price received in country B for exports of X is p_x and C seeks to maximize the value of its tariff revenues as given in (3)[8]

$$U^C = (p_x^C - P_x)(\omega_x^B - D_x^B) \tag{3}$$

In country A, domestic prices of Y and Z are $p_y^A = 1 + t_y^A$ and $p_z^A = p_z$ respectively, where t_y^A is A's specific tariff on imports of good Y from C.[9] In similar notation, internal prices of X and Z in B are $p_x^B = p_x$ and $p_z^B = p_z + t_z^B$ ff respectively. National income in country $i = A, B$, at domestic prices, is given in (4)

$$I^i = \sum_{j=X,Y,Z} [p_j^i \omega_j^i + t_j^i(D_j^i - \omega_j^i) - s_j^i(\omega_i^j - D_j^i)] \tag{4}$$

[8]Contrary to the common suggestion that the formation of a small CU leaves the rest of the world unaffected, even large trading partners will be affected through changes in tariff revenues, even though their prices are unchanged (which is why a large country's optimal tariff is non-zero in trade with a small one).

[9]As each country consumes only two goods, each faces only one relative price hence, by Lerner symmetry, we need consider only trade taxes as instruments.

Each country faces a balance of trade constraint at world prices

$$D_y^A - \omega_y^A = p_z(\omega_z^A - D_z^A)$$
$$p_z(D_z^B - \omega_z^B) = p_x(\omega_x^B - D_x^B) \quad (5)$$

Equations (4) can be rewritten, using (5). to yield expressions for I^A and I^B

$$I^A = p_y^A(\omega_y^A + p_z\omega_z^A) + (s_z^A - t_y^A p_z)D_z^A$$
$$I^B = p_x\omega_x^B + p_z\omega_z^B + t_z^B D_z^B \quad (6)$$

The representative consumer in each country seeks to maximize his/her welfare subject to the usual budget constraint that the value of consumption, at domestic prices, not exceed the value of income. This yields demand functions for each good in terms of domestic prices and income. Substitution back into (6) then enables us to solve for demands in terms of prices, taxes and endowments only. Finally, we require that the market for Z clear: (7) determines p_z in terms of endowments and other prices alone

$$\omega_z^A + \omega_z^B = D_z^A + D_z^B \quad (7)$$

We simulate this system of equations numerically[10] using endowments of $\omega_x^A = \omega_y^B = 0, \omega_z^A = 20, \omega_x^B = \omega_z^B = 10$, and $\omega_y^A = 0.2$. The model's constants take the values $\beta = 0.7, \gamma = 0.15$ and $\overline{D_y^A} = 0.1$. We first search over values of each country's tariff to find the unilateral tariff-setting (UTS) Nash equilibrium, when C's internal relative price of X is $p_x^C = 12$. Optimal tariffs for A, B, and C respectively are 0.863, 0.4015 and 2.853[11] and all resulting prices, demands and welfare levels are shown in Table 2.

Figure 2 illustrates the initial combined offer curve of countries A and B, in this UTS Nash equilibrium, as a dashed line labelled UTS OC. Country C's welfare contours here are just straight lines with a

[10]Simulations were run via grid-search techniques in GAUSS: the programmes and a description of the approach taken are available on request from the author.

[11]Optimal tariffs for A and B are non-zero, even though they are small countries relative to C, as each has market power with respect to the other and good Z is not traded with C.

Table 2. Simulation results for unilateral tariff setting

Unilateral tariff-setting $t_y^A = 0.863, t_z^B = 0.4015, t_z^C = 2.853$		Country A	Country B
Domestic price of good	X	—	9.1470
	Y	1.8630	—
	Z	0.1559	0.5574
Consumption of good	X	—	9.9746
	Y	0.4319	—
	Z	18.5123	11.4877
Welfare		1.8775	11.6835
		$U^C = 0.0723$	

slope of p_x^C and the optimal tariff of C just picks a trading point on the joint OC that has the same slope. The figure shows the resulting terms of trade presented by country C as the line labelled UTS ToT.

Suppose A and B now form a CU and abolish all taxes on trade between them so that $t_z^B = 0$. If the external tariff on good Y is left at 0.863 (as in the UTS configuration) then the joint offer curve facing C swings out, as shown in Fig. 2, to the solid line labelled CU OC CET = 0.863. The Vanek compensating tariff if C's tariff is unchanged is a little under 6.82 — this would them put the CU offer curve (the line consisting of short dashes in the figure) through the UTS equilibrium trading point, as shown. Call this outcome the compensating CU. Equilibrium prices, demands and welfare are shown in Table 3.[12] In particular, by construction, C is unaffected by this union.

That the KW theorem applies here is trivial: looking at Fig. 1, the pattern of trade is such that the only consequence of this compensating CU, if C's tariff is unchanged, is on the consumption of Z. In this endowment model the only allocation that leaves neither member country worse off is then exactly the UTS allocation. However,

[12]As only country A imports from C here, the CET is simply the same as A's tariff. Note that A gains from the CU as compared to UTS even though all domestic prices rise. This is because of large income effects from the abolition of B's tariff on, A's export and from increased tariff revenues from C.

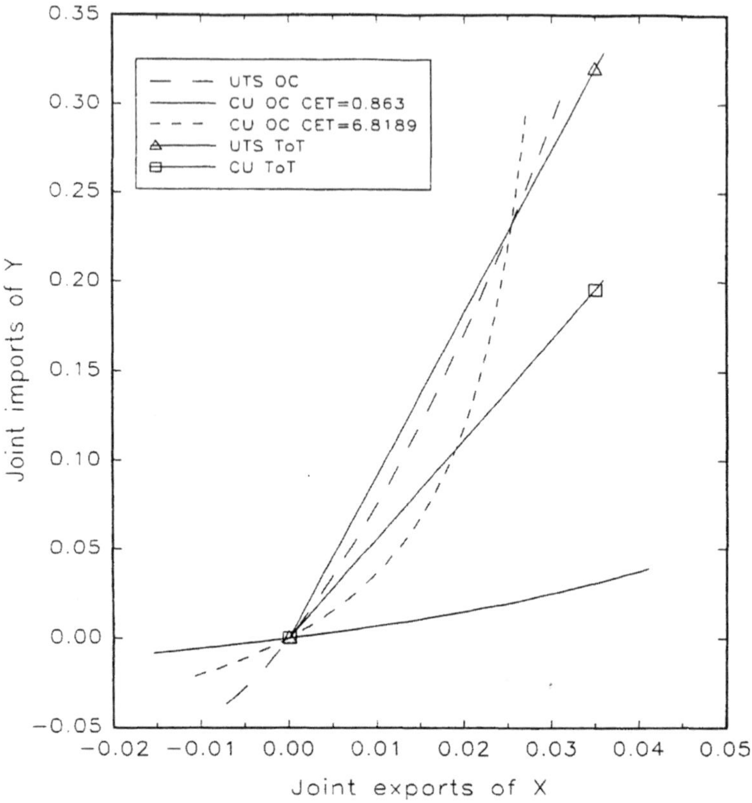

Fig. 2. Offer curves and terms of trade

it is also the case that C would not leave its tariff on X unchanged in the face of this compensating CU: even though the union's offer curve passes through the UTS point so that C's UTS welfare is still available to it, liberalisation of Z trade in the CU has made the whole offer curve less elastic. C is now best off with a higher tariff of 6.4075 which worsens the union's terms of trade and renders both A and B worse off than in the case of Table 3. The resulting CU external terms of trade are shown in Fig. 2 as the line CU ToT and prices, demands and welfare are all given in Table 4. Thus, while the KW theorem of course holds here, the common interpretation of it given above does not.

Table 3. Simulation results for the "compensating" CU where the CU offer curve passes through the pre-CU point and the non-member levies its pre-CU tariff

Compensating CU, C's UTS tariff $t_z^B = 0, t_x^C = 2.853$, CET = 6.818898		Country A	Country B
Domestic price of good	X	—	9.1470
	Y	7.8189	
	Z	0.6171	0.6171
Consumption of good	X	—	9.9746
	Y	0.4319	—
	Z	19.6242	10.3758
Welfare		1.9183	11.6123
		$U^C = 0.0723$	

Table 4. Simulation results for the "compensating" CU where the CU offer curve passes through the pre-CU point and the non-member levies its optimal tariff

Compensating CU, C's optimal tariff $t_z^B = 0, t_x^C = 2.853$, CET = 6.818898		Country A	Country B
Domestic price of good	X	—	5.5925
	Y	7.8189	—
	Z	0.3809	0.3809
Consumption of good	X	—	9.9811
	Y	0.3059	—
	Z	19.7220	10.2780
Welfare		1.8501	11.6121
		$U^C = 0.1213$	

In fact, grid search techniques reveal that, with this parameterization, if internal trade in Z is free there is no CET and pattern of internal transfers between A and B that could raise welfare in both countries compared to the UTS case, allowing for C's optimal reaction. So even optimal tariff-setting by the union cannot ensure mutual gains when the non-member is also behaving optimally.[13]

4. Conclusion

We have argued that the KW theorem does not imply that CU members alone can guarantee that their union be Pareto-improving, when the CET is chosen jointly and there are lump-sum transfers, in a setting in which the rest of the world responds optimally. We have provided an example to illustrate this. In defence of the more general interpretation of the KW theorem one could argue that country C is, in practice, a fiction that represents an amalgam of all non-member countries. If the union of A and B is truly small then a non-strategic reaction by C may be plausible as the coordination needed by non-members to generate an optimal response is impractical. For this reason, the practical implications of the KW theorem may be largely unaffected by the observations made in this paper except in cases where union trade is predominantly with a small number of outside countries.

Acknowledgements

The idea for this paper arose from a conversation with Ray Riezman and Costas Syropoulos. I am grateful to John McMillan and Murray Kemp for encouraging remarks and to the editor and an anonymous referee for helpful suggestions. Any errors, of course, are my own.

[13]Note that we are considering only a full CU wherein internal trade is completely free. It is possible that partial liberalisation combined with some CET and internal transfers may be mutually welfare improving even though full liberalisation is not. The latter, by changing the joint OC dramatically, induces a large tariff increase from the non-member which worsens the union's terms of trade so much that the gains from internal liberalisation are swamped and this effect can be lessened by only partial liberalisation. I am grateful to an Editor for raising this question.

References

Corden, W. M. (1984). The normative theory of international trade. In R. Jones and P. Kenen (eds.), *Handbook of International Economics*, Vol. I. Amsterdam: North-Holland.

Kemp, M. and Wan, Jr., H. (1976). An elementary proposition concerning the formation of customs unions. In M. Kemp (ed.), *Three Topics in the Theory of International Trade: Distribution, Welfare and Uncertainty.* Amsterdam: North-Holland.

Krugman, P. (1991). Is bilateralism bad? In E. Helpman and A. Razin (eds.), *International Trade Policy.* Cambridge MA: MIT Press.

McMillan, J. and McCann, E. (1981). Welfare effects in customs unions. *Economic Journal*, 91, 697–703.

McMillan, J. (1933). Does regional integration foster open trade? Economic theory and GATT's Article XXIV. In K. Anderson and R. Blackhurst (eds.), *Regional Integration and the Global Trading System*, pp. 292–310. London: Harvester-Wheatsheaf.

Chapter 10

Fortress Europe: Jericho or Château d'If?

Dominique Desruelle and Martin Richardson

Abstract: Traditional analysis of customs union formation suggests that it leads to an increase in members' external tariffs. This paper stresses two aspects of European trade and trade policy — a large volume of intra-industry trade between similar countries and a political motivation for tariffs — and highlights a role for tariff coordination in a model of differentiated products in which tariffs affect domestic costs and thus export prices and the magnitude of monopolistic rents. We show that when workers choose the tariffs and receive but a small portion of tariff revenues, the union's tariff wall falls.

1. Introduction

The notion that the European Community will become a "Fortress Europe" as it moves towards greater integration has become sufficiently popular that it is almost a cliché. Clearly, the consequences of such a union for the rest of the world are significant: fears of increased European insularity have been important in motivating the renewed interest of other countries in forming preferential trading blocs themselves. This paper considers the setting of external tariffs both before and after the formation of a customs union in a model with certain "European" features and considers whether forming the union leads tariffs against nonmembers to rise (the impregnable "Château

Originally published in *Review of International Economics*, 5(1), 32–46.

d'If" interpretation of Fortress Europe) or fall (the "Jericho" interpretation.)

The distinguishing features of our model are that (i) we consider trade between similar coutries in similar products and (ii) we suppose that tariffs are set for "political economy" reasons, rather than to maximize the welfare of a representative agent. The proximate motivation for these two features is the desire to capture essential elements of the European experience. However, the model is of interest beyond that direct application, given both the importance of intra-industry trade to many industrialized countries and the growing body of evidence[1] to substantiate the theroretical notion that protectionist trade polices are *politically* endogenous.

In the present model, countries produce and trade varieties of a differentiated good as well as a homogeneous good produced under constant returns to scale (CRS). The world consists of three countries endowed with labor and capital and peopled with two types of agents, workers and capitalists. Each country's tariffs are set according to a rule that accords different weights to the welfares of the different types of agents. Initially, countries are noncooperative and we find a Nash equilibrium in tariffs. Countries A and B, which are symmetric (a restriction that permits us to solve for analytical expressions for optimal tariffs), contemplate forming a customs union (CU) in which case they act together and we find a Nash equilibrium in tariffs between the CU and country C, the nonmember.

We demonstrate that the effects of forming a CU here depend not only upon who sets tariffs but also upon how tariff revenues are distributed. In particular, if the tariff is set to favor workers but workers receive only a small portion of tariff revenues (so the policymaker's central concern in setting tariffs is with their effects on workers' incomes through price changes) then formation of a CU will lead external tariffs to *fall*. In other results, we show that there are incentives to place tariffs on imports both of differentiated products

[1]See the survey of empirical evidence in Hillman (1989, ch. 11).

and of the CRS good and that full free trade within the union may not always be optimal.[2]

It is noteworthy that product differentiation and our political economy setup interact to produce our results. Indeed, in a Heckscher-Ohlin model with just the political economy specification embedded in it, the formation of a CU would have no effects at all on external tariffs in the small-country analog of our setting.[3]

The problem of how an external tariff is set *optimally* in a CU is one that has not been addressed in much detail in the economics literature. Most early analysis took the external tariff of the union as equal to the pre-union tariff of one or other of the members. Other writers, notably Kemp and Wan (1976) and Dixit and Norman (1980), come at the problem from a more general perspective, demonstrating the existence of Pareto-improving unions in some cases. Some recent work has focused directly on the issue of external-tariff setting. Kennan and Riezman (1990) run a number of simulations which indicate that a CU will tend to increase external tariffs compared to individual members' unilateral choices. This action is motivated by the internalization of a tariff externality between importers of the same good: a tariff imposed by one country depresses the world price and so benefits other countries that import that same good, as noted by Corden (1984, p. 122). Gatsios and Karp (1991) consider another motivation in tariff setting: the reaction of nonmembers.

---

[2]This phenomenon has been noted in other models, albeit for rather different reasons. See Ethier and Horn (1984) and McMillan and McCann (1981).

[3]In such a context, two identical CU members would have no trade in any equilibrium, be it one of unilateral tariff-setting (UTS) or a CU. The choice of external tariff of these relatively capital-abundant countries would then follow simply from Stolper-Samuelson considerations, ameliorated or reinforced by tariff revenue effects. E.g., if workers chose tariffs and received no revenues they would opt for autarky, both unilaterally and in a CU. If they also received tariff revenues they would generally choose some nonprohibitive tariff, but the CU would be inconsequential: there is no interaction between these countries and one's tariff has no effect on the other. Were the members to have some monopoly power against the rest of the world, of course, the CU would have consequences but, again, these are transparent: the only effect that one member's tariff has on the other is the externality mentioned above and the CU internalizes this, compared to the UTS outcome, so, in all cases, the CU would display a higher tariff than the countries individually.

However, even this modeling seems unnecessarily divorced from the reality of policy-making in a union (such as the EC) of generally similar and advanced industrial nations. In particular, it is usually assumed that trade occurs for reasons of comparative advantage and that tariffs are set, for traditional optimal-tariff reasons, to maximize the welfare of a representative individual. For both these reasons, the literature on external-tariff setting in a CU seems inadequate for an understanding of the likely consequences for nonmembers of the formation of blocs such as the EC.

Two recent papers have used models acknowledging these realities. However, they address issues different from those of this paper. Krugman and Venables (1990) consider a two-country, two-sector model in which a large country and a small one produce both a homogeneous good and many varieties of a differentiated product. They focus on the effects of partial bilateral trade liberalization on internal trade and incomes. Krugman (1992) presents a model of integration of similar countries, trading a set of differentiated products, into regional blocs of equal size and analyzes the issue of multilateralism versus regionalism. He focuses on the relation between the number of identical blocs and the welfare level achieved by each bloc.

2. The model

The basic structure of our two-good general equilibrium model is an expansion to a three-country world (essential for CU analysis) of the two-country, "no-entry" model of Helpman and Krugman (1989, ch. 7).[4] Good Y is a homogeneous good produced in each of the three countries by a CRS technology and good X is a differentiated product. Varieties of good X are produced in countries A and B, the future CU partners, but not in country C.[5] Countries A and B

[4]Their purpose is to show that, with monopolistic competition, a small tariff has a beneficial effect in increasing output of a good for which price exceeds marginal cost.

[5]We note in the Conclusion that allowing country C to produce X would be a useful extension. However, it would greatly complicate the already messy analysis and, at least as a first pass at this topic, the case under consideration provides valuable insights in

export domestic X varieties to each other and to country C and import good Y from country C.

To produce each variety of X requires one unit of capital and a^i_{Lx} units of labor for each unit of output in country $i, i = \mathrm{A}, \mathrm{B}$. Thus, if the wage rate is w^i, the marginal cost of production of a variety of X is $w^i a^i_{Lx}$. The production of good Y uses only labor and units are normalized such that one unit of Y requires one unit of labor. Hence, the marginal cost of a unit of Y is simply w^i. The wage in country C is our *numéraire*: $w^{\mathrm{C}} = 1$. Countries A and B are respectively endowed with n^{A} and n^{B} units of capital and L^{A} and L^{B} units of labor. Country C is endowed with L^{C} units of labor and no capital.

On the demand side, there are N^i people in country $i, i = \mathrm{A}, \mathrm{B}, \mathrm{C}$ and individual s has a utility function, over good Y and differentiated product X, given in equation (1):

$$U^i(D^{si}, D^{si}_y) = F^i \theta^{-1}(D^{si})^\theta + D^{si}_y, \tag{1}$$

where F^i and θ are constants, $F^i > 0$ and $\theta \in (0,1)$, D^{si}_y denotes consumption of good Y by consumer s in country i, and D^{si} is an index of consumption of varieties of X (where x subscripts are omitted for clarity):

$$D^{si} = \left[\sum_{m=1}^{n^*} (D^{si}_m)^\alpha\right]^{1/\alpha}. \tag{2}$$

Here D^{si}_m is consumption of the mth variety of X by consumer s, α is a constant between zero and one and $n^* = n^{\mathrm{A}} + n^{\mathrm{B}}$ is the total number of varieties of X worldwide.[6]

Consumers maximize utility. We assume the labor market is perfectly competitive in all countries. The market for good Y is also perfectly competitive. Since the number of varieties is fixed and since all varieties of X enter demand symmetrically, no two

itself. In the current setup country C could be thought of as a less-developed country (LDC) with A and B, the potential customs union partners, as developed industrial countries.

[6]Since consumers exhibit a preference for variety, it is optimal to produce as many varieties as possible in each country, i.e., as many as there are units of capital.

producers would choose to produce the same variety. We suppose that each firm producing a variety of X is sufficiently small in the market that it treats market aggregates as exogenous. Good X market behavior is thus like monopolistic competition but with no entry: firms are small and profit-maximizers, producing differentiated products.

As discussed in the introduction, it is important to consider motivations for tariff setting other than the goal of maximization of the welfare of a "representative" agent traditionally ascribed to governments in economic analysis. We suppose that the population of country A or B, $N^i(i = \text{A}, \text{B})$, is divided into two classes, workers and capitalists: L^i identical workers who derive income from labor supply plus any tariff revenues allocated to them and K^i identical capitalists who receive the monopolistic rents from the X sector and also may receive tariff revenues. Obviously, $K^i + L^i = N^i$ for $i = \text{A}, \text{B}$. In country C, as there is no capital and no X production, every individual is a worker. We let l^i denote the proportion of the population that are workers: $l^i = L^i/N^i$.

Following the political economy model of Long and Vousden (1991),[7] we suppose that the government's objective in countries A and B is to choose tariffs to maximize some objective function convex in the welfare of the different groups in society. Explicitly, if the representative worker in country i earns an income of I^{iw} and the representative capitalist an income I^{ik}, the government's maximand is:

$$G(q_y^i, \mathbf{q}_X^i, I^{iw}, I^{ik}) = \gamma^i V^i(q_y^i, \mathbf{q}_x^i, I^{iw}) + (l - \gamma^i) V^i(q_y^i, \mathbf{q}_x^i, I^{ik}), \quad (3)$$

where γ^i is an exogenous constant between zero and one, $V^i(\cdot)$ the indirect utility function corresponding to U^i, q_y^i the consumer price of good Y in country i, and $\mathbf{q}_x^i$ the n^* by 1 vector of consumers' prices of good X varieties in country i.

[7]This political objective function has recently been formalized in Grossman and Helpman (1994) whose model provides a microanalytic foundation for this sort of reduced-form political support function.

In each of the three countries, the government can impose *ad valorem* tariffs on imports. We denote the tariff on Y in country i by τ^i and the tariff in country i on all foreign varieties of X by t^i. We limit the set of policy instruments to import taxes only, partly for reasons of analytical convenience (the optimal policy of the nonmember country in our model is to be passive rather than to subsidize its exports) and partly for conformity with most existing literature on preferential trading arrangements. The main reason for this restriction, however, is simply empirical relevance. Direct export subsidies are generally illegal under the GATT while export taxes and import subsidies are rarely observed in practice. While the latter phenomenon may be due to latent mercantilism on the part of governments and would, ideally, emerge endogenously in a model of optimal policy, it is nevertheless convenient to restrict our attention in this paper to the use of import taxes alone.

To make the analysis tractable, we henceforth assume that A and B are identical: consumers in A and B have the same utility function and the endowments, populations and policy objectives of both countries are identical ($F^i = F, n^i = n, L^i = L, K^i = K, N^i = N$ and $\gamma^i = \gamma$ for $i = \mathrm{A}, \mathrm{B}$). All trade between A and B is then intra-industry. Also, we consider only two polar cases: where $\gamma = 1$ (the government cares only for capitalists) and where $\gamma = 0$ (the government cares only for workers). This specification of tariff setting combines with the symmetry of A and B to facilitate the comparison between a single country's choice of tariff and that of the CU: when acting together, the countries' aims are unchanged. Finally, we need to specify the allocation of tariff revenues; henceforth workers are assumed to get a fraction δ of tariff revenues, capitalists $(1 - \delta)$, and we consider alternative values of this share.[8]

[8]If δ is a choice parameter for the government it will simply allocate all revenues to the favored group in the cases we consider. The general difficulty with lump-sum transfers is that they are informationally demanding (see Dixit and Norman (1986, p. 121) for a cogent discussion) so we also consider reallocations of revenues through a lump-sum instrument that simply redistributes equal shares to all individuals. This approach requires no individual-specific information and it is therefore consistent with a setting in which more general lump-sum powers are infeasible. This case falls out here as the circumstance in which $\delta = l$.

Before we compute the impact of the formation of a CU on member countries' external tariffs, one convenient result should be noted. It turns out that C's optimal tariff on its imports of X is always zero: it produces only Y and has no terms-of-trade gain available from any tariff. This is because the price of X in A and B is a markup over marginal cost and this is unaffected by a tariff on X in C. As this is the case throughout the paper, we need only determine A's and B's optimal tariffs in order to describe the complete Nash equilibrium in each scenario.

3. Customs unions formation with different policy preferences

In this section, we analyze the impact of the formation of a CU between A and B on their tariffs on C's goods, under different governmental objective functions. We first solve the consumers' and producers' maximization problems.

The consumer's utility function is quasi-linear in Y. So there are no income effects on demand for X which, for an individual of country i, is just a share $(1/N^i)$ of country i's aggregate demand, regardless of income (supposing, as we do henceforth, that each individual has enough income to consume both goods). For an income of I^{si} and a price of good Y of q^i_y, maximization of U^{si} subject to the consumer's budget constraint yields the following demand for variety 1 of X, D^{si}_1:

$$D^{si}_1 = (N^i)^{-1} D^i_1 \quad \text{where} \quad D^i_1 = D^i(q^i_1/Q^i)^{-\sigma}, \tag{4}$$

where Q^i and D^i are indices of customer prices and consumption of X in country i:

$$Q^i = \left[\sum_{m=1}^{n^*} (q^i_{xm})^{\frac{\alpha}{(\alpha-1)}}\right]^{\frac{(\alpha-1)}{a}}, \tag{5}$$

$$D^i = \left(Q^i(N^i)^\theta / F^i q^i_y\right)^{-\varepsilon}, \quad \text{and}$$

$$\sigma = 1/(1-\alpha) > \varepsilon = 1/(1-\theta) > 1. \tag{6}$$

The parameter ε represents the overall price elasticity of demand for X and σ denotes the elasticity of substitution between varieties of X. To ensure that demand for a particular variety is increasing in Q^i we assume henceforth that $\sigma > \varepsilon$. (If this were not the case then holding the varietal price fixed but raising the price index would cause demand for the variety to fall.) Total expenditure on X in country i, $\sum_{m=1}^{n^*}(q_{xm}^i D_m^i)$, equals $Q^i D^i$, and expenditure by one individual is $(1/N^i)Q^i D^i$.

Turning to producers' decisions, as mentioned in the previous section, each firm producing a variety of X is sufficiently small in the market that it treats market aggregates as exogenous; in particular, σ and Q^i are treated parametrically by each firm. Given the constant price elasticity demand function above (with elasticity σ), each producer of X prices as a constant markup $\sigma/(\sigma-1)$ over marginal cost. Letting p_x^i denote the producers' price of X in country $i = \text{A}, \text{B}$,

$$p_x^i = w^i a_{Lx}^i(\sigma/(\sigma-1)), \quad i = \text{A}, \text{B}. \tag{7}$$

We note that this pricing rule is valid for any level of tariffs since they do not affect the price elasticity of demand. Equation (7) implies that, where X^i is total production of X in country i, total rents in the X sector can be written as

$$(p_x^i - w^i a_{Lx}^i)X^i = (p_x^i/\sigma)X^i. \tag{8}$$

As far as consumer prices are concerned, (7) implies that all varieties produced in country i have the same producers' price. Since we assumed that tariffs do not discriminate between varieties, all varieties produced in country i are sold for the same price to consumers of country j. We denote by q_x^{kj} the consumer price in country $k = \text{A}, \text{B}, \text{C}$ of all varieties of X produced in country $j = \text{A}, \text{B}$. Since we only consider tariffs, the relations between producer and consumer prices are $q_x^{jj} = p_x^j$ and $q_x^{kj} = (1 + t_x^{kj})p_x^j$ for $k \neq j, t_x^{kj}$ being k's *ad valorem* tariff on imports of j's varieties.

Turning to producers of Y, we assume throughout our analysis that total labor supplies (L^i) and aggregate demands are such that some Y is always produced in each country.[9] The Y sector is competitive. Therefore, producers' price equals marginal cost. In country C, where by assumption $\mathrm{w}^{\mathrm{C}} = 1$, and where Y is exported, $p_y^{\mathrm{C}} = q_y^{\mathrm{C}} = w^{\mathrm{C}} = 1$. Countries A and B both import from C. Given that they impose an *ad valorem* tariff of $\tau^i(i = \mathrm{A}, \mathrm{B}), q_y^i = (1 + \tau^i)$ for $i = \mathrm{A}, \mathrm{B}$. Equality between producers' price and marginal cost of the locally produced units of Y, in turn, implies that $w^i = q_y^i = (1 + \tau^i), i = \mathrm{A}, \mathrm{B}$.

Finally, denoting total production of X and Y in country i by X^i and Y^i respectively, the model is closed by full employment and trade balance conditions:

$$a_{Lx}^i X^i + Y^i = L^i; \tag{9}$$

$$(D_y^i - Y^i) + p_x^i D^{ij} = p_x^i (D^{ji} + D^{Ci}), \quad i, j = \mathrm{A}, \mathrm{B}, \quad i \neq j. \tag{10}$$

Here D^{ij} denotes demand in country i for varieties of X produced in country j. Equation (10) states that for country A, for example, the value at world prices of Y imports plus X imports from B equals the value of B's and C's demands for A's varieties of X.

An "Efficiency" Benchmark

We consider first a "traditional" case in which the government maximizes the welfare of a typical agent. This exercise is best thought of as seeking the optimal policy when lump-sum transfers are available and are used to equalize all agents' incomes — in this case we have a truly representative agent.[10] Without loss of generality (by symmetry) we consider the problem facing country A. We first compute the government's optimal tariff policy in the absence of a CU between A and B. We then do the same in the presence of the CU, and finally we compare these two policies.

[9] Given our interpretation of country C as a small LDC, this assumption is innocuous.

[10] While in the rest of the paper we only consider a welfare function in which one group or the other gets sole weighting, the present case is still a relevant benchmark. If we restricted attention here to, say, the case in which the government only cared about workers, its optimal trade policy, with lump-sum transfers available, would still be the same as if it cared only for capitalists or cared for the representative agent as in this section: it would set prices to maximize national income and then would use its lump-sum instrument to achieve its distributional goals.

From (8) and (10), aggregate incomes of workers and capitalists are as in (11):

$$I^{\mathrm{A}w} = w^{\mathrm{A}}L + \delta t^{\mathrm{A}} p_x^{\mathrm{B}} D^{\mathrm{AB}} + \delta \tau^{\mathrm{A}} \left[p_x^{\mathrm{A}} (D^{\mathrm{BA}} + D^{\mathrm{CA}}) - p_x^{\mathrm{B}} D^{\mathrm{AB}} \right];$$

$$I^{\mathrm{A}k} = (p_x^{\mathrm{A}}/\sigma) X^{\mathrm{A}} + (1-\delta) t^{\mathrm{A}} p_x^{\mathrm{B}} D^{\mathrm{AB}} + (1-\delta)\tau^{\mathrm{A}} \times \left[p_x^{\mathrm{A}} (D^{\mathrm{BA}} + D^{\mathrm{CA}}) - p_x^{\mathrm{B}} D^{\mathrm{AB}} \right]. \tag{11}$$

Incomes of the representative worker and capitalist are $I^{\mathrm{A}w}/L$ and $I^{\mathrm{A}k}/K$ respectively.

In the absence of a CU, the government chooses its external tariffs to maximize $V^{\mathrm{A}}(q_y^{\mathrm{A}}, Q^{\mathrm{A}}, (I^{\mathrm{A}}/N))$, where I^{A} is country A's total income, $I^{\mathrm{A}} = I^{\mathrm{A}w} + I^{\mathrm{A}k}$, taking the other countries' tariffs as given.[11] Consider first the choice of t^{A}, A's tariff on varieties of X imported from B. An increase will have no consequences for wages in any country, so long as Y is produced, no effects on the price of Y in any country and will also leave all foreign demands for A's varieties of X unaffected. But, as A's consumers must pay a higher price for B's varieties, there will be substitution away from the latter into both consumption of Y and of A's own varieties of X. From (10) and (11),

$$\frac{\partial (I^{\mathrm{A}}/N)}{\partial t^{\mathrm{A}}} = \left(\frac{\partial I^{\mathrm{A}}}{\partial t^{\mathrm{A}}} \right) \Big/ N = \left(\frac{p_x^{\mathrm{A}}}{\sigma} \frac{\partial D^{\mathrm{AA}}}{\partial t^{\mathrm{A}}} + p_x^{\mathrm{B}} D^{\mathrm{AB}} + (t^{\mathrm{A}} - \tau^{\mathrm{A}}) p_x^{\mathrm{B}} \frac{\partial D^{\mathrm{AB}}}{\partial t^{\mathrm{A}}} \right) \Big/ N. \tag{12}$$

Let λ^{A} denote the marginal utility of income. By Roy's identity and because q_y^{A} is unaffected by a change in t^{A} alone:

$$\frac{\partial V^{\mathrm{A}}}{\partial t^{\mathrm{A}}} = \frac{\lambda^{\mathrm{A}}}{N} \left(\frac{\partial I^{\mathrm{A}}}{\partial t^{\mathrm{A}}} - D^{\mathrm{A}} \frac{\partial Q^{\mathrm{A}}}{\partial t^{\mathrm{A}}} \right), \quad \text{where} \quad \lambda^{\mathrm{A}} = \frac{\partial V^{\mathrm{A}}}{\partial I^{\mathrm{A}}}. \tag{13}$$

Let s^{ij} denote the ratio of expenditure in country $i = \mathrm{A, B, C}$ on varieties of X from $j = \mathrm{A, B}$ to total expenditure in i on X so $s^{i\mathrm{A}} + s^{i\mathrm{B}} = 1 (i = \mathrm{A, B, C})$. Also, let $\phi^{\mathrm{A}} = \sigma s^{\mathrm{AA}} + \varepsilon s^{\mathrm{AB}}, \phi^{\mathrm{B}} = \sigma s^{\mathrm{BB}} + \varepsilon s^{\mathrm{BA}}$, and $\phi^{\mathrm{C}} = \sigma s^{\mathrm{CA}} + \varepsilon s^{\mathrm{CB}}$. Given that $\sigma > \varepsilon > 1, \sigma > \phi^i > \varepsilon$ and

[11] The indirect utility function depends upon the prices of varieties of X, q_x^{A}, only through the aggregate Q^{A}, as can be seen from the solution to the consumer's problem.

$\phi^i > 1 (i = \mathrm{A, B, C})$. Further, as A and B are identical, in equilibrium $s^{\mathrm{CA}} = s^{\mathrm{CB}} = 1/2$. Differentiation of the price index in A, Q^{A}, and of A's variety demands, D^{AA} and D^{AB}, then gives[12]:

$$\begin{aligned}\partial V^{\mathrm{A}}/\partial t^{\mathrm{A}} &= (\lambda^A/N)(p_x/(1+t^A)) \\ &\quad \times (((\sigma-\varepsilon)/\sigma)s^{\mathrm{AA}}D^{\mathrm{AA}} + \phi^{\mathrm{A}}(\tau^{\mathrm{A}} - t^{\mathrm{A}})D^{\mathrm{AB}}), \quad (14)\end{aligned}$$

where $p_x^{\mathrm{A}} = p_x^{\mathrm{B}} \equiv p_x$. As A and B are identical, both countries set identical tariffs in equilibrium and, therefore, face the same prices. Further, $s^{\mathrm{AB}} = s^{\mathrm{BA}}$, so $\phi^{\mathrm{A}} = \phi^{\mathrm{B}} \equiv \phi$. The right-hand side of (14) is positive at $t^{\mathrm{A}} = 0$ (as $\sigma > \varepsilon$) and decreasing in t^{A}. So we will observe a positive tariff on X, in the absence of any preferential trading agreement. Setting (14) to zero gives the optimal UTS tariff in this case,

$$\text{“Efficiency”}\ t^{\mathrm{UTS}} = \tau^{\mathrm{UTS}} + (\sigma - \varepsilon)s^{\mathrm{AB}}D^{\mathrm{AA}}/\sigma\phi D^{\mathrm{AB}} > \tau^{\mathrm{UTS}}. \quad (15)$$

Turning to τ^{A}, a tariff on Y raises not only the consumers' price of Y in A but also the wage, w^{A}, and the producers' and consumers' price of A's varieties of X. On the other hand, it does not affect the consumers' price of B's varieties of X. Therefore, a tariff on Y in A induces a consumption shift away from A's varieties of X and into B's varieties of X. It also increases the workers' real wage. Proceeding as with the tariff on X, one can derive (16):

$$\begin{aligned}\partial V^{\mathrm{A}}/\partial \tau^{\mathrm{A}} &= (\lambda^{\mathrm{A}}/N)\left[-((\sigma-\varepsilon)s^{\mathrm{AB}}/\sigma)D^{\mathrm{AA}}\right. \\ &\quad + ((1-(\phi/\sigma)) - (2\phi - 1)\tau^{\mathrm{A}} + t^{\mathrm{A}}\phi)D^{\mathrm{BA}} \\ &\quad \left. + ((1-(\phi^{\mathrm{C}}/\sigma)) - (\phi^{\mathrm{C}} - 1)\tau^{\mathrm{A}})D^{\mathrm{CA}}\right]. \quad (16)\end{aligned}$$

We can now substitute in (16) for the optimal tariff on X, from (15), and solve for the optimal unilateral tariff on Y in the “efficiency case”:

$$\text{“Efficiency”}\ \tau^{\mathrm{UTS}} = \frac{((\sigma - \phi^{\mathrm{C}})D^{\mathrm{CA}} + (\sigma - \phi)D^{\mathrm{BA}})}{\sigma((\phi^{\mathrm{C}} - 1)D^{\mathrm{CA}} + (\phi - 1)D^{\mathrm{BA}})}. \quad (17)$$

[12]These and all other derivations of the paper are available on request.

Equations (15) and (17) imply that in the "efficiency" UTS case the governments of A and B would choose to set positive tariffs on both goods with the tariff on the differentiated good being the higher. As in Helpman and Krugman (1989), the tax on imports of X shifts domestic demand out of foreign X varieties into both Y and domestic varieties of X and is beneficial as the latter effect increases the rents of that sector.[13] However, we also observe a tariff on imports of Y here, imposed for terms-of-trade reasons but of an odd sort: the tariff increases domestic costs and thus the export price in this imperfectly competitive setting.[14]

We now move to the case in which A and B set their tariffs jointly. While we refer to this as a CU throughout the paper, in some settings it may not be optimal to set intra-union tariffs to zero, as is implied by a CU; we are really considering an optimal preferential trading arrangement with internal tariffs set optimally.

To analyze a symmetric equilibrium of the CU, we have to consider the impact of a joint increase in $\tau(\tau^{\mathrm{A}} = \tau^{\mathrm{B}} = \tau_y)$ or in t $(t^{\mathrm{A}} = t^{\mathrm{B}} = t)$. Consider first the choice of t. The effect on welfare in A of an increase in t is the sum of the effect of an increase in t^{A} and the effect of an increase in t^{B}. The former is given in (14). An increase in t^{B} reduces the demand in B for A's varieties of X, D^{BA}, and with it the production of X in A, X^{A}, and the aggregate income of A, I^{A}. On the other hand, it does not modify consumers' prices in A. One can then show that

$$\begin{aligned}\partial V^{\mathrm{A}}/\partial t^{\mathrm{B}} &= (\lambda^{\mathrm{A}}/N)(\partial I^{\mathrm{A}}/\partial t^{\mathrm{B}}) \\ &= -(\lambda^{\mathrm{A}}/N)(p_x(\sigma^{-1} + \tau^{\mathrm{A}})\phi^{\mathrm{B}} D^{\mathrm{BA}}/(1+t)). \qquad (18)\end{aligned}$$

[13]This is also why the tariff on X exceeds that on Y: if both goods were taxed at the same rate, relative prices in A would be unchanged, as the tariff on Y raises both q_y^{A} and p_x^{A} by the same proportion.

[14]The tariff on Y raises the price of domestic varieties of X in country C versus those of country B and thus leads to decreased sales. However, this negative effect on rents is more than offset by increased tariff revenues, so rents *plus* tariff revenues rise for a small tariff.

From (14) and (18) the effect on V^{A} of a joint increase in t is given by

$$(\partial V^{\mathrm{A}}/\partial t^{\mathrm{A}}) + (\partial V^{\mathrm{A}}/\partial t^{\mathrm{B}}) = \lambda^{\mathrm{A}} p_x \left\{(\sigma - \varepsilon) s^{\mathrm{AB}} D^{\mathrm{AA}} - \phi(1+\sigma t) D^{\mathrm{BA}}\right\} / N\sigma(1+t). \quad (19)$$

This expression is negative at $t = 0$: if neither partner taxes imports of X then all varieties have the same price (as the tariff on Y is chosen jointly and applies in both A and B) so $D^{\mathrm{AA}} = D^{\mathrm{AB}}, s^{\mathrm{AB}} = 1/2, \phi = (\sigma + \varepsilon)/2$ and the bracketed term in (18) becomes $-\varepsilon D^{\mathrm{AA}}$. Intuitively, the CU would like to increase production of X to generate increased rents and this requires an increase in demand for X, i.e., a reduction in its relative price, not an increase through an import tax. In the absence of import subsidies, a joint internal tariff of zero is indeed optimal — the CU is the optimal form of preferential trading arrangement. In sum:

$$\text{“Efficiency” } t^{\mathrm{CU}} = 0. \quad (20)$$

We turn to the choice of the joint external tariff, τ. An increase in τ^{B} will affect I^{A} by raising the price of B's varieties, p_x^{B}, decreasing A's demand for those varieties, D^{AB}, increasing A's demand for its own varieties, D^{AA}, and thus increasing output of X in A, X^{A}. Furthermore, the fall in the relative price of A's varieties of X in country B also stimulates B's demand for those varieties, D^{BA}. Calculating as above,

$$\text{“Efficiency” } \tau^{\mathrm{CU}} = (\sigma - \varepsilon)/\sigma(\varepsilon - 1). \quad (21)$$

The last step in the analysis of the “efficiency” case is to compare the unilateral tariff on Y, τ^{UTS}, and the CU external tariff, τ^{CU}. Comparing (21) to (17),

$$\begin{aligned}
&\tau^{\mathrm{CU}} > \tau^{\mathrm{UTS}} \\
&\Leftrightarrow (\sigma - \varepsilon)\left[(\phi^{\mathrm{C}} - 1)D^{\mathrm{CA}} + (\phi - 1)D^{\mathrm{BA}}\right] \\
&\quad > (\varepsilon - 1)\left[(\sigma - \phi^{\mathrm{C}})D^{\mathrm{CA}} + (\sigma - \phi)D^{\mathrm{BA}}\right] \\
&\Leftrightarrow (\sigma - 1)\left[(\phi^{\mathrm{C}} - \varepsilon)D^{\mathrm{CA}} + (\phi - \varepsilon)D^{\mathrm{BA}}\right] > 0.
\end{aligned}$$

But this last condition is true. Thus the external tariff faced by the nonmember increases when the CU is formed.

In the "efficiency" case, a CU between A and B would choose free trade in varieties of X and impose a higher tariff on imports of Y than before the union. In the unilateral tariff-setting (UTS) context, the tariff on X is used to switch domestic demand away from the partner's varieties to domestic varieties, *given* the partner's tariff. While this imposes the usual consumption loss on domestic consumers, it is offset by the increased rents in the domestic X sector. Of course, the partner does the same thing — as A switches its own consumers into its own varieties so B switches its consumers *away* from A's varieties — and the net effect, symmetrically, is a decrease in demand and production of X in both countries as substitution into consumption of Y occurs. When the tariff is set jointly this wasteful competition is recognized and avoided, which explains why the intra-CU tariff falls to zero.[15] The tariff on Y, however, is increased. In the UTS case, an increased tariff by A alone, which raises A's production costs, makes its varieties less competitive in C compared to B's varieties. This, in turn, lowers the monopolistic rents A collects from C. When the tariffs are set jointly this effect is absent — both countries' export prices rise — and a higher tariff can be levied on imports from C. Turning the argument around, when A sets a unilateral tariff on Y it exerts a positive externality on B by raising the demand for B's varieties of X. This externality is taken into account when tariffs are set jointly but not when they are set unilaterally.

"Political Economy" Motives for Tariffs: the Case of Workers

For the remainder of the paper, we turn to what we consider to be a more realistic scenario for the determination of tariffs, one in which they are motivated by income-distribution considerations. The Long and Vousden (1991) framework we use is an optimal tax problem with an explicit social welfare function and severely restricted instruments: no lump-sum transfers are permissible, no domestic taxes or subsidies are available and, in our setting, only trade taxes are used. First we

[15]It should be noted that the solution for τ^{CU} does not depend on τ^{CU}, so setting the latter to zero (rather than the optimal *negative* level) does not affect our central result of interest: $\tau^{CU} > \tau^{UTS}$.

consider the extreme case in which only workers are considered in the government's objective function: $\gamma = 1$ in equation (3). This is equivalent to workers themselves setting tariffs.

The exercise proceeds in much the same fashion as in the previous section except that we are now concerned solely with the income of a typical worker. As before, we do the analysis for country A. Equation (11) gives aggregate income for workers; the typical individual earns a share $(1/L)$ of this. Workers also receive a fraction δ of tariff revenues. Proceeding as before yields the following expressions in the UTS case:

"Worker"

$$t^{\mathrm{UTS}} = \max\{0; (\delta(1+\phi\tau) - l)/(l + \delta(\phi - 1))\}; \tag{22}$$

"Worker"

$$\tau^{\mathrm{UTS}} = \begin{cases} \dfrac{((l/\delta)D^{\mathrm{BA}}) + D^{\mathrm{CA}}}{((2\phi - 1)D^{\mathrm{BA}} + (\phi^{\mathrm{C}} - 1)D^{\mathrm{CA}})}, & \text{if } t^{\mathrm{UTS}} = 0; \\ \dfrac{(D^{\mathrm{BA}} + D^{\mathrm{CA}})}{((\phi - 1)D^{\mathrm{BA}} + (\phi^{C} - 1)D^{\mathrm{CA}})} & \text{otherwise.} \end{cases} \tag{23}$$

Consider first the extreme case where workers get no tariff revenues so $\delta = 0$. While this case might seem odd given that tariffs are set to favor only workers, we think it is perhaps the most relevant of all the specifications considered in the paper. This case highlights the effects of tariffs on workers' incomes that are brought about through price changes rather than through direct income transfers. The notion that interest groups agitate for protection in order to generate tariff revenues for themselves seems far-fetched and this case isolates the more likely motivation for tariff seeking: protection of real incomes through changes in relative prices.

In this case, workers would choose, unilaterally, no tariff on X and a tariff on Y as high as possible.[16] The reason is that a tax on X serves no purpose when workers get none of the revenues, merely

[16]The expression for τ^{UTS} tends to infinity as δ tends to zero but as both A and B increase the tariff on Y symmetrically, even though trade with C will continue, we may hit a constraint in that home capitalist's incomes fall too low to purchase any X.

raising the consumption price; but a tariff on Y raises workers' real income: it raises the nominal wage and the prices of A's varieties of X and of Y all by the same percentage whilst leaving the price of B's varieties of X unaffected. (In equilibrium, of course, this strategy is ineffective as workers in B do the same thing but nevertheless the logic of the Nash equilibrium dictates this course.)

At the other extreme, if workers receive all tariff revenues, they will choose some positive tariff on each good. In this case they trade off the income gains of a higher tariff on Y against the transfer from capitalists they can effect through the tariff revenues they receive. Finally, if $\delta = l$ then a positive and equal tariff is set on each good. In this case there is no income-shifting effect and tariffs are set so that all relative prices are unchanged but tariff revenue is raised (on imports of both X and Y.)

When a CU is formed, the futility of attempts to increase real income through raising the tariff on Y is recognized and, as workers are unconcerned about the levels of rents generated in the X sector, the two countries simply set a tariff on Y that maximizes tariff revenues from C.[17] In the CU case we get, independent of δ,

$$\text{“Worker”}\ \tau^{\text{CU}} = 1/(\varepsilon - 1), \tag{24}$$

which is, indeed, the revenue-maximizing tariff against C. Finally,

$$\text{“Worker”}\ t^{\text{CU}} = \max\{0; (\delta - l)/(l + \delta(\phi - 1))\}. \tag{25}$$

The tariff on X is less than $1/(\phi - 1)$ and tends towards that value when workers get all tariff revenues and l tends to 0. Since $\phi > \varepsilon > 1$, the tariff on X is less than that on Y.

A comparison of (23) and (24) shows that when workers receive a small share of tariff revenues and the government only cares about

[17]In the limit, of course, if $\delta = 0$ and workers get no tariff revenues at all, then they are indifferent about the external tariff. It seems reasonable in that case to suppose that it will then be set to benefit capitalists and the same formula will follow. This could be formalized through government preferences lexicographic in workers' and then capitalists' welfare, and it seems unobjectionable. It should be stressed, also, that "national welfare" in this case is simply that of workers so the equivalence of the welfare-maximizing and revenue-maximizing tariffs should be read in this light.

workers, the common external tariff (CET) on Y *falls* when the CU is formed. The UTS equilibrium is plagued by each country's workers' futile attempts to raise their real wages at the expense of both capitalists and foreign workers (since a tariff on Y in A increases the price of A's goods in B). This negative externality between workers in the two countries is taken into account in a CU but not in the UTS case. When the CU is formed this competition to drive up real wages stops and the tariff is set jointly to maximize revenues.

When workers get a large share of tariff revenues (and when $\delta = l$), the CET on Y increases while the intra-CU tariff on X decreases. In this case, the results are similar to the "efficiency" case.

"Political Economy" Motives for Tariffs: the Case of Capitalists

We now summarize the other extreme in terms of policy-making: the case of $\gamma = 0$ in (3), which is equivalent to policies being chosen by the representative capitalist. We proceed as in the previous section except that income is now a fraction $(1/K)$ of I^{Ak} as defined in (11) and that capitalists receive a fraction $(1 - \delta)$ of tariff revenues. As this case yields rather messy expressions, we report only the extreme case of $\delta = 1$ where workers get all the tariff revenues;[18] the results of the other cases of $\delta = 0$ and $\delta = l$ are reported in Table 1 in the Conclusion. As before, we compute the optimal UTS tariffs first and the optimal CU tariffs second and finally we compare the two. Starting with the differentiated good, if l, the proportion of workers in the population, is less than some critical level the UTS tariff on X will be zero; otherwise it will be positive. In most economies, one might consider the latter case more relevant, as capital ownership is often concentrated in the hands of relatively few people. The reason for this tariff is, as in the "efficiency" case, to shift demand out of foreign varieties of X into domestic varieties in order to increase

[18] Again, we feel that this is of practical interest as it focuses on tariffs as redistributive tools via their effects on prices rather than through revenue transfers.

Table 1. Tariff-setting results

Tariff setters	Workers' tariff revenue share (δ)	UTS outcomes	CU outcomes	UTS and CU comparison of external tariff
"Efficiency"	—	$t > \tau > 0$[a]	$t = 0$	$\tau^{\mathrm{CU}} > \tau^{\mathrm{UTS}}$
	—		$\tau = \dfrac{\sigma - \varepsilon}{\sigma(\varepsilon - 1)}$	
Workers	$\delta = 0$	$t = 0$	$t = 0$	$\tau^{\mathrm{CU}} > \tau^{\mathrm{UTS}}$
($\gamma = 0$)		$\tau \to \infty$	$\tau = \dfrac{1}{\varepsilon - 1}$	
	$\delta = l$	$t = \tau > 0$	$t = 0$	$\tau^{\mathrm{CU}} > \tau^{\mathrm{UTS}}$
			$\tau = 1/(\varepsilon - 1)$	
			$t = \dfrac{1 - l}{l + (\phi - 1)} < \tau^{\mathrm{CU}}$	
	$\delta = 1$	$t > \tau > 0$	$\tau = 1/(\varepsilon - 1)$	$\tau^{\mathrm{CU}} > \tau^{\mathrm{UTS}}$
Capitalists	$\delta = 0$	$t > \tau > 0$	$t = 0$ if l "low"	$\tau^{\mathrm{CU}} > \tau^{\mathrm{UTS}}$
($\gamma = 1$)			$\tau = \dfrac{\sigma - \varepsilon}{\sigma(\varepsilon - 1)}$	
			$t = \dfrac{(\sigma - \varepsilon)s^{\mathrm{AB}}D^{\mathrm{AA}}}{(1 + \sigma(1 - \delta))D^{\mathrm{ba}}}$	
	$\delta = l$	$t > \tau \geq 0$	$\tau = \dfrac{1}{\sigma(1 - \delta)} \dfrac{(1 - \delta)\sigma - \varepsilon}{\varepsilon - 1}$	$\tau^{\mathrm{CU}} > \tau^{\mathrm{UTS}}$
		$t = 0$ if l "low"	$t = 0$	
	$\delta = 1$	$\tau = 0$	$\tau = 0$	$\tau^{\mathrm{CU}} = \tau^{\mathrm{UTS}} = 0$

[a] t, tariff on good X; τ, tariff on good Y.

capitalists' rents:

$$\underset{\delta = 1}{\text{“Capitalist”}} \quad t^{\mathrm{UTS}} \begin{cases} 0 & \text{if } l \leq l^*, \\ \dfrac{((\sigma - \epsilon)S^{\mathrm{AB}}D^{\mathrm{AA}} - \sigma(1 - l)D^{\mathrm{AB}})}{(\sigma(1 - l)D^{\mathrm{AB}})} & \text{if } l > l^*, \end{cases}$$

$$\text{where } l^* = \frac{(\sigma + \varepsilon)}{2\alpha}; \tag{26}$$

A's capitalists desire a unilateral tariff on X if workers are a sufficiently large fraction of the population: then the consumption loss of such a tariff is borne mainly by workers, whereas the increased rents stimulated by the substitution into domestic varieties of X accrue solely to capitalists. Turning to Y, when A's capitalists derive no share of tariff revenues, a unilateral tariff increase on Y is completely undesirable: it raises their costs, makes them less competitive in B and C *vis à vis* their foreign competitors from B, and lowers their rents.

$$\underset{\delta=1}{\text{“Capitalist”}} \quad \tau^{\text{UTS}} = 0. \tag{27}$$

Regarding the setting of joint tariffs, we obtain:

$$\underset{\delta=1}{\text{“Capitalist”}} \quad t^{\text{CU}} = \tau^{\text{CU}} = 0. \tag{28}$$

In this situation, where the government cares only for capitalists although they do not get any tariff revenue, the external tariff, τ, is always zero. A joint tariff on Y is undesirable because it increases the price of all varieties in C, thus decreasing demand in C and rents at home. Any tariff on X is also undesirable as it reduces sales and thus rents. The formation of a CU simply leads to the removal of a harmful internal barrier between A and B. This outcome highlights the role of tariff revenues in motivating a positive CET in the "efficiency" case earlier. In both cases, an increase in τ raises the cost and the price of X. Since the elasticity of demand for one variety of X with respect to a price increase of all varieties of X is greater than 1, this lowers the rents of domestic capitalists. However, in the efficiency case, this adverse effect on rents of a tariff on Y is compensated by the collection of tariff revenues.

4. Summary and Conclusion

In a model of intra-industry trade in which tariffs are determined by interest groups (workers or capitalists), we have considered the formation of a preferential trading arrangement and its effects on both internal and external tariffs, contrasting these effects to those of a purely efficiency-motivated policymaker. We have considered alternative allocations of tariff revenues to one group or the other and have derived three broad results, showing that in the presence of imperfect competition, tariff coordination in a CU is desirable in order to lower excessive competition for monopolistic rents in third countries, and that the consequences of CU formation for non-members depend on the nature of the groups that hold power in the CU members.

Table One summarizes our results. First, we have shown that the optimal preferential trading arrangement is indeed a CU (internal tariffs of zero) except when (1) workers set tariffs and receive all tariff revenues, or (2) capitalists set tariffs, receive all the revenues and are a relatively small group in the entire population. In these cases, an internal tariff remains to shift income to the policy-making group.

Second, in the unilateral tariff-setting equilibrium we observe that the tariff on the monopolistically competitive good is generally set higher than that on the CRS good, except when workers choose the tariffs and receive little of the revenues. This result follows from rent-shifting motives for tariffs in imperfectly competitive settings. Equal tariffs on all imported goods leave relative prices unchanged as the tariff on the CRS good pushes up costs and thus the price of domestic varieties of the differentiated good. It is then desirable to increase the tariff on foreign varieties of the differentiated good further to shift demand towards domestic varieties since production of the latter generates rents at home. The exception to this result is clear: when workers choose the tariff, the generation of rents is of no interest. If, in addition, they do not collect a large share of tariff revenues and so cannot use the tariff on X to transfer income away from capitalists, they lack any incentive to levy such a tariff.

Third, we note that the jointly chosen tariff on the CRS good will generally be *higher* (the "Château d'If" interpretation of Fortress Europe) than when chosen unilaterally except, again, in the case where workers choose the tariffs and receive but a small portion of tariff revenues. The general case of an increased tariff in the CU is due to the fact that a unilateral tariff by one member disadvantages it *vis à vis* the other producer of differentiated products by raising its costs and thus its price. This benefits the other country but, in the context of unilateral tariff setting, this external benefit is not taken into account when tariffs are chosen. In the CU this is considered. This general result is reminiscent of the tariff externality argument in perfectly competitive models of CU formation. It differs from it in the way the tariff operates (i.e., in the nature of the externality between the two tariff-setting nations): it is not by driving down the import price that one country's tariff benefits the other but by making the inactive country's *exports* relatively more competitive. This reasoning fails in the one case because workers do not care about any consequences for rents in the X sector and so care about the tariff on Y only as a means of raising tariff revenue (in both the UTS and CU cases) and of pushing up their real wage. When they receive little or no share of tariff revenues the real wage effect dominates the UTS outcome and their attempts to increase their real incomes drive the tariff exorbitantly high. This hurts the workers in the partner country by increasing the consumers' price of domestic varieties of the differentiated good in foreign markets. Coordination in the CU takes into account this externality and, indeed, removes the real wage effect entirely. This leaves only the revenue effect, which compels the choice of the lower revenue-maximizing tariff: the "Jericho" interpretation of Fortress Europe.

Two avenues for future research seem particularly useful. To more closely model the European example, at least from a U.S. perspective, one would like to allow the production of differentiated products in the third country as well. It would also be useful to consider the case in which workers and capitalists within the differentiated products sector share a common interest. If, as has been suggested by recent work in labor economics, workers in imperfectly competitive industries receive a portion of the rents generated in that sector, then workers and capitalists might not have different aims. This would be a useful extension and is the subject of ongoing research.

References

Corden, W.M. (1984). The normative theory of international trade. In R. W. Jones and P. B. Kenen (eds.), *Handbook of International Economics*, Vol. 1. Amsterdam: North-Holland Publishing Co.

Dixit, A. and V. Norman (1980). *Theory of International Trade.* Cambridge, UK: Cambridge University Press.

Dixit, A. and V. Norman (1986). Gains from trade without lump-sum compensation. *Journal of International Economics*, 21, 111–22.

Ethier, W. and H. Horn (1984). A new look at economic integration. In H. Kierzkowski (ed.), *Monopolistic Competition and International Trade.* Oxford, UK: Clarendon Press.

Gatsios, K. and L. Karp (1991). Delegation games in customs unions. *Review of Economic Studies*, 58, 391–7.

Grossman, G. and E. Helpman (1994). Protection for sale. *American Economic Review*, 84, 833–50.

Helpman, E. and P. Krugman (1989). *Trade Policy and Market Structure.* Cambridge, MA: MIT Press.

Hillman, A. (1989). *The Political Economy of Protection.* Chur, Switzerland: Harwood Academic Publishers.

Kemp, M. and H. Wan, Jr., (1976). An elementary proposition concerning the formation of customs unions. In M. Kemp (ed.), *Three Topics in the Theory of International Trade: Distribution, Welfare and Uncertainty.* Amsterdam: North-Holland.

Kennan, J. and R. Riezman (1990). Optimal tariff equilibria with customs unions. *Canadian Journal of Economics*, 23, 70–83.

Krugman, P. (1992). Regionalism vs. multilateralism: Analytical notes. Paper presented to World Bank and CEPR conference on New Dimensions in Regional Integration, Washington D.C.

Krugman, P. and A. Venables (1990). Integration and the competitiveness of peripheral industry. In C. J. Bliss and J. DeMacedo (eds.), *Unity with Diversity in the European Community: the Community's Southern Frontier.* Cambridge, UK : Cambridge University Press.

Long, N.V. and N. Vousden (1991). Protectionist responses and declining industries. *Journal of International Economics*, 30, 87–103.

McMillan, J. and E. McCann (1981). Welfare effects in customs unions. *Economic Journal*, 91, 697–703.

Part III

Trade and Competition Policy

Chapter 11

Trade and Competition Policies: *Concordia Discors*?

Martin Richardson

Abstract: In a simple model of trade and competition policies we show that the abolition of trade restrictions may lead to governments independently choosing more competitive competition policies. Subsequent co-ordination of competition policy involves encouraging less competitive behaviour than when such policies are not co-ordinated and may involve disharmonisation, in a sense made clear in the paper. Adding a third country, simulation results indicate that non-member concerns about customs union formation may be well-founded, particularly when the union goes beyond mere trade policy co-ordination (which may be needed to make it attractive to members in the first place).

1. Introduction

At the moment we are simply letting European industry be gradually destroyed by the superior power of American corporations... Only a deliberate policy of reinforcing our strong points — what demagogues condemn under the vague term of "monopolies" will allow us to escape relative underdevelopment (Jean-Jacques Servan-Schreiber, 1968, quoted in Scherer, 1994, pp. 64–5.)

[S]ome [enterprises] may attempt to insulate themselves from increased [international] competition through engaging in private anti-competitive practices... The possibility of negotiated trade

Originally published in *Oxford Economic Papers*, 51 (1999), 649–664.

liberalisation being undermined by restrictive business practices has long been recognised (Lloyd and Sampson, 1995, p. 693.)

These observations capture very nicely the idea that "slack" competition policy can achieve the same goals as trade restrictions: what has not been achieved through protection can be achieved through allowing domestic firms to cartelise or concentrate. As trade policy harmonisation (particularly in the form of preferential trading areas[1] (PTAs)) has become increasingly prevalent so has the fear that countries might be more tempted to tolerate non-competitive behaviour through slack national competition policy, with adverse consequences for other countries. In this paper we present a simple model in which trade liberalisation leads countries to adopt too strict a competition policy, even when they do not care about consumers.

The notion that the effects of trade policy co-ordination can be undone by other domestic tax instruments is not new (see, for example, Richardson, 1994) and has led to calls for co-ordination of these other policies as well as co-ordination of trade policies. Recent discussion of harmonisation issues has focused on policy areas such as labour and environmental standards as well as competition policy and, beyond the practical concerns of how harmonisation is defined and might be implemented (see Jacquemin, 1995, and references) this broader issue of whether harmonisation is per se desirable has also received some attention. Thus there are arguments for co-ordination of competition policies put forward, for example, by Scherer (1994). There are also arguments that environmental and labour standards provide exceptions to otherwise accepted principles governing trade, arguments that seem to constitute a potentially serious threat to existing multilateral as well as bilateral trade institutions.

The position suggested in our opening quotes really has two parts to it. First, there is the notion that the loss of trade policy as an instrument for a government will lead it to wish to change its competition policy and, second, that it will lead it to impose weaker

[1]The term "preferential trading area" is intended to capture all trading arrangements in which some form of discriminatory preference is given to certain partners. So it is intended to include not only cases of partial tariff preference but also customs unions and free trade areas in which trade between members is completely unrestricted.

competition policy unless otherwise constrained. The first of these, the idea that domestic competition policy has international consequences (so the variables impacted by trade and competition policies overlap), is surely beyond doubt:

(i) The USA has long argued that Japanese distributional and marketing practices within Japan amount to implicit protection and thus affect American exporters.
(ii) While most countries exempt certain desirable co-operative activities amongst firms from their cartel prohibitions, a domestic producers' cartel will still have consequences for export behaviour and therefore for foreign consumers.
(iii) Vertical restraints within industries (refusal to deal, vertical foreclosure and so on) can have direct consequences for foreign consumers. One of the first competition policy enforcements by the EC, in fact, was to prevent a West German electronics firm from prohibiting its EC distributors from shipping "parallel imports" into other EC nations: an attempt to segment the EC market.

It is on the second strand of the argument — that a country will wish to impose more lax competition policy when trade policy is lost — that the present model differs. We construct a two-country model, which captures competition policy in a simple manner and in which different national attitudes towards tolerance of non-competitive behaviour emerge endogenously. We show that countries may have an incentive to encourage increased domestic competition following the loss of trade policy as an instrument, even if they do not care about consumers. We also show that some degree of co-ordination is in the interests of both members of a PTA, again regardless of how the governments weight the welfare of consumers versus that of producers. Finally, we report some simulation results of a 3-country model to investigate how the introduction of a non-member might change the results of the 2-country analysis.

Regarding existing literature, there are a couple of features of competition policy in practice that suggest why analytical work is thin on the ground here. First, there is a wide variety of items that fall under the general heading of competition policy — everything from product standards laws to merger rules. A model of competition policy, to be useful, needs a simple policy instrument to proxy for the variety of instruments used in practice. Second, Levinsohn (1996) notes the wide divergence across different countries of tolerance of non-competitive behaviour by domestic firms. Whilst it is self-evident that different countries would have different optimal environmental and labour standards (due to different factor endowments, technologies, and so on) it is not so obvious that the optimal degree of competition policy should vary across countries and a successful model of policy harmonisation must capture this feature of reality.

In our model competition policy is captured by the choice of the number of domestic firms competing in an international oligopoly and different governments may have different preferences over the well-being of domestic firms and consumers. The reason this set-up leads to tighter competition policy when trade policy is removed is that each country perceives an increase in domestic firm numbers as a Stackelberg-like commitment to greater output. In equilibrium, of course, both countries think this way and no profit-shifting is achieved but, nevertheless, each country's best interest is served by increasing the numbers of domestic firms. In this sense competition policy acts as a substitute for strategic trade policy, *à la* Brander and Spencer (1984, 1985) and, indeed, we note later that the existence of alternative policy instruments would undermine the use of competition policy in this way.

Our model is close to the existing industrial organisation literature on mergers and divisionalisation as well as the trade theory work in this area. Our structure in which governments can choose the number of firms in a Cournot oligopoly has much in common with Baye *et al.* (1996a) looking at the strategic choice, by parent oligopolists, of the number of independent competing divisions they spawn. However, we look at the choices of two governments in the presence of sales in two countries and with other policy instruments also available and our results, most notably with respect to the optimal number of firms or divisions, are quite different.

In early work in this area Cowan (1989) considers a model where an exporting country can commit to firm numbers prior to a simultaneous trade policy setting stage of a game. He stresses that the shape of the demand curve in the importing country is important in determining optimal trade (and thus competition) policy. Interestingly, the linear version of his model implies, in contrast to our results, that trade policy liberalisation alone would encourage a more lax competition policy in the exporting country as it would then desire monopolisation of its export industry. The reason for the contrast is that in our model the countries are competing over market share and increased sales by one country come at the expense of the other whereas Cowan's exporters have no domestic competition in their export market.

Bliss (1996) considers a model very similar to ours but he uses it for rather different purposes. He also considers the effect of increasing firm numbers in a linear international Cournot oligopoly with increasing returns but his concern is with the level of exports of a country. Our focus is on the welfare consequences of such changes and on whether or not harmonisation in this setting is welfare-improving.

Horn and Levinsohn (1997), in subsequent work, consider merger policy in a general model of trade liberalisation. Their approach is similar to ours although they consider mergers that are marginal-cost reducing as well as the fixed-cost saving ones focussed upon here. Furthermore, they do not consider issues that arise in a preferential trading area setting.

In other related work, Gatsios and Karp (1992) look at the imperfect harmonisation of trade and industrial policies and note the possibility of welfare-reducing PTAs when industrial policy is not also harmonised. In particular, they consider a case in which a subset of countries, each characterised by a single firm, forms a PTA and consequently choose the same level of a policy instrument (a Brander–Spencer export subsidy/tax.) The firms in these countries are then essentially acting as one, merged firm (compared to the pre-union case) and the authors show that aggregate member welfare may fall as a consequence. They note that this result is also similar in spirit to the result that mergers amongst Cournot competitors may be welfare-reducing for the firms involved. (This is another related line of literature: the industrial organisation work on horizontal mergers, perhaps most notably represented by Salant *et al.* (1983) and

Kamien and Zang (1990), and its application to international issues, as in Barros and Cabral (1994) and Long and Vousden (1995). In the context of the model we use here, Salant *et al.* (1983) show that in the absence of fixed costs endogenous mergers between any two firms would not occur except in a duopoly. With a fixed cost saving from mergers, however, endogenous mergers will occur if that cost saving is high enough. Long and Vousden (1995) consider the case of mergers between firms with different cost structures, which also avoids this problem, and they consider how the incentives for such mergers are affected by exogenous changes in tariffs, either unilaterally or bilaterally).

Gatsios and Karp also consider 2- and 3-country versions of this model with an investment stage added and, prior to that, an industrial policy stage in which governments choose (non-cooperatively) investment subsidies/taxes. Their focus is on the strategic incentive that the CU gives to governments to increase subsidies on investment as a means of profit-shifting when the later export subsidy will no longer be chosen by virtue of co-operation on trade policy in the CU. In this respect their paper nicely illustrates a general result that also appears in the present paper (and elsewhere): co-operation in one dimension may be "more than undone" by "cheating" in other dimensions. Our concern here, however, is with the choice, by a government, of the degree of domestic competition and we are interested, amongst other things, in whether trade policy co-ordination induces less competitive behaviour or more.

The following section of the paper presents our two-country model and its results while Section 3 describes the numerical 3-country model and reports the simulation results. A final section summarises and concludes.

2. A two-country model

2.1. *The model*

A successful model of competition policy harmonisation needs at least two features: a simple way to capture competition policy as a government policy instrument and an explanation for why different countries might choose different levels of this instrument. Regarding the second of these, the model presented here assumes that national governments place different weights on the relative well-being of domestic consumers and producers. This approach is hinted at in Levinsohn (1996, p. 348) and in Bliss (1996, p. 318) who discusses the use of trade policy for income distributional goals in the absence of alternative instruments. It is difficult to explain the difference between competition policy in, say, Japan and the US without some reference to political economy (although Scherer (1994, p. 61) suggests that the evolution of tighter US competition policy may be due to the size of the US internal market leading to less concern for scale economy losses from structural fragmentation).

The current paper, like Levinsohn (1996), considers a partial equilibrium model of two countries producing a homogeneous good. However, we suppose that a national government can directly choose the number of domestic firms in the industry and that the industry is characterised by international Cournot competition. Thus competition policy is reflected in the number of domestic firms, which is a policy instrument for the government.[2] While this is a fairly heavy-handed representation of the nuances of competition policy in practice, it is simple and tractable and it does focus on a central element of competition policy — anti-trust control over mergers.

We suppose that there are two countries, A and B, and in each there is an identical inverse demand curve for this homogeneous product, given by (1)

$$p^i = \alpha - \beta(Q^{iA} + Q^{iB}) \tag{1}$$

where p^i is the price in country $i = \mathrm{A, B}$ and Q^{ij} denotes the total quantity sold in i by firms from $j, i, j = \mathrm{A, B}$. Each firm has a fixed cost of production, F,[3] and a constant marginal cost of c and there

[2]It might be objected that harmonisation then is of outcomes (firm numbers) rather than policies (the enforcement of competition law.) However, the debate on the desirability of harmonisation is cast in terms of outcomes and, although the mechanics of implementation is through policy, adjustments are driven by efforts to harmonise outcomes. The focus on firm numbers, then, does not seem inappropriate.

are n^i such firms in country i. Firms sell (potentially) in both markets and each is characterised by Cournot competition. There is no consumer arbitrage. Country i may levy a specific tariff t^i on sales in i by firms from country $j \neq i$.

The problem facing typical firm s in country A is to maximise (2)[4]

$$\pi_s^A = p^A[Q_{-s}^{AA} + q_s^{AA} + Q^{AB}]q_s^{AA} \\ + (p^B[Q^{BB} + Q_{-s}^{BA} + q_s^{BA}] - t^B)q_s^{BA} - c(q_s^{AA} + q_s^{BA}) - F \quad (2)$$

where Q_{-s}^{ij} denotes $\sum_{k \neq s} q_k^{ij} = Q^{ij} - q_s^{ij}$ and lower-case letters denote firm values, so q_s^{ij} denotes sales in country i by firm s from country j. We can use the symmetry of the countries to get expressions for equilibrium prices and sales that depend on the demand and cost parameters and on each country's tariff and firm numbers choices.

National welfare is given by a weighted average of traditional welfare (itself the simple sum of consumers' surplus (CS), aggregate profits ($\prod$), and government revenue (GR)) and aggregate profits accruing to domestic firms. That is

$$W^i = \omega^i(CS^i + \prod^i + GR^i) + (1 - \omega^i)\prod^i \\ = \omega^i(CS^i + GR^i) + \prod^i \quad (3)$$

where $\prod^i = \sum_s \pi_s^i = n^i \pi_s^i$. The parameters ω^A and ω^B can vary between zero and one where $\omega = 0$ indicates that the government cares only about aggregate profits and $\omega = 1$ indicates that the government maximises national welfare as traditionally defined.[5]

---

[3]This fixed cost serves two useful modelling purposes. First, it means the optimal number of firms is finite, regardless of the government's interests. Second, there is no pure strategy equilibrium to the governments' game if this fixed cost is zero.

[4]Throughout this paper, round brackets will denote products while square brackets will contain function arguments. Also, all results are derived in a technical appendix available from the author on request.

[5]We do not allow here for governments that are biased away from the traditional welfare measure in favour of consumers as it is not a case that has received any attention in the political economy literature, the usual presumption being that producer interests dominate. See Hillman (1989) for a survey and Grossman and Helpman (1994) for a model where this bias emerges endogenously from the political process.

Substituting for consumers' surplus, government revenue and aggregate domestic profits into (3), we get (4)

$$W^i = ((\omega^i(\omega - p^i)/2) + p^i - c)Q^{ii} + \omega^i(((\alpha - p^i)/2) + t^i)Q^{ij}$$
$$+ (p^i - t^j - c)Q^{ji} - n^i F \quad (4)$$

The problem facing the government in country i, then, is to maximise W^i by the choice of n^i and t^i, given n^j and t^j. We suppose that the two governments act simultaneously and we are looking for a Nash equilibrium in these four policy instruments. Clearly we must assume that there is not free entry here — with entry profits would be driven to zero and the problem for a government that cares only about profits is empty (and, of course, n^i is not then a choice variable.) We do, however, allow free exit — if the government sets the number of firms and the tariff in such a way that firms make losses, we allow that exit will occur until profits are non-negative.[6] The reason is that the choice of n^i is a modelling proxy for competition policy rather than a variable that is actually fixed by the government: it can permit entry but not force it. The results of Salant *et al.* (1983) indicate that mergers might not occur in our model, if fixed costs are low, unless they are forced by the government. This might seem rather extreme but, as Bliss (1996, pp. 319–20) notes, "[g]overnments have sometimes adopted the... policy [of] encouraging firms to merge and even subsidizing mergers" and our presumption is that governments can either force mergers or force exit. A final point is that n^i is, in practice, an integer. We ignore this constraint in order to characterise optima by equalities and to make reaction functions smooth so as to minimise the problem of multiple equilibria.[7]

We shall consider two general cases. First we provide a brief discussion of the unilateral tariff-setting case in which there are no restrictions on trade policy before turning to the case of bilateral

[6] Profits are non-negative in all the equilibria that follow: see the technical appendix available from the author on request.

[7] When the integer constraint is recognised, reaction functions in n^A/n^B space become broad step functions and many equilibria occur, even when the non-integer problem yields a unique solution. Note also that Baye *et al.* (1996b) demonstrate that, in their model, analysis of the continuous case, "reasonably approximates the equilibria of the discrete game."

liberalisation in which both tariffs must be set to zero. We refer to three general parameterisations for the governments: one in which both governments care only about their firms ($\omega^A = \omega^B = 0$), one in which they are both traditional governments ($\omega^A = \omega^B = 1$), and one in which one country (A) cares about welfare and the other cares only about its producers ($\omega^A = 1, \omega^B = 0$).

2.2. *The unilateral tariff setting case*

From the firms' first-order conditions we can rewrite (4) in terms of each government's choice variables, n^i and t^i, and choose these to maximise W^i, given the values of n^j and t^j. Where both governments care only about their firms' profits we can show, unsurprisingly, that both want a prohibitive tariff. Consequently, each chooses a small number of firms (less than one, in fact, unless there is no fixed cost or we respect the integer constraint.) Where both governments care equally about consumers' surplus, domestic firms' profits and government revenue (that is, $\omega^A = \omega^B = 1$ in (4)), they choose a positive — but not prohibitive — tariff. Each sets a competition policy that is more restrictive (i.e. has more firms) than in the previous case.

2.3. *The bilateral liberalisation (BL) case*

Suppose trade restrictions between A and B are abolished.[8] Thus $t^{\mathrm{A}} = t^{\mathrm{B}} = 0$. Competition policy is still chosen independently, however, and we wish to compare the resulting noncooperative outcome with cases of competition policy harmonisation.

[8]Neil Vousden has noted that ideally the decision to liberalise should be endogenised and, in a richer version of this model, might come about through an exogenous change in the weights in the government's objective function (through a change in government, perhaps). Such an exercise would then presumably have consequences for the optimal choice of competition policy. Here we have simply assumed that any internal liberalisation is complete, perhaps because of GATT Article XXIV restrictions, but in a richer analysis we might not expect this: if we were to think of liberalisation as a two-stage game in which negotiable instruments (tariffs) are set co-operatively prior to the noncooperative setting of competition policy *à la* Copeland (1990) then we might also anticipate non-zero internal tariffs in some cases as a constraint on subsequent competition policy.

With no trade restrictions the price of this good is given by (5) where $n^T \equiv n^{\mathrm{A}} + n^{\mathrm{B}} =$ the total number of firms

$$p^A = p^B = \frac{\alpha + n^T c}{1 + n^T} \tag{5}$$

As government revenue is zero in the BL case, we can rewrite W^i, substituting in for p and the (appropriately modified) expressions for equilibrium sales

$$W^i = \frac{(\alpha - c)^2}{\beta(1 + n^T)^2}(2n^i + (\omega^i(n^T)^2/2)) - n^i F \tag{6}$$

Differentiating with respect to n^i, setting to zero[9] and simplifying yields the following implicit function of n^i in n^j which defines a reaction function for country i

$$(\alpha - c)^2(2 + (2 + \omega^i)n^T - 4n^i) - \beta F(1 + n^T)^3 = 0 \tag{7}$$

Jointly solving (7) for i and j, we can characterise the Nash equilibrium in bilateral free trade by the following two equations

$$(\alpha - c)^2(2 + (2 + \omega^i)n^T - 4n^i) - \beta F(1 + n^T)^3 = 0 \tag{8}$$

$$(\omega^i - \omega^j)n^T = 4(n^i - n^j) \tag{9}$$

From (6) we can show that W^i is declining in n^j if $\omega^i n^T < 4n^i$. This is clearly the case if $\omega^i = 0$ and, from (9), if $\omega^1 = l$. Finally, if $\omega^i = \omega j = 1$ then $n^i = n^1$ so, again, this condition is satisfied. At the Nash equilibrium, then, each country's welfare is declining in the number of the other country's firms[10]: each would prefer that the other had fewer firms (i.e. less restrictive competition policy.)

Figure 1 illustrates a generic equilibrium for this model. The reaction function for country $i = \mathrm{A}, \mathrm{B}$ is denoted RF^i and the subscript indicates the value of w^i i.e. the weight placed on "traditional" welfare by the relevant government.

Take the case where A cares equally about surplus, profits and revenue but B cares only for domestic profits: the relevant reaction

---

[9]The second order conditions for a maximum are satisfied in this problem.

[10]Note that this is not true everywhere: domestic welfare is not monotonically declining in the number of foreign firms (see Dixit, 1984).

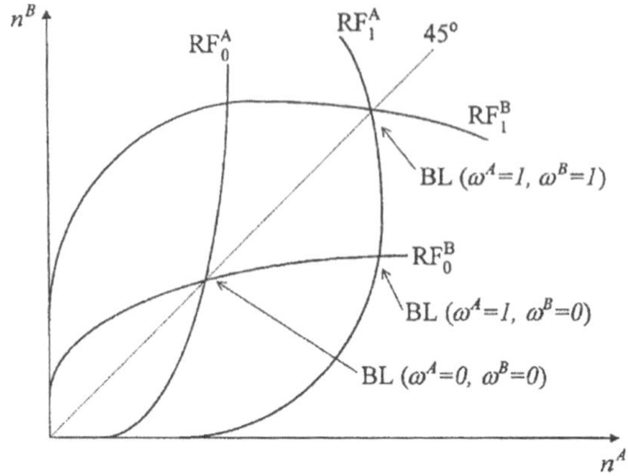

Fig. 1. Bilateral liberalisation (BL) equilibria in the 2-country case

functions are RF_1^A for country A and RF_0^B for country B.[11] Country A then chooses a more restrictive competition policy (a higher number of firms) than does country B but both would benefit from a mutual loosening of policy (a reduction in the number of firms).

Comparison of this outcome with the unilateral tariff setting solution indicates that BL may lead both countries to pursue tighter competition policies; that is, the number of firms in each country increases following the trade liberalisation. This depends on the magnitude of the fixed cost and occurs only when F is large.[12] This outcome is in contrast to the notion that the loss of trade restrictions can be compensated for by permitting increased domestic monopolisation. The explanation for this is postponed until we have considered the following symmetric case.

Suppose that both countries care only about the profits of their domestic firms. The appropriate reaction functions in Fig. 1 are those with 0 subscripts. By symmetry, $n^A = n^B \equiv n$ and we can solve (8)

[11]As mentioned earlier, the Nash equilibrium of this game tends to the competitive solution ($n = \infty$) as F tends to zero. If $F = 0$, the reaction function for A given in (7) would imply $n^A = 3n^B + 2$ while that for B in (7) would imply $n^B = n^A + 1$. These do not cross in the positive quadrant.

[12]When F is small and the unilateral tariff setting equilibrium is characterised by many firms, BL leads to a reduction in firm numbers in both countries.

for the Nash equilibrium

$$n = \left(\sqrt[3]{\frac{2(\alpha - c)^2}{\beta F}} - 1\right)\Big/2 \tag{10}$$

It can be shown here that the number of firms increases with bilateral free trade.

Why is this? Even though countries care only about domestic firms' profits, bilateral liberalisation means that it is impossible to keep foreign firms out of the domestic market. Accordingly, governments try to increase their own firms' share of profits being earned in the two markets by increasing the number of firms beyond the level that maximises total profits — given the number of foreign firms, this increases total domestic profits even though industry profits fall.

Note that the existence of alternative policy instruments would undermine the use of competition policy here. In particular, if the governments have access to production subsidies they would choose a single domestic firm and compete for market share in the subsidy dimension rather than incurring the additional fixed costs associated with encouraging entry. In this regard competition policy in our model is acting as a substitute for strategic trade policy.[13] This also highlights the significance of the Cournot assumption in this analysis. If there were strategic complementarity in the product market (e.g. imperfect substitute Bertrand) then additional entry would typically lead to lower profits as price leadership typically involves increasing price which requires less entry.

Another perspective on our results comes from the divisionalisation literature in industrial organisation. Baye *et al.* (1996a) show that Cournot parent companies have incentives to create

[13]I am grateful to a referee for this observation. We cannot say here that trade and competition policies are substitutes in the sense of strategic substitutability, however. The latter is characterised by the slope of a reaction function of the governments' strategic variables and there are no monotonic results on that in this setting. However, we can show that when governments are profit-maximisers an increase in t^i will lead to an increase in n^i, given n^j and t^j, around the symmetric Nash equilibrium. So, in this setting at least, a country's reaction function in n space will shift in if its tariff falls i.e. t^i and n^i are (locally) strategic complements. Thus restrictive trade policy (higher t^i) and slack competition policy (lower n^i) are here not substitutes in this sense.

independent, competing divisions in a two-stage game even though it reduces parent profits in equilibrium, as each perceives a possible Stackelberg-like commitment to greater output. This is what we are observing here (indeed, (10) is isomorphic to Eq. (7) in Baye *et al.* for a duopoly.)

It is also the case that both governments are worse off following the trade liberalisation than before. This follows from noting that total profits in a single country's protected market are concave in the number of firms. Thus total profits are higher for a given, small number of firms in a single, protected market than when two such markets are shared. That is, abolishing tariffs with no change in each country's firm numbers would reduce profits for both countries. In fact, firm numbers increase with a bilateral liberalisation which lowers profits even further.

One final case to consider is where both countries value surplus, profits and revenue equally. The appropriate reaction functions in Fig. 1 are those with 1 subscripts. By symmetry, $n^A = n^B \equiv n$ and we can solve (8) for the Nash equilibrium

$$(1+2n)^3 = (1+n)\frac{2(\alpha - c)^2}{\beta F} \tag{11}$$

In comparison to the unilateral tariff setting case, the number of firms will rise here too as bilateral liberalisation proceeds if F is sufficiently high that the initial number of firms is below some critical value. Otherwise trade liberalisation leads to a decrease in firm numbers. The intuition is that when governments care about welfare generally, they do not impose a prohibitive tariff but, rather, permit foreign sales domestically. Accordingly the incentive to encourage over-entry is present before trade liberalisation for the same reasons as it is present in the absence of trade restrictions. When F is low, however, the Nash equilibrium involves both countries choosing a large number of firms and also levying a tariff, which aids in profit-shifting.[14] When the tariff is lost the Stackelberg commitment incentive is decreased, in the Nash equilibrium, as no tariff revenue is gained from foreign firms.

[14]Note that greater numbers of domestic firms in the Nash equilibrium correspond to greater numbers of foreign firms too and thus greater revenue, *ceteris paribus*.

One final way to look at this is to note that the price-marginal cost distortion here has two relevant consequences, from the welfare-maximising government's perspective. First, it implies a consumption distortion. Second, it means pure profits exist which provides an incentive to shift them to domestic firms. Given the other country's policies, a tariff exacerbates the former but helps achieve the latter whereas an increase in domestic firm numbers, up to a point depending on the size of the fixed cost, reduces the consumption distortion and shifts profits away from foreign firms. When a tariff is available the worsened consumption distortion increases the marginal incentive to raise firm numbers so the removal of the tariff reduces that incentive. This is the force operating in conflict to the Stackelberg incentive. Comparison with (10) also makes it clear that the equilibrium number of firms here must be greater than in the case where countries care only about domestic profits. This contrasts with the striking result of Baye *et al.*(1996a) that, in a linear Cournot model, optimal divisionalisation in a duopoly gives the socially optimal number of competing units. Our results are rather different because we are essentially considering the decisions of "duopoly" social planners rather than the "monopoly" planners in Baye *et al.*[15]

2.4. *Harmonisation with bilateral liberalisation*

Is harmonisation of competition policy desirable with bilateral free trade? We consider two alternative definitions of harmonisation:

(i) weak: $\triangle n^A$ and $\triangle n^B$ so that $|n^A - n^B|$ falls.
(ii) strong: If $n^i > n^j$ in the BL outcome, $\triangle n^j \leq 0$ and $\triangle n^i \geq 0$ so that $|n^A - n^B|$ falls.

[15]Mike Baye provided this interpretation which is supported by noting that, if the countries were to act jointly, the socially optimal number of firms when $\omega = 1$ (which comes from setting equation (13) equal to zero) is the same as in Baye *et al.* (1996) and is given by the Nash equilibrium solution for when $\omega = 0$ i.e. by expression (10). Note also that allowing divisionalisation in the present model would leave matters unaffected. When $\omega = 0$ the government's choice of n corresponds to the optimal number of independent units from the firms' perspective already and when $\omega = 1$ the government's choice of n exceeds that desired by firms so that thy would have no incentive for further divisionalisation.

So if the BL outcome had $n^A = 2$ and $n^B = 3$, for example, then $n^A = n^B = 6$ would constitute weak harmonisation but not strong which requires that the final outcome chosen by the partner countries is some compromise on their initial stances.

Harmonisation is not an issue where the countries are fully symmetric as their choices are identical, so in these cases we just wish to identify what change in n^A and n^B will be mutually welfare-improving. As noted, the BL outcome has both countries choosing too lax a competition policy from their joint perspective. It is simple to verify that a mutual reduction in the number of firms, at the Nash equilibrium, will raise the profits of both countries and thus perceived (and, in fact, actual) welfare.[16]

The more interesting case here is where the countries' objectives are different so we return to $\omega^A = 1$ and $\omega^B = 0$ in (4). Starting at the BL equilibrium described in (8) and (9), consider $\mathrm{d}n^B = \gamma \mathrm{d}n^A$ for some constant γ. If there exists some $\gamma < 0$ for which (12) holds then strong harmonisation is mutually welfare-improving.[17]

$$\left.\frac{\mathrm{d}W^i}{\mathrm{d}n^A}\right|_{\mathrm{d}n^B=\gamma \mathrm{d}n^A} \leq 0, i = A, B \tag{12}$$

From (6) we can derive conditions under which both $\mathrm{d}W^A$ and $\mathrm{d}W^B$ are non-positive for changes in n^A and n^B such that $\mathrm{d}n^B = \gamma \mathrm{d}n^A$ and, evaluating these conditions at the Nash equilibrium, show that they require $\gamma \geq 0$. That is, mutually welfare-improving co-ordination of competition polices here requires, again, that both countries reduce the number of firms and there is no strong harmonisation that can raise welfare in both countries. Indeed, it is possible that both countries gain if we move in a direction of

[16] A referee has noted that Dixit (1984) shows that mergers under free trade generally have an ambiguous effect on welfare, depending on import shares. The difference here is that we are not evaluating the effect on welfare of a decrease in firm numbers at just any starting point but, rather, at the Nash equilibrium of the governments' competition policy game. That is, when n^A and n^B have been chosen optimally.

[17] As (8) implies that $n^B < n^A$ in equilibrium so our second definition of harmonisation requires that n^A be reduced ($\mathrm{d}n^A \leq 0$) which is why the required sign in (14) is negative. The required sign of γ is also negative because we require the numbers of firms to converge so that a decrease in n^A corresponds to an increase in n^B.

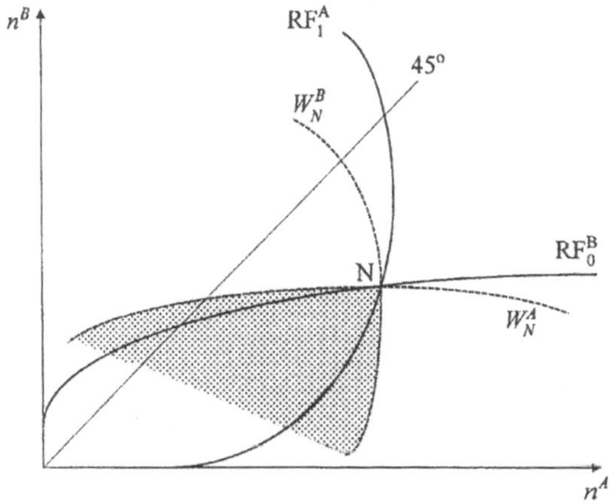

Fig. 2. Harmonisation in the asymmetric 2-country case

"disharmonisation" ($\gamma > 1$): decreases in n^A and n^B such that $|n^A - n^B|$ actually rises.

This result is illustrated in Fig. 2 which shows the BL Nash equilibrium (point N) and the level curves of W^B and W^A that pass through it (W_N^B and W_N^A respectively.) Nash equilibria are typically not Pareto optimal but the question of interest here is in what direction a Pareto improvement lies. Now, W_N^B must be vertical at N and W_N^A horizontal and it can be shown, from (6), (8), and (9), that $\partial W^i/\partial n^j < 0$ at N: each country would prefer that the other reduce its firm numbers at the Nash equilibrium. Thus, any "small" mutual reduction must be mutually welfare-improving; the shaded area illustrates a "trading lens" of mutually beneficial firm numbers. Beneficial disharmonisation is a move into the SSW octant from point N.

One final exercise is of some interest.[18] Our analysis above has essentially been positive, considering the effect on welfare as embodied in the actual objective functions of the governments. We can also address the more normative question of whether there exists some harmonisation that raises welfare in both countries as more usually understood; that is, can we find changes in n^A and n^B away from the Nash equilibrium such that $W^A|_{\omega^A=1}$ and $W^B|_{\omega^B=1}$ both rise? It can

[18] I am grateful to Neil Vousden for suggesting this exercise.

be shown that mutual welfare improvement requires a reduction in the number of firms in each country again but, interestingly, we need $\gamma \in [0, \frac{1}{2}]$ so any disharmonisation ($\gamma > 1$) here will not be mutually welfare improving.

3. A three-country model

We have also simulated a three country version of this model numerically. The importance of adding a third country is that trade policy is not now removed completely from the CU member countries. We augment the model of Section 2 by adding a third symmetric country, country C, which is not a member of the CU. We take a particular parameterisation of the model (see technical appendix) and look at a number of cases, described in an Appendix available on request. In each case we generate the unilateral tariff setting outcome and then consider both a free trade area (FTA) between A and B (i.e. with independently chosen external tariffs) and a customs union (CU) (with a common external tariff (CET).)

In the cases in which the non-member country cares only about its domestic firms, we are effectively back in the two-country world described above as C, not party to any agreements, chooses a prohibitive tariff and a low number of firms in every scenario. Most of our 2-country results carry over here, but co-ordination of competition policy in a CU (reducing firm numbers) is accompanied by an increase in the CET: reducing domestic firm numbers increases profit-shifting towards C's firms and this can be clawed back through an increased tariff. Also, the formation of a CU alone typically reduces the welfare of the two member countries but co-ordinating competition policy raises welfare back beyond the unilateral tariff setting level. This suggests a result seen in other contexts (see Gatsios and Karp, 1992; Richardson, 1994): for a CU to be welfare-improving it may require co-ordination of policies beyond just trade policy.

Suppose now that country C is a welfare-maximiser so the third-country interactions then become relevant. The two scenarios in which A and B are symmetric give us qualitatively similar results to those just discussed. But suppose A and B are asymmetric as in Section 2. Now in no arrangement (FTA or CU) alone does welfare increase in both A and B versus the unilateral tariff setting levels. But there are mutually welfare-improving changes in n^A and n^B which constitute harmonisation only in the looser sense defined earlier (a decrease in $|n^A - n^B|$) and only when C does not respond. If C reacts optimally to the formation of the CU then the only co-ordination of competition policy by members that raises welfare for both involves disharmonisation, by this measure.

Another point that emerges here is that when the members do co-ordinate their competition policy it makes the non-member worse off in every case, regardless of its response (or lack of it). This suggests that the concerns often expressed about the consequences for non-members of PTAs through their effects on members' trade policies (see the discussion in Desruelle and Richardson, 1997) might be reinforced when further policy co-ordination is considered.

Finally, it should be noted that in none of the CUs with co-ordinated competition policy are both members better off than in the absence of a CU altogether. While this result is an artefact of the assumptions about B's welfare function it highlights the observation that the gains from trade policy co-ordination may only be realised if members co-ordinate other policies too; in this case, even co-ordination of all policies is not sufficient to make the CU mutually beneficial as the member countries' objectives are too different.

4. Summary and conclusion

This paper has considered a very simple model of trade and competition policy in a Cournot oligopoly in order to examine the issue of harmonisation of competition policy in a preferential trading area. We present some analytical results for a two-country model and some numerical simulations for a three-country version of the same model. Our two-country results indicate a couple of rather surprising results: bilateral trade liberalisation may lead to more competitive competition policies, even if governments care only about domestic firms, but subsequent co-ordination of competition policy will involve less competitive outcomes. Furthermore, while co-ordination of competition policy must always be welfare-improving, we demonstrate that in the case where countries have different welfare objectives, such co-ordination may not involve harmonisation but rather disharmonisation, in a sense made clear in the paper. Finally, co-operation over competition policy generally involves less competitive behaviour than when such policies are not co-ordinated.

When a third country is added, these results still hold but our simulations indicate a number of interesting further results. First, our results indicate that non-member concerns about CU formation are well-founded, particularly when the CU goes beyond mere trade policy co-ordination. Second, if potential members' interests are too different (in that they weight different elements of their welfare function very differently) then there may be no CU that makes them better off than when all policies are set unilaterally, even with co-ordination of competition policies.

What to make of these results? The analytics of the 2-country model seem quite clear and illustrate the driving forces behind a lot of the results. While interpretation of the 3-country results is subject to the usual caveats concerning numerical simulations, the broad conclusion — that co-ordination of policies beyond trade policy may be needed to make a CU attractive to members but that such co-ordination increases the harm done to non-members by the CU — seems fairly general.

As far as future work is concerned, a number of extensions seem worthwhile. First, endogenising the decision to liberalise by considering the effects of changes in the weights placed by governments on the components of welfare might have interesting ramifications, as noted earlier, for both the choice of internal tariffs and the choice of competition policy. Second, setting liberalisation up as a two-stage game of co-operative tariff choice followed by the independent choice of competition policy might affect things substantially. In particular, the possibility of subsequent competition policy harmonisation might affect the initial choice of trade barriers.

References

Barros, P. and Cabral, L. (1994). Merger policy in open economies. *European Economic Review*, 38, 1041–55.

Baye, M., Crocker, K., and Ju, J. (1996a). Divisionalization, franchising and divestiture incentives in oligopoly. *American Economic Review*, 86, 223–36.

Baye, M., Crocker, K., and Ju, J. (1996b). Divisionalization and franchising incentives with integral competing units. *Economics Letters*, 50, 429–35.

Bliss, C. (1996). Trade and competition policy. In J. Bhagwati and R. Hudec (eds.), *Fair Trade and Harmonization: Prerequisites for Free Trade?* Vol. 1. Cambridge, MA: MIT Press.

Brander, J. and Spencer, B. (1984). Tariff protection and imperfect competition. In H. Kierzkowski (ed.), *Monopolistic Competition and International Trade.* New York, NY: Oxford University Press.

Brander, J. and Spencer, B. (1985). Export subsidies and international market share rivalry. *Journal of international Economics*, 18, 83–91.

Copeland, B. (1990). Strategic interaction among nations: negotiable and non-negotiable trade barriers. *Canadian Journal of Economics*, 23, 84–108.

Cowan, S. (1989). Trade and competition policies for oligopolies. *Weltwirtschaftliches Archiv*, 125, 464–83.

Desruelle, D. and Richardson, M. (1997). Fortress Europe: Jericho or Chateau d'If? *Review of International Economics*, 5, 32–46.

Dixit, A. (1984). International trade policy for oligopolistic industries. *Economic Journal*, 94, 1–16.

Gatsios, K. and Karp, L. (1992). The welfare effects of imperfect harmonisation of trade and industrial policy. *Economic Journal*, 102, 107–16.

Grossman, G. and Helpman, E. (1994). Protection for sale. *American Economic Review*, 84, 833–50.

Hillman, A. (1989). *The Political Economy of Protection.* Chur, Switzerland: Harwood Academic Publishers.

Horn, H. and Levinsohn, J. (1997). Merger policies and trade liberalization, mimeo. Ann Arbor, MI: University of Michigan.

Jacquemin, A. (1995). Towards an internationalisation of competition policy. *The World Economy*, 18, 781–89.

Kamien, M. and Zang, I. (1990). The limits of monopolization through acquisition. *Quarterly Journal of Economics*, 55, 465–99.

Levinsohn, J. (1996). Competition policy and international trade. In J. Bhagwati and R. Hudec (eds.), *Fair Trade and Harmonization: Prerequisites for Free Trade?* Vol. 1. Cambridge, MA: MIT Press.

Lloyd, P. and Sampson, G. (1995). Competition and trade policy: Identifying the issues after the Uruguay round. *The World Economics*, 18, 681–705.

Long, N.V. and Vousden, N. (1995). The effects of trade liberalization on cost-reducing horizontal mergers. *Review of International Economics*, 3, 141–55.

Richardson, M. (1994). Customs Unions and domestic taxes. *Canadian Journal of Economics*, 27, 537–50.

Salant, S., Switzer, S., and Reynolds, R. (1983). Losses from horizontal merger: the effects of an exogenous change in industry structure on Cournot–Nash equilibrium. *Quarterly Journal of Economics*, 48, 185–99.

Scherer, F.M. (1994). *Competition Policies for an Integrated World Economy.* Washington, DC: Brookings Institution.

Chapter 12

Trade Policy and Access to Retail Distribution

Martin Richardson

Abstract: The paper develops a model in which foreign and domestic manufacturers producing differentiated goods sell through spatially differentiated retailers. There is free entry into retailing but access to the retail distribution network (by manufacturers) may be controlled. The author considers a domestic vertical control mechanism in which domestic retailers carry only domestic brands (termed "domestic dealing") and compares the use of tariffs on imports and the enforcement of domestic dealing restrictions as means of increasing domestic welfare. It is shown that domestic dealing will always be prohibited when tariffs can be used. When trade policy is not available, however, domestic dealing may be desirable.

1. Introduction

It has long been noted that the beneficial consequences of trade liberalization can be lost when liberalizing countries can resort to other, uncontrolled domestic policy instruments. So nontrade-related instruments such as domestic taxes (Richardson, 1994) or labor and environmental policies (Bhagwati and Hudec, 1996) can undermine trade negotiations. One such group of policies being given increasing attention in this regard is competition policy.

In particular, there has long been concern that "exporters of some products may have gained access to markets in terms of the removal

Originally published in *Review of International Economics*, 12(4), 676–688.

of barriers at the border or lower tariffs, but attempts to export may be frustrated by inability to access distribution channels within the borders of importing countries" (Vautier and Lloyd, 1997, p. 8). This paper asks: under what circumstances might an explicit reduction in trade barriers lead an importing country to wish to permit domestic wholesalers to tie up the domestic retailing network? Our answer is that, while a country would never wish to allow the exclusion of foreign products when it can set its tariff freely, it may indeed wish to do this absent a tariff.

This issue has been particularly significant in the context of US/Japan trade relations, the distribution system in Japan being seen as an invisible structural barrier to foreign exporters stemming from "Japanese business organisations and their distinctive relationships with one another and with the Japanese government" (Tyson, 1992, p. 83). And Scherer writes:

> "Under prevailing Japanese legal interpretations, formal exclusive dealing... can be prohibited if competitors are excluded.... However, manufacturer-dealer relationships are seldom spelled out... and there are many reasons why retailers — and especially the typically small retailers with limited shelf space — might wish to maintain informally an exclusive arrangement with their suppliers." (Scherer, 1994, p. 76)

On retailers and manufacturers of apparel in large stores in Japan:

> "the traditional department store... has many of the characteristics of the typical traditional Japanese distribution system. *The distinctive feature of department stores is the diversity of products* kept in a relatively small number of shops. To secure such diversity... the retailer must seek the cooperation of the wholesaler... A considerable number of salesclerks working within department stores are not employees of the store but are assigned... by the manufacturers. The system of division of labor... cannot be founded only on a contract basis but must instead be nurtured as a long-term business relationship.... [so] products from overseas find it difficult to obtain access." (Itoh and Hatanaka, 1993, pp. 231–2; my italics)

Thus the relationship between wholesalers and retailers is complex and incompletely specified. Also, the diversity of products referred to in the previous excerpt suggests that this is *not* exclusive dealing as usually understood: the agreement between a retailer and a *single* manufacturer that the former will carry only the latter's brand.

What analytical modeling there is of the nexus between trade and competition policy is ill-suited to addressing this issue. Lloyd (1996) and Richardson (1999) both model competition policy as the choice of the number of domestic firms in an international Cournot oligopoly and then consider the interaction of this choice with trade policy. But, in this sort of setting, anticompetitive behavior by a subset of firms is beneficial for the rest: "[t]he merging firms, by cutting back the group's output, are providing a 'public' service, from which the rest of the industry enjoys free-rider benefit" (Dixit, 1984, p. 13). Raff and Schmitt (2000) consider a model of endogenous vertical restraints in an international setting and demonstrate that trade liberalization may make exclusive territories more attractive in their setting, depending on the uncertainty of trade barriers and the keenness of interbrand competition. In this paper, I model retail distribution explicitly. I consider the choice of enforcement of a policy that prohibits "domestic dealing": domestic manufacturers, as a group, contracting with domestic retailers to carry only domestic brands.

In this I am motivated partially by simplicity, and partially — and loosely — by the "stylized facts" of the Japanese experience. Scherer (1994) suggests that exclusive dealing is technically illegal in Japan but is largely unregulated. Accordingly, small retail firms have a wide degree of latitude in choosing to carry only certain brands; I simply assume those are domestic ones. Itoh and Hatanaka (1993) suggest that there are also relationships between domestic manufacturers and large retailers; I consider arrangements that permit only a subset of the existing foreign firms to have access to domestic retail distribution.These arrangements must be mutually profitable, of course, and I show that such a domestic dealing agreement can be, with appropriately chosen side-payments to retailers.

In a sense, the removal of a tariff constitutes the underlying comparative statics exercise in this paper, which seeks to address the impact of this on competition policy. I. I show that if a country loses the use of trade policy it may indeed be tempted to respond by permitting domestic firms to pursue anticompetitive practices that exclude foreign firms from retailing. By contrast, when trade policy is available this "slack" competition policy is never attractive. In this sense, commonly expressed fears that lax competition policy may "undo" the gains from trade liberalization find some support. However, the number of potential foreign firms is significant — the greater the number the more likely it is that their presence will be welfare-improving.

2. The Model

The model of retailing here is that of Salop (1979). It is a model in which retailers locate around a circle on which consumers are uniformly distributed. The literal interpretation of the model is that consumers incur a transport cost, but as usual this cost represents any disutility they incur in making a purchase. Accordingly, entry of "closer" retailers can be interpreted as entry of retailers that give greater surplus in some fashion other than price; perhaps through a service dimension. We consider first the case in which there is no domestic dealing. There are n domestic and n^* foreign "manufacturing" firms each producing a different "brand" of the good. All brands are sold through the R retailers who are symmetrically distributed around a unit circle. There is free entry into retailing at some fixed cost, F.

The L consumers, who each have unit demands, are uniformly distributed on the unit circle and a consumer located a distance s_i from retailer i obtains net utility from purchasing brand k from that retailer of

$$v + \varepsilon_k - p_{ik} - ts_i,$$

where v is a common value for all brands, ε_k is an idiosyncratic value for brand k, p_{ik} is the price of brand k at retailer i, and t is a per-unit (linear) transport cost. The idiosyncratic values (which give us product differentiation) are independently and identically distributed according to the double-exponential distribution function[1]

$$F(\varepsilon_k) = \exp^{\{-e^{-\varepsilon k/\mu}\}}.$$

[1]See Anderson et al. (1992, pp. 59–60) which is an excellent reference on all aspects of these discrete choice models.

Then $E[\varepsilon] = \mu\gamma$, where γ is Euler's constant $\simeq 0.577$ and $\text{Var}[\varepsilon] \equiv \sigma^2 = \mu^2\pi^2/6 \cong 1.645\mu^2$. With N products, a consumer purchases the one that yields the highest surplus.[2]

If we define z as the consumer's maximum surplus at retailer i, then $z = \max\{\nu+\varepsilon_1-p_{i1}-ts, \nu+\varepsilon_2-p_{i2}-ts, \ldots, \nu+\varepsilon_N-p_{iN}-ts\}$. The distribution function $G(z)$ of z is then $F(z-\nu+ts)\prod_k F(z-\nu+p_{ik}+ts)$ or

$$G(z) = \exp\{-e^{(\nu-ts-z)/\mu}D_i\} \quad \text{where} \quad D_i \equiv \sum_{k=1}^{N} e^{-p_{ik}/\mu}.$$

This is essentially a many-good version of Besanko and Perry (1994; BP henceforth) (partially developed in Richardson, 1998) in which firms may be asymmetric. The model of BP is a purely domestic one in which two manufacturing firms sell through spatially differentiated retailers. It is designed to investigate issues of exclusive dealing and the model developed here is similar to their nonexclusive dealing case in that differentiated manufacturers sell their goods through spatially differentiated retailers, there is free entry into retailing, and every retailer carries every brand that is made available. However, we allow that there may be more than two manufacturers and that some of these may be foreign firms. Note that the numbers of domestic and foreign manufacturers are exogenous throughout this analysis but the number of foreign manufacturers permitted to sell in the home country is not.[3] We also assume that all retailers are domestic in origin. As they earn zero profits this assumption has little direct impact; however, if foreign manufacturers could simply establish their own retail outlets then the entire problem would disappear here. The fact that it

[2]At this point I do not allow that a consumer may choose to make no purchase at all, but this is discussed later and, more fully, in a working paper version available from the author.

[3]With free entry into manufacturing, all profits go to zero and the profit-shifting motivation for policy disappears. However, it would permit another feature: entry of foreign manufacturers could have a welfare-enhancing effect by leading to the exit of the most inefficient domestic producers. Note also that FDI may be one means of evading restrictions on foreign manufacturers if a foreign manufacturer could buy into a domestic manufacturer. I do not consider that possibility in the present paper.

has been an important problem in practice — combined with a great deal of evidence that the establishment of foreign retail outlets in Japan is extremely difficult — suggests that our assumption is appropriate.[4]

As noted, I model competition policy in this setting as effectively controlling the number of foreign manufacturers through enforcement (or nonenforcement) of prohibitions on domestic dealing. It should be stressed again that this is *not* exclusive dealing, as usually understood or as discussed in BP, as each retailer here is still carrying the full range of the products that *are* available.[5] The timing of decisions here is as follows: the government makes its competition policy enforcement and tariff choices; retailers enter and locate symmetrically around the circle;[6] retailers and manufacturers do or do not enter into a domestic dealing contract; manufacturers set nondiscriminatory wholesale prices; retailers set (mill) prices for each brand. This timing is such that all market decisions are made in full knowledge of the government's policies; i.e., the government can make a commitment. Another feature of our timing is that the first "market" decision made is entry and location for retailers. In this sense, the retailing equilibrium is given as manufacturers make their decisions. First we consider the retailing equilibrium.

Retailing equilibrium

As BP note, while retailers are symmetric, so prices — and thus the spatial boundaries — will be symmetric in equilibrium, we need to calculate out those equilibrium prices so we allow asymmetric

---

[4]One simple way to formalize this is to suppose that retail technology is different in the domestic market than in foreign markets, and that it is sufficiently costly to acquire that profits from avoiding domestic dealing restrictions do not make foreign *retail* entry worthwhile.

[5]In our setup there is nothing to rule out collusion between domestic manufacturers and retailers over *prices*. However, vertical collusion over price does not seem to be a characteristic of Japanese retailing and, as a first approximation of an aspect of Japanese retailing that has drawn the attention of the US, I feel the present focus on domestic dealing as the vehicle of collusion is appropriate.

[6]See BP for a discussion of the optimality of symmetric locations.

retail boundaries. This is done in a mathematical appendix available on request where I demonstrate that, as in BP, the equilibrium is given by

$$p_k - w_k = m \equiv t/R \quad \forall k = 1, \ldots, N. \tag{1}$$

That is, regardless of the wholesale prices levied by the manufacturers, wk, the markup, m, for each brand is the same and is the standard Salop markup (that increases with the transport cost, t, and decreases with the number of retailers, R).

Letting x_k denote the probability of purchasing brand $k = 1, \ldots, N$, each retailer makes profits of

$$\pi_R = \frac{L}{R}\left[\sum_{K=1}^{N}(p_k - w_k)x_k\right] - F = (Lm/R) - F.$$

Free entry into retailing gives $\pi_R = 0$ which, from the markup m, solves for R:

$$R = (tL/F)^{\frac{1}{2}}. \tag{2}$$

Manufacturers' problem

For manufacturer k, profits are given as follows, as there is no fixed cost to manufacturing and a constant marginal cost of c_k:

$$\pi_{mk} = (w_k - c_k)x_k L, \tag{3}$$

where

$$x_k = e^{-pk/\mu}/E_N \quad \text{and} \quad E_N \equiv \sum_{j=1}^{N} e^{-p_j/\mu}. \tag{4}$$

The FOC for the choice of w_k is then

$$\frac{\partial \pi_{mk}}{\partial w_k} = x_k + (w_k - c_k)\frac{\partial x_k}{\partial w_k} = 0. \tag{5}$$

From (1) we get the following:

$$\frac{\partial p_k}{\partial w_k} = 1, \tag{6}$$

and thus the following FOC for wk:

$$w_k = c_k + \mu/(1 - x_k). \tag{7}$$

Note that this is not a closed-form expression for wk as x_k depends on prices.

From the preceding discussion we can see that retailers are unaffected by a change in the number of brands available. If one brand disappeared the market shares of all others would expand, from (1) retailers' markups do not depend on the number of products, and so retailers' profits would be unaffected. The remaining manufacturers, however, are each better off: each has an increased market share (from (4)) and so, from (7), an increased wholesale price.

So, can domestic dealing be an equilibrium practice in the sense that retailers would be willing to agree to carry only domestic brands? Suppose domestic manufacturers form a trade organization that negotiates with retailers in the collective interests of manufacturers. Manufacturers then offer a contract to individual retailers involving domestic dealing — an agreement to carry only domestic brands and not foreign ones — in return for a lump-sum payment. We wish to see whether there exists a payment such that domestic dealing is in the interests of the retailer and the manufacturers.[7]

In this case this is quite straightforward. Consider an initial equilibrium in the absence of domestic dealing. Suppose *every* retailer were to drop a single brand. Then profits would be unaffected: consumers previously choosing that brand will simply switch brands and the markup on every brand is constant. Consumers are worse off (and will also face a price increase, from (1) and (7)) but retailers are not. As the markup and sales of the remaining manufacturers have both increased, so their aggregate profits are higher. Accordingly, the joint profits of retailers and remaining manufacturers must

[7]Analogously to Bernheim and Whinston (1998), we might allow foreign manufacturers as a group to compete for exclusive access to domestic retailers. I do not consider this complication and, in a model with an international dimension, it is simple to note reasons why this might not happen.

strictly increase when one manufacturer is excluded. Thus there must exist a domestic dealing contract with a small payment from manufacturers to each retailer that is in the mutual interests of retailers and domestic manufacturers.[8] It should be stressed that this argument does depend on domestic manufacturers acting as a single cohesive group — to the extent that dropping foreign brands is mutually profitable, it must also pay $(n-1)$ domestic manufacturers to induce retailers to drop the nth domestic brand.[9]

Welfare

Finally, we can write welfare as the sum of domestic profits, consumers' surplus, and government revenue. Expected utility for a consumer located at s is

$$U(E_N, s) = \int_{-\infty}^{\infty} z dG(z),$$

where $G(z)$ is the distribution function of the variable z defined earlier: the maximum surplus of the consumer. Henceforth, I denote the consumer price of goods produced by the n^* symmetric foreign manufacturers as p^* and of goods produced by the n domestic manufacturers as p. Similarly, wholesale prices are w^* and w and manufacturers'

[8]Note that, in the usual way, this argument will fall to the holdout problem: if a single retailer can decline the contract their profits would then increase, as their market share increased, if all other retailers were domestic dealing. Accordingly this could not be a Nash equilibrium if retailers are free to deviate. However, with appropriate restrictions on retailers' beliefs domestic dealing *could* be supported as a Nash equilibrium. (An example could be a retailer who believes that their unilateral deviation would induce the withdrawal of the domestic dealing offer from *all* retailers. In such a case deviation reduces retail profits by γ.) An alternative (depending on the relative numbers of domestic and foreign brands) is if the domestic dealing is a take-it-or- leave-it offer in which turning the contract down means the retailer can carry *only* foreign brands. The domestic dealing I have described is thus somewhat fragile as an equilibrium, although no more so than any vertical restraint agreement subject to a holdout problem. Further, the precise nature of the domestic dealing relationship, while a very suitable field for study, is not a central focus of this paper, which looks instead at whether the regulatory authorities should tolerate any such behaviour — which seems to occur empirically—however supported.

[9]I am grateful to a referee for making this point.

marginal costs are c^* and c. Integrating,[10] we obtain

$$U(E_N, s) = (v + \mu\gamma) + \mu \ln (E_N) - t_s,$$

where $E_N = \text{n}e^{-p/\mu} + n^* e^{-p^*/\mu}$. The first term in $U(.)$ is the expected willingness-to-pay (as $\mu\gamma$ is the expected value of the idiosyncratic value). The second term is the value placed on diversity, in a sense: as more firms enter, the likelihood of getting a more valuable good (i.e., of making a higher draw from the distribution) goes up and this is more likely the more dispersed the distribution (the greater is μ). The third term is the transport cost. The typical consumer is halfway between a retailer and the spatial boundary for the next one, so she incurs transport costs of $(t/2R)/2$ or $t/4R$, so *total* expected consumer surplus is

$$U(p, p^*) = L\{v + \mu\gamma + \mu \ln (EN) - (t/4R)\}. \tag{8}$$

Total retail profits are given by $\Pi_R = R\pi_R = L\{nx(p - w) + n^* x^* (p^* - w^*) - RF/L\} = 0$ and the total profits of domestic wholesalers are $\Pi_M = nxL\{w - c\} = nxL\{p - m - c\}$. Finally, government revenue is just tariff revenue. If a specific tariff of τ is levied on foreign manufacturers, then $GR = \tau n^* x^* L$. Thus we can write welfare as

$$\begin{aligned} W &= L[\nu + \mu\gamma + \mu \ln(E_N) - (t/4R) + nx(p - w) + n^* x^* (p^* - w^*)] \\ &\quad - RF + L[nx(w - c) + \tau n^* x^*] \\ &= L[k + \mu \text{In}(E_N) + nx(p - c) + n^* x^* (p^* + \tau - w^*)], \end{aligned} \tag{9}$$

where $K = \nu + \mu\gamma - (t/4R) - (RF/L)$.

3. Tariffs versus Retail Access

No tariffs

We start with no tariff. Assuming all manufacturing firms have symmetric costs ($c = c^*$) then each manufacturing firm's market share is $x_k = x = x^* = 1/N$ and wholesale prices, from (7), are

[10] See BP appendix for details.

$w^* = w = c + \mu(N/(N-1))$. Thus final prices, from (1), are $p^* = p = w + m = w + (t/R) = c + (t/R) + \mu(N/(N-1))$. All spatial boundaries are equal (to $1/2R$), so $E_n = \sum_{j=1}^{N} e^{-pj/\mu} = Ne^{-p/\mu}$. Thus $\ln(E_N) = \ln(N) - (p/\mu)$ and, in the absence of tariffs, welfare can be written, from (9), as

$$
\begin{aligned}
W &= L[K + \mu\ln(n + n^*) - nxc - n^*xw] \\
&= L[K + \mu\{\ln(n + n^*) - n^*/(n + n^* - 1)\} - c].
\end{aligned}
$$

Suppose the regulator could actually choose the number of foreign firms. There are two reasons why foreign entry is desirable for consumers: it reduces prices and it increases welfare through increased diversity. On the other hand, it diverts profits away from domestic firms towards foreign firms (as $w > c$), which is a bad thing. Differentiating W with respect to n^* and simplifying, we obtain

$$
\frac{dW}{dn^*} = (\mu L/(N-1)^2 N)\{1 + N(n^* - 1)\}. \tag{10}
$$

This is negative at $n^* = 0$ but positive at $n^* \geq 1$, for any values of $n \geq 1$. Welfare is not monotonic in n^*, falling when $n^* = 0$ (but at a lower rate the higher is n, the number of domestic firms) but increasing at $n^* = 1$. However, we can establish the following.

Proposition 1. *When there is no tariff, the entry of a single foreign firm is welfare- reducing but entry of two or more foreign firms raises domestic welfare vis-á-vis the no-foreign-entry case. This holds regardless of the number of domestic firms. This is proved in the Appendix.*

Plotting $\Delta(n^*, n)$ (the change in domestic welfare from entry of n^* foreign firms versus no entry at all) over n^* gives Figure 1. The intuition for these results is as follows. A little bit of entry is harmful, for reasons of profit-shifting as wholesale price exceeds marginal cost. Further entry, however, is not harmful for two reasons. First, as entry occurs prices are falling, so the profits of domestic firms are smaller and the profit- shifting effect is of less concern. Second, more existing firms are foreign so less of the profit-shifting that follows marginal entry is away from domestic firms. This intuition helps explains the

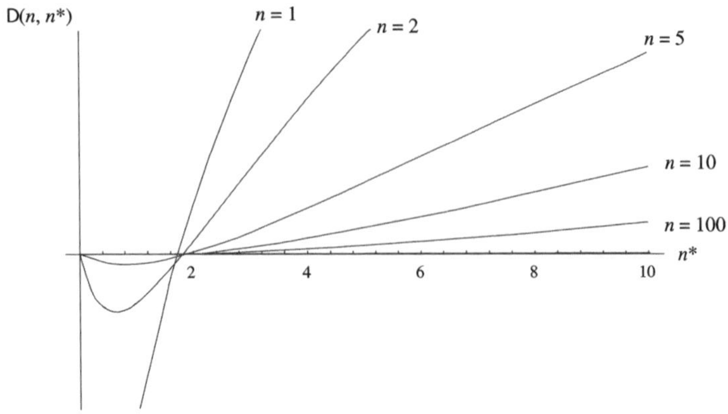

Fig. 1. Welfare in "No-Outside-Option" Case with Free Trade

shape of Δ as shown in Figure 1 as n changes: for higher n, the losses associated with a single foreign entrant are lower (as prices are lower so the profit- shifting is less) and the gains associated with multiple entry are lower (as the diversity value is reduced when there are already many domestic firms).

This general qualitative result — that a little foreign entry is harmful but a lot is welfare-improving — is not unique to the structure of this particular model. (Note that the retail equilibrium is unaffected by entry or exit at the manufacturing level as the markup m in (1) is unaffected and so is the equilibrium number of retailers R in (2).[11]) The intuition for the result depends only on profit-shifting and it can be shown that it carries over to other profit-shifting models.[12]

The implication of Proposition 1 is that whether or not a government wishes to permit domestic dealing depends only on the number of foreign brands. The issue of permitting *degrees* of foreign entry (which represents permitting degrees of domestic dealing by domestic

[11]This is because of the assumption that all consumers purchase the good.

[12]This holds in a pure logit-differentiation model without retailers but also in an international Cournot homogeneous-good oligopoly as well. See Dixit (1984) and Richardson (1998).

firms) does not arise in equilibrium here. *Given* the number of potential foreign entrants into manufacturing sales, a welfare-maximizing regulator will either wish to prohibit domestic dealing altogether (i.e., allow *all* foreign firms to enter) or to turn a blind eye to it (i.e., allow *no* foreign firms in at all).

Equilibrium with tariffs

The effect of a specific tariff of τ here is to increase the costs of foreign manufacturers. The retail markup is unaffected by this but the prices charged by foreign and domestic firms, respectively, will now be

$$w^* = c + \tau + (\mu/(1 - x^*)) \quad \text{and} \quad w = c + (\mu/(1 - x)),$$

where $x^* = e^{-p^*/\mu}/E < e^{-p^*/\mu}/E = x$ and $E = ne^{-p/\mu} + n^*e^{-p^*/\mu}$. Welfare is now a significantly more complicated expression as symmetry is lost and $\ln(E)$ does not break down so neatly. From $\Pi_M = nxL(w - c), \Pi_R = L(p - w - RF/L)$[13] and $GR = \tau n^* x^* L$, we have

$$\begin{aligned} W = L\{&v + \mu\gamma + \mu \ln[ne^{-p/\mu} + n^*e^{-p^*/\mu}] \\ &-(t/4R) + \tau n^* x^* + \mu n(x/(1 - x))\}. \end{aligned} \tag{11}$$

The complication here is that both x and x^* depend on prices which are expressed in terms of x and x^*. Nevertheless, we can derive the following expression:

$$\begin{aligned} \frac{1}{L}\frac{dW}{d\tau} &= \underbrace{\mu\frac{1}{E_N}\frac{dE_N}{d\tau}}_{(a)} + \underbrace{n^*x^*}_{(b)} + \underbrace{n^*\tau\frac{dx^*}{d\tau}}_{(c)} + \underbrace{\frac{\mu n}{(1 - x^2)}\frac{dx}{d\tau}}_{(d)} \\ &= n\left[\frac{\mu}{1 - x} + \frac{\mu(1 - nx)}{n^*(1 - x^*)^2} - \tau\right]\frac{dx}{d\tau}. \end{aligned} \tag{12}$$

---

[13]Note that there is no need to distinguish between retailers' profits made on foreign or domestic goods as the markup is the same in each case and every consumer is assumed to purchase the good (so $nx + n^*x^* = 1$).

The term labeled (a) represents consumer losses from higher prices, (b) is increased tariff revenue at a given level of foreign sales, (c) is decreased tariff revenues, at a given tariff, from lower foreign sales, and (d) represents the gain from profit-shifting from the tariff as the domestic share of the market increases.

Now, implicit differentiation gives the following expression:

$$\frac{dx}{d\tau} = \frac{x}{\mu}\left\{\frac{1}{1-nx} + \frac{x}{(1-x)^2} + \frac{n}{n^*}\frac{x}{(1-x)^2}\right\}^{-1} > 0, \tag{13}$$

which can be shown to imply that $0 < dp/d\tau < dp^*/d\tau < 1$.

Second, note that a small tariff must raise welfare. At $\tau = 0$, all firms are symmetric so $x = 1/N = x^*$ and $p = p^*$ and we can solve for

$$\left.\frac{1}{nL}\frac{dW}{d\tau}\right|_{\tau=0} = \frac{\mu N^2}{(N-1)^2}\frac{dx}{d\tau} > 0.$$

Thus, assuming the SOCs hold,[14] we have an optimal tariff defined implicitly by

$$\tau = \mu\left[1/(1-x) + (x^*/(1-x^*)^2)\right]. \tag{14}$$

Noting that in this model the consumer price is irrelevant to welfare (as it is simply a transfer from consumers to retailers), one might wonder why this expression is not infinite. The reason is that here there *is* a welfare loss from a tariff that is not offset by a transfer from consumers to domestic firms or the government, and that is the loss of surplus to consumers who now switch to a less-preferred brand as the price of foreign brands is driven up by the tariff.

Proceeding as before, we can write welfare when there are no foreign firms as

$$W_0^{\tau} = W_0 = L\{K - c + \mu\ln(n)\}.$$

When there is a single foreign firm, we have

$$W_1^{\tau} = L\{K + (t/R) + \mu\ln(E_N) + \tau x^* + (\mu nx/(1-x))\},$$

[14] We have seen that welfare is not well-behaved even in the absence of tariffs.

so that

$$\begin{aligned}\Delta^{\tau}(1,n) &\equiv (W_1^{\tau} - W_0^{\tau})/L \\ &= \mu\,\text{In}(E_N/n) + (t/R) + c + \tau x^* + \mu n x/(1-x). \quad (15)\end{aligned}$$

We can now establish the following result.

Proposition 2. *With an optimal tariff, the entry of a single foreign firm raises welfare vis-à-vis no foreign entry, regardless of the number of domestic firms. This is proved in the Appendix.*

Corollary. *With an optimal tariff, the entry of more than one foreign firm raises welfare vis-à-vis no foreign entry, regardless of the number of domestic firms.*

This corollary follows directly from Propositions 1 and 2, the fact that $\tau = 0$ is available, and the observation that, with no foreign entry, a tariff is redundant.

While Proposition 2 is familiar from the rent-shifting trade policy literature (Richardson, 1998), its significance here is that it contrasts starkly with the case when no tariffs are available.[15] The intuition comes simply from looking at why single-firm entry is harmful in the absence of tariffs: profit-shifting. When a tariff is available it can recapture some of these profits from the foreign firm while still enabling the gains to consumers from increased product diversity. The corollary implies that domestic dealing is never welfare-improving in this setting. Whether or not it is in the interests of domestic firms, a welfare-maximizing government would not permit it when tariffs can be chosen optimally.

The model with an outside option

While the analysis of the model above provides some analytical insight into the effects of foreign entry with and without trade policy, it does have the peculiar property that the retail sector is unaffected by either policy. This stems from the fact that consumers cannot

[15] Furthermore, as discussed below, even with no tariff entry may always be welfare-improving when consumers have an outside option.

choose to *not* buy the good: they have no "outside option". When all consumers buy the good, retail equilibrium involves a markup that is independent of the number of wholesalers or the wholesale price (and hence the tariff). Retailers simply pass on completely any increase in wholesale price, which has no consequences for total demand (as all consumers buy), so their profits are unaffected so the equilibrium number of retailers is unaffected.

When consumers *do* have an outside option this reasoning no longer holds. A tariff, for instance, increases the prices of all goods (foreign more than domestic) and so pushes more consumers out of the market.This reduces retailers' profitability and leads to retail exit with further welfare consequences through increased transportation costs. In this context we can show the following result.[16]

Proposition 3. *When consumers have an outside option, the entry of any number of foreign firms may raise domestic welfare vis-à-vis the no-foreign-entry case, even with no tariff. This is the case regardless of the number of domestic firms.*

The reason for this is that, as n^* increases, prices fall, the outside option becomes less attractive, and the number of retailers rises — which reduces transport costs.

4. Summary and Conclusion

This paper has presented an extension of the BP model of differentiated producers selling through differentiated retailers in which there are more than two manufacturing firms and there are foreign firms. I have compared the use of tariffs and competition policy in raising welfare where the competition policy considered has been the control of a vertical restriction between domestic manufacturers and retailers, dubbed "domestic dealing." I have shown that a country with tariff policy available will always permit foreign manufacturers to access the domestic retail network, but when tariffs cannot be used

[16]Available from the author.

it will prohibit domestic dealing only when there is more than one foreign entrant. I have also noted a result shown elsewhere; that in the presence of an outside option for consumers, entry may be always welfare-improving, tariffs or not, because it makes the outside option less attractive, thus encouraging retail entry which raises welfare.

One possible interpretation of these results is as follows. If a country loses the use of trade policy, perhaps through bilateral or multilateral negotiated trade agreements, it may be tempted to respond by permitting domestic firms to pursue anticompetitive practices that exclude foreign firms from retailing. In this sense, commonly expressed fears that lax competition policy may "undo" the gains from trade liberalization find some support. However, the results here also suggest that the number of potential foreign entrants is significant and that foreign entry has other consequences that are beneficial for domestic consumers — namely its effects on the retailing equilibrium — which reduce the attractiveness of slack competition policies. And if foreign manufacturing entry is also likely to stimulate retail entry, then this may further reduce the attractiveness of lax competition policies.

Of course, these precise results are sensitive to the assumptions I have made. In particular, two interesting next steps would be (1) to introduce the possibility of DFI and cross-ownership and ask to what extent the possibility of domestic dealing can trigger "tariff-jumping" investment, and (2) to allow free entry and exit into manufacturing to see how foreign entry affects domestic efficiency. One might also consider the possibility of interactions in more than one market, in which case domestic dealing may have beneficial profit-shifting effects *à la* other "import protection as export promotion" arguments (Krugman, 1984).

It should be stressed that this analysis is cast in a partial-equilibrium setting and I focus only on the policy choice facing an importing country. The pure profits earned by manufacturers here suggest that the home countries of foreign producers would be keen to have access to the domestic market. This fits well with the motivating example behind my analysis: countries' complaints that their firms are precluded from markets, despite the negotiated lowering of trade barriers, by the anticompetitive practices of domestic firms. Furthermore, in the case where foreign firms would be kept out,*sans* tariffs (i.e., when there is a single potential foreign entrant), it is clear that the joint welfare of the host and source countries is increased by such entry (as the profit- shifting is irrelevant from such a perspective and we are left with the benefits to consumers). This suggests that the issue of domestic competition policy is one that could very usefully be brought within the scope of multilateral or bilateral negotiations to avoid the same sorts of Prisoners' Dilemma outcomes that can equally plague unilateral trade policy setting.

Appendix

Proof of proposition 1

The following is adapted from Richardson (1998) (in which there is no retail sector). Suppose there are no foreign firms at all. Then $n^* = 0$ and domestic welfare is

$$W_0 = L\{K - c_{+}\mu \ln(n)\}.$$

With $n^* \geq 1$, however, we get

$$W_{n^*} = L\{K - c + \mu \ln(n + n^*) - \mu n^*/(n + n^* - 1)\}.$$

Define

$$\Delta(n^*, n) \equiv (W_{n^*} - W_0)/\mu L = \text{In}(n + n^*/n) - (n^*/(n + n* - 1)).$$

Then $\Delta(1,1) = \ln(2) - 1 < 0$ and $d\Delta(1,n)/dn = 1/n^2(n+1) > 0$, so Δ is everywhere increasing in n. But $lim_{n\to\infty}\Delta(1,n) = 0$. Thus $\Delta(1,n) = \ln((n+1)/n) - 1/n < 0$ for $n \geq 1$; so if there is only a single foreign firm, welfare is lower than if there are no foreign firms at all.

With two foreign firms, however, we have $\Delta(2,n) = \ln((n+2)/n) - 2/(n+1)$ and this is positive for all $n : \Delta(2,1) = \ln(3) - 1 > 0$ and $d\Delta(2,n)/dn < 0 \forall n \geq 1$, but $\lim_{n\to\infty}\Delta(2,n) = 0$ again. So welfare is higher with two foreign firms than with none.

Proof of proposition 2

With a tariff in place, we have $p^* = c + (t/R) + (\mu/(1 - x^*)) + \tau$ and $p = c + (t/R) + (\mu/(1 - x))$. If the tariff is set optimally, from (14), then we can write $p^* = p + \mu/(1 - x^*)^2$. Thus

$$E_N = ne^{-p/\mu} + e^{-p^*/\mu} = e^{-p/\mu}(k), \quad \text{where} \quad k = n + e^{\overline{\frac{1}{(1-x^*)^2}}} > n.$$

So $\mu \ln(E_N) = -p + \mu \ln(k)$. Thus, from (15) and (14), we have

$$\begin{aligned}
\Delta^\tau(1, n) &= \mu \ln(E_N/n) + (t/R) + c + \tau x^* + \mu n(x/(1 - x)) \\
&= \mu \ln(k/n) - \mu(1/(1 - x)) + \tau x^* + \mu n(x/(1 - x)) \\
&= \mu \ln(k/n) - \mu(1 - nx)/(1 - x) \\
&\quad + \mu[(x^*/(1 - x)) + (x^*/(1 - x^*))^2] \\
&= \mu \ln(k/n) + \mu(x^*/(1 - x^*))^2.
\end{aligned}$$

But this last expression is positive as $k > n$.

References

Anderson, S., A. de Palma, and J. Thisse (1992). *Discrete Choice Theory of Product Differentiation.* Cambridge, MA: MIT Press.

Bernheim, B.D. and M.D. Whinston (1998). Exclusive dealing. *Journal of Political Economy,* 106, 64–103.

Bhagwati, J. and R. Hudec (eds.) (1996). *Fair Trade and Harmonization: Prerequisites for Free Trade?* Vol. 1. Cambridge, MA: MIT Press.

Dixit, A. (1984). International trade policy for oligopolistic industries. *Economic Journal,* 94, 1–16.

Itoh, M. and K. Hatanaka (1993). Access to the Japanese market by Asian countries: A case study of the wool textile industry. In T. Ito and A. O. Krueger (eds.), *Trade and Protectionism,* Vol. 2. Chicago: University of Chicago Press for NBER.

Krugman, P. (1984). Import Protection as Export Promotion. In Henry Kierzkowski (ed.), *Monopolistic Competition and International Trade.* Oxford: Blackwell.

Lloyd, P.J. (1996). A link between international trade and international competition policy. Working paper 4/96, Institute of Applied Economic and Social Research, Melbourne.

Raff, H. and N. Schmitt (2000). Endogenous vertical restraints in international trade. Working paper 284, Munich: CESifo.

Richardson, M. (1994). Customs unions and domestic taxes. *Canadian Journal of Economics,* 27, 537–50.

Richardson, M. (1998). Foreign entry and welfare. *Weltwirtschaftliches Archiv*, 134, 250–62.

Richardson, M. (1999). Trade and competition policies: Concordia discors? *Oxford Economic Papers* 51, 649–64.

Salop, S. (1979). Monopolistic competition with outside goods. *Bell Journal of Economics*, 10, 141–56.

Scherer, F.M. (1994). *Competition Policies for an Integrated World Economy*, Washington, DC: Brookings Institution.

Tyson, L.D'A. (1992). *Who's Bashing Whom? Trade Conflict in High-technology Industries*. Washington, DC: Institute for International Economics.

Vautier, K.M. and P.J. Lloyd (1997). *International Trade and Competition Policy: CER, APEC and the WTO*. Wellington, NZ: Institute of Policy Studies.

Chapter 13

Private and Public Incentives for Mergers in the Face of Foreign Entry

Ryan Fang and Martin Richardson

Abstract: We consider private and public incentives for domestic firms to merge in the face of foreign entry. We consider the gains to two merging firms and to national welfare in a linear Cournot model. With heterogeneous firms and possible synergies, greater foreign entry tends to enhance both private and public incentives for domestic mergers. Thus, policymakers have no cause to doubt the intentions of firms seeking to merge: when it is in the firms' interests then it is also in the public interest. However, at least for certain parameterisations, private gains from mergers become positive at a lower level of foreign entry than do public gains. This suggests that private firms may have an incentive to overstate the degree of foreign competition they anticipate facing — for example, after liberalizing foreign investment rules — to persuade policymakers that a proposed domestic merger is in the national interest.

1. Introduction

In the run-up to — and immediate aftermath of — China's accession to the World Trade Organization (WTO), a number of high-profile mergers were proposed and undertaken in China. In commentary on these, Lu observes, "Once the [domestic] market is fully opened

Originally published in *Review of Development Economics*, 14(3), 520–532.

foreign capital is going to 'attack' and China is going to face international competition. Today's merger ... is to prepare for building our own commercial 'aircraft carriers.'" And Hua comments, "[t]his kind of concentration will help to improve the competitiveness of domestic firms ... [t]his is not an attempt for monopolising ... [i]n contrast to facing no competition, the new entity will face the challenge by much stronger foreign players."[1] Behind these mergers, frequently, is government encouragement, with many of these mergers a part of China's latest efforts to restructure the problematic state-owned enterprises (SOEs), but with an emphasis on preparing them for increased foreign competition. It is not only the large SOEs that are undertaking mergers, however, and nor are all mergers forced upon firms by the government. The individual causes for such initiatives may differ, but they seem to be generally motivated by China's admission to the WTO and the fact that Chinese domestic markets will increasingly be opened up to foreign capital.

The links between trade and competition policy are widely recognized by economists, and many are concerned that following trade liberalization countries may adopt too slack a competition policy in substitution for trade protection. However, Richardson (1999) and Horn and Levinsohn (2001) demonstrate that trade liberalization may lead countries to adopt too *strict* a competition policy. But Chinese experience seems to run counter to this, with recent mergers being seen as efforts to improve firms' "competitiveness." One way to capture this in a convenient shorthand is the idea that mergers create synergies; particularly, lower marginal costs. But why should such beneficial mergers be triggered by trade liberalization — why not reap the benefits of synergistic merger whatever the level of foreign competition? In an attempt to answer this question, this paper studies both the public and private incentives in horizontal mergers in an open-economy context.

There is a rich literature in industrial organization on horizontal mergers, from Salant *et al.* (1983) through Lahiri and Ono (1988) and Perry and Porter (1985) to Farrell and Shapiro (1990) and there

[1] Both cited in Zheng (2004), and translated by Ryan Fang.

is a corresponding literature on mergers in an international context including, *inter alia*, Barros and Cabral (1994), Richardson (1998), and Falvey (1998). In this paper, we analyze mergers with a focus on a particular comparative static effect, namely how changes in the level of competition affect both public and private incentives in horizontal mergers. In order to relate this to the Chinese example, we model the changes in competition as caused by foreign firms entering the domestic market.[2] The next section of the paper sets out the linear Cournot model that is considered in this paper. A "quantity equivalence" function is also introduced to assist in managing the asymmetries that arise as a consequence of introducing heterogeneity of firms. Section 3 then analyzes public and private incentives in a merger involving two domestic firms. We consider both nonsynergistic and synergistic mergers and show that, in general, an increase in the level of foreign entry will discourage nonsynergistic mergers, but encourage mergers that create synergies. We conclude with some proposals for further work.

2. The model

Consider a homogeneous good market with an inverse demand function given by $p(Q) = a - bQ$, where a and b are positive constants and Q is market (aggregate) output. Firms have cost functions of the form $C_i(q_i) = F + c_i q_i$, where c_i is the constant marginal cost which depends on the firm's type and F accounts for each firm's fixed costs. Let there be K types of firms, each with a marginal cost that is different from that of the other types. There are n_k type k firms in the market and each has marginal cost c_k, where $k = 1, 2, 3, \ldots, K$. The fixed cost is assumed to be equal across firms for simplicity. Finally, firms play Cournot, choosing their output levels to maximize profits, given their beliefs about the outputs of other firms.

Heterogeneity amongst firms' efficiency levels is required, as it will allow us to explore the effects of merger on average market efficiency

[2]Foreign entry is modeled exogenously and we do not specify the policy changes that trigger changes in the level of foreign entry in the first place.

as well as capture the idea of synergies created by a merger. But introducing heterogeneity into the Cournot model means losing symmetry, which makes firms' equilibrium outputs and market supply difficult to calculate. In order to manage this, we develop the "quantity equivalence" function.

The quantity equivalence function

We define the "quantity equivalence" of i in terms of j, E^i_j, as the ratio of a type i firm's equilibrium output to a type j firm's equilibrium output, i.e. one type i firm's output is equal to the sum of E^i_j type j firms' outputs.

Supposing there are only these two types of firms in the market and supposing that $c_i < c_j$, we can solve for the Nash equilibrium outputs in the usual way:

$$q_i = \frac{a + n_j c_j - (n_j + 1)c_i}{b(n_i + n_j + 1)} \quad q_j = \frac{a + n_i c_i - (n_i + 1)c_j}{b(n_i + n_j + 1)}. \tag{1}$$

Thus $q_i = E^i_j q_j$ and $q_j = E^j_i q_i$, where

$$E^i_j = \frac{a + n_j c_j - (n_j + 1)c_i}{a + n_i c_i - (n_i + 1)c_j},$$

$E^j_i = 1/E^i_j$ and clearly $E^j_i < 1 < E_j$. Note that quantity equivalence is defined over different types of firms' *equilibrium* outputs and, therefore, varies as market conditions change. Clearly it is a function of all the variables that define Cournot equilibrium.

Now, in Cournot, firms maximize their profits by choosing their outputs given their beliefs about the outputs of all other firms. So, if each firm believes that each type j firm will produce as much output as E^j_i type i firms, having n_j type j firms in the market is the same for them as having $n_j E^j_i$ more type i firms. Therefore, we can rewrite a type i firm's equilibrium output as:

$$q_i = \frac{a - c_i}{b(n_i + n_j E^j_i + 1)}. \tag{2}$$

Thus the quantity equivalence function allows us to "convert" other types of firms into one particular type and hence to write algebraic expressions for each type's equilibrium output and the aggregate market variables.

A more thorough introduction and discussion of quantity equivalence is provided in a Technical Appendix — see Fang and Richardson (2008) — where we extend it to accommodate many types of firms and derive a number of its properties for the case where there are n_k type k firms in the market and each has marginal cost c_k, where $k = 1, 2, 3, \ldots, K$. We report these properties here in two lemmata:

Lemma 1. *In a homogeneous good market with linear inverse demand curves, where there are many types of firms playing Cournot and each type of firm has a constant marginal cost that is different from that of others, the ratio of a low-cost firm's output to a high-cost firm's output is always greater than one. This ratio increases if: more firms enter the market; the difference between the two types of firms' marginal costs increases holding one of the marginal costs constant; both types' marginal costs increase holding their difference constant.*

Lemma 2. *For any i and j, the "aggregate quantity equivalence to type i firms," $\sum_i = \sum_{k=1}^{K} n_k E_i^k$, is equal to the market supply divided by the equilibrium output of the type i firms, and its derivative with respect to the number of type j firms is given by:*

$$\frac{d}{dn_j}\left(\sum_{k=1}^{K} n_k E_i^k\right) = \left(\sum_{k=1}^{K} n_k E_i^k + 1\right)\frac{E_i^j}{\sum_k n_k + 1}.$$

3. Horizontal Mergers and Foreign Entry

We turn now to study the profitability of horizontal mergers, to both the participating firms (private incentives for merger) and society as a whole (public incentives for merger) and how they change as we introduce different levels of foreign entry.

We categorize mergers based on the opportunities of cost savings they generate. Using subscript M to denote the new post-merger entity, m the number of firms merging, and P the set of merger participants, nonsynergistic mergers are those in which

$$C_M(q_M) = F_M + c_M q_M,$$
$$F_M = \sum_{i \in P} F_i = mF, \text{ and } c_M \geq \min_{\{i=P\}}(c_i).$$

Synergistic mergers are those for which

$$C_M(q_M) = F_M + c_M q_M,$$
$$F_M < \sum_{i \in P} F_i = mF, \text{ and/or } c_M < \min_{i \in P}(c_i).$$

Mergers that provide savings in fixed costs only we call "weakly synergistic," whereas mergers that improve firms' production technology we term "strongly synergistic."

It is beyond the scope of this paper to explore or discuss the actual existence or cause of any type of cost savings associated with mergers: for any particular type of merger, the nature of the cost savings it provides is exogenously assumed. Our main interest is to see whether foreign entry "encourages" or "discourages" any particular type of merger, i.e. creates or removes private and public incentives for such mergers.

Non-synergistic mergers

In a nonsynergistic merger, the cost function of the post-merger firm is $C_M(q_M) = F_M + c_M q_M$ for $F_M = \sum_{i \in P} F_i = mF$, and we will only analyze mergers involving two participants, so m will always be equal to two.[3]

First, we look at the private incentives for such mergers. In a nonsynergistic merger, effectively, the less efficient firm is closed down while the remaining participant incurs both the firms' fixed costs. Clearly, the merger will be profitable to the participants if the new entity's post-merger gross profit, defined as total revenue minus total

[3]Without loss of generality: mergers that involve $n > 2$ participants and do not create synergies can be viewed as $n - 1$ two-firm mergers. If the merger is synergistic, it is equivalent to $n - 2$ nonsynergistic two-firm mergers, and one synergistic one that creates the same amount of synergies. The net gains or losses from a multi-firm merger will hence be the sum of the gains and losses from all the "sub-mergers."

variable costs, is higher than the sum of the participants' pre-merger gross profits. Let the two participants be of type 1 and type 2, where firm 1 is no less efficient than 2. Formally, letting subscripts denote firm types and superscripts denote pre-merger (0) or post-merger (1) equilibria, the private gains from the merger are given by $G_p = \pi_1^1 - \pi_1^0 - \pi_2^0$. So we will examine, in particular, how the sign of G_p changes as we introduce different levels of foreign entry.

In our Cournot model, if one firm is removed from the market, the reverse of the *business stealing effect*[4] will increase each of the remaining firms' outputs while reducing market supply and pushing the market price up. So, upon the closure of the less efficient firm (firm 2), the remaining participant (firm 1) will produce a larger output and enjoy a higher price than before the merger takes place. We can then identify two main sources of (gross private) gains in this merger: firm 1's pre-merger output is now sold at a higher price and, in the presence of a higher price, the output of firm 1 is expanded. These gains are earned at the cost of firm 2's pre-merger profit, which is given up. The magnitudes of both the increases in firm 1's output and the market price will depend on two factors: firm 2's pre-merger output and the number of nonparticipating firms in the market. As noted by Falvey (1998), in Cournot with linear demand and constant marginal costs, if one firm is removed from the equilibrium, each remaining firm's output will increase — and the aggregate market supply will decrease — by exactly the level of the departing firm's output divided by the number of firms existing in the initial equilibrium. Therefore, the more merger nonparticipants there are in the market, the less firm 1's output and market price will increase in the post-merger equilibrium, and hence the smaller will be the profit gains to the participants. However, an increase in the number of merger nonparticipants will lower the market price as well as outputs by the participants in the pre-merger equilibrium, which will decrease both the (gross private) gains and the cost associated with the merger. Therefore, as we increase the number of nonparticipants

[4]This refers to the situation where introducing a new entrant into the market will reduce the output of all the existing firms (although increasing the total market supply).

the changes of the sign of the net private gains from the merger, G_p, will depend on the rates at which the gross gains and cost decrease respectively.

Using the quantity equivalence function, we can write G_p as follows:[5]

$$G_p = \frac{q_2^0}{\sum_k n_k}\left[(c_2 - c_1) - (a - c_2) \cdot \frac{\sum_k n_k - 1 - E_2^1 - \frac{1}{\sum_k n_k}}{\sum_k n_k E_2^k + 1}\right], \quad (3)$$

where $\sum_k n_k$ is the total number of firms in the market, and $\sum_k n_k E_2^k$ the aggregate quantity equivalence to type 2 firms. Note that $q_2^0/\sum_k n_k$ is always nonnegative so the sign of G_p is determined by the term in the square brackets of (3). When there are no merger nonparticipants in the market, i.e. the merger involves two firms forming a monopoly, the merger is always profitable: $\sum_k n_k = 2$ and $E_2^1 \geq 1$, as firm 1 is (weakly) more efficient than firm 2. But as the number of nonparticipants increases, firm 2's pre-merger output falls, as do the net gains from the merger. The sign of G_p depends on both firm 2's absolute level of efficiency (hence the $(a - c_2)$ term) as well as its level of efficiency *relative to the other firms* (hence the $(c_2 - c_1)$ term and the quantity equivalence ratios E_2^k).

Calculating out these effects we find that, so long as firm 2 is not so inefficient that it cannot survive entry,[6] G_p will become — or remain — negative and then approach zero as we increase the number of nonparticipant (either domestic or foreign) firms in the market, within the relevant range (i.e. so long as firms' output remains positive). As we keep introducing nonparticipants, firm 2's pre-merger output will fall to zero and, as it approaches zero, G_p will become positive. Note that we have firms of different efficiencies here, so a nonsynergistic merger may be privately profitable in

[5] Derivations are relegated to the Appendix to Fang and Richardson (2008).

[6] Otherwise, merging the firms in the face of foreign entry will just mean closing down a firm that does not produce, which is obviously trivial in our analysis. Furthermore, it is technically possible that the high-cost firm is so inefficient relative to the low-cost firm and the nonparticipants, in which case the existence of a very small number of nonparticipants will see the high-cost firm's output fall to zero, while the merger could be always profitable until this (small) number of nonparticipants is reached. However, for similar reasons, we think such cases are not interesting for our analysis here.

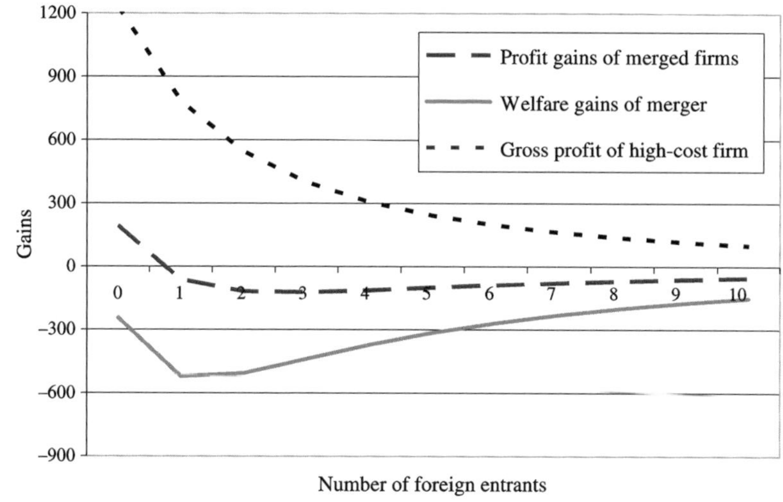

Fig. 1. Nonsynergistic merger

contrast to the results of Salant *et al.* (1983), even if it is not to monopoly.

A numerical illustration is given in Figure 1,[7] where we also show the gross profitability of a high-cost firm: from this one can infer the level of foreign entry that would lead the high-cost firm to shut down. Figure 1 depicts the general case where foreign entry renders the merger unprofitable and the gains from a merger approach zero from below as we increase foreign entry within the relevant range.[8]

Note, too, that this analysis tells us that for a merger to be privately profitable it must provide some form of cost savings, with the only exception being where the merger creates a monopoly. If there are no cost savings from the merger then $c_1 = c_2$ in expression (3) so, by our earlier reasoning, G_p must be negative if $\sum_k n_k > 2$.

[7]Parameter values for all numerical illustrations are reported in the Appendix to Fang and Richardson (2008).

[8]Note that close to zero output and hence positive profit gains, with the chosen parameters, correspond to a very large number of foreign entrants. The graph has been truncated for presentational purposes.

That is, we have the result of Salant *et al.* (1983), although without nonparticipants in a merger necessarily having equal costs.

We now turn to the public incentives for nonsynergistic mergers. The merger is profitable to the public if it increases social welfare, so the net social gain from mergers is given by $G_s = W^1 - W^0 = CS^1 - CS^0 + \Pi^1 - \Pi^0$. As established earlier, in a nonsynergistic merger one domestic firm (firm 2) will be closed down, which will increase each of the remaining firms' outputs but decrease the total market supply (by the same amount, in this particular model). So consumer surplus must fall after the merger, while all the remaining firms will enjoy a profit gain (without counting the loss of firm 2's pre-merger profit to the participants). Using the quantity equivalence function, we can write G_s from a nonsynergistic merger as:

$$G_s = \frac{q_2^0}{\sum_k n_k}\left[\sum_{k\neq f}(c_2 - c_k)\cdot n_k - (a - c_2)\cdot \frac{n_f E_2^f + n_f + \frac{2n_f+1}{2\sum_k n_k} + 1}{\sum_k n_k E_2^k + 1}\right]. \tag{4}$$

Clearly, in contrast to the case for private incentives, nationalities of nonparticipants do matter here. We assume there is only one type of foreign firm, type f, hence changes in the level of foreign entry are represented by changes in n_f.[9] We can interpret c_f as the average marginal cost of foreign firms, which reflects the average "size" of the foreign firms.

First, we examine the profitability of nonsynergistic mergers to the society as a whole when there are no foreign firms in the market. Lahiri and Ono (1988) suggest that, under Cournot oligopoly, removing a firm with a sufficiently low market share is welfare improving. Without foreign entry, (4) becomes:

$$G_s = \frac{q_2^0}{\sum_k n_k}\left[\sum_{k\neq f}(c_2 - c_k)\cdot n_k - (a - c_2)\cdot \frac{2\sum_k n_k + 1}{2\sum_k n_k(\sum_k n_k E_2^k + 1)}\right]. \tag{5}$$

[9]This is for simplicity only and will not affect the analysis: as far as the net domestic welfare gain from the merger is concerned, only the number of foreign entrants and their joint output matter.

Clearly, if all domestic firms are of type 2, then the merger will always reduce domestic welfare, even when there are many firms in the pre-merger equilibrium and firm 2's market share is very small. From the expression above, we need $\sum_{k \neq f}(c_2 - c_k) \cdot n_k$ to be large for the merger to be welfare improving. In other words, we need enough nonparticipants that are significantly more efficient than firm 2: we need firm 2's pre-merger market share to be both absolutely small — closing it down will not then cause activity to fall by too much — and relatively small, so that there is enough efficiency gain to offset the loss due to the fall in activity. A more accurate qualification of the conditions for the closure of firm 2 to be welfare improving, then, is that the average quantity equivalence to a type 2 firm be higher than some threshold defined as a function of the total number of firms in the market, where the threshold will fall as the total number of firms increases.

To determine the effects of changes in the level of foreign entry on the sign of the net social gain from nonsynergistic mergers, we have the following lemma:[10]

Lemma 3. *So long as the high-cost firm can survive foreign entry (i.e. its output remains positive in the pre-merger equilibrium), a sufficient condition for the net social gain to be negative is for foreign firms to aggregately have higher market share than domestic firms in the pre-merger equilibrium.*

Essentially, as foreign entry increases more of the profit of the shutdown domestic firm and the lost consumer surplus accrues to foreign firms (a bad thing). The exact algebraic condition specified in the lemma follows from the linear setting of the model. However, even with more general settings, foreign entry will still render the merger socially unprofitable once foreign firms' aggregate market share increases beyond a certain threshold. Moreover, a further increase in foreign entry will not reverse the trend. Last, we note that the magnitude of the social loss will decrease and approach zero as n^* rises and firm 2's pre-merger output falls to zero.

[10] See the Appendix to Fang and Richardson (2008) for a more detailed discussion.

So, we have the general behavior of the G_s function: G_s will be negative initially (or will become negative as n^* rises) and will then approach zero from below. Therefore, initially publicly attractive nonsynergistic mergers may become unattractive with foreign entry, but never the converse, as long as firm 2 survives foreign entry. (In the case where sufficient foreign entry renders a merger privately profitable when firm 2's output approaches zero, mergers will not be approved since they are not publicly profitable.) A numerical illustration is given in Figure 1 where a little foreign entry makes the merger unattractive, even when it was otherwise desirable, but further entry lessens the social loss from the merger.

Proposition 1. *In a homogeneous good market, where firms have potentially different marginal costs and play Cournot, introducing foreign entry will, in general, discourage mergers that are nonsynergistic and will not encourage such mergers.*

Synergistic mergers

We start by looking at weakly synergistic mergers. Essentially, these are the same as nonsynergistic mergers, except they also provide some savings in fixed costs to the participants. In terms of the graphs, this is tantamount to shifting the G curves up in a parallel fashion. If the fixed cost savings are large enough the merger may always be profitable. Alternatively, with small fixed cost savings, we are back to the nonsynergistic mergers case. Accordingly, the net gains from merger will now approach some positive number, so low levels of foreign entry *may* remove public and private incentives for weakly synergistic mergers, if such incentives exist without the entry, but high levels of foreign entry *will* create public and private incentives for weakly synergistic mergers if such incentives do not exist without the entry.

We now turn to strongly synergistic mergers. We will only analyze strongly synergistic mergers that do not provide fixed cost savings, as the effects of adding the latter are obvious. First, we look at the private incentives for strongly synergistic mergers. In such a merger, the new entity's marginal cost is lower than that of the more efficient participant. This is equivalent to a two-step process: first, a nonsynergistic merger occurs that closes down the less efficient participant (firm 2); and second, the remaining participant (firm 1) becomes a new entity that is even more efficient. Clearly this second step must be profitable for the participants.

So the net private gain, G_p, from a strongly synergistic merger equals that of the corresponding nonsynergistic merger plus something positive. However, we still need to examine how G_p changes as we vary the level of foreign entry. We recognize that, if we keep increasing the number of firms in the market, the new entity's output in the post-merger equilibrium will become greater than or equal to the sum of the participants' pre-merger outputs. For future reference, we use $\tilde{n}^*$ to denote the infimum of the set of n^* that satisfy this condition. Moreover, we denote the infimum of the set of n^* that will render the new entity to produce zero output in the post-merger equilibrium by $\hat{n}^*$ We now have the following lemma:[11]

Lemma 4. *In a strongly synergistic merger, G_p is strictly positive for all $n^* \in (\tilde{n}^*, \hat{n}^*)$.*

Therefore, for any relevant level of foreign entry that is higher than some threshold level,[12] the net private gain from a strongly synergistic merger is strictly positive. The magnitude of this gain will depend on the level of synergies and the participants' marginal costs. As before, if mergers create large enough synergies, they may be profitable at any level of foreign entry. In sum, low levels of foreign entry *may* remove private incentives for strongly synergistic mergers, if such incentives exist without the entry, but high levels of foreign entry *will always* create private incentives for strongly synergistic mergers, if such incentives do not otherwise exist. A numerical illustration is given in Figure 2.

Now consider the effects on public incentives for strongly synergistic mergers, G_s, of increasing n^*. As in the case for private incentives,

[11]See the Appendix to Fang and Richardson (2008) for proof of the lemma.

[12]Given the continuity of G_p in n^*, the threshold will generally be lower than $\tilde{n}^*$.

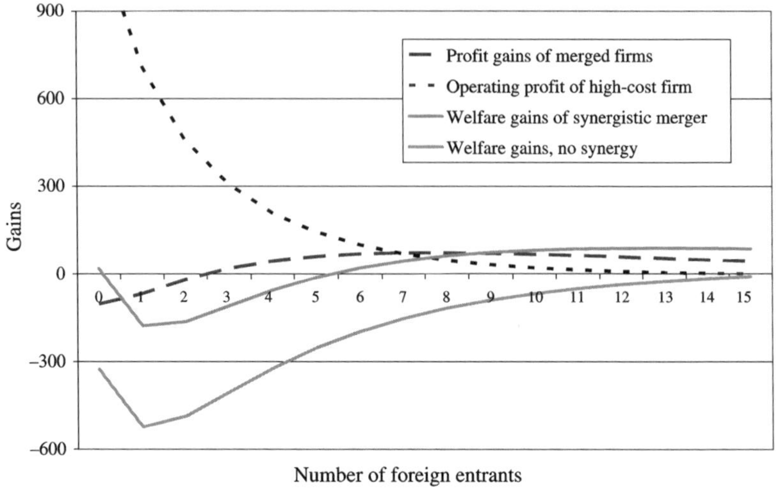

Fig. 2. Synergistic merger

a strongly synergistic merger can be decomposed into a two-step process but, unlike in the case of private incentives, the effect of the second step is now not clear: if the lower cost of the two merging firms is not the lowest-cost firm in the market then a reduction in its costs may be welfare reducing.[13]

Recall that the new entity's output in the post-merger equilibrium will become greater than or equal to the sum of the participants' pre-merger outputs for all $n^* \geq \tilde{n}^*$. When the new entity's output in the post-merger equilibrium is exactly equal to the sum of the participants' pre-merger outputs, the nonparticipants' aggregate output as well as the market supply will not be changed by the merger. So consumer surplus and all nonparticipating domestic firms' profits are unchanged by the merger, while the participants' joint profit rises: at this point G_s must be positive.

[13]Falvey (1998) argues that the gains from merger are greatest for the lowest-cost firm so we should expect to see such a firm involved in any mergers. This is not clear with synergistic mergers, as the gains from a merger depend on the level of synergy which may in turn depend on the participants' identities. However, it is true that, given a fixed amount of synergy, the gains from a merger are greatest for the lowest-cost firm. Clearly, if the lowest-cost firm is always involved in any merger, the second-step welfare effect will always be positive. However, we discuss the general case for completeness.

Given that the new entity is more efficient, we know — using superscript 1 to denote the post-nonsynergistic-merger equilibrium, and superscript 2 the equilibrium after the "second step" of the synergistic merger — that $q_M^2 > q_1^1$. So the expansion of firm 1's output will reduce all the other firms' outputs and increase the market supply (by $(q_M^2 - q_1^1)/\sum_k n_k$). The welfare effects of this will include a gain due to the increase in market activity, gains from transfers of foreign firms' profits to both domestic consumer surplus and a domestic firm (the new entity), a potential loss due to the business stealing by the new entity from the other domestic firms (which might result in a potential efficiency loss if the new entity is less efficient than the other domestic firms), and, of course, a welfare gain due to the fact that firm 1's output in the old equilibrium is now produced by the new entity at a lower cost.

Clearly, if the level of synergy is "large," all the gains will become "large" and the potential efficiency loss will either become "small" or even turn into an efficiency gain, so G_s must be positive. In fact, the welfare effect of this second step is eventually strictly increasing in the level of synergy but, if the synergy is small, it may be positive or negative given different market conditions.

Recall that, in general, G_s in a nonsynergistic merger will either be negative at $n^* = 0$ or will become negative as n^* rises and will then approach zero as n^* rises further. However, as discussed before, with positive synergies, at some critical level of foreign entry the new entity's post-merger output will be equal to the sum of the participants' pre-merger outputs and at this critical point the merger must be socially profitable. Now, if the synergy is close to zero, that critical point will occur only at high levels of foreign entry where firm 2's pre-merger output is also close to zero. Here, G_s in the corresponding nonsynergistic merger will be negative and, therefore, the "second-step welfare effect" must be positive. Since the quantity equivalence ratio of the new entity to type 2 firms is increasing in both the level of foreign entry and the level of synergy, if we increase the latter then this critical level of foreign entry will decrease. We can show that, if the "second-step welfare effect" is positive, it must be strictly increasing in the level of synergy. So, given that the "second-step welfare effect" is continuous in both the level of foreign entry and the level of synergy, as we increase the level of synergy from zero, the critical level of foreign entry will decrease and, for any levels of foreign entry higher than that, the "second-step welfare effect" will be increasing and hence will stay positive. If we keep increasing the level of synergy, the critical level of foreign entry will keep decreasing and the synergistic merger will eventually become socially profitable at any level of foreign entry. So we have the two extreme cases: if the synergy is really large, the merger will always be socially profitable; and, if the synergy is close to zero, the merger will only become socially profitable at a very high level of foreign entry, where firm 2's pre-merger output will be close to zero. The more general case, given a moderate level of synergy, is where G_s will initially be either positive or negative when there is zero foreign entry and will become negative as we increase foreign entry; however, as n^* increases further, the net social gain will become positive (and significantly greater than zero) and will stay positive over the relevant range of the levels of foreign entry.

So we can again conclude that low levels of foreign entry *may* remove public incentives for strongly synergistic mergers, if such incentives exist without the entry, but high levels of foreign entry *will* create public incentives for strongly synergistic mergers, if such incentives do not exist without the entry. A numerical illustration of the net social gain from a strongly synergistic merger is given in Figure 2. We also show the welfare effect of the same merger in the absence of any synergies, in which case it is never desirable. Combining the results we have for both the private and public incentives for synergistic mergers, we have the following proposition:

Proposition 2. *In a homogeneous good market, where firms have potentially different marginal costs and play Cournot, introducing foreign entry at low levels may discourage mergers that are synergistic; however, high levels of foreign entry will encourage such mergers.*

One final exercise we consider is to ask: when the private and social gains have the shapes we have described, at what critical level

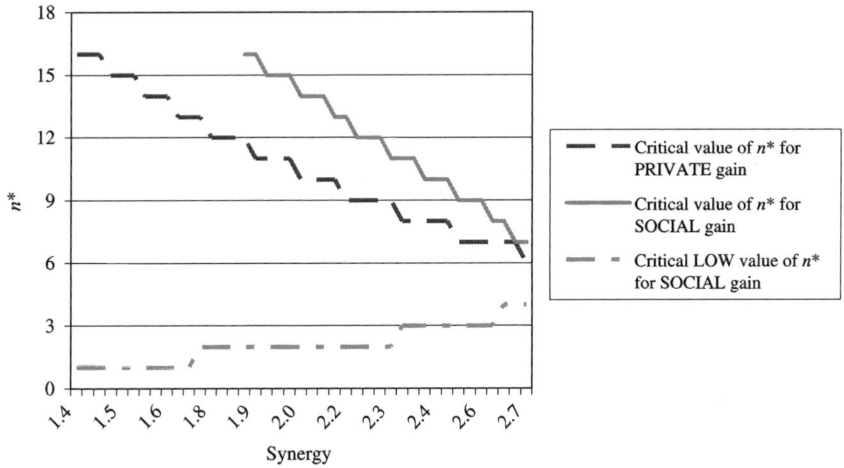

Fig. 3. Critical values of n^* for different level of synergies

of foreign entry does a merger become privately attractive and at what level does it become socially attractive?

Figure 3 illustrates this exercise for one configuration. Synergies greater than those plotted are such that the merger is socially attractive for any level of foreign entry. As the social gain from the merger is typically U-shaped, so zero or a little foreign entry will typically make the merger attractive, higher levels make it unattractive, but higher levels of n^* still might make it attractive again.

The plot labeled "Critical low value of n^* for social gain" indicates a level of n^* such that, for any lower level of foreign entry, the merger would be socially desirable, and the plot labeled "Critical value of n^* for social gain" indicates any level of n^* such that, for any *higher* level of foreign entry, the merger would again be socially desirable. Finally, the plot labeled "Critical value of n^* for private gain" indicates any level of n^* such that, for any *higher* level of foreign entry, the merger would be privately profitable. For example, when the synergy is 2.06 this merger would be socially desirable if $n^* \geq 2$ *or* $n^* \geq 14$ but is privately profitable for any $n^* \geq 10$. The point to note here is that, for this particular simulation, the threshold level of foreign entry above which the merger is always socially attractive, for any particular synergy, is greater than that above which the merger is always privately profitable to participants. This suggests that merger partners might generally be keener to promote a merger than should be the regulator.

We conclude this section by relating our findings to the Chinese experience mentioned in the introduction. Although throughout the paper we have been using the term "level of foreign entry," this should not be interpreted as referring only to the *number* of foreign firms entering the market. As we have seen in our earlier analysis, both the number of foreign entrants and their levels of efficiency matter in determining the profitability of domestic mergers. For that reason, in the context of this paper, the term "level of foreign entry" is better interpreted as the "level of foreign competition."

With that clarification, Chinese experience seems quite consistent with the findings in this section. In China, it is widely believed that foreign firms are far more efficient than domestic firms, which means, for a given "number" of foreign entrants, that the "level of foreign competition" is going to be very high. Also, managers and government officials, as well as economists, often make the claim that these mergers will enhance domestic firms' "competitiveness," which suggests that the mergers are, at least, believed to be synergistic. These all seem to back our explanation of what is happening in China. However, the fact that these mergers are justified by a perceived higher level of foreign entry and perceived level of synergies also raises more questions, as discussed in the next section.

4. Conclusion

This paper attempts to understand the private and public incentives for horizontal mergers given the presence, or prospect, of foreign entry and how these incentives change as the level of foreign entry varies. We found that while low levels of foreign entry may discourage both nonsynergistic and synergistic mergers, high levels of foreign entry will encourage the latter but not the former. These results are not surprising. The profitability of nonsynergistic mergers relies on the abilities to increase price significantly (for private incentives) and to shift production from a specific firm to other targeted firm(s) (for both private and public incentives). The presence of foreign firms constrains and diminishes such abilities and hence renders the mergers unprofitable. However, the size of the gains provided by a given amount of synergy increases, in a relative sense, as the level of foreign entry increases, so a high enough level of such entry will render synergistic mergers profitable.

Chinese experience can be interpreted in a way that is consistent with these findings: although mergers were perceived to generate synergies, these were not large enough to justify mergers given the initial market conditions. But China's WTO admission created the prospect for foreign entry, the level of which was *perceived* to be high, and the mergers consequently became attractive both to the participants and the economy and hence were undertaken by firms, encouraged by the government.

We say "perceived," since in practice the amount of synergy a merger creates and the level of prospective foreign entry (competition) are both rarely known with certainty. Given incomplete information, there are risks that mergers are undertaken when they should not be. This suggests a useful avenue for further research. In the context of a principal–agent relationship between shareholders and the management of firms, informational asymmetries make it harder for shareholders to determine whether proposed mergers are in their best interests or just those of management. In fact, given their impacts on the profitability of mergers, these asymmetries may be the cause of certain conflicts of interest, if the principal and the agent have different attitudes towards risk. Market-wide, uncertainty regarding the level of synergy created by any particular merger makes it harder for nonparticipants to form expectations of the new entity's efficiency level and hence to work out their best responses. With the prospect of future entry, and if incumbent firms have private but incomplete information about the level of that entry, a merger between two particular firms may send signals about the participants' belief of the entry level to nonparticipants, who may then be led themselves to merge. In the Chinese example, merger between some firms, citing prospective foreign entry as the reason, may just lead other firms in the market to believe that they should do the same.

References

Barros, P.P. and L. Cabral (1994). Merger policy in open economies. *European Economic Review*, 38, 1041–55.

Falvey, R. (1998). Mergers in open economies. *The World Economy*, 21, 1061–76.

Fang, R. and M. Richardson (2008). Private and public incentives for mergers in the face of foreign entry. *ANU School of Economics discussion paper 494*, July. Available at http://www.ecocomm.anu.edu.au/research/papers/pdf/wp494.pdf.

Farrell, J. and C. Shapiro (1990). Horizontal mergers: An equilibrium analysis. *American Economic Review*, 80, 107–26.

Horn, H. and J. Levinsohn (2001). Merger policies and trade liberalisation. *Economic Journal*, 111, 244–76.

Lahiri, S. and Y. Ono (1988). Helping minor firms reduces welfare. *Economic Journal*, 98, 1199–202.

Perry, M.K. and R.H. Porter (1985). Oligopoly and the incentive for horizontal merger. *American Economic Review*, 75, 219–27.

Richardson, M. (1998). Foreign entry and domestic welfare. *Weltwirtschaft liches Archiv*, 134, 250–62.

Richardson, M. (1999). Trade and competition policies: Concordia discors? *Oxford Economic Papers*, 51, 649–64.

Salant, S.W., S. Switzer, and R.J. Reynolds (1983). Losses from horizontal merger: The effects of an exogenous change in industry structure on Cournot–Nash equilibrium. *Quarterly Journal of Economics*, 48, 185–99.

Zheng, H. (2004). The strengthened functions of the capital market. *Jie Fang Daily*, 9 April.

Part IV

Parallel Imports

Chapter 14

An Elementary Proposition Concerning Parallel Imports

Martin Richardson

Abstract: This paper demonstrates that, when countries individually choose whether or not to prohibit parallel imports, a global Nash equilibrium involves the permitting of parallel importing into all relevant foreign markets i.e. global uniform pricing. This result is sensitive in a straightforward way to the tariff-setting powers of countries and to the specification of a government's objective function (i.e. political economy considerations). We also show that when countries can prevent "parallel exports" then any Nash equilibrium involves global price discrimination.

Keywords: Grey markets; Parallel imports

1. Introduction

The phenomenon of parallel imports (or grey markets) — "the importation genuine ... goods for resale by an agent other than the local authorised distributor"[1] — is one that has gained increasing prominence in recent years. A number of countries — including Australia, New Zealand and Singapore — have recently liberalised restrictions on parallel importing and the European Union is very active in preventing restrictions on *internal* parallel imports.[2] Scherer (1994) notes that the first major competition policy enforcement

Originally published in *Journal of International Economics*, 56, 233–245.

[1]NZIER (1998) at http://www.moc.govt.nz//cae/parallel/parallel-01.html#P227_9191.

in the EC concerned an attempted dealership territoriality within the EC and Malueg and Schwartz (1994, MS henceforth) suggest that, "[g]enerally, policies worldwide firmly support parallel imports" (p. 169).[3] The size of the grey market in the US as far back as the mid-1980s has been estimated at $US7b (MS p. 168) and grey market car sales alone in Germany have been estimated at US$6b (Gallini and Hollis, 1999, p. 2).

The economics of grey markets are, in principle, straightforward. The literature considers two broad reasons[4] why grey markets might arise: one is to arbitrage away international price discrimination, the other is to free-ride on investments made by intellectual property right (IPR) holders. In the first of these, a holder of an IPR in some good (by definition a monopolist) would like to set different prices in different markets with different elasticities of demand. Parallel imports remove that ability and enforce uniform pricing on the monopolist.

---

[2]But a number of recent decisions have supported the view that restrictions on parallel imports originating outside the Union are quite permissible. In *Silhouette International Schmied GmbH & Co KG v. Hartlauer Handelsgesgesellschaft GmbH* [1998] ETMR 539 the European Court of Justice (ECJ) ruled that a trademark proprietor's rights in the European Economic Area (EEA) were only exhausted once the goods were placed on the market in the EEA. This was re-affirmed in *Sebago Inc and another v. GB-Unic SA* [1999] All ER (D) 706 when the ECJ stressed that the relevant part of the European Trade Marks Directive meant that trademark rights were only exhausted when products were placed on the EEA market (although another decision suggests that initial sale outside the EEA can give implied consent for goods to be sold on into the EEA depending inter alia on relevant local laws. See *Zino Davidoff SA v. A&G Imports Ltd* [1999] All ER (D) 502.)

[3]See Maskus and Chen (1999) for a recent discussion of parallel import policy in a number of countries.

[4]There are many other explanations too, of course. Frequently, parallel imports simply arbitrage "fire sales" internationally — rather than being a long-phenomenon, parallel importers spceialise in one-off job lots. Another possibility is that international price discrimination reflects differing intellectual property regimes so that in countries that are lenient towards pirating, authentic distributors will optimally charge lower prices. Parallel imports then arbitrage these policy differences, sourcing in the low-price countries to sell in those where pirating is more strictly controlled. And, Maskus and Chen (1999) have recently shown that parallel imports can arise endogenously in a situation of vertical price control between a manufacturer and a downstream distributor: efficient two-part pricing might dictate a low per-unit wholesale price but this makes parallel exporting attractive if it is less than the retail price abroad (less trade costs). They find some empirical support for this argument.

It is well known that imposing uniform pricing on a 3rd degree price discriminating monopolist might reduce aggregate welfare if it leads to small markets — that would otherwise be served — being dropped. In what ie perhaps the leading theoretical analysis of this issue in an international setting, MS note that uniform pricing may be welfare-reducing, from a global perspective, if demand dispersion is high enough. The losers from uniform pricing are, of course, the small countries[5] that might be dropped. Yet the countries listed above as recent liberalisers of parallel import restrictions — New Zealand, Australia and Singapore — are all *small* countries (in the sense of international economics).[6]

Why is this? MS note that a "mixed" system in which countries are grouped and each group faces a uniform price internally will, for appropriately chosen groups, typically welfare-dominate (from a global perspective) any pure system of either global uniform pricing or global price discrimination. But what would we anticipate if we look not at global welfare but rather at the incentives facing individual countries? Would some countries — low elasticity, high price onces — allow grey markets while others do not?

This paper considers an international policy-setting game in which countries choose, simultaneously and non-cooperatively, domestic policy on grey markets. In the next section we set up a simple model focusing only on price discrimination as a rationale for parallel imports to argue that any Nash equilibrium to such a game effectively involves de facto global uniform pricing. Section 3 considers some extensions and qualifications of the basic insights looking

[5]In their analysis "smaller" corresponds to "more elastic demand" as they look at linear inverse demand curves of the form $p = a(1-q)$ and look at dispersion in a affecting both the slope and the price intercept of the demand curve. In such a linear model aggregate output is unaffected by a switch from discrimination to uniform pricing so long as all markets are still served so welfare would rise in such a case.

[6]To focus on one of these, in May 1998 New Zealand unilaterally removed prohibitions on parallel imports of copyright goods. The US immediately responded by announcing a special 301 out-of-cycle review of New Zealand. While there are some special circumstances in the New Zealand case given the extensive reach of its copyright legislation (see Richardson (1999) and Wood and Scholes (1998)), it is by no means alone in permitting parallel imports.

at tariff-setting, political economy issues and the effects of allowing restrictions on re-exports. A final section concludes.

2. The Basic Result

Consider a world of $n+1$ countries indexed by $i = 0, 1, \dots, n$. A monopolist firm in country 0 produces a homogeneous good sold, potentially, in all $n+1$ countries under the canonical conditions of international trade theory: zero transport costs, non-decreasing production costs and full information on (well-behaved) demand conditions. Demand for the product in country $i = 0, 1, \dots, n$ is given by $x_i(p_i)$ where p_i is the price charged in country i. The firm's costs are given by $C(X)$ where $X \equiv \sum_{i=0}^{n} x_i$, $C'(X) > 0$ and $C''(X) \geq 0$. Welfare in country $i = 1, 2, \dots, n$ is simply consumers' surplus whereas in country 0 welfare includes the global profits of the monopolist. If we denote by a_i the "choke price" in country i (the price at which demand just falls to zero, so $a_i = x_i^{-1}(0)$) then $W_0 = CS_0 + \pi = \int_{p_0}^{a_0} x_0(s)ds + \sum_{i=0}^{n} p_i x_i - C(X)$ and $W_i = CS_i = \int_{p_i}^{a_i} x_i(s)ds$ for $i = 1, 2, \dots, n$. Thus $\partial W_i / \partial p_i = -x_i(p_i) < 0, i = 1, \dots, n$ and $\partial W_0 / \partial p_0 = [p_0 - C'(X)]x_0' < 0$ when p_0 is chosen to maximise profits. Note too that $\partial W_0 / \partial p_i = x_i + (p_i - C')x_i'$ for $i > 0$. This last expression is zero, either because the country is not served, or by the firm's FOC. We assume that the firm's problem has an interior solution for at least some markets: $a_i > C(0)$ for some i.

Suppose the monopolist can price discriminate across all markets. Let $S \equiv \{i : x_i(p_i^*) > 0$ denote the set of countries that are served in this case where p_i^* is the price charged to country i under price discrimination: so S is the set of countries in which there are strictly positive sales under global price discrimination. Denote its complement by N so that $N \equiv \{i : x_i(p_i^*) = 0\}$. Suppose that, under global uniform pricing in $i = 0, \dots, n$ (that is, when the monopolist must charge the same price in every market) it maximises profit by setting $p_i = \underline{p}$ and sells $\underline{x}_i(\underline{p})$ in country i for total sales of $\underline{X}$. Let $\underline{S} \equiv \{i; x_i(\underline{p}) > 0\}$ denote the set of countries that are served in this case and denote its complement by $\underline{N}$ so that $\underline{N} \equiv \{i; x_i(\underline{p}) = 0\}$. Finally, we consider first only two policy extremes for countries: either parallel imports are permitted with no restrictions or they are prohibited outright. Let I_i be an indicator variable, which takes the value 1 for countries that permit parallel imports and 0 for countries that do not.

Our conclusions depend on the following:

Key assumption. Consider any two countries, i and j, which are both served under price discrimination and face prices $p_i^* > p_j^*$, respectively. Under our maintained assumptions, if these two were to be treated as a single market they would face a common price $p \in [p_j^*, p_i^*]$ and welfare in country $i(j)$ would be weakly higher (lower) than with price discrimination.[7]

We assume henceforth that $x_i' < 0$ and $x_i'' \leq 0$. This is assumed simply to give a unique global maximum to the firm's problem. In fact, our propositions will apply in any world where our Key assumption holds (for which these restrictions are sufficient).

We consider a simple two-stage game with the following structure: first, all governments simultaneously choose whether to permit or prohibit parallel imports; second, the monopolist sets a price in each country. If this involves a higher price in a country that permits parallel imports than in some other country then arbitrage will occur from the latter to the former (parallel imports) and the monopolist's profits will be lower than if it were to set a uniform price that "groups" the two countries together in the sense of treating them as a single market. Suppose, initially, that either $0 \in \underline{N}$ or $0 \in \underline{S}$ and $p_0^* < \underline{p}$ We can now state our central result.

Proposition 1. *Consider the one-shot policy game involving the simultaneous and non-cooperative choice of parallel import policy by all countries. In any Nash equilibrium to this game, only countries* $i \in \underline{S}$ *are served and* $p_i = \underline{p}\ \forall i, j > 0, i, j \in \underline{S}$.

Proof. Suppose not. Consider some country $i \neq 0, i \in M$ where M denotes the set of countries other than the monopolist's home country facing the highest price in a discriminating equilibrium: $M \equiv \{k\colon p_k^* = \max\{p_1^*, \ldots, p_n^*\}\}$. Similarly, let J denote the set of countries facing the lowest price in a discriminating equilibrium:

[7]See Tirole (1988, pp. 137–138).

$J \equiv \{k\colon p_k^* = \max\{p_1^*, \ldots, p_n^*\}\}$. While J and M may be singletons, they are clearly non-empty. So no country (other than possibly the monopolist's home country) faces a higher price than country i or a lower price than any country $j \in J$. This can only occur if $I_i = 0$. Suppose country i were instead to set $I_i = 1$ i.e. it were to permit parallel imports. It would then be grouped by the supplier with some country $j \in J$ and treated as a single market. By our Key assumption, welfare in country i would be higher than with price discrimination i.e. $I_i = 0$ could not be a Nash equilibrium. Accordingly, all countries $i > 0$ that are served must face the same price and $p_i = p_j \forall_i, \in \underline{S}$, as claimed.[8] Furthermore, $I_i = 1\ \forall i \in \underline{S}$ such that $p_i^* > p_i$. □

This result says that we effectively observe global uniform pricing[9] and the intuition behind it is very simple. The countries that would like to permit parallel importing are those that are discriminated against in its absence. So "high-price" countries can "undo" price discrimination. While high-elasticity demand countries might favour discrimination, in this set-up they cannot enforce it globally when high-price countries permit grey markets.[10]

---

[8] A referee has noted that allowing parallel imports is, in fact, a weakly dominant strategy for every country in that a country can do no worse allowing parallel imports than prohibiting them regardless of the policy choices of other countries.

[9] Technically there are multiple equilibria here depending on the policy choices of both the countries in $\underline{N}$ and those in $\underline{S}$ that would face $p_i^* < \underline{p}$ in the absence of parallel imports (these latter might prohibit parallel imports but with no effect on the equilibrium price). Clearly these equilibria are all equivalent to global uniform pricing. The only exception that might arise is if $0 \in \underline{S}$ and $p_0^* > p_E$ where $p_E < \underline{p}$ is the uniform price that would be charged to all export markets if $0 \in \underline{S}$ but country 0 prohibits parallel imports. If country 0 then permits parallel imports it will lead to a uniform price of $\underline{p}$ — lower at home but higher in the rest of the served markets than p_E. While the sum of consumers' surplus and profits in its own market must increase with this, if the decrease in profits from the served export markets is substantial it *could* more than offset this. In that case the source country would prohibit parallel imports. Nevertheless, all foreign markets will still face a uniform price, as in Proposition 1.

[10] This result seems robust to repeated game complications. The usual complication repetition adds to a one-shot full information game is that, while repetition of any Nash equilibrium to the one-shot game is still a Nash equilibrium in the repeated game, there is a much richer variety of strategies agents can play and this can sustain other mutually-beneficial outcomes through appropriately chosen punishment strategies. However, in the

We close this section with a final observation. As noted earlier, MS show that world welfare may be higher than with either complete price discrimination or uniform pricing in a "mixed" system in which countries are grouped. The monopolist can then discriminate between the groups but charges a uniform price within a group. Clearly this does not affect the world of Proposition 1.

3. Extensions and Qualifications

Our initial query was motivated by the observation that real-world practice does not conform to the predictions of economic theory: it is frequently small countries who have pursued parallel import liberalisation most eagerly. This might be attributed to free-rider behaviour in the broad area of intellectual property (see Barfield and Groombridge (1998)) but we have suggested, in a very simple and stylised model, that there is a case for all importing countries, large or small, to permit parallel imports. However, of course, we do not observe this in practice either. In this section we consider three extensions and qualifications to the above analysis: tariff setting, political economy considerations and the effects of "parallel export" restrictions.

3.1. *Tariffs and parallel imports*

The model of the previous section is one in which countries have a single policy instrument: prohibition or permission of parallel imports. In a more realistic setting countries can also choose other instruments such as tariffs. Knox and Richardson (1999) consider a two-country model in which tariffs are also available to governments and show that while permitting parallel imports is always attractive in the absence of tariffs (e.g. due to multilateral or bilateral trade agreements) it

simple setting of this section in which the strategic players are governments only, repetition changes nothing. The reason is that no combination of actions by the countries can raise the welfare of the country facing the highest price in any discrimination equilibrium compared to the equilibrium of Proposition 1. Hence, as in Proposition 1, any other outcome "unravels" iteratively.

may not be attractive at all if even a small country can levy an optimal tariff against the monopoly. In any case, the *relative* attraction of permitting parallel imports is always greater when tariffs are not available. This does not automatically invalidate Proposition 1, however. While tariffs reduce the return to the monopolist, allowing parallel imports is always attractive to high price countries. Only if the range of prices that would prevail in the absence of parallel imports is not too great will the availability of tariffs disrupt the logic of Proposition 1 (in that a relatively high price country might prefer to prohibit parallel imports).

3.2. *Political economy considerations*

In this model (and in Knox and Richardson (1999)) countries desire to be low-price destinations for the monopolist's exports. This is based on the government maximising economic welfare as traditionally understood but the reality of trade policy setting in most countries is that it is driven by "political economy" factors. There are a number of complications involved in introducing such issues into the parallel import setting, however. First, many such models are driven by the concerns of import competing producers but, in this setting, the imported product is necessarily produced by a monopoly. Further, internal resistance to parallel imports in practice has typically been expressed by local distributors of IPR goods, not by import-competing producers. As the surplus accruing to distributors can be extracted by the monopolist wholesaler through licensing fees, one might suspect there is little to be gained from lobbying in an equilibrium model where policy is fully anticipated. We show now, however, that in a simple model in the spirit of Grossman and Helpman (1994) (G&H henceforth) parallel imports may be prohibited by active lobbying.

Consider a two-country model in which countries A and E both consume a good produced by a monopolist in country B. Suppose that country A faces the higher price if the markets are segmented. The monopolist licenses the sale of the product to a local distributor in country A and charges a license fee, L. The local distributor realises a profit of π_A and retains $\rho = \pi_A - L - \lambda$ where λ is a lobbying payment to the government of A. The government in country A seeks, *à la* G&H, to maximise $U_A = \lambda + \gamma[CS_A + \pi_A - L]$ where CS_A denotes consumers' surplus in A and γ is a weight placed on economic welfare.[11]

We suppose that the timing of actions is as follows. In the first stage the monopoly producer sets the license fee, L. The second two stages constitute a G&H-type game: the licensee in A determines its lobby contribution, λ, to offer the government and, in the third stage, the government decides whether or not to permit parallel imports and collects the associated lobby payment, the monopolist provides the good to the distributor and the market clears. If parallel imports are prohibited optimal behaviour by the monopolist is to supply the good at marginal cost (extracting what it can through the license fee); otherwise it supplies it at the optimal uniform price across the two markets, $\underline{p}$. We seek a subgame perfect equilibrium to this game; accordingly, we solve backwards.[12]

Suppose, in the third stage, that no lobbying were done ($\lambda = 0$) so parallel imports were permitted. The payoffs to the monopolist, the distributor and the government in A are then, respectively:

$$\begin{aligned} \pi_T^{pi} &= L + \pi_B(\underline{p}) \\ \rho^{pi} &= \pi_A(\underline{p}) - L \\ U_A^{pi} &= \gamma[CS_A(\underline{p}) + \pi_A(\underline{p}) - L] \end{aligned} \tag{1}$$

[11]As in G&H this comes from maximising a weighted sum of lobby contributions and economic welfare in which the post-contribution (net) profits of the domestic firm appears, so long as the weight on the former exceeds the weight on the latter. Our model has little of the richness of G&H, note, as we do not consider rival lobby groups due to the nature of the monopoly market considered here. Nevertheless, the timing, objective function of the government and the rationale for lobby payments are much as in the G&H model and the interested reader is referred there for a more complete explanation of the underlying model.

[12]Issues of the government "reneging" — accepting the contribution but then allowing parallel imports anyway — do not arise here as the lobby paymentis only made contingent on the parallel import regime chosen: the distributor's choice in the second stage is simply a (binding) offer — a menu of options for the government.

where a *pi* superscript indicates that parallel imports are permitted and π_{T} denotes the total profits of the monopolist wholesaler.

Now suppose, instead, that lobbying occurs and in the third stage parallel imports are *not* permitted. The corresponding payoffs will then be as follows:

$$\begin{aligned} \pi_{\mathrm{T}} &= L + \pi_{\mathrm{B}}(p_{\mathrm{B}}) \\ \rho &= \pi_{\mathrm{A}} - \lambda - L \\ U_{\mathrm{A}} &= \lambda + \gamma[CS_{\mathrm{A}}(p_{\mathrm{A}}) + \pi_{\mathrm{A}} - L] \end{aligned} \tag{2}$$

where the lack of superscripts indicates that parallel imports are *not* permitted and p_j denotes the (discriminatory) retail price in country $j = \mathrm{A}, \mathrm{B}$.

The government in A will prohibit parallel imports iff $U_{\mathrm{A}} \geq U_{\mathrm{A}}^{pi}$ i.e. from (1) and (2), if $\lambda + \gamma(\Delta\pi_{\mathrm{A}} - L) \geq \gamma(\Delta CS - L)$ where $\Delta CS = CS_{\mathrm{A}}(p_{\mathrm{A}}) > 0$ and $\Delta\pi_{\mathrm{A}} = \pi_{\mathrm{A}}(p_{\mathrm{A}}) - \pi_{\mathrm{A}}(p) > 0$. So in the second stage, given L, the distributor in A maximises its payoff (ρ in (2)) by minimising λ subject to this "participation" constraint for the government,[13] implying that the latter holds with equality:

$$\lambda = \gamma(\Delta CS - \Delta\pi_{\mathrm{A}}). \tag{3}$$

Having parallel imports barred is only desirable for the distributor if $\rho > \rho^{pi}$ i.e. from (1) and (2), if $\lambda \leq \Delta\pi_{\mathrm{A}}$ or, from (3), if:[14]

$$\Delta\pi_{\mathrm{A}} \geq \frac{\gamma}{1+\gamma}\Delta CS. \tag{4}$$

[13]Note that the maximised value of π_{A} is unaffected by the choice of λ as the latter is a lump sum payment to the government.

[14]An alternative way to solve this problem is to recognise, as noted earlier, that the final two stages constitute a very simple and limiting version of the common agency game adapted by G&H and Konisihi *et al.* (1999) in which there is a single principal only. By Proposition One of Konishi *et al.* (1999), any coalition-proof equilibrium here will involve a parallel imports policy choice that maximises the joint welfare of the distributor and the government in A. That is, parallel imports will be prohibited iff $U_{\mathrm{A}}^{pi} + \rho_{\mathrm{A}}^{pi} = \gamma[CS_{\mathrm{A}}(\underline{p}) + \pi_{\mathrm{A}}(\underline{p}) - L] \leq \gamma CS_{\mathrm{A}}(p_{\mathrm{A}}) + (1+\gamma)(\pi_{\mathrm{A}}(\pi_{\mathrm{A}}(p_{\mathrm{A}}) - L) = U_{\mathrm{A}} + \rho_{\mathrm{A}}$ which can be rewritten as condition (4) in the text. The lobby payment is simply a transfer that affects the distribution of that joint surplus across these two players. Further, the structure of our problem is one of a single principal so it (the distributor) can extract the entire surplus from the lobbying relationship. It will therefore set its lobbying payment such that the government's surplus is reduced to its reservation level, which gives us condition (3).

Subject to this condition (which is purely parametric) in the first stage the monopolist maximises π_{T} in (2) by maximising L given the distributor's "participation" constraint ($\rho \geq 0$) implying that the latter also holds with equality or, from (2):

$$L = \pi_A - \lambda. \tag{5}$$

Violation of (4) implies that there is no value of λ that the subsidiary is willing to offer that would induce the government to prohibit parallel imports. So long as (4) does hold, the equilibrium lobby payment and license fee are given in (3) and (5).

Consider a linear case in which the monopolist produces at a constant marginal cost c and (inverse) demand in each country is given by:

$$\begin{aligned} p_{\mathrm{A}} &= a - bD_{\mathrm{A}} \\ p_{\mathrm{B}} &= \alpha - \beta D_{\mathrm{B}} \end{aligned} \tag{6}$$

Our presumption that A faces the higher discriminatory price now requires $a > \alpha$ and without loss of generality we henceforth set β to unity. It is straightforward to show that

$$\Delta\pi_{\mathrm{A}} = \frac{b(a-\alpha)^2}{4(1+b)^2} > 0$$

and

$$\Delta CS = \frac{(a-\alpha)}{8(1+b)^2}[b(a-\alpha) + 2(1+b)(a-c)] > 0.$$

Hence we can rewrite condition (4) as (7):

$$\gamma \geq \left(\frac{2b(a-\alpha)}{2(1+b)(a-c) - b(a-\alpha)}\right) \equiv \underline{\gamma} \tag{7}$$

Thus if $\gamma \leq \underline{\gamma}$ we will observe the prohibition of parallel imports; otherwise parallel imports will be permitted. Inspection of (7) reveals some intuitive results: a prohibition on parallel imports is more likely, ceteris paribus, the lower is γ (the weight on economic welfare), the lower is α (the price intercept in the other country) and the higher is a (the domestic price intercept), c (marginal cost) and b (the slope of the domestic demand curve). The lower is γ the more important to the government are lobbying contributions hence prohibition of parallel imports is more likely (although, from (3), the government is no better off in equilibrium with such imports than without: although it receives lobby payments these exactly equal the welfare-weighted loss of consumer surplus and gain in distributor's profit from prohibiting parallel trade). The other results all follow for the same reason: for instance, a lower α (greater dispersion of the demand curves in terms of choke prices) indicates increased profitability from price discrimination and thus greater lobbying.

Finally, from (5), the domestic distributor makes zero net profit in equilibrium here, even though parallel imports are prohibited: the license fee extracts all profit that is not contributed as lobby payments to the domestic government.

How does this tie into the model and results of the previous section? This analysis suggests that if governments are motivated by political economy concerns then even high price destinations may choose to prohibit parallel imports. In such a case, of course, Proposition 1 would no longer apply. However, the lower the demand dispersion (in terms of choke prices) the less likely is prohibition of parallel imports in high-price countries (in contrast to the tariff-setting case) because of the reduced gains from discrimination and thus lower lobbying expenditures.

3.3. *Parallel export restrictions*

The third and final extension of our earlier model that we consider relates to what might be called "parallel exports": the re-export of licensed sales from low price countries. Proposition 1 suggests that one set of beneficiaries of parallel import restrictions — countries that face low price in a discriminatory outcome — cannot do anything to prevent global uniform pricing in equilibrium. As MS note, however, there is one way that countries that are favoured by international price discrimination *can* encourage it, even when others permit grey markets, and that is by prohibiting the re-export of licensed sales. Thus a prohibition on parallel exports could retain international price discrimination. So consider the one-shot policy game involving the simultaneous and non-cooperative choice of I_i by all countries *along with* the choice of whether or not to prohibit parallel exports. In this case we get the following result:

Proposition 2. *Consider the one-shot policy game involving the simultaneous and non-cooperative choice of parallel import* **and** *export policy by all countries. In any Nash equilibrium to this game, only countries $i \in S$ are served and are charged prices p_i^*.*

Proof. If any served countries are grouped together and charged a uniform price then, by our Key assumption, any country in the group which would receive a lower price if discrimination were permitted can obtain that price by prohibiting parallel imports and exports. So no dissimilar countries can be grouped in equilibrium. □

So now it is "low-price" countries that "undo" uniform pricing and we effectively observe global price discrimination.[15]

While this is a theoretical possibility, the prohibition of parallel exports is not a policy one sees enacted in practice, perhaps for reasons of policing difficulties, latent mercantilism and a perception that this is a policy that serves private rather than national interests. Our analysis to date has taken the behaviour of the monopolist as essentially passive. And yet one might anticipate that the monopoly manufacturer would desire to take steps to prohibit parallel trade, perhaps through closer integration into or control over distribution channels (as has been suggested in the case of Japan where government policies might permit parallel imports de jure while private practices prohibit them de facto)[16] or through explicit controls on re-exports. Indeed, there is evidence that some manufacturers do attempt to control this behaviour (see Michael (1998)).[17] Interestingly, however, a recent decision in Spain has questioned such

[15] Again there are multiple equilibria here depending on the policy choices of the countries in N but now they are all equivalent to global price discrimination. I am grateful to a referee for noting, too, that the choice of parallel *import* regime in this setting is redundant: whether or not countries permit parallel imports, parallel export restrictions ensure that they do not occur.

[16] See also the analysis of Maskus and Chen (1999).

[17] "However, only 18% of respondents in Michael's (1998) survey of US manufacturers reported that they would prohibit parallel exports of their products under all

steps — pharmaceutical company (Glaxo Wellcome) employed a dual pricing system with one price for products sold through Spanish pharmacies and a higher price for those sold to Spanish wholesalers who were deemed to be the source of parallel exports into the rest of Europe. Spanish legal authorities ordered in December 1998 that this dual pricing scheme be suspended pending a further ruling; since then the European Commission's competition directorate, DGIV, has notified the company that it perceives this pricing system to be a restriction of competition in violation of European competition rules.

4. Conclusion

We began by noting that recent policy reforms by a number of countries have involved relaxing restrictions on parallel imports and that it has frequently been small countries that have liberalised in this fashion. This runs counter to the observation that under uniform pricing it is small countries that might suffer from being "dropped" by a monopolist supplier. In this paper we have argued that, in a simple price discrimination model where countries choose their parallel importing regime simultaneously and non-co-operatively, any Nash equilibrium is effectively one of global parallel importing. This perhaps renders less surprising the observation that policy-makers globally are sympathetic to grey markets, despite their ambiguous consequences for global welfare.

Our result begs the question of why we do not then observe all countries permitting parallel imports. One explanation, of course, is that parallel imports may be driven by more than arbitrage across a discriminating monopolist's markets. Even in such a setting, however, we have examined a number of other qualifications and extensions which would temper the stark and rather stylised result derived here.

---

circumstances, indicating that it can serve international marketing purposes other than simply arbitraging third degree price discrimination.

References

Barfield, C. and M. Groombridge (1998). The economic case for copyright owner control over parallel imports. *Journal of World Intellectual Property*, 1, 903–939.

Gallini, N. and A. Hollis (1999). A contractual approach to the gray market. *International Review of Law and Economics*, 19, 1–21.

Grossman, G. and E. Helpman (1994). Protection for sale. *American Economic Review*, 84, 833–850.

Knox, D. and M. Richardson (1999). *Trade policy and parallel imports.* University of Otago, Dunedin, New Zealand, Mimeo.

Konishi, H., K. Saggi and S. Weber (1999). Endogenous trade policy under foreign direct investment. *Journal of International Economics*, 49, 289–308.

Malueg, D. and M. Schwartz (1994). Parallel imports, demand dispersion and international price discrimination. *Journal of International Economics*, 37, 167–195.

Maskus, K. and Y. Chen (1999). Vertical price control and parallel imports. University of Colorado at Boulder, CO, Mimeo.

Michael, J. (1998). A supplemental distributional channel? The case of US parallel export channels. *Multinational Business Review*, 6, 24–35.

NZIER (1998). In: Parallel Importing: A Theoretical and Empirical Investigation. Report to NZ Ministry of Commerce, Contract 1441, February 1998. New Zealand Institute of Economic Research (Inc), Wellington, New Zealand, http: //www.moc.govt.nz//cae/parallel/index.html.

Richardson, M. (1999). *Some observations on parallel imports.* University of Otago, Dunedin, New Zealand, Mimeo.

Scherer, F.M. (1994). *Competition Policies for an Integrated World Economy.* Washington DC: Brookings Institution.

Tirole, J. (1988). *The Theory of Industrial Organisation.* Cambridge, MA: MIT Press.

Wood, P. and K. Scholes (1998). Parallel importing — the legal and commercial consequences of the Government's decision to lift the ban. NZ Intellectual Property Journal, 5, August.

Chapter 15

Trade Policy and Parallel Imports

Daniel Knox and Martin Richardson

Abstract: We consider the simultaneous choice of parallel importing regime and tariff policy in a setting of international price discrimination by a monopolist. We show that an importer's optimal tariff decreases when parallel imports (PIs) are permitted. This may lead to the monopolist benefiting from PIs. Allowing PIs is always attractive for a country whether or not it sets an optimal tariff. In a political economy modification, we show that the prohibition of PIs is more likely to emerge (where it would not otherwise) the more the government cares about lobby contributions and the greater are profits from price discrimination.

Keywords: grey markets; parallel imports; commercial policy

1. Introduction

In the late 1990s, a number of countries such as Australia, New Zealand, and Singapore relaxed restrictions on parallel imports (PIs) — the importation of genuine goods into a country without the authorisation of the intellectual property right (IPR) holder in that country. Richardson (2002) offers an explanation for countries permitting PIs: when all countries simultaneously choose their PI regime, any Nash equilibrium involves the abolition of restrictions on PIs by all countries served by the monopolist. From this perspective, one would anticipate that any high-price country in a world without PIs would wish to liberalise its PI regime. From a global

Originally published in *European Journal of Political Economy*, 19, 133–151.

welfare perspective, the analysis of Malueg and Schwartz (1994) suggests that the likely *losers* from a global regime of uniform pricing (a consequence of global PI liberalisation) are small low-price markets who are likely to be dropped.[1] This might seem to describe the liberalising countries identified above, so why have these particular countries been leading recent global moves to liberalise PIs?

One possible explanation is that it is a consequence of the countries being small: allowing PIs is seen as being weak on IPRs[2] and large countries are more likely to represent the interests of IPR holders. We focus on another argument, however, noting that the countries we have mentioned above have all liberalised their international trade regimes in recent years. We consider a model in which an importing country chooses both its PI regime *and* its trade policy and we show that allowing PIs is always attractive to a country with no trade barriers. We also show that if the country is setting a tariff, the optimal tariff is lower in the presence of PIs than in its absence. Nevertheless, the intuition that high-price countries would wish to permit PIs still holds in the tariff-setting context. So a country facing a higher price, net of its optimal tariff, in a segmented market can always do better still by permitting PIs and adjusting its optimal tariff appropriately. While facing a high price under price discrimination is sufficient for a country to favour uniform pricing, it is not necessary. However, if a country faces a lower price, then its PI regime is irrelevant in determining whether or not the monopolist will segment the two markets, whether or not the country favours uniform pricing.

Further, we show in the context of welfare-maximising governments that the reduction in the optimal tariff following the legalisation of PIs is sufficiently beneficial to the monopolist that overall profitability might be higher in the presence of PIs than in their absence. We then look at political economy arguments and show

[1]In their model, small countries are also low-price countries.

[2]This is certainly the perspective of the US, which launched an out-of-cycle review of NZ's IPR regime when NZ liberalised its PI legislation in 1998 and placed NZ on its IP "watchlist".

that these might overturn our earlier findings. In particular, a government that would otherwise choose to permit PIs might prohibit them if it is sufficiently concerned with the profitability of a domestic distributor or if it is subject to lobbying by the monopoly. The latter is more likely in exactly the case where permitting PIs is most attractive to the country — when discrimination is more profitable to the monopolist.

While there is a growing literature on parallel imports in this setting,[3] our analysis is perhaps most closely related to the literature on market integration (see Ishikawa, 2000 for a summary). The key distinction in our analysis, however, is the endogeneity of tariff setting as tariffs are chosen optimally in our model.

2. A two-country model

While PIs might arise for a number of reasons,[4] we focus on international price discrimination by a monopolist. If the monopolist is able to segment markets on the basis of geographical location, then it will maximise profits by charging a higher price in markets with lower demand elasticity. Permitting PIs then allows entrepreneurs to purchase the product in the high-elasticity low-price market and sell it in the low-elasticity high-price market, which leads to the monopolist charging a uniform price and thus arbitrages away price discrimination.[5]

Consider a country that is facing a high price under a system of international price discrimination. This country has two broad tools available to reduce the effects of price discrimination by the IPR holder.[6] One option is to tax imports of the good in question. This allows the government to capture some of the monopoly rent

[3]See Gallini and Hollis (1999), Maskus and Chen (1999), and Malueg and Schwartz (1994).

[4]See the references in the previous note as well as Richardson (2002).

[5]Maskus and Chen (1999) provide an insightful model in which PI goods may flow from high- to low-price countries: they note that the relevant margin for PI goods arbitraged by retailers is the difference between retail price in the destination country and wholesale price in the source.

as tariff revenue. Alternatively, it can remove restrictions on parallel imports so that the monopolist is "constrained by the threat of arbitrage to set a uniform price" (Malueg and Schwartz, 1994, p. 171): entrepreneurs can import the good from a low-price country. A third option is both to allow parallel importing and to use tariffs. Thus, there is interaction of parallel import and tariff policy. The model developed in this paper examines the optimal parallel import and trade policy for a high-price country in a two-country framework.[7] To obtain closed-form solutions for the optimal tariff, we consider a linear model but the intuition for our results does not hinge significantly on this linearity.

Consider a monopolist based in the foreign market, which produces a final good at a constant marginal cost, c, for sale in both the domestic and foreign markets. It faces the following inverse demand curves in the domestic and foreign markets, respectively:

$$p = a - bq$$
$$p^* = a^* - b^*q^* \tag{1}$$

where a represents the domestic country's choke price — the price where demand in that market goes to zero — and p and q denote domestic price and quantity, respectively. Foreign market values are denoted with an asterisk. Henceforth, without loss of generality, we normalise the value of b^* to unity. The restriction required for the domestic market to face the higher free trade price when markets are segmented is:

$$a > a^* \tag{2}$$

The authorised channel into the domestic market can be characterised by either the monopolist granting a domestic firm the exclusive right to import the good or the right to produce it under license,

[6]The firm that holds the IPR is by definition a monopolist, since it has control over production of the unique good. Malueg and Schwartz (1994, p. 171) note that parallel imported products are usually differentiated products, with high fixed costs (such as R&D, advertising and marketing costs) which indicates an imperfectly competitive market.

[7]The market we are interested in is the country facing high free trade prices under a system of international price discrimination. This market will be referred to as the home, or domestic, market. The other market will be referred to as the foreign market.

or the monopolist selling the good directly itself. Either way, in this full-information setting in equilibrium, the monopolist can appropriate any producer surplus created in the domestic market.[8] Therefore, welfare in the domestic market can be thought of as the sum of consumers' surplus (CS) and government revenue (GR).[9] The timing of moves is as follows: first, the domestic government sets its PI policy and any tariff; then the monopolist sets its prices to each or both markets (if PIs are prohibited or allowed, respectively), and finally markets clear. We assume throughout the analysis that tariff policy in the foreign country is fixed — we normalise the foreign tariff to zero (alternatively, we can think of a^* as being the foreign choke price minus the foreign tariff.) We also suppose that the foreign country — the home country of the monopolist — prohibits PIs throughout. This is only relevant if the domestic country sets a tariff such that it faces a net-of-tariff price below p^*, of course, as no arbitrage from the domestic to the foreign country would otherwise be attempted. As PIs are still legal trade they, too, are subject to any tariff levied by the home country.

2.1. *No parallel imports*

We consider first the case in which the domestic country levies no tariff and prohibits all PIs. The discriminating monopolist will maximise profits by equating marginal revenue and marginal cost in each market and it is straightforward to calculate closed-form expressions[10]

[8]The monopolist is able to appropriate all producer surplus in the domestic market, since the maximum amount a rational domestic firm would be willing to pay for the right to distribute/produce the good would be the total amount of surplus it could derive from the market.

[9]As we discuss below, allowing parallel imports may have a once-off wealth effect on the domestic IPR holder if the contractual arrangement between that firm and the foreign IPR owner was based on producer surplus under the parallel import restrictions. This would reduce the benefit to the domestic country of removing parallel import restrictions and may change the optimal policy choice.

[10]The basic linear model we use here is a very familiar one and our results hinge on sometimes messy and tedious but always simple algebraic manipulations. As there are no technical innovations here, we have chosen to leave the paper as uncluttered as possible — we summarise all of our analytics in Appendix A and our complete calculations are in a further Technical Appendix available from the authors on request.

for the variables of interest: $p_{\text{ft}}, q_{\text{ft}}, CS_{\text{ft}}, GR_{\text{ft}}, W_{\text{ft}}, \pi_{\text{ft}}$ and Π_{ft}, where π denotes the profits earned by the monopolist in the domestic market, Π denotes its aggregate profits and the ft subscript denotes free trade, no PIs.

If the government can levy a specific tariff of t, we can rewrite welfare in terms of the tariff, maximise to find an optimal tariff of $t = (a - c)/3$ and solve out once more for the variables of interest. We subscript these with a t to denote values under the optimal tariff and let p_t be the price to domestic consumers ('world' price plus the tariff). We can show that, compared to free trade, there is a positive tariff, domestic price is higher and quantity less but the tariff revenue more than offsets the decreased consumers' surplus. Thus, welfare increases. This is simply the well-known observation that a country facing a monopolist can gain from a tariff by extracting some of the monopoly profit: the domestic price increases by less than the tariff.

2.1.1. *Parallel imports permitted*

By construction, the domestic market benefits from allowing PIs, *absent trade policy*, as it faces the higher price in the segmented markets case. If PIs are allowed, then the monopolist treats the two countries as one aggregate market and maximises profits off the (horizontal) summation of their individual demand curves. It now faces the inverse demand curve given below:

$$\begin{aligned} &p = a - bq - t \quad \text{if } p \geq a^* \\ &p = (a + b(a^* - Q) - t)/(1 + b) \quad \text{otherwise} \end{aligned} \tag{3}$$

where $Q \equiv q + q^*$. From this, we can find the profit-maximising price, the quantities sold in each market and the other variables of interest. First, suppose there are no tariffs so $t = 0$. Again we can solve for the values of the variables of interest, where a 'pi' subscript alone denotes free trade but with PIs allowed. But when the domestic government can levy a tariff, we find that the uniform price is decreasing in t and that, again, the domestic price increases by less than the tariff. Indeed, denoting the domestic consumer price with parallel imports and a tariff by $p_{\text{pi},t}$:

$$\frac{\partial p_{\text{pi},t}}{\partial t} = \frac{1+2b}{2(1+b)} \in \left(\frac{1}{2}, 1\right) \tag{4}$$

Finding the optimal tariff is somewhat messier here than in the absence of PIs but doing so demonstrates our first result:

Result 1. The optimal tariff is lower when PIs are permitted than when they are prohibited.

Note first that this result applies far more generally than to just the linear model studied here (see Appendix A). The intuition for this is simply that under the threat of PIs, a given tariff has less of an effect on the monopolist's price [$\partial(p_{\text{pi},t} - t)/\partial t < 1/2$ in the linear model] than when markets are segmented ($\partial p_t/\partial t = 1/2$) as a given price cut must be extended to both markets under uniform pricing. As the only source of gain from the tariff is this "terms of trade" effect, the optimal tariff is lower as this effect is lessened.

2.1.2. *Model implications*

The domestic country's welfare in each policy regime is summarised in Table 1. From this, we can see our next two conclusions.

Result 2. A tariff is welfare-improving for the domestic country given its PI regime — $W_t > W_{\text{ft}}$ and $W_{\text{pi},t} > W_{\text{pi}}$.

This is as it must be, of course: setting the tariff optimally can be no worse than setting it to zero (free trade). More interestingly, however, permitting PIs is (weakly) welfare-improving whatever the tariff regime:

Result 3. While allowing PIs is always attractive for a free trading country — $W_{\text{pi}} > W_{\text{ft}}$ — uniform pricing will only be attractive for a country setting the optimal tariff when the following condition holds: $6(1 + b)(a - c)(a - a^*) + 3b(a - a^*)^2 < (b + 2)(a - c)^2$. However, this condition implies that $p_t - t < p^*$ so the domestic country cannot induce global uniform pricing by permitting PIs in such a case.

Table 1. Welfare comparisons of policy regimes

PI policy	Trade policy	Welfare
Prohibited	No tariffs	$W_{\text{ft}} = (a-c)^2/8b$
	Tariffs	$W_t = (a-c)^2/6b$
Unrestricted	No tariffs	$W_{\text{pi}} = [(1+b)(a-c)+b(a-a^*)]^2/8b(1+b)^2$
	Tariffs	$W_{\text{pi},t} = [(1+b)(a-c)+b(a-a^*)]^2/$ $[2b(1+2b)(3+2b)]$

So prohibiting PIs can never be attractive for a country that faces the higher price from the monopolist in the segmented markets case under an optimal tariff.[11] Appendix A demonstrates that $p_t - t > p^*$ is sufficient for $W_{\text{pi},t} > W_t$ where p_t is the domestic price cum tariff, p^* the foreign price, and t the domestic country's optimal tariff. The reason is that PIs must still then be attractive — even with an unchanged tariff, PIs would further reduce the price charged by the monopolist and thus raise domestic welfare. And while uniform pricing (and therefore, so it might seem, permitting PIs) is *less* likely to be attractive for a tariff-setting country, the lower is a and the higher is a^*,[12] in fact there is nothing the country can do to induce uniform pricing when it is desirable: in such a case, it is the low-price country and PIs, were they to flow at all, would be *from* the domestic country, not to it. Under our maintained assumption of a PI prohibition in the foreign country, domestic liberalisation has no effect.[13,14]

[11] We are very grateful to a referee for suggesting this possibility.

[12] The intuition being that the beneficial consequences of PIs on the price charged by the monopolist are greater the greater the choke price (as it leads to a greater difference between the prices charged to the two countries when the markets are segmented). This price fall from uniform pricing more than offsets the increased monopolist price due to the reduction in the domestic tariff.

[13] If, instead, the foreign country were to *permit* PIs, then we would observe global uniform pricing in this case regardless of the home country's PI regime. Our result still holds: liberalising PIs is never worse than prohibiting them.

[14] It is also the case that a quantitative restriction on PIs can never be attractive to a country. While PIs lead to uniform pricing by the monopolist, a quota on PIs will not, generically: it will reduce the price discrimination margin but, if the quota is quite tight, the monopolist may prefer not to undercut PI arbitrage entirely. Now, totally prohibiting PIs can only be attractive when a country can set a tariff and, by our discussion of

Note that a higher domestic price in segmented markets with an optimal tariff is sufficient but not necessary for global uniform pricing to be attractive to the home country — it is just that such pricing cannot be induced through PI liberalisation unless the home country is the high-price country. So uniform pricing can still be welfare-improving for a "low-price" country as, even though it yields a worsening in the terms of trade (the function of the optimal tariff), it permits a smaller tariff, which lessens the latter's consumption loss.

We have stressed that our results do not depend on country size (which, in this setting, is inversely related to b). Nevertheless, permitting PIs is likely to be *more* attractive for a small country than a large one, ceteris paribus, when it can set a tariff optimally. The reason is a general one: the uniform price set by a monopolist serving two markets will be closer to the discriminatory price faced by a particular country the larger that country is. This is still the case here (the gain from liberalising PIs is increasing in b) even though the home country's optimal tariff under PIs is increasing in its size ($dt/db < 0$). Thus, given the size of the other country, a high-price country that liberalises PIs will experience a greater reduction in price — and so a greater welfare gain — the smaller it is.

Another interesting conclusion concerns the effects of PIs on the monopolist:

Result 4. When a country sets its tariff optimally, allowing PIs may benefit the foreign monopolist.

So permitting PIs can benefit the monopolist — while the restriction of uniform pricing alone reduces its profits, the decrease in the domestic tariff raises them by even more.[15]This might seem counterintuitive: if uniform pricing yields higher profits, why does the

Result 3, when the country faces a lower price from the monopolist, absent PIs, than does the foreign market. PIs are not then attractive because they lead to worse terms of trade, after the tariff is adjusted optimally. This is still the case even if the volume of PIs is restricted so PIs under a quota cannot raise welfare in a case where prohibition is preferred to unrestricted PIs. If, on the other hand, PIs *are* attractive, then a quantitative restriction will again not be used as it leads only to a partial price reduction. We are grateful to a referee for suggesting this line of enquiry.

profit-maximising monopolist not simply charge each country the same price even when discrimination is feasible? The answer lies in the timing of the game: the firm acts when the PI regime and tariff have been chosen. So if the domestic government prohibits PIs and levies a tariff, then *given* this, the best the firm can do is price discriminate. Even if the firm was somehow to commit to not discriminating against the home country, it would still face a tariff and, in a sense, a regime of allowing PIs can be thought of as a commitment by the country to a lower tariff.

3. Political economy considerations

We have argued that a welfare-maximising country will choose to permit PIs whether or not it is free to set its own tariffs. In this section, we consider two objectives a government might pursue and ask whether these might constrain a country to prohibit PIs.

In our analysis above, it was assumed that the legitimate domestic license-holder had no interest in prohibiting PIs: while the possibility of PIs affects profits earned in the domestic market, these can be entirely appropriated by the parent company through its licensing fee. While an unanticipated change of PI regime would have an impact on the subsidiary, in a fully specified equilibrium the optimal PI regime would be fully anticipated. The trigger for a regime change could be, as we have noted, a liberalisation of a country's trade policy (perhaps through bilateral or multilateral agreement).

The New Zealand experience following PIs liberalisation has been that considerable opposition has been expressed by domestic holders of foreign IPRs. This suggests (correctly, as it turns out) that the liberalisation was not anticipated. In such a setting, where license fees have been paid in anticipation of PI prohibitions, there will be a once-off wealth loss to domestic IPR holders when PIs are permitted. If the domestic government has agreed not to impose

[15]The comparison of total profits under an optimal tariff with and without PIs is a messy one that yields few clear-cut comparative static results. We can show that the firm is more likely to benefit from allowing PIs the lower is c, its marginal cost, but little else — the gain in profits from allowing PIs is nonmonotonic in a and a^*.

tariffs but is motivated by a concern for the profitability of the domestic IPR holder, it is a simple matter (see Appendix A) to see that PIs might not be attractive. As in Result 3, a free trade government that cares only about consumers will permit PIs. But a government that cares only for domestic profits will prohibit PIs. Furthermore, some manipulations show that the gain from prohibiting PIs is monotonically increasing in the weight placed on domestic profits so there is a range of such weights under which PIs would be prohibited.

A second political economy scenario to consider is one based on the common agency model exposited by Grossman and Helpman (1994). In this model, the domestic government chooses its IP regime and, if permitted, its tariff subject to lobbying by industry interests. Richardson (2002) has considered the free trade version of this model in which the foreign IPR holder charges a license fee to the domestic licensee who lobbies through a financial contribution. We now summarise a modification of this model when the government can also choose a tariff.

To make the problem tractable, we suppose that it is the foreign monopolist who lobbies the domestic government directly, rather than through the medium of a domestic licensee.[16] While this structure differs somewhat from that of Grossman and Helpman (1994) in that it allows for foreign lobbying, it is similar to —if somewhat simpler than — Konishi et al. (1999).

The home country government seeks to maximise $U = \lambda + \gamma[CS + GR]$ where CS denotes consumers' surplus, GR denotes government revenue, λ is a lobbying payment, and γ is the weight placed by the government on economic welfare. The timing is as follows: the monopoly producer first determines its lobby contribution, λ; second, the government sets a tariff and decides whether or not to permit parallel imports and finally the market clears.[17] By Proposition 1

[16]Little is changed through this simplification as a domestic licensee would be susceptible to the international IPR holder extracting all of the former's surplus through the license fee.

[17]Technically, the lobbying contribution is a schedule of offers $C(\alpha, t)$ dependent on the subsequent trade policy actions, α and t, of the government where $\alpha \in$

of Konishi et al. (1999), an equilibrium to this game will involve a trade policy choice that maximises the joint welfare of the IPR holder and the government and the lobby payment is simply a transfer that affects the distribution of that joint surplus across the two players. The monopolist's payoff here is its joint profits in both the home and foreign countries ($\Pi = \pi + \pi^*$) as profits in the foreign market are affected by domestic tariff policy when PIs are permitted. The home country government's payoff is the value of consumers' surplus plus revenues: $\gamma[CS + GR]$.

Unsurprisingly, in light of Results 3 and 4 above, maximising the sum of total profits and government welfare may or may not favour PIs. We know from Malueg and Schwartz (1994) that PIs would maximise global surplus in this setting: with low demand dispersion, all markets are still served and with linear demands, total output is unchanged. But in our exercise, we are ignoring that foreign consumer surplus and prohibition of PIs may be attractive if the weight on domestic surplus (γ) is sufficiently low. It may also be attractive if aggregate profits from price discrimination are sufficiently great. Whether PIs are prohibited or allowed, the structure of this problem is such that the entire surplus from the lobbying relationship is extracted by the firm — it will set its lobbying payment such that the government's surplus is reduced to its reservation level in each case.

The case of greatest interest here is where, in the absence of lobbying, PIs would be permitted but they are prohibited in the political equilibrium. If it is optimal for the government to permit PIs in the absence of lobbying, then setting the optimal tariff as in Section 2 allows us to solve for government welfare (see Appendix A). But when PIs are prohibited, the optimal tariff *with* lobbying is given by:

$$t = \frac{\gamma - 2}{3\gamma - 2}(a - c) \tag{5}$$

{allow PI, prohibit PI} and $t \in [\underline{t}(\alpha), t^{\mathrm{P}}]$ where $\underline{t}(\alpha)$ is the (negative) tariff that yields a zero price to consumers and t^{P} is the prohibitive tariff. The government then selects α and t and the firm contributes the corresponding λ. So apparent issues of time consistency (that the government would renege, given λ) do not arise.

which varies from a large subsidy at low γ[18] through free trade at $\gamma = 2$ up to the optimal no-lobbying tariff in the limit as γ goes to infinity. We can then calculate the surplus achieved by the government in the presence of lobbying and thus derive the level of lobby payments from the monopoly that drives government surplus down to that which prevails *absent* lobbying.

Turning to the firm, we calculate its profits in the absence (and facing PIs) and in the presence of lobbying (with PIs excluded, the optimal tariff given in Eq. (5) and the lobbying payment just calculated). We can demonstrate that we do get solutions such that $\lambda > 0$ and the firm is, indeed, better off in the lobbying outcome, i.e.

$$\Pi|_{\text{lobbying, no PIs}} - \Pi|_{\text{PIs,no lobbying}} - \lambda > 0 \tag{6}$$

So while we would see PIs permitted in the absence of lobbying, they are excluded in the political equilibrium. The monopoly captures the entire surplus from this arrangement, however, although it pays a lobby payment to the domestic government.

When is this more likely? A government allowing PIs sans lobbying is more likely the smaller is a^* relative to a (as the fall in price following PIs is then greater) but the prohibition of PIs in the lobbying equilibrium is then also more likely as the relative profitability of price discrimination is greater. Similarly, prohibition of PIs in the lobbying equilibrium is more likely the lower the weight placed on consumer welfare, γ, as lobby payments are then relatively more significant and the effective weight placed on aggregate profits is increased.

4. Conclusion

In this paper, we have shown, in a model in which a country chooses both its PI regime *and* its trade policy, that allowing PIs is always

[18]Second-order conditions for the government's problem hold unambiguously at the tariff specified only when we confine our attention to the case of $\gamma > 2/3$ which we do henceforth. Further, at $\gamma = 1$, the optimal tariff is $-(a - c)$ which yields a domestic price of $p = c$.

(weakly) attractive to a country whether or not it is also setting a tariff. We also consider political economy arguments, however, and show that the attractions of allowing PIs can be overcome by other considerations, notably a sufficient concern for (i) the profits of domestic license holders, or (ii) the political contributions of the global monopolist.

Finally, while our arguments have been made in the context of a simple linear model, the intuition for them does not depend on that linearity. The most significant feature of our model is that allowing PIs leads to a lower optimal tariff against the monopolist and this is a consequence of the fact that a price reduction induced by a tariff under PIs must be extended to all markets, not just the domestic market. This is a very general property.

Acknowledgements

We are grateful to the editor and three referees, to participants at the 2000 RIEB Trade Conference, Kobe University, Japan, particularly Arye Hillman, Jota Ishikawa, and Toru Kikuchi, and to seminar participants at the University of Otago.

Appendix A

A.1. *Parallel imports*

We consider first the case in which the domestic country levies no tariff and prohibits all PIs. It is straightforward to show[19] that we then get the following values for variables of interest, where, as in the text, the 'ft' subscript denotes free trade, no PIs:

$$\begin{aligned} p_{\text{ft}} &= (a+c)/2 \quad q_{\text{ft}} = (a-c)/2b \\ \text{CS}_{\text{ft}} &= (a-c)^2/8b \quad \text{GR}_{\text{ft}} = 0 \\ \pi_{\text{ft}} &= (a-c)^2/4b \quad \Pi_{\text{ft}} = [(a-c)^2 + b(a^*-c)^2]/4b \\ W_{\text{ft}} &= (a-c)^2/8b \end{aligned} \tag{1A}$$

[19]All omitted calculations are in a Technical Appendix available from the authors on request.

where π_{ft} denotes the profits earned by the monopolist in the domestic market and Π denotes its aggregate profits.

If the government can levy a specific tariff of t then:

$$\begin{aligned} p &= (a+c+t)/2 \quad q = (a-c-t)/2b \\ \text{CS} &= (a-c-t)^2/8b \quad \text{GR} = tq = t(a-c-t)/2b \\ W &= (a-c-t)(a-c+3t)/8b \end{aligned} \tag{2A}$$

Maximising welfare over t gives an optimal tariff of $t = (a-c)/3$ and solving out for the variables of interest then yields:

$$\begin{aligned} p_t &= ((a+c)/2) + ((a-c)/6) \quad q_t = (a-c)/3b \\ \text{CS}_t &= (a-c)^2/18b \quad \text{GR}_t = (a-c)^2/9b \\ \pi_t &= (a-c)^2/9b \quad \Pi_t = [(a-c)^2 + (9b(a^* - c)^2)]/9b \\ W_t &= (a-c)/6b \end{aligned} \tag{3A}$$

where the t subscript denotes values under the optimal tariff and p_t is the price to domestic consumers ('world' price plus the tariff).

A.2. *Parallel imports permitted*

First suppose there are no tariffs. From the aggregate demand curve given in the paper,

$$\begin{aligned} p &= a - bq \quad \text{if } p \geq a^* \\ p &= (a + b(a^* - Q) - t)/(1+b) \quad \text{otherwise} \end{aligned} \tag{3}$$

we find the following, where the 'pi' subscript denotes free trade but with PIs allowed:

$$\begin{aligned} p_{\text{pi}} &= [(a+c) + b(a^* + c)]/2(1+b) \\ q_{\text{pi}} &= [(1+b)(a-c) + b(a-a^*)]/2b(1+b) \\ \text{CS}_{\text{pi}} &= [(1+b)(a-c) + b(a-a^*)]^2/8b(1+b)^2 \\ \text{GR}_{\text{pi}} &= 0 \\ W_{pi} &= [(1+b)(a-c) + b(a-a^*)]^2/8b(1+b)^2 \end{aligned}$$

$$\pi_{\text{pi}} = \{(a-c)+b(a^*-c)\}[(1+b)(a-c)+b(a-a^*)]/4b(1+b)^2$$
$$\Pi_{\text{pi}} = [(a-c)+b(a^*-c)]^2/4b(1+b) \tag{4A}$$

But when the domestic government can levy an optimal tariff we can solve for it as:

$$t_{\text{pi}} = [(1+b)(a-c)+b(a-a^*)]/[(1+2b)(3+2b)] > 0 \tag{5A}$$

To see Result 1 — that this tariff is lower than that in the absence of PIs:

$$t \text{ exceeds } t_{\text{pi}} \text{ as } (a-c)/3 > \frac{[(1+b)(a-c)+b(a-a^*)]}{[(1+2b)(3+2b)]}$$
$$\text{or } (1+2b)(3+2b)(a-c) > 3[(1+b)(a-c)+b(a-a^*)]$$
$$\text{or } [5+4b](a-c) > 3(a-a^*) \tag{6A}$$

But this last expression is true by assumption since $(a-c) > (a-a^*)$ and $5+4b > 3$. Plugging t_{pi} into our expression for welfare yields:

$$W_{\text{pi},t} = [(1+b)(a-c)+b(a-a^*)]^2/[2b(1+2b)(3+2b)] \tag{7A}$$

To see Result 3 — that allowing PIs will not be attractive for a country setting the optimal tariff when $6(1+b)(a-c)(a-a^*) + 3b(a-a^*)^2(b+2)(a-c)^2$:

$$W_{\text{pi},t} - W_t = \frac{[(1+b)(a-c)+b(a-a^*)]^2}{[2b(1+2b)(3+2b)]} - \frac{(a-c)^2}{6b}$$
$$= \frac{(3[(1+b)(a-c)+b(a-a^*)]^2 - (1+2b)(3+2b)(a-c)^2)}{(1+2b)(3+2b)}$$
$$= \frac{(6(1+b)(a-c)(a-a^*)+3b(a-a^*)-(b+2)(a-c)^2)}{(1+2b)(3+2b)}$$

The numerator of this last expression is clearly decreasing in a^* and it is straightforward to verify that it is increasing in a.

We claim in the paper that a country imposing an optimal tariff that, in the segmented markets case, still has a higher price than the foreign country must gain from allowing PIs. To see this, note from the expression for P_t and the optimal tariff ($t = (a-c)/3$) that

$$p_t - t > p^* \Leftrightarrow \frac{2}{3}(a+2c) > (a^*+c) \Leftrightarrow (2a+c) > 3a^*$$

From above, allowing PIs is attractive when:

$$\begin{aligned}
W_{pi,t} - W_t > 0 \Leftrightarrow\ & 3[(1+b)(a-c)+b(a-a^*)]^2 \\
& > (1+2b)(3+2b)(a-c)^2 \\
& \Rightarrow (1+b)(a-c)+b(a-a^*) \\
& > (a-c)\sqrt{\frac{(1+2b)(3+2b)}{3}} \\
& \Rightarrow \left\{(1+b)-\sqrt{\frac{(1+2b)(3+2b)}{3}}\right\} \\
& \times (a-c)+b(a-a^*) > 0 \\
& \Rightarrow 3\left\{\frac{1}{b}+1-\sqrt{\frac{(1+2b)(3+2b)}{3b^2}}\right\} \\
& \times (a-c)+3a > 3a^*
\end{aligned}$$

This last inequality will hold, when $p_t - t > p^*$, if its LHS exceeds $2a+c$ or:

$$3\left\{\frac{1}{b}+1-\sqrt{\frac{(1+2b)(3+2b)}{3b^2}}\right\}(a-c)+a > c$$

But this is always the case:

$$\begin{aligned}
& 3\left\{\frac{1}{b}+1-\sqrt{\frac{(1+2b)(3+2b)}{3b^2}}\right\}(a-c)+a > c \\
& \Leftrightarrow 3\left\{\frac{1}{b}+1+\frac{1}{3}-\sqrt{\frac{(1+2b)(3+2b)}{3b^2}}\right\}(a-c) > 0 \\
& \Leftrightarrow 3+3b+b-\sqrt{3(1+2b)(3+2b)} > 0 \\
& \Leftrightarrow (3+4b)^2 > 3(1+2b)(3+2b)
\end{aligned}$$

$$\Leftrightarrow 9 + 24b + 16b^2 > 9 + 24b + 12b^2$$

$$\Leftrightarrow b \neq 0$$

A simple example establishes that the reverse — that a low-price country must lose from uniform pricing — does not apply. Suppose $c = 0, b = 1, a^* = 22$, and $a = 30$. Then $p_t = 20, t = 10, p_t - t = 10$, and $p^* = 11$. So the domestic country faces the lower price from the monopolist in the absence of PIs and gets $W_t = 150$. However, under global uniform pricing, it would set an optimal tariff of $t_{\text{pi}} = 4\frac{8}{15}$ which induces a world price from the monopolist of $p_{\text{w}} = 11\frac{13}{15}$ and domestic welfare of $W_{\text{pi},t} = 154\frac{2}{15} > W_t$.

A.3. *The generality of result 1*

Result 1 is an application of a far more general result. Suppose demand is given by some downward-sloping function $q = q(p), p' < 0$ and marginal costs are constant: $C(Q) = cQ$. Then the absolute value of the optimal tariff is lower in the presence of PIs than in their absence. To see this, note that in the absence of PIs, the monopolist's profit-maximising choice of price in the domestic market yields:

$$q + (p - t - c)q' = 0$$

This implies that:

$$\frac{dp}{dt} = \frac{q'}{\{2q' + (p - t - c)q''\}} < 0$$

where the sign follows from the firm's SOC: $\{.\} < 0$. Now, domestic welfare is given by

$$W = tq(p) + \int_p^a q(p)dp$$

where a again denotes the choke price: $q(a) = 0$. Thus,

$$\frac{dW}{dt} = q + (tq' - q)\frac{dp}{dt}$$

and we can solve, using the firm's FOC, for an expression that implicitly defines the optimal tariff which we shall denote t^*:

$$t^* = \frac{q}{(q')^2}(q' - \{2q' + (p - t^* - c)q''\}) = \frac{q}{(q')^3}(q''q - (q')^2)$$

So, in the linear case $q = (a - p)/b, q' = -1/b$ and $q'' = 0$, the firm's FOC yields $a - p = 1/2(a - t - c)$ and we get $t = -q'/q = (a-p) = 1/2(a-t-c)$ and solving for t yields $t = (a-c)/3$, as in the text. For other demand functions, however, the optimal tariff may be negative, e.g. if $q = p^{-\varepsilon}$ for $\varepsilon > 1$, which solves for an optimal tariff of $t = -p/\varepsilon^2$. The intuition for this is that $dp/dt > 1$ under this demand system so our argument in the text does not apply and it is optimal to subsidise the monopolist as more than 100% of the subsidy is passed on to consumers.[20]

Now suppose PIs are permitted. With $\underline{p}$ denoting the consumer price in the home country, square brackets indicating function arguments and $\underline{p}-t$ denoting the uniform price charged by the monopolist, the firm's profits are:

$$\pi_{\text{pi},t} = q[\underline{p}](\underline{p} - t) + q^*[\underline{p} - t](\underline{p} - t) - c(q[\underline{p}] + q^*[\underline{p} - t])$$

From the firm's FOC we now find the following:

$$\frac{d\underline{p}}{dt} = \frac{q' + 2q^{*\prime} + (\underline{p} - t - c)q^{*\prime\prime}}{[2(q' + q^{*\prime}) + (\underline{p} - t - c)(q'' + q^{*\prime\prime})]}$$

where $[2(q'+q^{*\prime})+(\underline{p}-t-c)(q''+q^{*\prime\prime})] < 0$ by the firm's SOC. Again choosing the tariff to maximise domestic welfare yields $(dW_{\text{pi},t}/dt) = q + (tq' - q)(dp/dt)$ but now $d\underline{p}/dt$ is as above. To demonstrate our result, suppose we evaluate $dW_{\text{pi},t}/dt$ at the no-PIs optimal tariff:

$$\left.\frac{dW_{\text{pi},t}}{dt}\right|_{t=t^*} = q + (t^*q' - q)\frac{dp}{dt} = \frac{q}{q'}\left[q' - \{2q' + (p - t^* - c)q''\}\frac{dp}{dt}\right]$$
$$= \left(-\frac{1}{q'}\right)\frac{q(2q^{*\prime} + (p - t^* - c)q^{*\prime\prime})}{[2(q' + q^{*\prime}) + (p - t^* - c)(q'' + q^{*\prime\prime})]}$$
$$\times (q' + (p - t^* - c)q'')$$

The first (bracketed) term here is positive and, assuming the firm's SOCs hold globally, the second term is positive (as both numerator and denominator are less than zero). Thus, the sign of this overall

[20]We are grateful to a referee for suggesting this case.

expression is the same as the sign of the third term: if negative (positive) then the optimal tariff under PIs is lower (higher) than that with segmented markets. Using the FOC from the no-PIs case, we can rewrite this last term as follows:

$$q' + (p - t^* - c)q'' = q' - \frac{q''q}{q'} = \frac{1}{q'}((q')^2 - q''q)$$

so the sign of this term is the opposite of that of the optimal tariff. Thus, if the optimal tariff is positive allowing PIs leads to a reduction in the tariff; if negative, allowing PIs leads to an increase (i.e. a less negative tariff). Either way the absolute value of the tariff falls when PIs are permitted, as claimed.

A.4. *Political economy considerations*

Consider our first political economy model in which the government places a weight of δ on domestic profits and a weight $(1 - \delta)$ on consumers' surplus and revenue. Then, from our earlier calculations, in the absence of PIs the government's maximand is given by:

$$W_{\text{ft}} = \delta\pi_{\text{ft}} + (1-\delta)\text{CS}_{\text{ft}} = (1+\delta)(a-c)^2/8b \tag{8A}$$

When PIs are allowed, however, we can calculate the government's objective function:

$$W_{\text{pi}} = \frac{2\delta\{(a-c) + b(a^* - c)\} + (1-\delta)[(1+b)(a-c) + b(a-a^*)]}{8b(1+b)^2}[.] \tag{9A}$$

The gain from prohibiting PIs is $W_{\text{ft}} - W_{\text{pi}}$. As already shown, this is negative at $\delta = 0$:

$$W_{\text{ft}} - W_{\text{pi}}|_{\delta=0} = -\frac{(a-a^*)}{8(1+b)^2}(2(1+b)(a-c) + b(a-a^*)) < 0 \tag{10A}$$

At the other extreme, however, we get the following:

$$W_{\text{ft}} - W_{\text{pi}}|_{\delta=1} = \frac{b(a-a^*)(a-c) - b(a-a^*)(a^*-c)}{4(1+b)^2}$$

$$= \frac{b(a-a^*)^2}{4(1+b)^2} > 0 \tag{11A}$$

That is, a government that only cares for the profits of the firm in the domestic market will, not surprisingly, prohibit PIs. Further manipulations show that:

$$\frac{\partial}{\partial\delta}(W_{\text{ft}} - W_{\text{pi}}) = \frac{(a-a^*)}{8(1+b)^2}(2(1+b)(a-c) + 3b(a-a^*)) > 0 \tag{12A}$$

Our second political economy scenario is one based on Grossman and Helpman (1994). The monopoly offers a schedule of contributions to the domestic government, which is contingent on the subsequent trade policy choice of the government. Equilibrium occurs where the payment schedule and trade policy choices are best responses to each other, leading to an actual payment we denote λ. In more complicated versions of this structure with multiple principals (lobbying firms), the equilibrium concept commonly invoked is that of coalition-proof Nash equilibrium. While coalition-proofness makes little sense in our two-player context, a number of features of such an equilibrium will still hold: the equilibrium involves a policy choice that maximises the sum of the payoffs to all the players and no player is worse off than their reservation utility level. The first of these features amounts to there being no unrealised gains from the relationship (no money is left "on the table") and the second is individual rationality.

Absent PIs, total surplus (S) is the sum of the monopolist's profits at home and abroad plus the γ-weighted sum of home consumers' surplus and government revenue:

$$S_{\text{no}}\text{PI} = \pi + \pi^* + \gamma(\text{CS} + \text{GR}) \tag{13A}$$

We can write this out as:

$$S_{\text{no}}\text{PI} = \frac{(a-t-c)^2}{4b} + \frac{(a^*-c)^2}{4} + \frac{\gamma}{8b}((a-c-t)(a-c+3t)) \tag{14A}$$

Choosing t to maximise this solves for an optimal tariff, as in the paper, of:

$$\frac{dS_{\text{no}}\text{PI}}{dt} = 0 \Rightarrow t = \frac{(2-\gamma)}{(2-3\gamma)}(a-c) \tag{15A}$$

Note that $t > (< 0)$ as $\gamma > (<)2$ and that, intuitively, $lim_{\gamma \to \infty} t = (a - c)/3$ which is the optimal tariff in the absence of lobbying. Note also that

$$\frac{d^2 S_{\text{no}}\text{PI}}{(dt)^2} = \frac{(2 - 3\gamma)}{4b} \tag{16A}$$

so Eq. (15A) identifies a surplus maximising tariff for $\gamma > 2/3$, a restriction we impose henceforth. Substituting from Eq. (15A) into Eq. (14A) and simplifying yields the following expression for maximised surplus in the absence of PIs:

$$S_{\text{no}}\text{PI} = \frac{\gamma^2}{(3\gamma - 2)} \frac{(a - c)^2}{2b} + \frac{(a^* - c)^2}{4} \tag{17A}$$

Turning to when PIs are permitted, we now get the following total surplus:

$$\begin{aligned} S_{\text{PI}} &= \pi + \pi^* + \gamma(\text{CS} + \text{GR}) \\ &= \frac{1}{2b}[(p_c - t - c)\{(a - c) + b(a^* - c) - t\} \\ &\quad + \gamma(a - p_c)^2 + 2t\gamma(a - p_c)] \end{aligned} \tag{18A}$$

where p_c denotes the consumer price in the home country: $p_c = \underline{p} + t$ where $\underline{p}$ is the common price set by the monopolist to both markets. Solving out for $\underline{p}(t)$, maximising the expression in Eq. (18A) and simplifying yields an optimal tariff:

$$t_{\text{PI}} = \frac{\begin{array}{c}\gamma[(a - c)(1 + b) + b(a - a^*)] \\ +(1 + b)(2b - 1)\{(a - c) + b(a^* - c)\}\end{array}}{\gamma(1 + 2b)(3 + 2b) - 2(1 + b)} \tag{19A}$$

Again, it is straightforward to show that the SOC for a maximum is satisfied if $\gamma > 2/3$.

Consider a case in which PIs are permitted absent lobbying but prohibited in the political equilibrium. Suppose, for concreteness, that $\gamma = 1.3, a = 20, a^* = 15, b = 2$, and $c = 0$. Then, in the absence of lobbying, government welfare when PIs are permitted is:

$$\gamma(\text{CS} + \text{GR})|_{\text{PIs, no lobbying}} = \gamma \frac{[(1+b)(a-c) + b(a-a^*)]^2}{[2b(1+2b)(3+2b)]}$$
$$= \frac{91}{2} = 45.5 \tag{20A}$$

If PIs were prohibited it would yield government welfare of:

$$\gamma(\text{CS} + \text{GR})|_{\text{no PIs, no lobbying}} = \gamma \frac{(a-c)^2}{6b} = \frac{130}{3} = 43\frac{1}{3} \tag{21A}$$

Thus, PIs would be permitted in the absence of any political activity by the monopoly. (This is also easily confirmed by noting that, absent political economy considerations, these parameters yield $p_t - t = 6\frac{2}{3} < 7\frac{1}{2} = p^*$ in the absence of PIs. As shown in the paper, this condition is sufficient for PIs to be attractive under optimal tariff setting.) The optimal tariff is $t = 2$ and the firm's profits would then be:

$$(\pi^* + \pi)|_{\text{PIs, no lobbying}} = \frac{\{(a-c) + b(a^*-c) - t\}^2}{4b(1+b)} = \frac{(48)^2}{24} = 96 \tag{22A}$$

and total surplus is $(96 + 45.5) = 141\frac{1}{2}$.

But when lobbying is introduced, the optimal tariff with PIs is, from Eq. (19A),

$$t_{\text{PI}} = \frac{2(13/10)[70] + 18\{50\}}{(79)} = \frac{1082}{79} (\cong 13.7) \tag{23A}$$

This yields a consumer price of $p_c = 1560/79 (\cong 19\frac{3}{4})$ and, from Eq. (18A), a total surplus of:

$$S_{\text{PI}} = \pi + \pi^* + \gamma(\text{CS} + \text{GR}) = \frac{356922}{(79)^2} (\cong 57.19) \tag{24A}$$

But if PIs were prohibited in the political equilibrium, then the optimal tariff would be $t = -140/19$ [a subsidy of about 7.37, from Eq. (15A)] and total surplus is, from Eq. (17A):

$$S_{\text{no}}\text{PI} = \frac{11035}{76}(\cong 145.2) \tag{25A}$$

Hence, total surplus is greater when PIs are prohibited than when they are permitted, in this case. Total profits for the monopolist are:

$$\begin{aligned}(\pi^* + \pi)|\text{lobbying, no PIs} &= \frac{(a^* - c)^2}{4} + \frac{(a - c - t)^2}{4b} \\ &= \frac{225}{4} + \frac{(20 + (140/19))^2}{8} \\ &= \frac{216425}{1444}(= 149.88) \end{aligned} \tag{26A}$$

and government surplus is a little under -4.68 (as subsidy payments are large). We have already seen that the best the government can do outside of the lobbying relationship is to permit PIs and set the optimal tariff in which case, from Eq. (20A), it gets a surplus of 45.5. Thus, the firm must pay a lobby payment of:

$$\lambda = 45.5 + \frac{1690}{361} = \frac{32851 + 3380}{722} = \frac{36231}{722}(\cong 50.18) \tag{27A}$$

The retained profits of the firm, then, are:

$$(\pi^* + \pi)|\text{lobbing, no PIs} - \lambda = \frac{216425}{1444} - \frac{36231}{722} = \frac{143963}{1444}(\cong 99.7) \tag{28A}$$

This exceeds the profit it would make in the absence of lobbying, 96 (from Eq. (22A)).

References

Gallini, N. and A. Hollis (1999). A contractual approach to the gray market. *International Review of Law and Economics*, 19, 1–11.

Grossman, G. and E. Helpman (1994). Protection for sale. *American Economic Review*, 84, 833–850.

Ishikawa, J. (2000). From segmented markets to integrated markets. Discussion Paper Series # 1000-1, Graduate School of Economics, Hitotsubashi University, Japan.

Konishi, H., K. Saggi and S. Weber (1999). Endogenous trade policy under foreign direct investment. *Journal of International Economics*, 49, 289–308.

Malueg, D. and M. Schwartz (1994). Parallel imports, demand dispersion and international price discrimination. *Journal of International Economics*, 37, 167–195.

Maskus, K. and Y. Chen (1999). Vertical price control and parallel imports. Mimeo, University of Colorado at Boulder, CO, USA.

Richardson, M. (2002). An elementary proposition concerning parallel imports. *Journal of International Economics*, 56, 233–245.

Part V

Miscellaneous

Chapter 16

Quality and Congestion in Environmental Goods

The Road to the Wangapeka

Martin Richardson

Abstract: An increasing complaint heard among New Zealand residents is that their enjoyment of local environmental resources is being diminished by increased congestion from foreign visitors. This paper considers a model of vertical differentiation in which foreign high-value and domestic low-value consumers incur congestion costs in using a common resource. We demonstrate that reducing quality in the face of increased foreign demand is optimal absent discriminatory prices (but not otherwise). We also consider the provision of multiple environmental goods and demonstrate that providing differential qualities may be optimal even if domestic consumers do not use the high-quality resources at all.

Keywords: vertical differentiation; environmental access; congestion.

1. Introduction

The Wangapeka River is a tributary of the Motueka River in the upper South Island of New Zealand. A fine trout stream, it is also the access point for the Wangapeka track, a 54-km hike which winds up largely through lush bush over from the Motueka valley to the west coast of the South Island, emerging near Karamea. Unlike many New Zealand tracks, however, the Wangapeka is not particularly well

Originally published in *Journal of Environmental Economics and Management*, 43, 477–496.

developed. Huts are frequent and adequate but rudimentary[1] and access to the track is not always easy:

> The road [at the eastern end of the track] includes a major ford at the Dart River which becomes impassable in heavy rain. Following close to the river, the road occasionally washes away, making for a long walk to the start of the track... The otherwise easy walk out includes two deep fords. [A] small section of [the Wangapeka Road] at the very end of the Track crosses private land, and access arrangements have failed. In high river conditions where the fords to avoid this brief section are not possible, a 3.2 km detour has been provided. This steep track struggles around the hillsides for $1\frac{1}{2}$ hr, taking you 500 m past the end of the Wangapeka Track and certainly souring your memories of it." (Archipelago guide at http://hike.org/walks/Wangapeka.html.)

One might think that the amenities of the Wangapeka could be far more successfully utilised by *all* consumers if these roads and access were improved but numerous writers have argued exactly the opposite: "foreign visitors ... are seen to be overwhelming facilities on easier tracks. A sense of equity suggests the Department of Conservation should [not] ... develop the facilities. Walks such as the Wangapeka ... should remain free from over-development and over-the-top promotion" [16].

This is an illustration of a problem that occurs widely, from access to national parks around the world to local beach access[2] and it is an old problem: Fairbrother [7] notes that Wordsworth, some 200 years ago, "waged an angry campaign against the Windermere railway and its effect of 'transferring at once uneducated persons in large bodies' to the [English] Lakes."[3] It is a fairly general problem: how to restrict uses of a public resource so as to preserve the quality

[1]They range from DOC (Department of Conservation) category 2 (Intermediate. Have bunks or sleeping platforms with mattresses, water supply, toilet, and hand washing facilities. May have cooking and heating facilities) to category 4 (Shelters and bivouacs. Huts with limited facilities. Do not have bunks or sleeping platforms, toilet, or water supply).

[2]Indeed, one could argue that it also applies in the context of highway access.

[3]She continues that Wordsworth, "only liked uneducated persons as solitary reapers or leech-gatherers or similar examples of local colour and preferably hard at work, certainly not as 'parties of pleasure out- of-doors' " (p. 143). Furthermore, he had a "belief in an absolute difference of kind between the worthy few who could appreciate mountains and

of the "wilderness experience"? An economist's first reaction would be to use prices to ration access but there are a number of constraints in this setting that render them unavailable. The question, then, is whether reducing the quality of the good is a sensible means of rationing access, given that this alone reduces the value of the experience to all users. Or, in terms of our example, as the number of foreign visitors increases, should we worsen the huts on and the roads to the Wangapeka?

In this paper we construct a model of vertical differentiation in which foreign high-value and domestic low-value consumers incur congestion costs in consuming a common resource. We consider optimal policy in terms of quality when there are prohibitions on the use of prices. In the next section we motivate our model with a brief discussion of the New Zealand experience before going on to construct a formal model. We consider two separate cases. In the first only one good is provided and consumed by all and its quality must be chosen. It is shown that quality downgrading may be an optimal response to increased foreign demand in the constrained, second-best setting of this problem. In the second case there are two goods available and there may potentially be cases in which consumers of different origins will self-select into consumption of different goods. We discuss the implicit use of congestion costs as a means of separating consumers and establish that full separation can never be optimal. We show that, nevertheless, in some circumstances (depending on the relative demands and tastes for quality of domestic versus foreign consumers) a partial separation may apply where only foreign consumers use the highest quality good. A final section summarises and concludes.

2. The New Zealand example

New Zealand (NZ) is famous for its environmental tourism and has many miles of walking (tramping) tracks available to almost anybody

the unworthy many who could not — artisans and labourers and the humbler classes of shopkeepers' who should not be encouraged 'to ramble to a distance'!" (pp. 153–154).

who cares to use them. Among these tracks are a group known by the Department of Conservation (DOC) as the Great Walks which are heavily promoted and particularly popular with foreign tourists. In 1990/1991 DOC estimated that 76% of visitors to the Routeburn track were foreign and 56% of walks taken on the Abel Tasman track were by international visitors [15]. Furthermore, there were less than 24,000 international trampers in New Zealand in 1990/1991 but this was projected to be over 53,000 by the year 2000 with a *target* (based on Tourism Board targets for overall visitor numbers) of 82,800 [15]. This has led in recent years to increasing complaints by New Zealanders that the walks are congested:[4] In some cases entry[5] is difficult because of the heavy pressure of foreign visitors and the enjoyment of the tramping experience is lessened.

The obvious economic solution to this is to set prices appropriately. However, in the NZ outdoor recreation context (as in many others) there are severe restrictions on the use of prices at all, let alone discriminatory prices. Indeed, the relevant legislation in New Zealand[6] prohibits DOC from charging for tracks or entry to national parks or reserves. It is permissible, however, to charge for the use of "improvements" which suggests that users could be charged more for higher "quality" walks than others. This is done to a very limited extent currently and it is clear that prices are set neither to control congestion[7] nor to cover costs.[8] Part of the reason for this is that one of DOC's missions is to foster the use of natural resources

[4]See Kearsley et al. [12] for recent survey evidence.

[5]Cullen [5] distinguishes usefully between "access" — the "process of reaching a natural area" — and "entry" which "describes events beyond the carpark." So physical remoteness can be a high access cost, even if entry is unrestricted.

[6]The 1980 National Parks Act, the 1977 Reserves Act, and the 1987 Conservation Act.

[7]Fees do vary dramatically across the tracks, however: three nights on the Milford track (a "Great Walk") costs NZ$90 (and, as access is principally by boat, numbers are controlled through a booking system and camping is not permitted so all Milford trampers must use the DOC huts). By contrast, a night in a hut on the Wangapeka track can be had for NZ$4–8 and camping is free. Nevertheless, DOC makes it clear that these prices are not set to determine user numbers.

[8]Cullen [5] reports that national park operating expenditures in 1993/1994 were over NZ$36 million and revenues less than NZ$12 million.

for recreation and to allow their use for tourism (insofar as this is consistent with conservation).[9]

While there is some debate concerning the use of entry fees to the NZ conservation estate [5], there is also strong opposition to the idea, rooted in the notion that open access is a "right." So the Minister of Conservation could state in 1997, "[c]harging for access to our National Parks and conservation areas would deprive thousands of New Zealanders of their birthright. Free public access is a core concept of the National Parks Act and is here to stay" (press release, December 18, 1997, Hon. Dr. Nick Smith). Some go further:

> These attitudes [maintaining a sense of equity between users of the conservation estate and the principle of freedom of access] were founded and remain immersed in an ideology of open democracy where the state protects all peoples' equal rights to wild places and which can claim a clear lineage of language, from the slogans of the French Revolution,[10] to the United States constitution and the National Parks Acts of most countries. ([16])

Even proponents of charges see little rationale for discriminatory charges based on national origin of the user. So the Tourism Policy Group of the Ministry of Commerce has argued that if user charges are introduced correctly then there is no need to distinguish between domestic and overseas visitors [18]. They do allow, however, that there may be equity reasons for discriminating against foreigners in suggesting a "discount card" available to New Zealanders only: "Such discounts are primarily for equity purposes, on the expectation that New Zealanders face tighter income constraints than overseas visitors, and that local users are more price sensitive" [19]. Cullen [5] disagrees: "[g]iven the GST [NZ's Goods and Services Tax] receipts per visitor day in NZ and the restricted range of taxpayer provided services they consume, it seems likely that tourists meet their share of parks and reserves costs... discriminatory charges for tourists are difficult to justify on equity grounds." Interestingly, visitors themselves

[9]Of course, it is recognised that congestion is largely *not* consistent with conservation and one of the main arguments for the introduction of access charges is to preserve the conservation estate. We do not address this issue in this paper.

[10]Liberty! Equality! Brotherhood! Hiking!

disagree: Kearsley et al. [12] found that of international track users surveyed who believed that more visitor management was needed in New Zealand, 53% favoured increased prices for non-taxpayers and only 10% favoured increased prices for all users! (The corresponding numbers for domestic users were 91% and 27%, perhaps unsurprisingly.)

It is recognised that quality control as we are referring to it is a means of rationing. Indeed, Cullen [4] suggests that requiring greater effort of users, "is the New Zealand way of rationing!" An obvious problem, of course, is that the effort cost is simply dissipated whereas it could be monetised through a fee.

To summarise the situation in New Zealand, then, we have a setting in which the provision of services related to outdoor recreation is constrained by the inability to discriminate between users of different national origins and, indeed, the inability to set prices to ration access at all. In terms of the distribution of foreign trampers across tracks, it appears that foreign visitors have a greater taste for "high quality" resources than do local consumers but that the increasing demand for these resources is leading to congestion costs borne by all. While there is some self- selection of consumers into different quality goods it is not clear that this separation is a deliberate policy choice at all.

3. A model

Based on this brief description of the NZ case, this paper models a walking track, for example, as a good that embodies a certain (endogenous) quality[11] on which different types of consumers place different valuations. In particular, we model this as a case of vertical differentiation in which domestic and foreign consumers place different valuations on quality. Furthermore, consumers incur disutility

[11]Some readers have suggested that environmental quality is easily downgraded but not so easily restored. In the context of walking tracks or other environmental goods, then, the quality referred to here is perhaps best thought of as ease of access, as in the discussion above, rather than the inherent environmental quality of the resource.

from congestion. In this setting we are interested in optimal policy but subject to the constraints discussed above which mirror the reality of policy setting in this context.

Note that this modelling choice captures a consumer's willingness to exert effort as a greater willingness to pay. We do not include a physical cost in the modelling, however; rather we think of access difficulties as being embodied as a lower quality good for a given price. We noted earlier that requiring high effort for consumers to access a resource means the dissipation of that effort so that a reduced quality (more effort) would be harmful for that reason. In the modelling here reduced quality has a direct disutility effect (it also is beneficial in reducing congestion and because costs are increasing in quality).

In effect, our model is equivalent to a two-stage structure in which the government first chooses quality, knowing the consequences this will have for the flow of tourists, and then consumers (both domestic and foreign) decide whether or not to consume the environmental good in question. In this sense, we endogenise the decision of foreign tourists to visit the country in the first place.

We allow that more than one quality may be provided and we show that a separating outcome is then possible even in the absence of prices. There are four idiosyncratic features of our model that contrast to the existing literature in this area and should be borne in mind in what follows. First, dollar prices are zero for both types of consumers. Second, we are concerned with the optimum of a government that maximises national welfare so it does not care about the surplus of foreign consumers per se (except insofar as it can extract it; given our first point, however, it cannot do this de facto). It is concerned, however, with the number of foreign visitors (which depends on the quality of environmental goods provided) who are assumed to provide some benefit to the country. Thus, in contrast to the existing literature on vertical differentiation, our policy-maker is neither a monopolist nor a planner that cares about the welfare of all consumers. Third, our model features congestion costs from consumption of the good. Fourth, and in order to capture congestion, our model features heterogeneity not just across the two types of consumers (domestic and foreign) but also *within* each of these populations.

In terms of the existing literature, our model is one of vertical differentiation but the problem we consider has been most closely examined in the club goods literature.[12] However, there are some critical features of our analysis that distinguish it from that literature. First, the club goods literature supposes that the provision of the good is funded across club members and this cost will typically affect the membership decision. In our model there is no such decision as the good is provided to all who wish to consume it. Second, the analysis of clubs typically considers optimal pricing by the club — be it a private club or the application of club theory to problems such as transportation economics. In our model all dollar prices are zero. Third, much of the recent club literature (see [3] for a thorough survey) has been concerned with the efficiency and existence (or otherwise) of competitive equilibrium among multiple providers; again, this is not an issue in our analysis.

3a. *Demand*

Consider a good for which there are two types of consumers. There are domestic consumers who each derive utility of $U = a\theta q - p - g(s)$ from consuming this good of quality q at a price p, where $a < 1, \theta$ is a taste parameter, and $g(s), g' > 0, g'' \leq 0$, measures disutility from congestion when there are s total users of the good in question.[13] The parameter θ measures an individual's marginal

---

[12]See also [2, 6, 13, 14]. Glazer and Niskanen [9] argued that congested public facilities might be "desirable" in a model in which costs are spread across all taxpayers. Their model is one of political economy, however, and they suggested that poorer individuals might favour poor-quality public facilities to drive the rich into private consumption, thus reducing public crowding. Feldman [8] also considered rationing by taste for quality but his model is one in which "quality" is exactly synonymous with "lack of congestion" and so is not an exogenous choice variable. He considered provision of a good in which quality and quantity are traded off and argued that as the taste for quality in some consumers increases this lowers their consumption, thus increasing that of others and leading to an increased quality over all. But the prime beneficiaries of this are those with a lower taste for quality whose consumption increases.

[13]It is worth noting that congestion enters utility here as a linear cost, akin to price. If it were multiplicative instead, then, while utility would fall as congestion increased, demand would not be affected particularly when prices are zero.

valuation of quality and we assume that consumers' tastes are distributed uniformly on an interval $[0, \underline{\theta}]$. The density of domestic consumers on this interval is normalised to one.

There are also foreign consumers with taste parameters distributed uniformly over the same interval who derive utility of $U^{\mathrm{f}} = \theta q - p^{\mathrm{f}} - g(s^{\mathrm{f}})$ for the good at quality q^{f}. The density of foreign consumers on this interval is L. Note that any foreign consumer has a higher valuation of quality than his or her domestic counterpart with the same θ (for the same quality $q^{\mathrm{f}} = q$ and if the total number of consumers in each market is the same so $s^{\mathrm{f}} = s$) because of the assumption that $a < 1$. Nevertheless, all consumers incur congestion disutility in the same fashion. Under the same conditions, the increase in surplus for a higher θ consumer is less for domestic consumers than for foreign consumers ($\partial U/\partial\theta < \partial U^{\mathrm{f}}/\partial\theta$) and consumers of given θ get less out of an increase in quality, holding price fixed, if they are domestic than if they are foreign ($\partial U/\partial q < \partial U^{\mathrm{f}}/\partial q^{\mathrm{f}}$).

Why assume $a < 1$? There are two reasons. First is the observed evidence that foreign consumers in New Zealand are found primarily on high-quality walks [12]. While this may reflect the marketing effort of NZ tourist authorities, it may also reflect a selection effect (see below) and is most easily captured in this model as a generically higher taste for quality. A second reason is that a common interpretation of θ in vertical differentiation models is that it represents income (so higher taste for quality simply reflects higher income). In this context, again, the assumption of higher income in foreign visitors than in the local population is not unreasonable. Household survey data suggest that in 1998, for example, the average household income for the top U.S. quintile was U.S.$127,529, whereas the top NZ quintile had an average household income of only around NZ$38,250 or less than U.S.$20,600. Furthermore, the top quintile of U.S. households *began* at an income of U.S.$75,000, while the top *decile* of NZ households had an *average* income of NZ$49,096 or less than U.S.$27,000.[14]

[14] I am grateful to Srikanta Chatterjee for NZ income data from the Statistics NZ Household Economic Survey. The U.S. income data are taken from U.S. Census Bureau Historical Income Tables — Households. The exchange rate used is a simple average of monthly rates from NZ Reserve Bank data.

One further endogenous reason for the assumption of higher income in foreign visitors than in the local population is that foreign consumers must incur a substantial cost simply to access local walks so there is a selection effect on the distribution of tastes that actually present at the local resource.[15]

For any given qualities q and q^{f}, prices p and p^{f}, and demands s and s^{f}, we can determine critical domestic and foreign consumers, denoted θ^* and $\theta^{\mathrm{f}*}$, respectively, for whom there is zero surplus.[16] Setting $U = U^{\mathrm{f}} = 0$ and solving gives

$$\theta^* = \frac{p + g(s)}{aq} \quad \text{and} \quad \theta^{\mathrm{f}*} = \frac{p^{\mathrm{f}} + g(s^{\mathrm{f}})}{q^{\mathrm{f}}}. \tag{1}$$

Demand for the good, then, is just the measure of consumers with non-negative surplus, i.e., those domestic consumers for whom $\theta \in [\theta^*, \underline{\theta}]$ and those foreign consumer for whom $\theta^{\mathrm{f}} \in [\theta^{\mathrm{f}*}, \underline{\theta}]$. Note that if prices (and congestion) were the same for both groups there would be a smaller range of domestic consumers in that $\theta^* > \theta^{\mathrm{f}*}$ in that case. These relationships are all made clear in Fig. 1, which illustrates surplus for the different types of consumers for given prices and quality.

Denoting by x and x^{f} the total numbers of domestic and foreign consumers, respectively, the uniform distribution of θ implies that $x = (\underline{\theta} - \theta^*)$ and $x^{\mathrm{f}} = L(\underline{\theta} - \theta^{\mathrm{f}*})$. Thus we have

$$x = \underline{\theta} - \frac{p + g(s)}{aq} \quad \text{and} \quad x^{\mathrm{f}} = L\left(\underline{\theta} - \frac{p^{\mathrm{f}} + g(s^{\mathrm{f}})}{q^{\mathrm{f}}}\right). \tag{2}$$

Following the literature we suppose that costs are increasing and weakly convex in quality but marginal costs are constant in output.

[15]Of course, this represents a truncation of the distribution of foreign consumers from below rather than the model we have chosen in which the upper end of the support of the domestic distribution is lower than that of the foreign distribution, a choice which reflects the actual income distribution. We have also analysed a model in which $a = 1$ and foreign consumers explicitly incur a transport cost of T in coming to the domestic country. This does effectively truncate the distribution of foreign consumers downward and we get similar — though even messier — results from an increase in foreign demand.

[16]Aggregate demand for a good depends on the identity of the marginal consumer which, in turn, depends on aggregate demand (through the congestion cost). While this suggests the possibility of multiple equilibria, in fact there is a unique outcome for each parameterisation: higher demand raises congestion which curtails the increased demand.

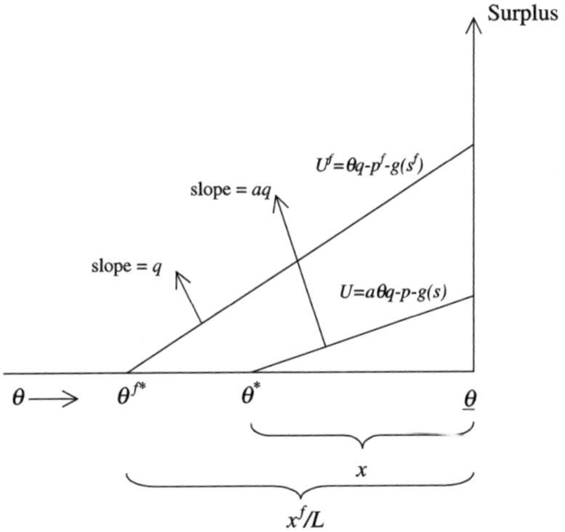

Fig. 1. Surplus to foreign and domestic consumers with a single quality.

Thus the total cost of providing this good is $c(q)x + c(q^{\mathrm{f}})x^{\mathrm{f}}$, where $c' > 0$ and $c'' \geq 0$.

3b. *Welfare*

We assume a modification of the usual welfare function for the policy-setting authority where welfare (W) is simply the sum of domestic consumer surplus and profits. We also allow that foreign visitors are valued. Certainly in the NZ case foreign tourists are valued for their consumption of domestic goods and services. There are two extreme approaches to modelling this, however. One is to suppose that these visitors arrive anyway, regardless of the provision of environmental goods, so this benefit is exogenous to our analysis. The other extreme is that they only come to the domestic country because of the provision of environmental goods.[17] In either case, note that

[17]As always, reality probably lies somewhere between the extremes — some tourists visit New Zealand only because of the walks; others visit regardless. Presumably, those in the first category are those who obtain the highest surplus so one might model this with some threshold level of surplus, say $\underline{s}$. The country then derives the value V only for those foreigners who obtain surplus above $\underline{s}$. If s is sufficiently high then it will be irrelevant to our analysis and equivalent to the $V = 0$ case; if lower, it may be affected

the *levels* of surplus achieved by foreign consumers are irrelevant to the policy-maker, except insofar as they determine the *extent* of consumption of environmental goods in the second case.

We suppose that policy-makers derive some value V from each foreign visitor so for $V > 0$ this indicates the second of these approaches as it only accrues from foreign visitors who consume the environmental good. The first extreme is captured by $V = 0$.[18] So our welfare function is given by

$$W = \int_{\theta^*}^{\underline{\theta}} [a\theta q - p - g(s)]d\theta + p^{\mathrm{f}}x^{\mathrm{f}} - c(q)x - c(q^{\mathrm{f}})x^{\mathrm{f}} + Vx^{\mathrm{f}}. \quad (3)$$

Integrating, expanding, and substituting from (1) and (2), we can derive the following[19]:

$$\begin{aligned} W &= (p^{\mathrm{f}} + V - c(q^{\mathrm{f}}))x^{\mathrm{f}} + (p - c(q))x + \frac{1}{2}aqx^2 \\ &= (P^{\mathrm{f}} + V - c(q^{\mathrm{f}}))L\left\{\underline{\theta} - \frac{p^{\mathrm{f}} + g(s^{\mathrm{f}})}{q^{\mathrm{f}}}\right\} \\ &\quad + (p - c(q))\left\{\underline{\theta} - \frac{p + g(s)}{aq}\right\}\frac{aq}{2}\left(\underline{\theta} - \frac{p + g(s)}{aq}\right)^2. \end{aligned} \quad (4)$$

4. Policy

Existing literature on vertical differentiation with heterogeneous consumers suggests that a monopolist will typically effect a separating equilibrium in which different price-quantity packages are offered that induce self-selection by the appropriate consumer groups.[20] In our model, however, we have heterogeneity *within* the different consumer groups as well as between them. Furthermore, prices cannot be chosen which would seem to make separation infeasible. We show later that this is not the case, however.

by quality degrading and so enter the policy-maker's problem. We do not model this complication.

[18]"Accordingly, the $V = 0$ version of our model might be argued to apply more readily to cases such as municipal care of beaches and local or state parks.

[19]This and all other omitted calculations are in an Appendix available from the author.

[20]Acharyya [1] makes it clear that this result depends on restrictions on costs and on the distribution of consumers across the types.

We wish to consider two cases. First, by way of a benchmark, we look at the case in which the policy-maker can identify the two different groups, provide a different good to each group, and price discriminate between the groups. We then turn to the case in which all prices must be set to zero. In this setting we consider an outcome in which all consume a single quality and outcomes in which more than one quality is offered.

4a. *Costless separation*

Suppose the policy-maker can costlessly separate domestic and foreign consumers and it can price discriminate across the two goods they consume. In this case domestic (foreign) consumers incur congestion only from other domestic (foreign) consumers (so that $s = x$ and $s^{\mathrm{f}} = x^{\mathrm{f}}$) and consume a good of quality $q(q^{\mathrm{f}})$.

Maximising (4) by the choice of q, q^{f}, p, and p^{f} yields four first-order conditions (FOC's) which can be written as

$$\begin{aligned} &\text{(i)}\ \ p = c(q) + g'(x)x, \\ &\text{(ii)}\ \ p + g^{(\mathrm{x})} = c'(q)q - \tfrac{1}{2}aqx, \\ &\text{(iii)}\ \ V + p^{\mathrm{f}} = c(q^{\mathrm{f}}) + g'(x^{\mathrm{f}})x^{\mathrm{f}} + (q^{\mathrm{f}}x^{\mathrm{f}})/L, \\ &\text{(iv)}\ \ V + p^{\mathrm{f}} + g(x^{\mathrm{f}}) = c'(q^{\mathrm{f}})q^{\mathrm{f}}. \end{aligned} \tag{5}$$

While direct comparisons of these expressions are complicated by the different arguments of the $g(\cdot)$ and $c(\cdot)$ functions, if $V = 0, a = L = 1$, and both groups were offered the same quality, then (5)(i) and (5)(iii) imply the domestic price would be lower. No surprises there: the policy-maker cares about domestic consumers' surplus but if $V = 0$ it is a pure profit-maximiser against foreign consumers.

Henceforth we assume that the congestion function is linear, for tractability, so $g(s) = Gs$ for some positive constant G. Hence $g'(\cdot) = G$ and $g''(\cdot) = 0$. We now wish to determine what the change in optimal quality would be if foreign demand were to increase. Formally, we are looking for the signs of dq/dL and dq^{f}/dL from the system of equations in (5). Note first that, in this setting, nothing should be done to domestic quality or price: changes in foreign demand have no congestion spillover into the domestic market in this case. As for the foreign market, total differentiation of (5)(iii) and (5)(iv) demonstrates that an increase in L leads to increases in both optimal q^{f} and p^{f}. That is, as foreign demand increases, the optimal response in this case is to increase the quality provided to foreign consumers and also to increase the price charged to them. Hence,

Proposition 1. *A welfare-maximising government that can costlessly separate and provide different qualities of good at different prices to domestic and foreign consumers will optimally increase the quality and price of the good provided to foreign consumers as their demand increases.*

Note that this is also welfare improving: as foreign demand increases, domestic profits from foreigners increase, with no impact on domestic consumers at all.

4b. *Constrained: Zero prices and separation unenforceable*

In a rather different setting to that which we have constructed here, Acharyya [1] noted three general types of equilibria in a vertical differentiation model. First is a pooling equilibrium in which all consumers get the same quality and price. Second is a separating equilibrium in which the two types of consumers self-select across two price-quality bundles. Third is an equilibrium in which the policy-maker serves only the high-valued consumers. We can immediately rule out the third possibility — serving only foreign consumers[21] — as uninteresting here.

The high-demand types in this setting are foreign consumers and, absent prices, if $V = 0$ the policy-maker cannot extract surplus from them and so does not care about them at all. On the other hand, if $V > 0$ then an equilibrium serving only foreigners could occur if V

[21]Serving only the domestic consumers is not feasible, of course, as if their participation constraints are satisfied then so too must be those of higher valued foreign consumers.

was sufficiently high. However, the comparative statics of an increase in foreign demand are trivial: if quality is chosen optimally initially then an increase in demand can only lead to a decrease in quality (which is costly to provide). We consider the other two alternatives in turn.

1. *Single quality*

Now we provide a single quality q to be consumed by all consumers. Accordingly, congestion will depend on total demand $X = x + x^{\mathrm{f}}$ and total cost is $c(q)X$. The problem facing policy-makers is

$$\operatorname*{Max}_{\{q\}} W = \frac{1}{2}aqx^2 - c(q)X + Vx^{\mathrm{f}}, \tag{6}$$

where

$$x = \underline{\theta} - \frac{g(X)}{aq}, \quad x^{\mathrm{f}} = L\left(\underline{\theta} - \frac{g(X)}{q}\right),$$

and

$$X = x + x^{\mathrm{f}} = \underline{\theta}(1+L) - \frac{g(X)(1+aL)}{aq}.$$

With the linear congestion function, we can solve for explicit solutions for x, x^{f}, and X. From (6) we get the following FOC:

$$W_q \equiv \frac{\partial W}{\partial q} = \frac{1}{2}ax^2 - c'(q)X + V\frac{dx^{\mathrm{f}}}{dp} + aqx\frac{dx}{dp} - c(q)\frac{dX}{dq} = 0. \tag{7}$$

Equation (7) defines optimal quality as an implicit function of the underlying parameters and, assuming second-order conditions (SOC's) hold, we have

$$\left.\frac{dq}{dL}\right|_{W_q=0} = -\frac{dW_q/dL}{dW_q/dq} \equiv -\frac{W_{qL}}{W_{qq}}.$$

But the SOC's imply $W_{qq} < 0$ so the sign of $(dq/dL)|_{(7)}$ is the same as that of W_{qL}. Differentiating (7), we can show after considerable manipulation that $W_{qL}|_{v=0} < 0$.[22] Hence, by continuity,

[22]This does not depend on $a < 1$.

Proposition 2. *A welfare-maximising government providing a single quality of good and unable to charge prices for its use will, for sufficiently low values of V, optimally reduce quality as foreign demand increases.*

So, in contrast to the costless separation case, it may be optimal in this zero-price, pooling situation to *reduce* quality as foreign demand increases. Also, in contrast to the previous case, increasing foreign demand may be welfare reducing. The intuition for these results is as straightforward as the algebra is messy. Suppose $V = 0$. When foreign demand increases, its effects are to worsen congestion (recall that prices are zero) and to increase the marginal social cost of quality provision at the current level of quality.[23] The marginal social gain from providing quality, however, has fallen: increased congestion reduces domestic demand and consumer surplus.[24] Thus the optimal response is to decrease quality.

2. *Two qualities*

Would a government ever wish to provide goods of different qualities? This remains to be seen, but note first that the provision of two *goods* as opposed to one will always be attractive because of the reduced congestion that follows (which may also be achieved by providing them at the same quality, of course). In this setting we can think of the number of goods (parks, beaches, walks, or whatever) as being exogenous and the policy-makers' choice is to decide on the qualities of those goods. In this section we are considering the case where that exogenous number of goods is 2.

We have noted that, with the inability to enforce separate consumption and in the absence of prices, a separating equilibrium

---

[23]Total costs are $c(q)X$ so the marginal cost of quality is $c'(q)X + cX_q$ (thinking of congestion increases as a mitigation of benefits rather than a direct cost). An increase in L alone increases both X and its responsiveness to changes in q, X_q, so MC rises, given q.

[24]While the effect on the marginal impact of quality on domestic demand is ambiguous, the decreased domestic demand itself swamps this.

might seem unlikely: if two qualities are provided, how can the provider induce consumers to self-select into the appropriate good? The answer is that there is a limited ability to separate through congestion costs.

Heuristically, suppose we have two goods available with qualities $q^{\mathrm{H}} > q^{\mathrm{L}}$, respectively. With no monetary prices the demand for the high-quality good will exceed that for the low-quality good but then congestion costs will be higher which, in turn, will lessen the relatively high demand. Given that domestic consumers get less surplus from a given quality good than do their foreign counterparts but that the congestion costs impinge equally on both, it is possible that differential demands for the goods will lead to a separation of domestic and foreign consumers. This possibility depends, clearly, on the numbers of consumers and the relative valuations of domestic and foreign consumers and in this sense the ability to separate is limited by these exogenous factors.

This effect has been noted before, most clearly by Donaldson and Eaton [6] and Nichols *et al.* [14]. The focus of Nichols et al. is very different from ours, however, as they consider the joint use of money prices and waiting times for a publicly provided good and, more significantly, they do not consider the optimal setting of waiting time as a consequence of price setting. In our model (as in theirs) the government cannot separately choose a feature of the good (quality here, price in Nichols et al.) and the congestion (waiting) costs but rather the latter flows endogenously from the former. Donaldson and Eaton [6] consider the joint choice of prices and waiting times as explicit instruments of price discrimination by a monopolist. The setting is very different from ours in a number of ways and fits more into the standard price discrimination literature [1] in that there are two types of consumers but within each type all consumers are identical. This makes pure separation more feasible, of course.

To make our argument a little more formal, define $X^J, J = \mathrm{L}, \mathrm{H}$, as the total demand for the good with quality $J, \Delta X \equiv X^{\mathrm{H}} - X^{\mathrm{L}}$, and $\Delta q \equiv q^{\mathrm{H}} - q^{\mathrm{L}} \geq 0$. Now, it is clear that if a domestic consumer buys the high-quality good then foreign demand for it must also be positive[25] and if no domestic consumer purchases it and nor does any foreign consumer then there is no point in providing it. If we denote by x^{iJ} the demand for good $J =$ H, L (quality high and low) by consumers $i =$ d, f (domestic and foreign) (so $X^J = x^{\mathrm{d}J} + x^{\mathrm{f}J}$, $J =$ L, H) then clearly we have $x^{\mathrm{fH}} > 0$. Now, domestic consumers will buy the high-quality rather than the low-quality good if $aq^{\mathrm{H}}\theta - GX^{\mathrm{H}} > aq^{\mathrm{L}}\theta - GX^{\mathrm{L}}$ or, after rearranging, if $a\theta > G(\Delta X/\Delta q)$. They will buy the low-quality good rather than nothing, by identical reasoning, if $a\theta > G(X^{\mathrm{L}}/q^{\mathrm{L}})$. So domestic demand for the low-and high-quality good respectively is x^{dL} and x^{dH}:

$$x^{\mathrm{dL}} = \begin{cases} \max\left\{\dfrac{G}{a}\left(\dfrac{\Delta X}{\Delta q} - \dfrac{X^{\mathrm{L}}}{q^{\mathrm{L}}}\right), 0\right\} & \text{if} \dfrac{G}{a}\dfrac{\Delta X}{\Delta q} \leq \underline{\theta}, \\ \underline{\theta} - \dfrac{G}{a}\dfrac{x^{\mathrm{L}}}{q^{\mathrm{L}}} & \text{otherwise,} \end{cases} \tag{8}$$

$$x^{\mathrm{dH}} = \max\left\{\underline{\theta} - \frac{G}{a}\frac{\Delta X}{\Delta q}, 0\right\}.$$

A similar exercise for foreign consumers gives foreign demand for the low- and high-quality good, respectively, as x^{fL} and x^{fH}:

$$x^{\mathrm{fL}} = \max\left\{GL\left(\frac{\Delta X}{\Delta q} - \frac{X^{\mathrm{L}}}{q^{\mathrm{L}}}\right), 0\right\}, \tag{9}$$

$$x^{\mathrm{fH}} = L\left(\underline{\theta} - G\left(\max\left\{\frac{\Delta X}{\Delta q}, \frac{X^{\mathrm{H}}}{q^{\mathrm{H}}}\right\}\right)\right).$$

There are three possible cases here that we can ignore directly.

- First as noted above, the problem here is only of interest if $x^{\mathrm{fH}} > 0$ and if we do not have $x^{\mathrm{dH}} = x^{\mathrm{dL}} = 0$.
- Second, we cannot have $x^{\mathrm{dL}} = 0$ and $x^{\mathrm{dH}} > 0$, i.e., domestic consumers consuming only the high-quality good. If they did then either foreign consumers use only the high-quality good as well, in which case there is no reason to provide the other good at a

[25]It should be clear that the results that follow do depend on the assumption that $a < 1$: if this were not the case, then alternative configurations in which domestic consumers consume the high-quality good and foreigners do not might be possible.

lower quality, or foreigners also consume the low-quality good. But $x^{\text{fL}} > 0$ implies $(\Delta X/\Delta q) > (X^{\text{L}}/q^{\text{L}}), x^{\text{dH}} > 0$ implies $\underline{\theta} > (G/a)(\Delta X/\Delta q)$, and so $x^{\text{dL}} = 0$ implies $(\Delta X/\Delta q) \leq (X^{\text{L}}/q^{\text{L}})$, which is a contradiction.

- Third, we cannot have $x^{\text{fH}} > 0, x^{\text{fL}} = 0, x^{\text{dH}} > 0$, and $x^{\text{dL}} > 0$. As above, $x^{\text{dH}} > 0$ implies $a\underline{\theta}/G > (\Delta X/\Delta q)$ so

$$x^{\text{dL}} = \frac{G}{a}\left(\frac{\Delta X}{\Delta q} - \frac{X^{\text{L}}}{q^{\text{L}}}\right) > 0$$

implies $(\Delta X/\Delta q) > (X^{\text{L}}/q^{\text{L}})$. But $x^{\text{fL}} = 0$ implies $(\Delta X/\Delta q) \leq (X^{\text{L}}/q^{\text{L}})$, again a contradiction.

Thus we are left with only three possibilities. The first we term *pure* separating, in which foreigners consume only the high-quality good and domestic consumers use only the low-quality good. The second we call *impure* separating, for obvious reasons: foreigners consume both goods but domestic consumers use only the low-quality good. The last possibility is the *non*-separating case in which both types of consumers consume both goods. To summarise, our three possibilities are as shown in Table 1.

We can now establish the following result concerning pure separation.

Proposition 3. *Qualities cannot be chosen such that pure separation applies.*

Proof. First note that in any pure separating outcome the marginal foreign consumer must get zero surplus from the high-quality good. Accordingly, $q^{\text{H}}\theta^{\text{f}*} - GX^{\text{H}} = 0$, where $\theta^{\text{f}*}$ defines the marginal foreign

Table 1. Possible Consumption Patterns of Two Qualities, Domestic and Foreign Users

	x^{fH}	x^{fL}	x^{dH}	x^{dL}
Pure separating	+	0	0	+
Impure separating	+	+	0	+
Non-separating	+	+	+	+

consumer and can be solved for as $\theta^{f*} = G(X^H/q^H)$. But this individual must get non-positive surplus from the low- quality good, i.e., $q^L\theta^{f*} - GX^L < 0$ or $\theta^{f*} \leq G(X^L/q^L)$ so that, from the definition of θ^{f*},

$$\frac{X^L}{q^L} \geq \frac{X^H}{q^H}.$$

Similarly, the marginal domestic consumer must get zero surplus from the low-quality good so $aq^L\theta^* - GX^L = 0$, where θ^* defines the marginal domestic consumer and can be solved for as $\theta^* = G(X^L/aq^L)$. But this individual must get non-positive surplus from the high-quality good, i.e., $aq^H\theta^* - GX^H \leq 0$ or $\theta^* \leq G(X^H/aq^H)$ so that, from the definition of θ^*,

$$\frac{X^L}{q^L} \leq \frac{X^H}{q^H}.$$

These two inequalities imply that

$$\frac{X^L}{q^L} = \frac{X^H}{q^H} \Rightarrow \frac{X^L}{q^L} = \frac{X^H}{q^H} = \frac{\Delta X}{\Delta q}.$$

Thus

$$0 < x^{dL} = \underline{\theta} - \frac{G}{a}\frac{X^L}{q^L} = \underline{\theta} - \frac{G}{a}\frac{\Delta X}{\Delta q} \Rightarrow a\Delta q\underline{\theta} > G\Delta X$$

or

$$aq^H\underline{\theta} - aq^L\underline{\theta} > GX^H - GX^L \quad \text{or} \quad aq^H\underline{\theta} - GX^H > aq^L\underline{\theta} - GX^L.$$

But this last inequality states that the highest value domestic consumer gets greater surplus from the high-quality good than from the low-quality good, a contradiction.

Thus we are left with only two generic possibilities: foreign consumers consume both the high- and the low-quality goods; domestic consumers certainly consume the low-quality good but domestic consumers may (the non-separating case) or may not (the

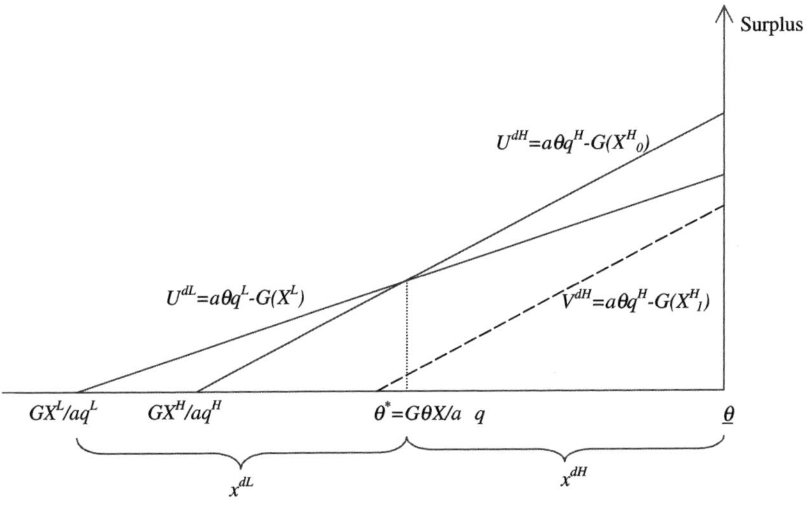

Fig. 2. Surplus to domestic consumers with two qualities.

impure separating case) consume the higher quality good.[26] Figure 2 illustrates a possible configuration of surplus for domestic consumers. If the relative aggregate demands (with corresponding congestion in each good) are, say, X^{L} and X_0^{H}, and are such that the surplus curves are U^{dH} and U^{dL}, then domestic consumers use both kinds of goods and demands are as shown. Alternatively, if congestion in the high-quality good is too great, say, X_1^{H}, leaving a surplus curve V^{dH}, then we get the impure separation case in which domestic consumers use only the low-quality good.

Of course, X^{L} and X^{H} are endogenous and depend on the chosen qualities. We turn to this next.

[26] As noted previously, one can also consider a model in which $a = 1$ but foreign consumers face a transport cost of T to access domestic resources, which has the effect of truncating the distribution of foreign consumers downward. In such a case, pure separation is again impossible, but because the domestic and foreign distributions are coincident at the top end. Further, in such a model we can get a kind of impure separation that does not occur in our present case: one in which foreign consumers use only the high-quality good and domestic consumers use both high- and low-quality goods.

a. *Optimal quality*

When domestic consumers use two goods of different qualities, we obtain the following expression for domestic consumers' surplus:

$$CS = \frac{a}{2}[q^{\mathrm{L}}(x^{\mathrm{dL}} + x^{\mathrm{dH}})^2 + \Delta q(x^{\mathrm{dH}})^2]. \tag{10}$$

Thus the government's problem is

$$\underset{\{q^{\mathrm{L}},q^{\mathrm{H}}\}}{\mathrm{Max}}\ W = \frac{a}{2}[q^{\mathrm{L}}(x^{\mathrm{dL}} + x^{\mathrm{dH}})^2 + \Delta q(x^{\mathrm{dH}})^2]$$
$$+V(x^{\mathrm{fH}} + x^{\mathrm{fL}}) - c(q^{\mathrm{L}})X^{\mathrm{L}} - c(q^{\mathrm{H}})X^{\mathrm{H}}, \tag{11}$$

where demands are given in (8) and (9).

As we cannot determine this unambiguously in analytical form, we turn to some numerical simulations to shed light on whether or not providing different qualities is attractive and under what conditions we are more likely to get impure separating or non-separating outcomes when qualities *are* different.

b. *Simulation results*

To get some indication of when impure separation is more attractive than non- separation, we have simulated this model numerically.[27] Figure 3 presents our results. Note from panel a (which illustrates the quality regimes chosen) that under no parameterisation in terms of a and L is a single quality chosen: it always pays to set $q^{\mathrm{H}} > q^{\mathrm{L}}$. Panel d shows the percentage difference between the qualities chosen and indicates that this is seldom very great except when a is very small and L is very large. In that case, as panel a shows, we get impure separation — the qualities are set sufficiently far apart that domestic consumers do not use the high-quality good at all. Panel b demonstrates that welfare is increasing mono- tonically in a, not a surprising result. However, when a is low, domestic welfare increases monotonically in L — this is the value of foreign consumers as

[27]The details of the simulation are discussed in an Appendix available from the author on request.

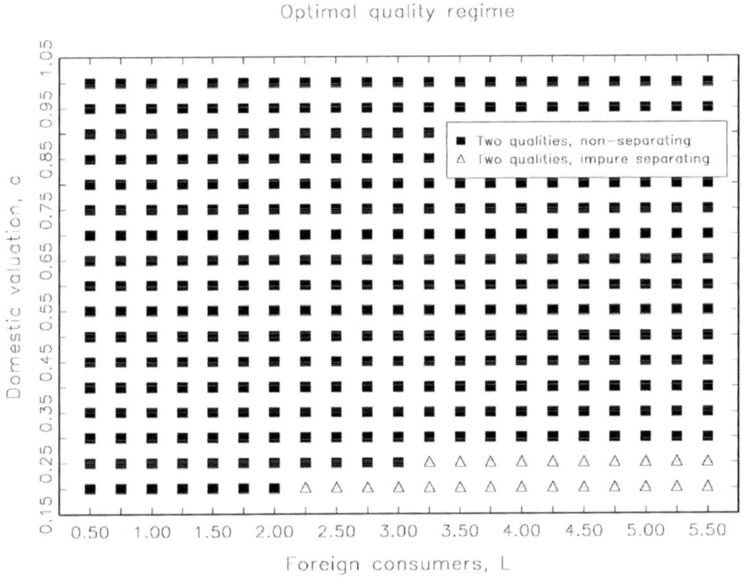

(a)

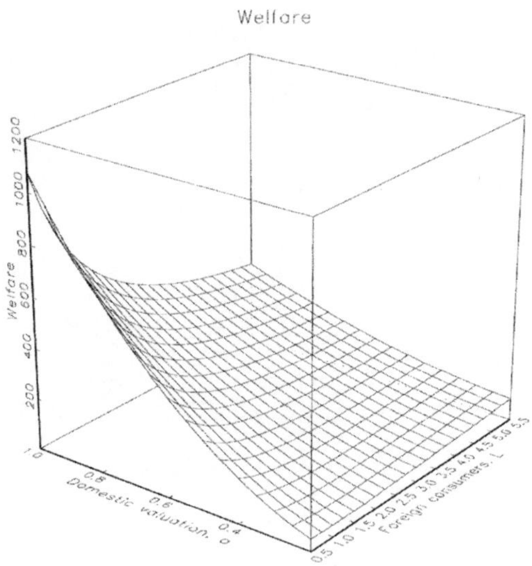

(b)

Fig. 3. (a) Choice of quality regime, foreign numbers, and the value of quality. (b) Welfare, foreign numbers, and the value of quality.

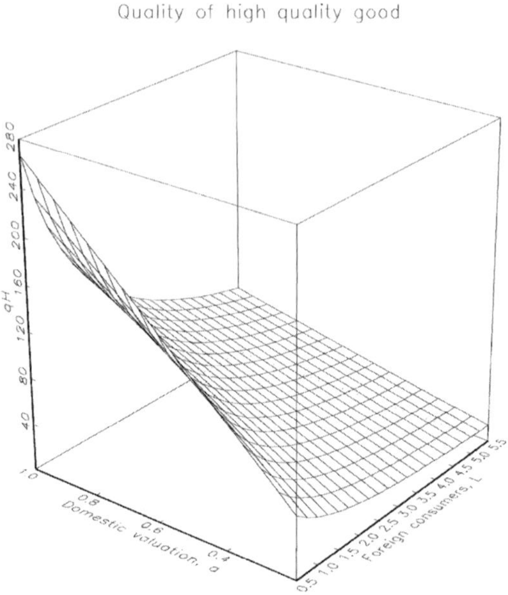

(c)

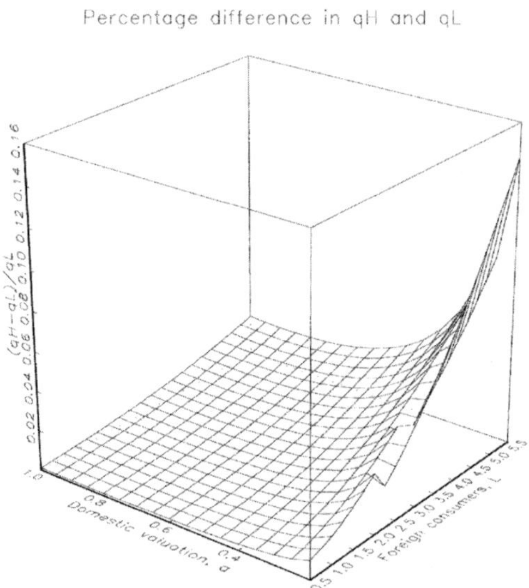

(d)

Fig. 3. (*Continued*) (c) Quality of the high-quality good, foreign numbers, and the value of quality. (d) Percentage difference in qualities, foreign numbers, and the value of quality.

represented by V — but when a is high, welfare decreases monotonically in L. In this case, the congestion effects of increased foreign demand are more costly. The convexity of welfare in a is a consequence of the quality adjustments made as domestic consumers value quality more highly: panel c shows that the high-quality good is upgraded as a increases (and a similar plot shows the same thing for the low-quality good).

These same panels also show our earlier result coming through here again: it is optimal to reduce the quality (of *both* goods) as the number of foreign consumers increases. We can also show that domestic consumption of the low-quality good is decreasing in a when non-separation holds and is generally increasing but concave in L. The concavity is driven by congestion — as L increases domestic demand for the high-quality good falls but foreign demand for *both* goods rises so congestion worsens on both goods.

4c. *Quantity rationing: A brief discussion*

In this paper we have been concerned with the use of quality alone as a means of controlling congestion. An alternative that might be used, however, even when prices are unavailable, is physical rationing. That is, the policy-maker could issue permits to domestic and foreign residents and restrict the number of permits issued. How might this affect the incentive for quality downgrading?

First note that having this extra instrument costlessly available must be (weakly) welfare improving. However, the club goods literature notes that there are costs associated with exclusion[28] and, indeed, the relative absence of such schemes in the contexts we have been considering suggests that these costs might be quite significant

[28]See [3] for a survey and [17] for an example of analysis of clubs with costly exclusion. These costs include the costs of identifying foreign versus domestic users and of policing access and, as such, are typically modelled as fixed costs which, in this case, would be borne by the government. I am grateful to a referee for suggesting this line of enquiry and these references. I do not undertake a complete analysis of this topic here, however, partly because we simply do not observe such rationing in practice. This begs the question "why not?" of course, and examining this issue more completely is a useful topic for future research.

in practice. While a full analysis of this is beyond the scope of this paper, we can note a few features of rationing in this context. We suppose throughout that a binding rationing constraint leads to efficient rationing, i.e., permits go to the highest value users.

First, consider the single-good case. Our results will still go through if exclusion costs — denoted e following Silva [17] — are sufficiently high. Suppose that e is too high for rationing to be used in some initial equilibrium, and we then experience an increase in foreign demand ($dL > 0$ in our model). Then quality downgrading leads to a smaller welfare loss than no action at all and this may still be optimal if e is high and the welfare gains of an exclusionary regime are small.

On the other hand, suppose e is sufficiently low that access *is* controlled in equilibrium. Now an increase in foreign demand will have no effect on optimal quality as the initial optimum will be unaffected with the (optimal) rationing level on foreign consumption unchanged. Of course, in the presence of rationing the marginal foreign consumer who is excluded is a relatively "low taste" consumer whereas the $dL > 0$ exercise adds consumers across the entire range of quality tastes in the market. But this makes no difference — the policy-maker does not care about the surplus of foreign consumers per se, only the total number of them, and whether they are high taste or low taste makes no difference to their optimum number.[29]

It is also quite possible in this context that it is domestic consumers who will be rationed. To see this, suppose there is no rationing and consider restricting the number of domestic consumers marginally. Each marginal consumer gains zero surplus so losing a few domestic consumers has approximately no effect on the surplus but it reduces congestion, drawing in new foreign consumers, each of which is worth V to the policy-maker. If rationing is costless this must be welfare improving for $V > 0$.

[29] Formally, consider maximising (6) over q, x, and x^{f} subject to the inequality constraints that x and x^{f} cannot exceed the values specified in (6). If we confine our attention to the regime in which both domestic and foreign consumers are rationed (i.e., the inequality constraints do not bind), then this yields FOC's which do not depend on L since x^{f} is itself a choice variable.

Second, consider the two-good case. In the presence of rationing we now might be able to sustain pure separation, even though the marginal foreign consumer need not have zero surplus.[30]

5. Conclusions

In this paper we have constructed a model of demand for quality-differentiated products in which domestic consumers generically have a lower valuation of quality than their foreign counterparts. Four critical features of our model, driven by the realities of environmental resource provision, are that (i) there is consumer heterogeneity within consumer populations, (ii) all consumers incur disutility from congestion, (iii) the provider of the resource cannot use monetary prices to allocate it, and (iv) they care only for the surplus of domestic consumers. We demonstrate that, in such a setting, an appropriate response to increased foreign demand is to reduce the quality of the goods being provided. Welfare still falls as foreign demand increases but quality downgrading mitigates that loss to some extent. This is in contrast to the case in which monetary prices are available and explicit separation of domestic and foreign consumers is possible. In that case an appropriate response to increased foreign demand is to increase quality and welfare rises too. We also show that a government will generally have an incentive to provide different qualities if two goods are available in which case congestion costs can act as a separating device. It is never in the government's interests to separate consumers fully, but if foreign demand is high and domestic valuations low then a partial separation may be attractive.

[30]A welfare-maximising government would always wish to downgrade the high-quality good in such a case until either (a) the marginal foreign consumer does, indeed, have zero surplus or (b) the highest value domestic consumer is exactly indifferent between the high- and low-quality goods. In case (a) if domestic consumers are not rationed, then the marginal domestic consumer gets zero surplus and our proof of Proposition 3 still goes through: pure separation cannot hold. Otherwise, however, a relaxation of the constraint on domestic consumers might be unattractive because it increases congestion on the low-quality good, thereby making the high-quality good more attractive and, potentially, destroying the separating outcome. Hence separation could be maintained with an appropriate constraint on domestic consumption. In case (b), separation could also be maintained with the appropriate constraint on *foreign* consumption.

It should be stressed that our analysis is very much in a constrained, second-best environment and caution needs to be exercised in interpreting our results. While we have shown that quality downgrading may be an optimal response in the absence of prices and while we have not considered it explicitly (except in the single-good case with costless separation) the ability to charge differential prices to domestic and foreign consumers must be (weakly) welfare improving here (by revealed preference arguments). Furthermore, in the case of multiple goods, differential pricing across *goods* must similarly be (weakly) welfare improving as well. So the first-best solution will involve the use of monetary prices. Nevertheless, it will very likely also involve differential quality provision and the strategic use of congestion costs a la Donaldson and Eaton [6].

Finally, an interesting extension of this work would be to consider the provision of more than two goods. One would conjecture from our results that it would pay to differentiate them all but it may then be the case that some goods would be consumed only by domestic users, some by both types, and some by foreigners only; i.e., we might get a more complete form of separation than in the current analysis.

References

Acharyya, R. (1998). Monopoly and product quality: Separating or pooling menu? *Economics Letters*, 61, 187–194.

Barro, R. and P. Romer (1987). Ski-lift pricing, with applications to labor and other markets. *American Economic Review*, 77, 875–890.

Cornes, R. and T. Sandler (1996). *The Theory of Externalities, Public Goods and Club Goods*, 2nd ed. Cambridge, UK: Cambridge University Press.

Cullen, R. (1985). Rationing recreation use of public land. *Journal of Environmental Management*, 21, 213–225.

Cullen, R. (1998). Zero prices, equity and natural areas. *International Journal of Social Economics*, 25, 1300–1309.

Donaldson, D. and C. Eaton (1981). Patience, more than its own reward: A note on price discrimination. *Canadian Journal of Economics*, 14.

Fairbrother, N. (1970). *New Lives, New Landscapes.* Penguin, Harmondsworth.

Feldman, R. (1978). Rationing congested goods by preferences on quality. *Public Finance*, 33, 225–231.

Glazer, A. and E. Niskanen (1997). Why voters may prefer congested public clubs. *Journal of Public Economics*, 65, 37–44.

Glazer, A., E. Niskanen and S. Scotchmer (1997). On the uses of club theory. *Journal of Public Economics*, 65, 3–7.

Hull, B. (1987). The effect of foreign and local visitors on granting park concessions. *New Zealand Economic Papers*, 21, 83–96.

Kearsley, G., D. Coughlan, J. Higham, E. Higham and M. Thyne (1998). Impacts of tourist use on the New Zealand backcountry. Research Paper 1, Centre for Tourism. Dunedin, New Zealand: University of Otago.

Knight, F. (1924). Some fallacies in the interpretation of social cost. *Quarterly Journal of Economics*, 38, 582–606.

Nichols, D., E. Smolensky and T. Tideman (1971). Discrimination by waiting time in merit goods. *American Economic Review*, 61, 312–323.

NZ Tourism Board (1993). *New Zealand Conservation Estate and International Visitors*. Wellington, NZ.

Potton, C. (1998). Equity and Access in Natural Areas, NZ Ministry of Tourism. Available at http://www.otsp.govt.nz/oldweb/pubs/equity3.html.

Silva, E. (1997). A-la-carte or smorgasbord? Multiproduct clubs with costly exclusion. *Journal of Urban*, 41, 264–280.

Tourism Policy Group (1994). *Funding Options for the Provision of Facilities in Natural Areas*. Wellington, NZ: Ministry of Commerce.

Tourism Policy Group (1998). Existing Examples of Economic Instruments in Natural Areas. NZ Ministry of Tourism. Available at http://www.otsp.govt.nz/oldweb/pubs/econinst.html.

Chapter 17

Fair Trade

Martin Richardson and Frank Stähler

Abstract: This chapter analyses a setting in which a vertically integrated fair-trade firm competes against vertically disintegrated, profit-maximising oligopolists. Consumers of the fair-trade product derive a "warm glow" that depends on the wage paid to fair-trade producers; the firm returns all surplus to its farmers. Trade integration will unambiguously increase the size of the fair-trade firm, but the relative size compared to oligopolists may shrink. Furthermore, we show that the "warm glow" effect may support a marginal expansion of the volume of fair trade, but for rather perverse reasons.

1. Introduction

In recent years, many countries have seen a sharp increase in the prevalence of so-called fair trade (FT) products[1] and yet there is very little analysis of this trade in the economics literature. In this paper, we model the operation of FT firms in competition with non-FT firms — motivated mainly by the structure of the coffee market, in which FT first became a significant factor — to try to understand the origins and growth of FT as a structure. Our aims are to understand

Originally published in *Economic Record*, Economic Society of Australia.

[1]The term "fair trade" has been used to refer to a number of things, such as the imposition of trade policy motivated by ethical concerns, but we use it to refer to trade by intermediary firms, which undertake to pay higher returns to primary producers than the latter receive in the market. Worldwide sales of FT coffee, cocoa, tea, rice, sugar, honey, fruit, textiles and other handicrafts grew at over 3 per cent annually in the 1990s and demand for FT coffee in particular has grown much more rapidly than demand for coffee overall.

why FT has arisen and grown, particularly in the coffee industry, and to consider the welfare implications of supporting such trade. To these ends, we construct a model of FT that captures certain essential features of the reality of FT structures while, at the same time, is relatively parsimonious.

In our model, an (effectively) vertically integrated FT firm competes against a number of oligopolistic competitors selling a product processed from an agricultural input. There are two quality-differentiated markets, the products in them being imperfect substitutes in demand and the FT firm competes in one only (the high-quality market) with or without non-FT rivals (depending on parameter values). The FT firm contracts with an endogenously chosen number of farmers, but the cost of transforming their inputs into high-quality output depends (negatively) on the quality of the inputs and this, in turn, depends on unobservable farmer effort. This yields a "moral hazard in teams" problem (hereafter, moral hazard) facing the FT firm that is not faced by its rivals which deal with growers on a spot market. The moral hazard problem endogenously limits the optimal size of the FT collective. The FT firm also returns all surplus from its operations to its growers in the form of a wage premium over the wages paid by rivals and, in turn, induces a higher willingness-to-pay from consumers who derive a "warm glow" from the knowledge that they are delivering more to growers. That is, consumers' welfare is improved by the knowledge that primary producers are receiving higher incomes — this makes consumers feel good about themselves and they are suffused with a "warm glow" of satisfaction (see Andreoni, 1990). Finally, all firms incur trade costs in shipping the growers' outputs to their processing plants in the final country of consumption.

In this setting, we show first that a FT firm will arise if trade costs are sufficiently low and/or the "warm glow" effect is sufficiently high. Given such a firm, we show that there are two possible generic outcomes: one in which the FT firm faces no competition in the high-quality sector and one in which the non-FT firms are active in both sectors. We demonstrate that, if trade costs fall, while the FT firm will expand, its market share may fall if its moral hazard problem is sufficiently severe. With competition in the high-quality sector, a change in consumer attitudes such that high-quality and low-quality coffees are seen as less perfect substitutes (arguably, a phenomenon we have observed in the last decade) can actually lead the FT firm's market share to fall, if the relative market potential of the high-quality sector is large. Neither of these results holds out much promise for the continued growth of FT.

Unsurprisingly, an increase in the "warm glow" effect will lead to an expansion of the FT firm at the expense of any non-FT rivals in the high-quality sector, but, perhaps not so obviously, we show that a marginal expansion in the FT sector would be beneficial in terms of its effect on consumers' overall surplus only if the "warm glow" component of consumer welfare is ignored. This occurs because it leads to a fall in the FT wage for inframarginal FT farmers and, therefore, in the overall FT wage bill. If the "warm glow" is taken into account in welfare, then the laissez-faire solution is efficient with respect to the "warm glow".

Commencing in the Netherlands in 1973 (although the fair trade label had its origins in 1988), the FT movement has been most successful in Europe. In Switzerland, for example, fair trade products accounted for 55% of the banana market, 17% of the pineapple market and 15% of all sugar sold in 2006.[2] These FT organisations essentially offer a certification to producers who meet certain standards (see Mohan, 2010, p. 20) for a summary). Howley (2006) describes the operation of TransFair USA, the US operation of the 1989 Dutch company, as certifying fair trade products and auditing the production chain from grower to final retailer. The certification of farms is undertaken by the Fairtrade Labeling Organization (FLO), a collective organisation that specifies criteria that farms must satisfy to receive the stamp of approval.

The carrot offered to induce members to comply with these costly criteria is that the FLO guarantees a minimum floor price for certified members that not only provides stability in an extremely volatile

[2]These figures on Switzerland are from Krier (2008), p. 102.

market but also ensures a premium on the market price.[3] It is important to note that FT firms do not simply pay farmers a premium over the market price: obtaining FT certification for a coffee-grower, for example, requires that a farm must be strictly a family concern (employing no long-term hired labour) and must be a member of a large cooperative[4]: the FLO does not deal with individual farms, but with collectives of small farms. Once producers comply with the eligibility criteria, they receive approval to contact licensed importers. These importers are expected to supply credit to growers, but pay no certification fee, while roasters and distributors pay a license fee for the right to use the fair trade logo.

The fact that FT firms require farmers to make a number of significant undertakings suggests two things of importance in modelling them. First, it suggests that any "warm glow" that FT firms supply to consumers derives from more than just providing higher returns to farmers, as the latter could be done simply by appropriate transfers. Instead, FT firms have elaborate and costly requirements of participating farmers, which indicates that the uses to which any premium is put must also be valued by consumers.[5] Second, these undertakings require FT farmers to make commitments to their production technology *before* they produce and sell their output, and this has implications for the timing of actions in these markets.[6]

---

[3]For Arabica coffee, for example, it pays \$1.26 if the New York price is less than \$1.21; otherwise, it pays the New York price plus five cents. Since 2000, there have only been two brief periods during which the latter price was the relevant one. In the Robusta coffee market, the relevant market price has not reached the Fairtrade floor price in over 10 years.

[4]Rice (2001) states directly, concerning the price premium paid to farmers, "[t]he fair price is conditional" and goes on to list the production criteria discussed here that need to be met to obtain FT certification. Other requirements imposed on cooperatives include restrictions on their political structure and independence and requirements regarding openness to new members: see Rice (2001) and Milford (2004). We discuss the international coffee market more fully in Appendix SA.1.

[5]For example, Wilkinson (2006, p. 1) suggests that, "the nature of fair trade... [is] a variegated social movement mobilized around a range of objectives".

[6]While this corresponds to a Stackelberg game, in the present setting, the timing is solely to capture an essential structural difference between FT and non-FT firms: the former must pre-commit to output by contracting farmers in advance, whereas the latter do not. While it is generally true that a first mover in a quantity-setting game is better off than it would be in the equivalent simultaneous move game, there is no presumption

At the same time that FT has become such a phenomenon, we have also observed a bifurcation in coffee consumption along quality lines, with FT firms operating exclusively in the "gourmet" sector of the roast and ground market, the high-quality segment of the coffee market (the low-quality segment being the market for instant and non-specialty coffee). It is also the case that the high fixed costs of coffee processing (see Sutton, 1991) have yielded a high degree of concentration in the coffee processing and wholesaling market. For these reasons, the international coffee market is best characterised as an oligopoly (see Ponte, 2002) across at least two quality-differentiated sub-markets.

The collective structure of FT farmers is an important feature of FT production and is central to our analysis. Milford (2004) finds "clear evidence" that co-ops use "membership regulations actively to obtain a specific level of membership and a corresponding volume of coffee" (p. 52). That is, while, in principle, these FT cooperatives are meant to be open to all new members willing to produce by the FT guidelines, *de facto* they do constrain output. She also examines the efficiency of co-op operations and finds evidence of "free-rider" problems in the management and control of co-ops. This moral hazard problem is a key feature of the model of this paper.

There is a growing literature on the economics of "ethical" consumption. Besley and Ghatak (2007) present a model of corporate social responsibility (CSR) as the private provision of a public good, the latter being valued by some subset of consumers. They also consider the use of firm reputation to sustain CSR when consumers cannot perfectly observe their compliance and show that the sustainable level of CSR is then reduced. Finally, as does Kotchen (2006), they compare CSR with other institutional means to provide a public good such as government regulation and the activities of non-profits. A central aspect of much of this literature is demonstrating the possibility of competitive equilibria in models where some consumers

---

that it is better off than a second mover, particularly in a case like ours where the first mover has increasing marginal costs in contrast to the second's constant costs.

are willing to pay a premium for some feature of a good's production and others are not. The focus of our analysis, by contrast, is on an FT firm establishing against oligopolistic non-FT competitors. The feasibility of such a firm in this setting is not an issue, due to the oligopolistic rents in the sector.[7] Most of the existing literature on FT markets is largely non-analytical. A number of authors (Maseland & de Vaal, 2002; Milford, 2004; Hayes, 2006) have observed that an FT organisation can offset monopsonistic behaviour in an input market. Leclair (2002) documents the increasing significance of FT generally while Milford (2004) provides a discussion more focused on coffee in particular.

To our knowledge, there are only a few papers which provide an analytical model of FT markets. Becchetti and Adriani (2002) consider the role of consumers willing to pay a premium for FT products. In their model, the FT firm hires those workers with the lowest outside options, thereby forcing the monopsonist to pay more than it otherwise would. However, in contrast to the present paper, Becchetti and Adriani do not model the cooperative nature of FT production and nor is there any responsiveness of consumer welfare to the level of Southern wages: the good is simply considered to be fairly produced or not.[8]

Piyapromdee *et al.* (2008) develop an oligopsony model with an upward-sloping input supply curve in which FT firms maximise a linear combination of producer surplus and profits. They show in

[7]A number of FT analysts have argued that the "warm glow" premium is not essential to the success of FT firms, which exist primarily to shift oligopsonistic rents to farmers. As we shall see, it is not essential in our model either, although it helps. Implicitly, there are fixed costs associated with establishing a FT firm, which constrain entry. We do consider the impact of multiple FT firms in what follows. Furthermore, we consider the activities of FT firms as involving a natural bundling of higher returns to FT farmers with restrictions on production techniques, and this makes the separation of buying coffee and donating to such constrained coffee farmers, for example, less efficient than just buying FT coffee.

[8]Their analysis is similar to that of papers that consider the impact of eco-labeling on trade (see e.g., Graeker, 2006, and Mälkönen, 2005 and, for models incorporating green consumers, Conrad, 2005, and Eriksson, 2004). Fair trade is more concerned about factor rewards than about the production process, although, as noted above, FT certifying organisations do impose a significant number of restrictions on their members in terms of the organisation of production. See Appendix SA.1 and the references therein.

a calibration that the existence of FT firms will drive up producer incomes, but only by a small margin. They also assume that final commodity prices are given, whereas we employ a model of imperfect competition between the FT firm and profit-maximising non-FT oligopolists.

Finally, Chau *et al.* (2009) describe a model of spatially differentiated farmers in which there are transport costs associated with delivering to an export hub. Chau *et al.* model the entry of poverty-averse non-profits in competition with middlemen and show that they tend to work in the most distant regions, raise the average export price received by farmers and reduce average farmer poverty. Their stress on the role of non-profits as competing against the market power of middlemen underscores our earlier discussion of the role of FT firms in agricultural markets, but their focus and analysis are quite different from ours, as they do not model the mechanism by which higher prices are delivered to farmers at all.

The remainder of the paper is organised as follows: In the next section, we present our model and Section III discusses the equilibrium, while Section IV undertakes a number of comparative statics and policy exercises of interest. Section V concludes. For expositional convenience, we have relegated the main bulk of our proofs to an Appendix S1, available on request, along with a discussion of the structure of the world coffee market, which drives some of our modelling choices.

2. The model

Motivated by the coffee market, we suppose there are two countries, home and foreign, with all initial production in the foreign country, but all consumption at home. There are also two qualities of the good for sale and they are perceived by consumers as imperfect substitutes. We distinguish two types of firms: a fair-trade firm (henceforth labeled as FT) and other firms, which we will label non-FT firms. The FT firm serves the high-quality market only and its supply is equal to z, whereas all non-FT firms produce, in aggregate,

$X(Y)$ for the low- (high-)quality market.[9] There are L households in the home country, and each of them inelastically supplies one unit of labour such that aggregate labour supply is equal to L with L large so that consumers take prices as given. Demand behaviour can be determined by considering the optimal consumption plan of consumer i. The utility function of consumer i is quasi-linear and given by

$$\tilde{U}_i = U(X_i, Y_i, z_i) + Q_i, \quad U(X_i, Y_i, z_i) = A_i X_i + \alpha_i (Y_i + z_i)$$
$$-\frac{1}{2}(X_i^2 + 2\gamma X_i (Y_i + z_i) + (Y_i + z_i)^2) + \delta_i w z_i,$$
$$\gamma, \delta_i \in [0, 1], A_i, \alpha_i > 0, \tag{1}$$

where X_i denotes consumption of the low-quality commodity, $Y_i(z_i)$ denotes consumption of the high-quality commodity which is produced by non-FT firms (by the FT firm), and Q_i is the consumption of a commodity which is produced under perfect competition and is the numeraire in our model. The term $\delta_i w z_i$ is the "warm glow" effect, which is explained below in detail.

We assume that one unit of labour is required to produce one unit of commodity Q. Accordingly, consumer i maximises expression (1) subject to the budget constraint $pX_i + qY_i + rz_i + Q_i = 1$ where p, q and r denote the respective prices for X, Y and z. Maximisation by all consumers leads to the inverse demand functions

$$\begin{aligned} p &= A - X - \gamma(Y + z), \\ q &= \alpha - (Y + z) - \gamma X, \\ r &= \alpha - (Y + z) - \gamma X + \delta w, \end{aligned} \tag{2}$$

where $X = \sum X_i/L$, $Y = \sum Y_i/L$, $z = \sum z_i/L$, $A = \sum A_i/L$, $\alpha = \sum \alpha_i/L$ and $\delta = \sum \delta_i/L$. Utility maximisation gives rise to the existence of two markets, a low-quality market and a high-quality market, because the price for the high-quality commodity received by the FT firm differs from the price received by the non-FT firms only by a

[9]Empirical evidence suggests that FT firms serve only one market segment. However, our results would not change qualitatively if we allowed the FT firm to produce for both markets.

wage premium.[10] Hence, we will use

$$p = A - X - \gamma(Y + z),\ q = \alpha - (Y + z) - \gamma X \tag{3}$$

only and add a wage premium for the FT firm. High- and low-quality commodities are (weak) substitutes and the parameter γ measures the degree of substitutability. Furthermore, $A(\alpha)$ measures the average quality of commodity $X(Y$ and $z)$ as perceived by consumers. Hence, our model will allow us to discuss the effects of both changes in substitutability *between* commodities and of changes in perceived quality of a *single* commodity.

We assume that the number of firms is fixed such that there is only one FT firm, but n non-FT firms. In Appendix SA.9, we show that none of our results changes qualitatively if we assume more than one FT firm. The assumption of n non-FT firms allows us to discuss the effects of more or less competition on FT behaviour. Our non-FT firms are profit-maximising firms, and they are able to serve both the high- and the low-quality markets. On the production side, they are vertically disintegrated and simply acquire inputs on the international spot market. Without loss of generality, we assume that each non-FT firm requires one unit of input to produce one unit of output. The marginal cost of producing the low-quality final commodity is normalised to zero, but the high-quality commodity warrants a marginal cost of size c with $c > 0$.[11]

[10]The essence of the FT phenomenon is that consumers do not consider one bag of coffee to be *inherently* different from another, but are willing to pay more for one purely because of the manner in which it has been produced (indeed, purely because of the manner in which its producers have been remunerated). So, we focus our analysis on the case where this is most apparent: where the goods are perceived as perfect substitutes aside from the manner of their producers' pay. We also believe that this is a compelling assumption as an empirical matter.

[11]While we have normalised the oligopolists' costs of producing the low-quality good to zero, our focus is on the cost premium of producing high-quality goods (those that compete with the FT firm) and this is captured in c. Note that our modelling approach is equivalent to one in which all farmers have the same technology requiring higher effort for production of high-quality output. But non-FT firms operate on a spot market and so can observe the quality of the goods they are purchasing and higher quality inputs will receive a premium. This can be determined endogenously and depends on the parameters of the effort function; as these are given, we simply characterise this premium as c. We are grateful to a referee for noting this equivalence.

The market for intermediate inputs is competitive from the supply side as there is are large number of producers. These producers are located in the foreign country, and each can produce one unit of the intermediate input. If the producer is not offered a contract with the FT firm, it has to decide whether to produce one unit of the intermediate input, which will be sold on the international market, or to pick an outside option whose payoff we have normalised to zero. Accordingly, the price of the intermediate input on the international market will be zero irrespective of the demand by non-FT firms.[12]

This practice and, in particular, the monopsony power of oligopolists, is felt to be unfair by consumers of the final commodity, and this discomfort gives rise to the establishment of a different type of firm — the FT firm — which has a different objective. It produces high-quality commodities only[13] and guarantees credibly that all proceeds net of production costs are given back to producers through a restrictive cooperative. The FT firm is effectively vertically integrated with producers, as it produces the final output solely with the input of producers with which it has signed an exclusive contract. Hence, the FT firm does not use the international market, and producers signing a contract with the FT firm (henceforth labeled as FT producers) will exclusively produce the intermediate input for the FT firm.[14]

---

[12]If producers were heterogeneous in terms of their outside options, supply would not be perfectly elastic and the existence of the FT firm would also affect the input prices of oligopolists. See Piyapromdee *et al.* (2008). See also Becchetti and Adriani (2002) where the FT firm contracts with the farmers with the lowest outside options, thus driving up the prices that must be paid by the oligopoly firms. Finally, if producers were heterogeneous in terms of their productivity (and this was *ex ante* observable), then we would face the problem that the FT firm would, as first mover, seek to sign up the most efficient farmers, an option in contradiction with the principles of FT operation. In this model, then, we suppose that producers are homogeneous.

[13]As discussed by Sutton (1991), production of instant coffee involves substantial fixed costs in comparison with production of roast coffee beans, either whole or ground, so, in the coffee market at least, this explains the fact that FT firms operate only in the latter, high-quality, sub-sector.

[14]An empirical feature of FT firms' operations is that the contract between suppliers and licensed buyers involves a premium on the market price, supported by a floor price. While it is the case (see, e.g., Imhof & Lee, 2007, p. 100) that FT cooperatives may

In our model, then, the non-FT firms use the spot market for buying the intermediate input, whereas the FT firm uses explicit contracts with producers. One rationale for this difference is that a key feature to enable the FT business to be credible is that it is transparent and can be seen to be delivering returns to farmers, hence the direct contracting. Furthermore, in terms of timing, contractual arrangements with agricultural producers must occur before the actual contracted delivery of the output, and so must precede any activity on the anonymous spot market, so it is natural that the FT firm commits to its (contracted) input choices before non-FT firms decide on their (spot market) input decisions.[15]

Finally, profit maximising non-FT firms choose to be vertically disintegrated, because vertical integration comes with an additional cost. The contract between the FT firm and the FT producer is incomplete, as it specifies the delivery of one unit of the intermediate input, but not the effort of each producer to reduce the overall production cost of the final (high-quality) commodity. This effort is not observable and thus FT production suffers from a moral hazard problem due to vertical integration. So this feature of our model fits very well with the observed reality that non-FT firms are not vertically integrated, whereas FT firms are (at least, through contractual arrangements). Table 1 gives the sequence of decisions of the game, which we solve in the usual backward induction fashion.

The other notable difference between FT production and production by non-FT firms is the "warm glow" effect of FT production. Because the FT firm can credibly guarantee that it gives all profits back to the producers, it is able to earn a premium on top of the high-quality price q. The FT good can be regarded as bundling a service and a private good. The service is similar to a private charity contribution and allows consumers to make a donation to increase

---

occasionally produce more output than their FT contract specifies (the surplus being sold on spot markets), our focus is on the FT-contracted quantity.

[15]Numerous case studies illustrate the accuracy of these timing assumptions — see Milford (2004) and Imhof and Lee (2007), for example. We assume that they incur some added costs in doing this, beyond those incurred by other firms, as they still need to screen their farmers to ensure that they are producing according to the wishes of the FT firm.

Table 1. Game structure

Stage I:
FT firm decides on the number of FT producers.
Stage II:
Each FT producer decides on efforts to reduce production costs.
Stage III:
Non-FT firms decide simultaneously on their production levels in both markets.

FT producers' income.[16] We assume that consumers are willing to pay δw on average more per unit of the high-quality commodity for this service offered by the FT firm, where w denotes the wage premium paid to each FT producer (and thus, given that the wage of non-FT firms is normalised to zero, the wage itself) and $\delta \in [0, 1]$.[17]

3. Fair trade equilibrium

In this section, we discuss the behaviour of the FT firm and the non-FT firms by solving the three-stage game. Note that the FT firm and the non-FT firms determine their inputs by contracts or on the spot market respectively. Our fixed-coefficient production technology means that an input choice is equivalent to a firm-specific capacity constraint and therefore we model firm behaviour as a Cournot game.[18] The non-FT firms move last in this game and, due to the transparency of the FT business, they know how many FT producers

[16]In this sense, bundling successfully prevents fraudulent use of donations as the FT firm guarantees that all proceeds are returned to FT producers.

[17]As noted earlier, we assume that the consumer perceives the two high-quality goods to be perfect substitutes in all respects other than the preference for "fair" production techniques. An alternative way of modelling the effect of FT labeling would be to drop the "warm glow" effect completely and suppose that an FT product is simply perceived as an imperfect substitute for its oligopoly rival products. While we do not pursue it in this paper, we are grateful to Peter Neary for this observation.

[18]It is well known that Cournot games can be strategically equivalent to capacity-constrained price games so that this assumption is not too restrictive. For the pioneering paper, see Kreps and Scheinkman (1983). We do not go into the details of the set of requirements, which are necessary to establish strategic equivalence in our model as this is beyond of the scope of this paper. It should be noted, however, that FT firms do not in practice commit to sell all FT-certified output in periods when the price floor is binding.

have been hired by the FT firm. To make the problem interesting, we assume that the non-FT firms will be active at least in one market. Let z^* denote the optimal number of FT producers (for which we will not be able to derive a closed form solution). We require:

Assumption 1. $z^* < \frac{A-t}{\gamma}$.

Assumption 1 guarantees that the non-FT firms are at least active in the low-quality market. Stages II and III take z as given, but firm-specific and aggregate outputs depend on z in Stage I. In Stage III, each non-FT firm maximises its profits $\Pi_i \equiv (p-t)x_i + (q-c-t)y_i$ where t denotes the per-unit trade cost of the intermediate input. The Kuhn–Tucker conditions are

$$\begin{aligned} p - t + p_X x_i + q_X y_i &= 0, \\ q - c - t + q_Y y_i + p_Y x_i &\leq 0, \ y_i \geq 0, \\ y_i(q - c - t + q_Y y_i + p_Y x_i) &= 0, \end{aligned} \tag{4}$$

where the subscripts denote the partial derivatives of the inverse demand function w.r.t. respective aggregate output levels.[19] Note that non-FT firms have to take a cannibalisation effect into account: an increase in output in one market will decrease the price in the other market, and this effect is stronger with a larger γ. Based on condition (4), we now have to distinguish two cases, depending on whether or not the non-FT firms serve both market sectors. In this paper, we consider only the case where they do; Richardson and Stähler (2007) consider the other case as well.[20] If $y_i > 0$, non-FT firms serve both markets and their output levels (denoted by a double

[19] It can easily be shown that the second-order conditions $\Pi_{xx}, \Pi_{yy} < 0$, $\Pi_{xx}\Pi_{yy} > \Pi_{xy}^2$ are fulfilled.

[20] From (6), we can infer the critical level of z which makes the FT firm monopolise the high-quality market. Monopolisation will (not) occur if z is larger (smaller) than

$$\hat{z} \equiv \frac{(\alpha - c - t) - \gamma(A-t)}{1-\gamma^2}. \tag{6}$$

Note that $y_i^* = 0$ and $\gamma \to 1$ is the case of both types of firms competing in one market only. This case could easily be extended to both types of firms competing in both markets without further insights except a potential cannibalisation problem for the FT firm, too.

star) are equal to

$$
\begin{aligned}
x_i^{**} &= \frac{(A-t) - \gamma(\alpha - c - t)}{(n+1)(1-\gamma^2)}, \\
y_i^{**} &= \frac{(\alpha - c - t) - \gamma(A-t)}{(n+1)(1-\gamma^2)} - \left(\frac{1}{n+1}\right) z.
\end{aligned}
\tag{5}
$$

Note that z affects y_i^{**} only but not x_i^{**}. In particular, an increase or decrease in z will not change x_i^{**}. The reason is that an increase in z has two effects on firm behaviour in the low-quality market, a direct and an indirect effect. First, this market becomes less attractive as more, albeit imperfect, substitutes are now available (despite the decline in y_i^{**}), and this direct effect would make x_i^{**} decrease. However, y_i^{**} and x_i^{**} are strategic substitutes, and because y_i^{**} decreases, the cannibalisation effect has been reduced and x_i^{**} should increase. In our model with an identical γ across quality types and linear demand, these effects cancel each other out.

We now turn to Stage II. To determine each producer's payoff, let c_0 denote the production cost of the FT firm.[21] Because each producer produces one unit, its wage is determined by the price in the high-quality market, complemented by the wage premium and corrected for costs.

That is, $w = r - c_0 - t$, or:

$$
\begin{aligned}
w &\equiv \alpha - z - Y - \gamma X + \delta w - c_0 - t \\
\Leftrightarrow w &= \frac{\alpha - z - Y - \gamma X - c_0 - t}{1-\delta}.
\end{aligned}
$$

As for the production cost, we assume that each FT producer j can make a contribution by individual efforts e_j such that

$$
c_0 = \theta - \frac{\lambda \sum e_j}{z}
$$

with $\theta, \lambda > 0$, where this specification is known to all producers. The typical FT producer j correctly anticipates the number of all fellow

[21]Note that our analysis does not warrant that the FT firm's marginal cost is higher than the marginal cost c. However, $c_0 > c$ might be the result of vertical disintegration being the most efficient production method.

FT producers and, in Stage II, maximises its payoff

$$v_j \equiv w - \frac{\mu e_j^2}{2},$$

where the quadratic term gives the individual disutility of the producer's (unobservable) effort. Maximising over individual effort leads to

$$e_j^* = \frac{\lambda}{\mu z(1-\delta)}, \quad v_j^* = \frac{\alpha - z - Y - \gamma X - \theta - t}{1-\delta} + \frac{2z-1}{2z^2}\frac{\lambda^2}{\mu(1-\delta)^2} \equiv v^*. \tag{7}$$

The asterisks denote optimal levels, and v^* is written using symmetry among FT producers. Expression (7) shows that the FT producer's surplus consists of two parts, the price–cost margin and the reduction in production cost due to producers' effort. The price–cost margin declines with the number of FT producers and the aggregate output of non-FT firms, while the production cost reduction also gets smaller with z, as the moral hazard problem becomes more severe with an increase in FT producers. *Ceteris paribus*, the moral hazard problem is exacerbated by an increase in the term λ^2/μ as this term measures the decline in producer payoff caused by an increase in the size of the FT firm. If λ is large, individual efforts contribute strongly to reductions in the FT firm's costs; if μ is small, the marginal disutility of effort is small, and hence a substantial FT cost reduction could be attained easily without a significant moral hazard problem.

The FT firm correctly anticipates the behaviour of each FT producer and, in Stage I, chooses their number to maximise the sum of payoffs of all FT producers, which is equal to

$$S(z) \equiv zv^* = z\left(\frac{\alpha - z - Y(z) - \gamma X(z) - \theta - t}{1-\delta} + \frac{2z-1}{2z^2}\frac{\lambda^2}{\mu(1-\delta)^2}\right). \tag{8}$$

Expression (8) takes into account the fact that the FT firm is well aware that it precommits to its high-quality output z before the non-FT firms become active. This is the reason why both X and

Y depend on z.[22] Given that each FT producer is relatively small, we will ignore the integer constraint in the remainder of the paper. However, it takes at least one FT producer to establish a vertically integrated FT firm so we do require that $z \geq 1$.

The FT firm will maximise its surplus (8), correctly anticipating the non-FT firms' output levels. The marginal surplus is given by

$$\frac{dS}{dz} = v^* - \frac{z}{1-\delta}\left(\frac{1+n(1-\gamma^2)}{n+1} + \frac{z-1}{z^3}\frac{\lambda^2}{\mu(1-\delta)}\right). \tag{9}$$

Lemma 1. *$S(z)$ is a strictly concave function.*

Proof. See Appendix SA.2. □

The first-order condition $dS/dz = 0$ gives the behaviour of the FT firm only if this firm is viable. Lemma 2 shows that at least one FT producer who is better off compared to producing for the spot market is required to establish an FT firm.

Lemma 2. *A fair trade firm will not be established if $v^*(1) < 0$.*

Proof. According to (9), $dS/dz < v^*$, and if $v^*(1) < 0$ surplus will be negative for all $z > 1$. □

From Lemma 2, we may derive conditions under which an FT firm will (not) be established:

Corollary 1. *A fair trade firm will not be established if trade costs are too high and/or the "warm glow" effect is too small.*

Proof. This follows from Eq. (8) for $S(1) < 0$. With non-FT firms serving the high-quality market, as assumed here, $S(1) < 0$ for output

[22]Our assumption of linear demand has the advantage of leading to clean results. If demand were non-linear, the existence of the FT firm would also have a direct impact on the low-quality market: an increase in z could make x_i^{**} decrease if the direct effect is stronger than the reduced cannibalisation effect. In this case, the FT firm would also be able to take away market shares from the low-quality market, and vice versa if the direct effect is weaker than the reduced cannibalisation effect. Thus, linear demand allows us to focus on the high-quality market as the relevant target market for FT products.

levels according to (6) warrants

$$\frac{\alpha - 1}{n+1} + \frac{nc}{n+1} - \theta - \frac{t}{n+1} + \frac{\lambda^2}{\mu(1-\delta)} < 0.$$

We may already conclude from Corollary 1 that some combination of economic integration and the "warm glow" effect is an essential prerequisite for the existence of an FT firm. Of course, even with $\delta = 0$ we can still sustain an FT firm, but this requires a sufficiently low t. In the remainder of the paper, we will assume that parameters are such that the FT firm will be viable.[23] □

Finally, let us briefly discuss how non-FT firm competition affects the behaviour of the FT firm. If $n = 1$, it does not matter whether the FT firm's rival sets prices or quantities because it maximises its profit over the FT firm's residual demand. For a very large n, *i.e.*, $n \to \infty$, the price in the high-quality (low-quality) market will be equal to $c(0)$.[24] The "warm glow" effect will continue to allow the FT firm to earn a premium above c. It will crucially depend on the FT firm's costs, and hence on the severity of the moral hazard problem, how large the FT firm will be. In general, the response of the FT firm to an increase in the number of non-FT firms depends on its initial size.

Lemma 3. *An increase in the number of non-FT firms, given rivalry in the high-quality market, makes the FT firm larger* (*smaller*) *if*

$$z^* > (<) \frac{\alpha - (c+t)}{2}$$

Proof. See Appendix SA.3. □

It is a well-known result that first movers increase output in response to an increase in the number of their followers if their cost

---

[23]We have assumed that the FT firm incurs only variable costs of operation, but one might also model the establishment of an integrated FT network as a fixed cost. Doing so will obviously lower the threshold level of trade costs above which and/or increase the threshold level of δ below which an FT firm cannot operate, but it would not obviously add anything further to the analysis of this paper.

[24]This result would also emerge from pure price competition between two or more oligopolists.

is comparably low. Consequently, low FT costs translate into a large FT firm size, and this is the reason why the FT firm grows further in size when it is already large. Note that the size requirements are quite demanding. For the case of rivalry in the high-quality market, $(\alpha-(c+t))/2$ coincides with the monopoly output in the high-quality market, both ignoring cannibalisation effects. This does not conflict with Assumption 1.

4. Integration, substitutability and fair trade

In this section, we consider first how changes in parameter values will affect the fair trade equilibrium and, second, whether a small increase in the volume of FT can be welfare improving.

4.1. *Comparative statics*

We are in particular interested in how economic integration, measured by a decline in trade cost t, will affect the fair trade equilibrium. Our next result extends Corollary 1.

Proposition 1. *A decrease in trade cost increases the number of FT producers.*

Proof. See Appendix SA.4. □

Proposition 1 shows that the FT firm becomes larger with integration. While this result supports our finding that integration is crucial for the establishment of an FT firm, we would also like to enquire how the market share of an FT firm changes with integration. Proposition 2 demonstrates that the absolute increase in size with integration does not necessarily imply an increase in relative size.

Proposition 2. *A decrease in trade costs increases the market share of non-FT firms and decreases the market share of the FT firm if the moral hazard problem implies substantially increasing marginal costs of the FT firm.*

Proof. The size of dz^*/dt can be determined by using the implicit function theorem and (A.6) and (A.8) in Appendices SA.2 and SA.4. The change in the number of FT producers is equal to

$$\frac{dz^*}{dt} = -\frac{(1-\delta)\mu z^{*3}}{2(1-\delta)\mu z^{*3} + \lambda^2(n+1)} = -\frac{1}{2 + \frac{\lambda^2(n+1)}{(1-\delta)\mu z^{*3}}},$$

and the change in non-FT production in the high-quality market can be derived as

$$\frac{dy_i^{**}}{dt} = \frac{\partial y_i^{**}}{\partial t} + \frac{\partial y_i^{**}}{\partial z}\frac{dz^*}{dt} = -\frac{1}{(n+1)}\left(\frac{1}{1+\gamma} + \frac{dz^*}{dt}\right).$$

Hence,

$$\frac{dY}{dt} = -\frac{n}{(n+1)}\left(\frac{1}{1+\gamma} + \frac{dz^*}{dt}\right) > \frac{dz^*}{dt}$$

if

$$\frac{\lambda^2}{\mu z^{*3}} - (1-\delta)\left(\left(\frac{n}{n+1}\right)^2 + \gamma(n+1)^2\right) > 0. \tag{10}$$

□

There are two conflicting effects at work here. As the first mover, the FT firm potentially has an advantage in responding to a decrease in t. On the other hand, its moral hazard problem means that it faces an upward-sloping marginal cost curve in contrast to its rivals' constant marginal costs. If an FT firm suffers seriously from the moral hazard problem, an expansion of FT producers necessarily implies that the marginal cost of production goes up, whereas non-FT firms continue to produce with the same marginal cost. In this case, the FT firm is still in a first-mover position, as it contracts with growers before any transaction takes place on the spot market, but this strategic advantage is more than eaten up by increasing marginal costs. Note that this will not drive the FT firm out of the market, but integration will benefit non-FT firms overproportionally and the FT firm underproportionally. As the second term in (10) is large in absolute terms if n is large, a lower market share of the FT firm is likely if the non-FT market is very competitive. In this case, a reduction in t will boost non-FT firms' output. In any case, all firms, including the FT firm, will produce more, which will result in a rise in non-FT firms' profits and the FT firm's surplus (distributed back to producers).

It is unlikely that it is integration alone which has contributed to the establishment of FT firms in recent years and the boom in the "boutique" coffee market. So we also consider (i) the impact of a perceived lessening of the degree of substitutability, by consumers, between the two qualities of good being produced and (ii) the impact of a higher appreciation of the high-quality product. Starting with a decrease in substitution as perceived by consumers, we conduct comparative statics on γ. We find, perhaps surprisingly, that the substitutability parameter γ does not appear in the FT firm's first-order condition (see (A.5) in Appendix SA.2). Hence, any change in γ will not affect the optimal number of FT producers.

This result warrants an explanation. In our linear setting, the impact of the aggregate output of the rival non-FT firms due to a change in γ will just neutralise each other. In fact, define $\Omega \equiv n(\gamma X + Y)$, and we find that $d\Omega/d\gamma = n(X + \gamma dX/d\gamma + dY/d\gamma) = 0$ (see (A.9) in Appendix SA.5). Thus, any change in market shares is driven by changes in output levels of non-FT firms.[25] Proposition 3 shows that the effect depends on the relative market potential of the high-quality market, defined as

$$\frac{\alpha - c - t}{A - t}.$$

Proposition 3. *An increase in* γ

1. *will not change the number of FT producers,*
2. *will decrease (increase) the non-FT firms' output in the low- (high-)quality market if*

$$\frac{\alpha - c - t}{A - t} < \frac{1 - \gamma^2}{2\gamma},$$

[25]With non-linear demand, results would change as the FT firm would also gain (or lose) market share from (or to) the low-quality market directly. With linear demand, the relevant target market for the FT firm is the high-quality market; see also footnote 22.

3. *will increase the non-FT firms' output in both markets if*

$$\frac{\alpha - c - t}{A - t} \in \left[\frac{1-\gamma^2}{2\gamma}, \frac{1+\gamma^2}{2\gamma}\right],$$

4. *will increase (decrease) the non-FT firms' output in the low- (high-) quality market if*

$$\frac{\alpha - c - t}{A - t} > \frac{1+\gamma^2}{2\gamma},$$

Proof. See Appendix SA.5. □

Proposition 3 demonstrates that a decrease in substitutability has a non-monotonic impact on market shares. If the relative potential of the high-quality market is large, a decrease in γ will make the non-FT firms' output in the high-quality market larger. Because the number of fair trade producers stays constant, the market share of the FT firm will decline and the market share of non-FT firms will rise. On the other hand, if the relative market potential of the high-quality market is small, y_i^{**} will decline, so that the FT firm's market share will rise and the non-FT firms' market share will decline. Hence, we may expect a decline in the FT firm's market share if the relative potential of the high-quality market is large or has become larger over time, when these two commodities have become less substitutable at the same time. One might consider this to be an accurate description of the coffee market over the last two decades: consumers see high- and low-quality coffees as much less perfect substitutes than they once did (before the rise of boutique coffees) and the high-quality segment has experienced significant growth in size. Remarkably, Proposition 3 does not depend on the number of non-FT firms; hence, the changes in market shares do not qualitatively depend on the degree of competition.

We now turn to a change in quality differentiation and consider how an increase in α — that is, an increase in the high-quality reserve price — affects equilibrium outputs.[26] This is different

[26]Note that we do not need to assume that $\alpha > A$ although this would be consistent with our notion of high- versus low-quality markets. However, all our results hold also for $\alpha < A$.

from the effect of integration, which makes both markets more attractive.

Proposition 4. *An increase in α increases the number of FT producers and decreases non-FT firms' output in the low-quality market. With the non-FT firms active in the high-quality market,*

1. *their individual output increases with α in this market and*
2. *their individual output increases more than the FT firm's output if $\gamma \geq \sqrt{n/(n+2)}$ or if $\gamma < \sqrt{n/(n+2)}$ and the FT output is sufficiently small.*

Proof. See Appendix SA.6. □

Hence, a higher appreciation of the high-quality good will increase outputs in this market and reduce outputs in the other market. As for the change in market shares, the market share of the FT firm shrinks and that of non-FT firms increases if γ is sufficiently small or the FT firm is sufficiently small. In the first case, both commodities are strong substitutes, and a non-FT firm will be able to decrease output in the low-quality market so as to increase output in the high-quality market substantially. In the second case, a small size of the FT firm indicates a severe moral hazard problem, which will be exacerbated by the output increase, which thus has to be underproportional. However, an increase in the FT market share is possible if the FT firm is large and γ is low. If the FT firm is not too small, and if competition among non-FT firms is fierce such that $\sqrt{n/(n+2)}$ is close to one, the FT firm's market share will increase. Furthermore, Proposition 4 depends crucially on the assumption of a single FT firm, as we demonstrate in Appendix SA.9 that an increase in the number of FT firms may decrease high-quality non-FT firms' output (see eq. (A.16) in Appendix SA.9). However, the existence of more than one FT firm leaves all other results, including the other ones in Proposition 4, qualitatively unchanged.

Next, we consider the effects of changes in consumers' willingness to pay a premium for FT products: a warmer glow. Not surprisingly, this will lead to an expansion of the FT firm and the number of FT producers and a decline in the operations of the non-FT firms.

Proposition 5. *An increase in δ*

1. *will increase the number of FT producers and*
2. *will decrease the non-FT firms' output in the high-quality market.*

Proof. See Appendix SA.7.[27] □

In sum, while the number of FT producers in our model will rise with a fall in trade costs, overall FT market share may still fall (due to the moral hazard problem.) Similarly, an increased perception by consumers of differentiation between the different qualities of product can also decrease the FT market share (although it has no effect on the number of FT producers) and an overall increase in demand for the high-quality product can also reduce FT market share.

4.2. *Fair trade and welfare*

Finally, given that integration increases FT production and enhances consumers' "warm glow", we consider whether a small increase in FT at the margin — perhaps through a quota on non-FT trade or a small subsidy to FT production — could raise world welfare.[28] This analysis draws upon trade policy papers, which determine under which conditions imports of a foreign firm should be supported (or discouraged).[29] The increase in consumer surplus must be balanced against the decline in aggregate profits, and the outcome is unclear in general. Without any "warm glow" effect, the effect of an increase in z is similar because an FT firm gives all net revenues back to growers.[30] Let us label the incentive or disincentive to

---

[27]Proposition 5 also offers some guidance regarding what happens if the FT firm can only pass on a part of the operating profits to growers, perhaps because FT wholesaling and retailing is less efficient and eats up part of the profit. In this case, it can be shown that if the share of operating profits passed on to growers declines, the FT firm will reduce the number of growers at the same time, and non-FT output will increase in the high-quality market.

[28]We do not model the dynamic consequences of FT firms, particularly the danger of encouraging growers to overly postpone exit from a declining industry. Accordingly, our welfare analysis, while looking at global welfare, is static in nature only.

[29]For an overview, see Feenstra (2004), Chapter 7.

[30]A further complication of our model is that the FT firm is a first mover and an increase in z affects both markets.

increase z marginally without any "warm glow" effect the *marginal import effect.* We would now like to explore how this incentive is changed when fair trade is considered, and thus we call any further effect a *marginal "warm glow" effect.*

We do this exercise by considering a marginal expansion of FT production above the laissez-faire number of FT growers chosen by the FT firm. Hence, the marginal FT surplus will be equal to zero and any marginal change will have only second-order effects on the FT firm's surplus. Using (4), we may write the maximised profits of a non-FT firm as $\Pi_i^{**} = x_i^2 + y_i^2 + 2\gamma x_i y_i$ and, since x_i does not change with z, the change in profit is equal to

$$\frac{d\Pi_i^{**}}{dz} = (2y_i + 2\gamma x_i)\frac{dy_i}{dz} = -\frac{2(y_i + \gamma x_i)}{n+1} < 0, \quad \frac{d\Pi_i^{**}}{dz}$$
$$= -\frac{2(Y + \gamma X)}{n+1} < 0,$$

where Π^{**} denotes the aggregate profits on the industry level. As expected, aggregate profits will decrease with FT production (*i.e.*, $dz > 0$).

As for consumer surplus, Andreoni (2006) suggests cogently that, while "warm glow" effects clearly need to be considered in analysing the incentives facing and behaviour of agents in these sorts of markets, they should, for a number of reasons, be ignored in welfare analysis. The debate on this question is by no means settled and we consider both positions here. If the "warm glow" effect *is* considered then it simply washes out of consumer surplus: any "warm glow" utility that accrues to consumers is exactly offset by the higher prices they pay to farmers. To see this, note from (5) that $r = q + \delta w$ so that $CS \equiv U - pX - qY - rz - Q$ becomes, from (1),

$$CS \equiv AX + \alpha(Y + z) - \frac{1}{2}(X^2 + 2\gamma X(Y + z) + (Y + z)^2) - pX - q(Y + z). \tag{11}$$

On the other hand, if the alternative position is adopted and the "warm glow" benefit is ignored in welfare calculations, then it only enters into consumer surplus *negatively*: the higher payments to farmers are a financial loss to consumers. Where the "warm glow" *is* considered in welfare, we have

$$\frac{dCS}{dz} = \frac{\partial CS}{\partial z} + \frac{\partial CS}{\partial X}\frac{dX}{dz} + \frac{\partial CS}{\partial Y}\frac{dY}{dz} = -X\frac{dp}{dz} - (Y+z)\frac{dq}{dz}$$

$$- \left(X\frac{dp}{dY} + (Y+z)\frac{dq}{dY}\right)\frac{dY}{dz} = (\gamma X + (Y+z))\left(1 + \frac{dY}{dz}\right)$$

where the second and third equalities follow from (2) and the fact that X does not respond to changes in z when non-FT firms operate in the high-quality sector (see (6)). But $Y = ny$ so, from (6) again, we have $dY/dz = -n/(n+1)$. In the case where we ignore any welfare gains to consumers from the "warm glow", the change in CS is the same as that just expressed less a term representing any change in wage payments to farmers. Consequently,

$$\frac{dCS}{dz} = \underbrace{\frac{1}{n+1}(\gamma X + (Y+z))}_{\text{(a)}} - \underbrace{\delta\left(w^* + z\frac{dw^*}{dz}\right)}_{\text{(b)}}. \tag{12}$$

In this expression, the second term applies only if we ignore the welfare gain of the "warm glow" and dw^*/dz gives the marginal change of the equilibrium FT wage with FT output. Defining world welfare as $W \equiv \Pi^{**} + CS + S(z)$, and since $dS(z = z^*)/dz = 0$, we arrive at

$$\frac{dW}{dz} = \underbrace{\frac{z - (Y + \gamma X)}{n+1}}_{\text{(I)}} \underbrace{-\delta\left(w^* + z\frac{dw^*}{dz}\right)}_{\text{(II)}}. \tag{13}$$

Term (I) is the marginal import effect, the sign of which is ambiguous without further assumptions, and term (II) is the marginal "warm glow" effect, which we are able to sign to prove Proposition 6.

Proposition 6. *The marginal "warm glow" effect is positive.*

Proof. Appendix SA.8 shows that

$$w^* + z\frac{dw^*}{dz} = -\frac{\lambda^2}{2\mu z^2(1-\delta)^2} < 0. \tag{14}$$

□

Proposition 6 demonstrates that *ceteris paribus* the "warm glow" effect might warrant a marginal increase in FT production in our second specification of welfare only, subject to concerns about the size of the marginal import effect. Hence, if the marginal import effect is positive, the overall effect is positive irrespective of the size of γ. Furthermore, a negative but moderate marginal import effect may be overcompensated by the positive "warm glow" effect.

Why does the "warm glow" effect make promotion of FT products more attractive in our second case when the welfare benefits of the "warm glow" to consumers are ignored? The reason is the increasing marginal cost which the FT firm faces due to the moral hazard problem. We may rewrite the marginal "warm glow" effect in terms of the elasticity of wages w.r.t. FT production:

$$\delta\left(w^* + z\frac{dw^*}{dz}\right) = \delta w^*\left(1 + \frac{dw^*/w^*}{dz/z}\right).$$

Eq. (14) demonstrates that this elasticity is less than -1. Hence, a relative output increase implies an overproportionally large relative decrease in the wage rate. A marginal increase in FT output leads to less efforts by each FT grower and thus an increase in marginal cost.[31] In conclusion, if the moral hazard effect of FT production works for favourable treatment of FT products, it is solely because it reduces the total payments made to FT farmers.

Finally, we can see that a small increase in FT will necessarily be welfare-improving if the FT sector is relatively large (which, in turn, follows from a small moral hazard cost i.e. large λ and/or low μ).

5. Concluding remarks

This chapter has developed a model of the behaviour of fair trade organisations, taking into account the apparent fact[32] that consumers

[31]In fact, the marginal "warm glow" effect would disappear if the marginal cost of FT production were constant, contrary to our assumptions. In this case, $\lambda = 0$ and $(dw^*/w^*)/(dz/z) = -1$ according to eq. (14).

[32]See Hiscox and Smyth (2005) for semi-experimental evidence on this. We are grateful to Steve Matusz for this reference.

are willing to pay more for a fair-trade product, because consumption of fair-trade products gives rise to a "warm glow" effect. However, fair-trade production comes with an additional cost, as any fair-trade organisation must be effectively vertically integrated. This limits the size of the fair-trade organisation compared with its rivals in international markets. In particular, while economic integration will make the fair-trade organisation absolutely larger in size, its size shrinks relative to that of its rivals if the moral hazard problem is sufficiently substantial.

Hence, while we conclude that economic integration will support the establishment and the increase in size of fair-trade organisations, our analysis suggests that there is a limit to the size that a fair-trade firm can attain — at least, under the ownership structures that current fair-trade firms impose — which constrains its ability to expand in competition with non-vertically integrated rivals.

Furthermore, our analysis lends support, albeit only partial, to the contention that "[t]he ethical consumer and the fair trade premium are not the core of fair trade" (Hayes, 2006, p. 466). It is true that one of fair trade's central impacts is on the input market. However, a sufficiently large "warm glow" effect is necessary for the establishment of the fair-trade firm if trade costs are insufficiently low (particularly if the fair-trade firm also has to carry some fixed start-up costs). Hence, either economic integration and/or the "warm glow" effect must be sufficiently strong to make fair-trade production worthwhile. However, where the "warm glow" effect is present, it does not necessarily imply that fair-trade production warrants any favourable treatment by the importing country. If fair-trade production were supported, the wage paid to fair-trade growers would decrease overproportionally because each fair-trade grower will reduce its efforts and marginal costs will increase.

In terms of future work, fair-trade production has become more and more visible and deserves further academic attention. In particular, we did not take into account the fact that fair-trade production may make fair-trade growers less sensitive to market signals. We have also assumed that fair-trade growers have identical abilities. If they differ in terms of productivity, should the fair-trade firm sign contracts with the most efficient growers, so as to maximise the aggregate surplus, or does that contravene the spirit of the fair-trade movement?

Furthermore, we have assumed only one fair-trade firm and a single collective operated by that firm, although our results remain by and large unchanged if more than one fair-trade firm is in the market so long as the "warm glow" effect is not jeopardised by competition in the fair-trade business. But if fair-trade production continues to boom, will more fair-trade firms be established and will competition undermine the "warm glow" effect? Indeed, Nicholls and Opal (2004, p. 246 ff.) note that the fair-trade "movement" already faces threats both from within (competing fair trade certification bodies) and without (from self-certification by farmers or low-cost independent certification). The long-run entry dynamics of this sort of market are an important and promising area for future research.

Finally, we have not looked explicitly at the use of trade policy by an importing country both to affect the price set by non-FT firms and to affect "warm glow" gains to consumers from FT consumption. A tariff that discriminates according to the nature of the production process might be an interesting topic in the context of discussions about the use of trade policy to promote environmental and labour standards in exporting countries.[33]

Supporting Information

Additional Supporting Information may be found in the online version of this article:

Appendix S1: Background and Proofs.

References

Andreoni, J. (1990). Impure altruism and donations to public goods: A theory of warm-glow giving. *Economic Journal*, 100, 464–77.

[33]We are grateful to a referee for raising this point.

Andreoni, J. (2006). Philanthropy, Chapter 18. In S.-C. Kolm and J.M. Ythier (eds.), *Handbook of the Economics of Giving, Altruism and Reciprocity*, Vol. 2, pp. 1201–69. Amsterdam: Elsevier.

Becchetti, L. and F. Adriani (2002). Fair trade: A "Third Generation Welfare" mechanism to make globalisation sustainable. Working Paper, University of Rome Tor Vergata, Department of Economics. Available from: http://www.art.torvergata.it/bitstream/2108/274/1/170.pdf.

Besley, T. and M. Ghatak (2007). Retailing public goods: The economics of corporate social responsibility. *Journal of Public Economics*, 91, 1645–63.

Chau, N.H., H. Goto and R. Kanbur (2009). Middlemen, non-profits, and poverty. Working Paper 55931, Cornell University, Department of Applied Economics and Management.

Conrad, K. (2005). Price competition and product differentiation when consumers care for the environment. *Environmental and Resource Economics*, 31, 1–19.

Eriksson, C. (2004). Can green consumerism replace environmental regulation? A differentiated-products example. *Resource and Energy Economics*, 26, 281–193.

Feenstra, R. (2004). *Advanced International Trade.* Princeton, NJ: Princeton University Press.

Graeker, M. (2006). Eco-labels, trade and protectionism. *Environmental and Resource Economics*, 33, 1–37.

Hayes, M. (2006). On the efficiency of fair trade. *Review of Social Economy*, 64, 447–468.

Hiscox, M.J. and N.F.B. Smyth (2005). *Is There Consumer Demand for Improved Labor Standards? Evidence from Field Experiments in Social Labeling.* Department of Government, mimeo: Harvard University.

Howley, K. (2006). Absolution in Your Cup: The Real Meaning of Fair Trade Coffee. Reason March 2006. Available from: http://www.reason.com/archives/2006/03/01/absolution-in-your-cup.

Imhof, S. and A. Lee (2007). Assessing the Potential of Fair Trade for Poverty Reduction and Conflict Prevention: A Case Study of Bolivian Coffee Producers. Swiss Peace Foundation. Available from: http://www.swisspeace.ch/fileadmin/user_upload/Media/Topics/Further_Topics/Business_and_Peace/Imhof_Sandra_Assessing_the_Potential_of_Fair_Trade_for_Poverty_Reduction_and_Conflict_Prevention.pdf.

Kotchen, M.T. (2006). Green markets and private provision of public goods. *Journal of Political Economy*, 114, 816–34.

Kreps, D. and J. Scheinkman (1983). Quantity pre-commitment and bertrand competition yield Cournot outcomes. *Bell Journal of Economics*, 14, 326–337.

Krier, J.-M. (2008). Fair Trade 2007. Dutch Association of Worldshops: Culemborg: 2008. Available from: http://www.european-fair-trade-association.org/efta/Doc/FT-E-2007.pdf.

Leclair, M. (2002). Fighting the tide: Alternative trade organizations in the era of global free trade. *World Development*, 30, 949–958.

Mälkönen, V. (2005). Harmonization versus mutual recognition of national eco-labels. Helsinki Center of Economic Research Discussion Paper No. 45.

Maseland, R. and A. de Vaal (2002). How fair is fair trade? *De Economist*, 150, 251–272.

Milford, A. (2004). Coffee, Co-Operatives and Competition: The Impact of Fair Trade. CMI Report R 2004: 6. Chr. Michelson Institute, Bergen, Norway. Available from: http://www.cmi.no/publications/ publication/?1802=coffee-co-operatives-and-competition.

Mohan, S. (2010). *Fair Trade without the Froth*. London: Institute of Economic Affairs.

Nicholls, A. and C. Opal (2004). *Fair Trade: Market-Driven Ethical Consumption*. London: SAGE Publications Ltd.

Ponte, S. (2002). The 'Latte Revolution'? Regulation, markets and consumption in the global coffee chain. *World Development*, 30, 1099–1122.

Piyapromdee, S., R. Hillberry and D. MacLaren (2008). 'Fair trade' coffee and the mitigation of local oligopsony power. Working Paper 1057, Department of Economics, University of Melbourne.

Rice, R. (2001). Noble goals and challenging terrain: Organic and fair trade coffee movements in the global marketplace. *Journal of Agricultural and Environmental Ethics*, 14, 39–66.

Richardson, M. and F. Stähler (2007). 'Fair Trade'. Working Papers in Economics and Econometrics 481, School of Economics, CBE, Australian National University.

Sutton, J. (1991). *Sunk Costs and Market Structure*. Cambridge, MA: MIT Press.

Wilkinson, J. (2006). Fair trade moves central stage. Working Paper No. 3. The Edelstein Center for Social Research. Rio de Janeiro, Brazil. Available from: http://www.centroedelstein.org.br/PDF/Working Papers/WP_3_English.pdf.

Chapter 18

Buy Local? Governmental Incentives to "Inform" Consumers

Martin Richardson and Frank Stähler

1. Introduction

CAMPAIGNS to promote the purchase of domestic goods are fairly common — the Australian government, for example, created a certification trade mark in 1986 to promote Australian made products[1] — and are frequently driven by concerns for domestic employment. These sorts of campaigns have the intention of shifting out the demand for domestic products relative to that for imports. But information campaigns can have other consequences for demand; in particular, if consumers learn more about some aspect of the domestic/import comparison, it can also affect the variance of willingness to pay across consumers.

Consider the so-called food miles and eco-labelling debates. The notion that "food miles" are an important indicator of the environmental cost or carbon footprint of consumer choices is one that has been debated and promoted fairly widely, including in the US: see http://at-tra.ncat.org/farm_energy/food_miles.html. Whilst one can

Originally published in *The World Economy* (2016).

[1]It was assigned to Australian Made Campaign Ltd in July 2002, a not-for-profit company that now funds its campaigns through levies on those authorised to use the logo.

understand why domestic firms might be keen to publicise information that appears to work in their favour, Saunders and Hayes (2007) note, "[t]he food miles debate, initially started by NGOs with environmental concerns has gradually involved a range of government organisations. In the United Kingdom, the Department for Environment, Food and Rural Affairs has a dedicated team undertaking food miles related research and policy development. In Germany, the Federal Ministry for Consumer Protection, Food and Agriculture has sought EU legislation requiring food labelling indicating the product's origin. At a recent meeting of the EU Agriculture and Fisheries Council in Brussels there was support from a number of EU member states for Germany's call for more comprehensive labelling of food product origin information". But the idea that food miles are a useful indicator of environmental worthiness is one that has apparently been debunked (see Desrochers and Shimuzu, 2008; Wilson, 2007; Saunders and Hayes, 2007). Consequently, some consumers initially willing to pay a high premium for local goods might, on being informed more accurately, value such goods somewhat less. This paper focuses on the incentives domestic governments have to provide information to consumers about the relative merits of local versus foreign goods and considers both shifts and rotations of demand curves.

The existing literature on the economics of eco-labelling typically supposes that there are two methods of production available to producers, one of which is more costly but is also "greener" than the other (see Robertson, 2007; Podhorsky, 2008 for exemplars, where the former is a deliberately minimalist model). Consumers have a preference for green production over the relatively less environmentally friendly "brown" production, captured in an increased willingness to pay for goods that are certified as green, and the introduction of eco-labelling can induce firms to undertake the more costly green production method where they otherwise would not. This may be beneficial to consumers, both because they care about the way in which a good is produced and because of its environmental consequences. In most models, however, each firm can choose between the green and brown technologies and the general application of these analyses is to issues like dolphin-safe tuna fishing, turtle-safe shrimping, organic versus non-organic farming and so on. For the case of food miles, however, as well as many other dimensions of a production process carbon footprint,[2] the production technology is essentially exogenous to the firm.[3]

In this paper, we suppose that, all other things being equal, consumers are willing to pay some premium for the local product that is due, for instance, to the perceived environmental aspect of production. This premium is distributed across consumers on some support and we assume that the domestic government can, for example through an information campaign, affect both the mean and the distribution of that support. This is our proxy for a government's commitment to promoting and publicising the idea of food miles, for example, but it can equally capture the promotion of other features of the good that can be used to advantage the domestic firm in a "buy local" campaign. An important feature of our analysis, however, is that a consumer's actual valuation of the good in question depends on features of the good that are not evident from the act of consumption alone. Examples of such features might be whether the good's production jeopardises turtles or dolphins, involves child labour, pays a farmer too low a wage, overexploits a natural resource and so on. (Indeed, it might also be the case that the consumer cannot identify a relevant feature during the good's use such as the energy efficiency of a refrigerator.) If this were not the case, then a consumer would discover their "true", possibly idiosyncratic, valuation immediately on consumption and there is no obvious rationale for a government to intervene prior to purchase. Also, in contrast to the eco-labelling literature in which firms simply inform

[2]For example, British apples sold in Britain out of the growing season (when they compete with Southern hemisphere apples produced and shipped immediately) must be kept in energy-intensive coolstores from their time of harvest until the point of sale. British producers selling at that time have effectively no alternative means for doing so.

[3]There is a branch of the eco-labelling literature that considers the exogenous technology case — see Mason (2006) — but does not consider the resource-allocation decision involved in promoting helpful labelling.

consumers of a product feature over which the latter already have preferences, a "buy local" campaign is modelled here as both informing consumers of a product feature and educating them about the desirability (or otherwise) of that feature.[4]

Our analysis can also be seen as contributing to the literature on the "re-creation" of border barriers to trade through domestic policy. As trade costs have fallen globally in recent decades, both through technological change and regulatory changes (such as harmonisation that reduces the resource costs of trading internationally and through negotiated reductions in tariffs), governments have found alternative means to protect domestic firms, such as internal domestic taxes and subsidies, and SPS and other "green" restrictions. A question of some interest here, then, is what happens to any incentive a government has to provide an information campaign of the sort we analyse when trade costs fall. Does trade reform increase a government's incentive to intervene in this fashion on behalf of domestic firms?

An early contribution to this literature in Chiou *et al.* (2003) looks at the reverse causality, arguing that an upward shift in the distribution of a consumer preference for local goods will reduce the optimal tariff such a country would levy for profit-shifting reasons in a Bertrand duopoly. In contrast to that paper, we consider the effects of trade liberalisation on the incentives for such a campaign, and we consider both shifts and rotations of demand curves, as well as attempting some welfare analysis. There is also a small literature on country-of-origin labelling (COOL), see Dinopoulos *et al.* (2010).

There is an extensive literature on the private provision of information by firms to consumers about the latter's valuations of a good — see McCracken (2012) for a recent review. In most of that work, the supposition is that consumers genuinely have different specific and particular valuations of a good but can only know their true

[4]However, as we demonstrate in Section 2, our model is strategically equivalent to a model in which a private and a public good are consumed jointly, and in which consumer preferences with respect to the public good provision are heterogeneous.

willingness to pay once the good has been purchased. Producers know the distribution of these valuations across the consumer population and can provide information to those consumers, in some fashion, that better enables the consumer to know *ex ante* their true valuation. The general thrust of the literature is to ask whether or not firms wish to provide such information. Our approach is quite different, in that we are not considering experience goods. We suppose not that a consumer has a given valuation that will be uncovered when the good is consumed but that each consumer's valuation depends on what they know about aspects of the good's production process and that this is affected *ex ante* by the government's information campaign.[5] So consumers can learn something new about the products they are buying in our model, independent of the act of consumption. In Johnson and Myatt's (2006 — JM henceforth) terminology, we consider a government to be providing both real information as well as hype: it can rotate consumer demand curves as well as shift them out.

Our approach is related to the more general analysis in JM of shifts and rotations of a demand curve, but is placed in an international context. Furthermore, when we look at demand curve rotations, we consider only mean-preserving spreads with a uniform distribution of tastes and we explicitly model changes in the support of the distribution, a feature that is captured in JM's general structure, but is not necessary there (see their footnote 8). Our analysis focuses on governmental incentives to provide information, as opposed to the JM analysis in which it is firms themselves who undertake information campaigns (or not). The implicit assumption in our analysis is that domestic firms suffer from insurmountable credibility problems in providing information that is clearly self-serving. It is nevertheless the case that, even in the context of the non-experience goods that we consider, there may be other ways in which utility-relevant information can be brought to the attention of consumers.

[5]An alternative perspective on this can be taken that preserves the more traditional view: see footnote 11.

There are a number of so-called fair trade certifying agencies (such as the FLO) and there are similar non-governmental organisations for certifying child-labour-free products (e.g. GoodWeave) and goods produced in various environmental ways (such as the Forest Stewardship Council.) Furthermore, there are also industry-level certification authorities (such as The National Association for Sustainable Agriculture, Australia (NASAA).) The question still arises as to how these agencies gain credibility in the eyes of consumers and, in some cases at least, the answer might lie in the non-market origins of the agency: if its objective is charitable, for example, then its incentive to misinform consumers might be considered negligible. For others, though, the credibility problem is significant and there is likely to still be a role for governmental provision of relevant information.[6]

JM show that, in many cases, a firm's profits will be U-shaped (more accurately, that they will be quasi-convex) in the dispersion of demand and suggest the following interpretation: at low dispersion, where consumers have similar valuations, the firm has a limited ability to vary its price but can sell to a large number of consumers (a mass market strategy), whereas when dispersion is high, it can sell to fewer consumers but charge a higher price (a niche marketing strategy). These results generally carry over to our context. Finally, JM restrict their analysis to unit demands; we do not. Hence, in our analysis, all consumers will respond to price changes, and not just those switching from one supplier to the other. This is an important point of distinction.

In this setting, we initially consider the autarky solution, to generate some understanding of the intuition of the model. For expositional clarity, we present our analysis in terms of shifts in the distribution, turning to demand rotations in Section 5 of the paper. We then look at an equilibrium with trade in which both international and domestic products are sold and we consider

[6]We are grateful to an anonymous referee for comments stimulating this discussion.

a government's incentives to undertake an information campaign promoting the domestic good. We also consider the response of a foreign government through an (implicit) export or production tax/subsidy. We address a number of questions including the effects of a small decrease in trade costs facing foreign producers (be they through falling transport costs or tariffs) and we look at questions of welfare.

2. The model

Suppose we have a firm in a small, open economy producing a good for sale in the home country that, aside from certain features we discuss below, is considered by domestic consumers to be a perfect substitute for the imported good. The preferences of consumer i are given by $\ln(\beta_i \gamma_i)$ if she buys a quantity y_i from the domestic firm, and $\ln(x_i)$ if, instead, she buys the quantity x, from a foreign supplier. The parameter $\beta_i = \beta + \delta_i > 1$ is an individual taste parameter that measures the consumer's preference for the home good and we assume that δ_i is distributed uniformly on an interval $[-\varepsilon, +\varepsilon]$. The domestic firm chooses its price p, and we assume that the foreign price in this small, open economy is given by p^*: this may be affected by trade costs and foreign policy variables, as we discuss later; nevertheless, it is given to the consumer.

So the mass of consumers, normalised to unity, is distributed uniformly on an interval of length 2ε centred on some $\beta > 1 + \varepsilon$. We consider the impact of an information campaign by the domestic government to be captured by changes in either β or ε: a shift in the former is just a general shift in the demand for the home good, but we also allow that an informational campaign could be such that a more intensive campaign leads to a more compact support for δ (that is, finer information for consumers). This is a very simplified version of the more general analysis of information provided in JM, simplified in the interests of tractability so that we can determine explicit solutions for our variables of interest, but the general set-up (of information affecting the support of the distribution of preferences) is one we adopt by virtue of its intuitive appeal. Consider the case of "food miles", as discussed earlier. Absent an information campaign, we suppose that some consumers are aware of the issue — but might have an exaggerated sense of its environmental significance — whilst others are less aware. An informational campaign can better inform both types of consumers and thus lead to a homogenisation of the premium that all consumers place on the domestic good, *vis-a-vis* its foreign rival, accordingly.

As shown in the Appendix,[7] solving the consumer's maximisation problem yields a consumer indifferent between the domestic good and the import, denoted henceforth by $\tilde{\beta} = \frac{p}{p^*}$. All consumers with β_i greater than this will buy the domestic product and all others the import. Assuming interior solutions and that p^* is such that the market is covered, we can then derive the market share of the foreign good and the domestic product. The home firm faces a constant marginal cost of c and it sells $(1/p)$ units to each of its consumers. Consequently, it faces a downward-sloping demand curve that has the properties that, as in JM, it shifts out with increases in β and falls in p^* and rotates clockwise with increases in ε. The latter occurs because the highest-valuation consumers value the good even more highly when ε increases and the lowest-valuation consumers value it even less. This is all illustrated in Figure 1.

We can then solve for the domestic firm's optimal price[8] — which is, unsurprisingly, increasing in β, c, p^* and ε — and for the resulting equilibrium marginal consumer.

[7] All omitted calculations are provided in an online Appendix to this paper, available on request.

[8] For the market to be covered we require that every consumer would make non-negative surplus from the foreign good; this implies a restriction on p^*. Furthermore, in order to ensure an interior solution in which both domestic sales and imports are positive, we require that the marginal consumer lies strictly between $(\beta - \varepsilon)$ and $(\beta + \varepsilon)$ and it transpires that this follows from restricting the home firm's costs to a certain non-empty range. We maintain these restrictions throughout our analysis.

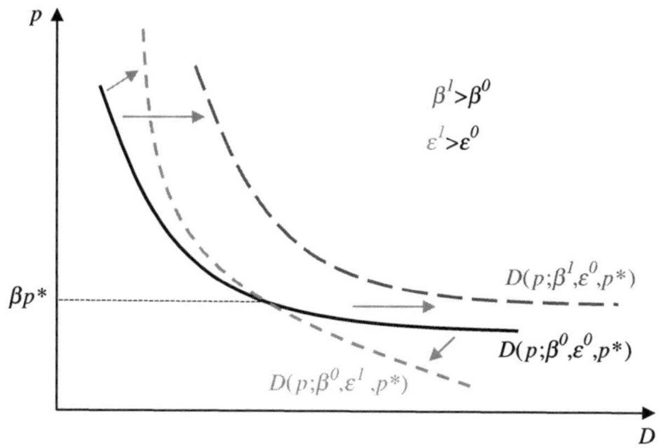

Fig. 1. Domestic demand.

a. *Welfare*

Assessing welfare in this model raises the issue that a change in β or ε might be thought of as representing a change in consumers' utility functions.[9] The question of how to assess a welfare change in this context has been discussed at some length in the advertising literature and there are essentially two major approaches (see Bagwell (2007) for a discussion). Consider some advertising that shifts out a demand curve. One approach, perhaps exposited most clearly in Dixit and Norman (1978), takes the view that advertising changes the welfare function and so welfare change is appropriately measured by looking at surplus changes measured either off the preshift or off the postshift demand curve, but not combining both.[10] The other approach, well articulated by Bagwell (2007), directly compares the preshift surplus, measured off the preshift demand curve, with the postshift surplus measured off the postshift curve.

[9]JM do not analyse the welfare effects of demand rotations, perhaps for this reason.

[10]The reasoning is analogous to the following: if the temperature rises from 0°C to 41°F, one could say that it has increased by 5°C, using the initial scale, or that it has increased by 9°F, using the subsequent metric, but not that it has increased by 41°, as the latter is a meaningless combination of the two alternative measures.

In this paper, we adopt the latter approach. Our modelling strategy is based on the notion that the β_i term in a consumer's utility function represents actual willingness to pay and that a change in β or ε effectively represents a change in the good itself. In our approach, if a consumer, at the initial level of β_i, values a particular carpet, say, at \$1,000 but, once they learn that it was produced with child labour (β_i falls), value it at only \$600, then they are \$400 "worse off" as a consequence of the information and, to the extent that we are attempting to measure subjective valuations when we consider consumers' surplus, this \$400 is appropriately included in welfare as a loss. In a Lancasterian view, the carpet features, as one of its characteristics, the consumer's perception of this aspect of its production and this is explicitly altered by changes in ε or β.[11]

While our analysis focuses on the role of information campaigns, note that our model can also be regarded as a contribution to the literature on the joint consumption of private and public goods. This literature has mainly dealt with the private provision of a public good, jointly consumed with a private good (for the seminal paper, see Kotchen, 2006). Our model is strategically equivalent to a set-up in which the government provides a public good that affects the utility of consuming the private good (if sourced locally) differently across consumers.[12] In this sense, the government's decision on public good provision is two-dimensional: it decides on the average utility contribution of the public good (by determining β), and it decides on the heterogeneity of its policy on consumers (by determining ε). From this view, our model set-up is more general than in

[11]One can also view this approach as capturing the following situation. Suppose there is a continuum of goods, indexed by γ, that could be produced and that differ in, for example, the environmental impact of their production. One of these is, in fact, produced by the domestic firm. A consumer has a stable and fixed set of preferences defined over γ. The distribution described by β and ε can then be thought of as a distribution of beliefs that consumers hold about which good is being produced, yielding different valuations. An information campaign then alters those beliefs and the consequent change in welfare corresponds exactly to the change in welfare associated with consuming not one good on the γ spectrum but another.

[12]We are grateful to a referee for this observation.

its application here and it could also be adapted to analyse policies beyond information campaigns.

3. Autarky

To provide a benchmark and some intuition for the working of this model, consider first the case of autarky in which there is only a domestic firm. If there is no foreign good — perhaps due to a prohibitive tariff — then the marginal consumer purchasing from the domestic firm is one who gets zero surplus. Now, if ε is sufficiently large that consumer tastes are very heterogeneous, then the firm may choose not to cover the market entirely, as to do so would require too low a price.

Graphically, we can represent the consumers' equilibrium as shown in Figure 2. This solution requires that demand be no greater than one, the mass of consumers. In particular, this solution only holds if the marginal consumer defined here strictly exceeds $\beta - \varepsilon$. If this condition does not hold, the firm could, if profitable, raise its price to ensure that the lowest-value consumer will get zero surplus.

So, in principle, we have two cases to consider here: an unconstrained choice of p in which the market is covered and all consumers get weakly positive surplus and an alternative in which the marginal

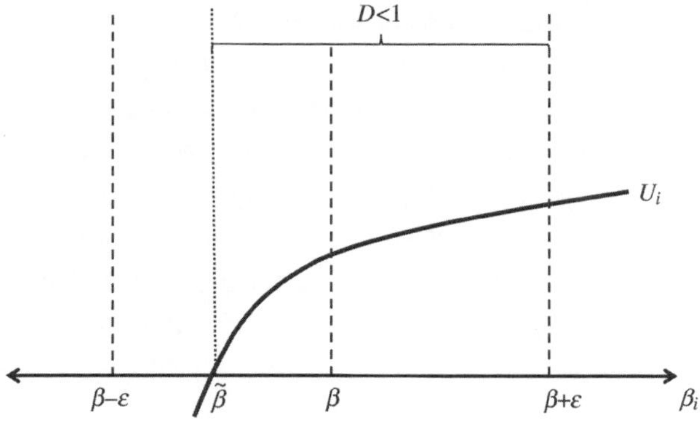

Fig. 2. Market size in autarky.

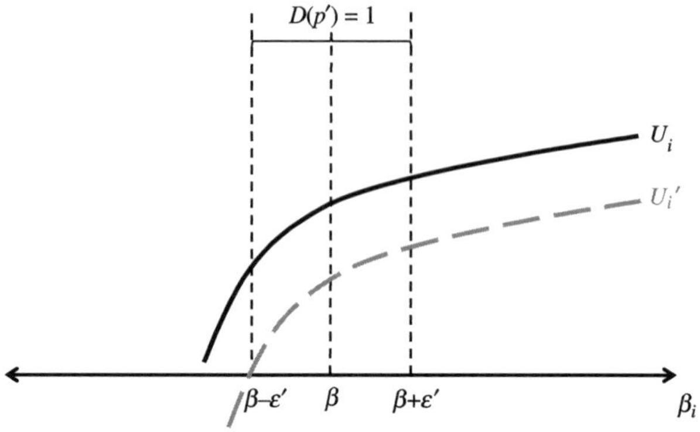

Fig. 3. Market coverage in autarky with low ε.

consumer strictly exceeds $\beta - \varepsilon$. Figure 3 illustrates two options in the first subcase: the firm does or does not extract all surplus from the lowest-value consumer.[13]

It is not immediately obvious in this model that a firm would wish to choose the latter strategy, because we do not assume unit demands; hence, such a price increase will lead to lower demand from infra-marginal consumers. However, each consumer's demand for the good is $1/p$ so, when all consumers buy the good, total demand is just $1/p$ and the firm's profits are this multiplied by their markup, $p - c$. So profits are still monotonically increasing in p and the firm will, indeed, optimally extract all surplus from the marginal consumer.

That consumer has a valuation of $\beta - \varepsilon$ and gets surplus of $\ln(\beta - \varepsilon) - \ln(p) - 1$ so setting this to zero solves for the optimal price and maximised profits, as functions of β and ε. Consequently, we can write welfare (the sum of domestic profits and consumer surplus) in terms of β and ε. Differentiating with respect to β yields an expression that is comprised of the overall negative effect of the induced price increase (which hurts consumers more than it benefits the firm) and the positive consequences for consumers of an increase in their valuations. Overall, the relative strengths of these effects

[13]Note, too, that $\mathrm{d}U_i/\mathrm{d}p = -1/p$ for all consumers i, so a price increase results in a parallel shift of the surplus function in the space of Figure 2.

cannot be determined, so the effect of an increase in β on welfare is indeterminate.

But if we turn to the case in which the solution to the firm's problem yields an outcome in which the market is not covered, we can show that an increase in β is unambiguously welfare-improving. This occurs despite the consequent price increase and is due to the fact that market coverage increases with the rise in β. As β rises, the firm will eventually choose to cover the entire market; further increases in β are then ambiguous in their effects on welfare as the price increase squeezes demand by each consumer. All in all, then, for changes in β, it is typically more attractive to serve the entire market only for higher β; profits are then monotonically increasing in β, but welfare is non-monotonic, due to the higher prices and this lower demand. Some numerical simulations illustrate these results. Figure 4 illustrates a typical case looking at changes in β.[14]

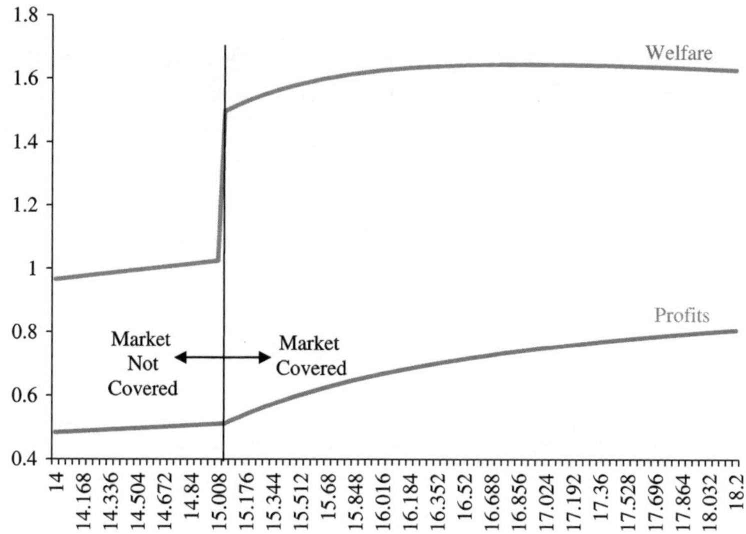

Fig. 4. Autarky changes in β.

[14]This example sets ε to 13 and c to 1 and plots profit and welfare over a range of β from 14 to around 18.

So what would be the choice of a government if it could control the distribution of consumer valuations in autarky? Ignoring, for the moment, the costs associated with any campaign to raise β, note that welfare is always maximised where the market is completely covered. Consequently, a welfare-maximising government would either raise β or leave it unchanged, depending on the laissez-faire β^0. This would also raise firm profits and so would also be undertaken by a government biased towards producer interests. The latter sort of government, however, would pursue a more extreme policy — a higher β — than a welfare-maximising government.

Once we consider the costs of such policies, however, we get a number of possibilities which we explore more fully in the case of trade. But note here that, if there are no fixed costs associated with these campaigns, there is still a general presumption that, in autarky, a government would wish to (weakly) increase β.

We summarise these findings for the autarky case in the following proposition:

Proposition 1. *In autarky, the domestic firm will always price such that the marginal consumer makes zero surplus and (i) if the market is covered, increases in β raise the firm's profits but have ambiguous consequences for welfare and (ii) if the market is not covered, increases in β raise profits, market coverage and welfare. Consequently, there is a presumption that, in autarky, a government would wish to (weakly) increase β.*

4. Trade

With this benchmark of autarky in mind, we now turn to the case where there is a foreign firm as well.

a. *Shifting demand: The choice of β*

It transpires that the marginal consumer is increasing in β: while a consumer initially indifferent between the two goods will favour the domestic product if their valuation of that product rises and prices are unchanged, the domestic firm will, in equilibrium, raise its price sufficiently that the marginal consumer will switch to purchasing the import. Furthermore, the increased domestic price means that all consumers of the domestic product will buy less of the good, given the downward-sloping individual demand curves. Nevertheless, considering the maximised utility of a consumer buying the domestic product, we can show that they are better off as β rises: the direct impact on welfare of their increased valuation is not offset by the induced price increase. Finally, all consumers who purchase the foreign good before an increase in β and continue to do so after the increase are unaffected by it. In sum, continued import buyers are unaffected by an increase in β, those who switch from the domestic good to the import are worse off (by revealed preference arguments) and those who continue to buy the domestic good are better off.

We can also show, unsurprisingly, that domestic profits are increasing in β as the domestic firm can charge more now that their good is more highly valued by consumers. The situation overall, then, is similar to the autarky case with incomplete market coverage except that the marginal consumer here is lost to the import good and not dropped from the market altogether. As in that case, we can show that welfare in trade is strictly increasing and convex in β.

This is in contrast to the autarky case with complete market coverage. Note that, with trade, as domestic consumers drop out of buying the domestic good (due to the induced price increase), they switch to purchasing the foreign good, rather than getting zero surplus, so the market is, in fact, covered. Nevertheless, an increase in β shrinks the foreign market share: the lower limit of their sales — the consumer with valuation $\beta - \varepsilon$ — is increasing in β more rapidly than is their upper limit at $\tilde{\beta}$. This is still attractive to a welfare-maximising government, however, for profit-shifting reasons.

Suppose the economy is endowed with laissez-faire values of β and ε given by (β^0, ε^0). If the cost of an information campaign to shift out demand for the local good in this fashion is $C(\beta - \beta^0)$ with $C(0) = C'(0) = 0, C' > 0$ and $C'' > 0$, then a domestic government would wish to raise b to the point where $\mathrm{d}W/\mathrm{d}\beta = C'(\beta)$.[15] Note, too, that a government in the pocket of the local firm and committed to maximising domestic profits would also wish to raise β, given that profits are monotonically increasing in β here too. However, it can be shown that welfare with trade is increasing in β more rapidly than is profit so the optimal level of β is higher than that which would be chosen by a profit-maximising government.

It is useful at this point to consider what actions, if any, might be taken by a foreign government in response to such a "buy local" campaign. While the world price of the foreign export is given, the consequence of this campaign is a reduction in the volume of exports. Clearly, foreign market share is also decreasing in p^* so, if there is any rent component in the export trade, a foreign government has an incentive to intervene to reduce the import price in the home country. An optimising foreign government will choose its intervention s^* so that $\frac{\mathrm{d}w^*}{\mathrm{d}p^*}\frac{\mathrm{d}p^*}{\mathrm{d}s^*} = 0$, where W^* denotes foreign welfare. Unsurprisingly, foreign exports are declining in p^* and we can show that a foreign government's optimal reaction to a "buy local" campaign in the home country is to adjust its intervention to reduce p^*. That is, the marginal effectiveness of a fall in p^* in increasing exports is increased by the domestic campaign. In such a case, a buy local campaign by the home government will trigger a foreign response that leads to a lower import price at home, at least partially undoing the campaign's efforts to induce greater sales, but reinforcing any positive welfare effects of the campaign through what is in essence a terms of trade effect.

Figure 5 presents some simulations for welfare as functions of β and ε in trade — a plot of profits is qualitatively isomorphic.[16] It turns out that both welfare and the profits of the domestic firm are increasing in β (as established) but, as discussed in Section 5 below, are non-monotonic in ε: for low values of β, both welfare and profits

[15]This assumes an interior solution, but the convexity of welfare in β means that the optimum may be reached only when imports have been driven to zero. If costs are sufficiently more convex than welfare, then we can meet this condition.

[16]Note that values in the simulations are set to zero where the parameters violate the cost or market share constraints.

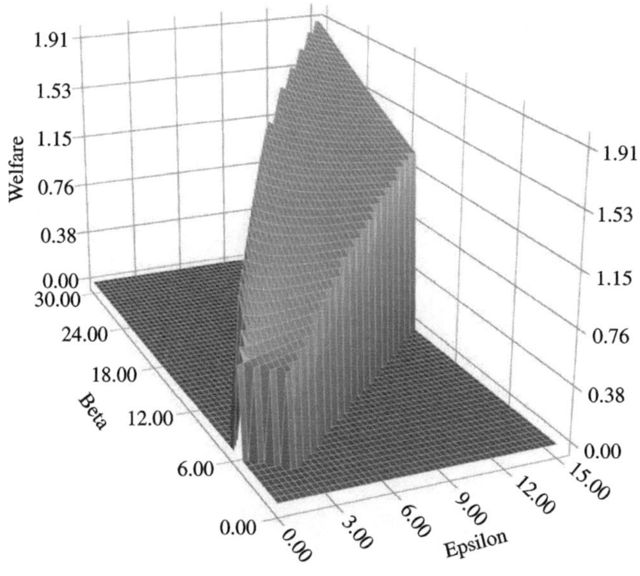

Fig. 5. Welfare in trade.

are increasing in ε, but when β is sufficiently high, profits decline monotonically in ε. As noted, the domestic market share rises with β and in Figure 5 it covers almost the entire range of [0,1].

We summarise this in the following proposition:

Proposition 2. *With trade, so long as imports are non-zero, increases in β raise both the firm's profits and welfare.*

b. *Trade liberalisation*

We turn now to consider how a policymaker might respond to falling trade costs (or export subsidies from trading partners). As noted before, we suppose there is some cost associated with an informational policy intervention. The government starts from some initial endowment (β^0, ε^0). An information campaign is costly with the costs increasing and convex in the fineness of information — that is, increasing in β.

Suppose, then, that the government is choosing some optimal informational campaign such that the marginal welfare gain of an increase in β is equal to its marginal cost. The online Appendix demonstrates that the marginal welfare gain from increasing β is itself increasing in p^*. Consequently, reduced trade costs or foreign policies that lead to a reduction in the price of the import good reduce the incentives for the local government to engage in an informational campaign that raises β. This is because a reduction in the world price reduces the marginal increase in profits from an increase in β: as the foreign good becomes more attractive so the incentive to increase demand for the domestic good falls.

We summarise this finding in the following proposition:

Proposition 3. *With trade, so long as imports are non-zero, falls in p^* will reduce the incentives of either a welfare-maximising or a profit-maximising government to raise β.*

We noted earlier the possibility that a "buy local" campaign might constitute the "re-creation" of border barriers to trade through domestic policy. But our results do not support this notion; on the contrary, trade liberalisation here reduces a government's interest in promoting a domestic industry through this sort of informational campaign. This occurs partly because the losses to consumers switching from imports to the domestic good are greater, the lower is the import price and partly because the market share of the domestic firm is lower, the lower the import price, so the profit-shifting gains from persuading consumers to buy the domestic good are smaller than if the market share was high to begin with.

This result might seem a little surprising on its face: that increased pressure on local producers, from a falling world price, reduces their government's incentives to invest in an informational campaign that benefits these domestic firms. We have already noted that domestic profits are increasing in β but it can also be shown straightforwardly that the responsiveness of profits to such an increase in demand is itself increasing in the world price, a result that is due to the fact that the domestic price — and thus mark-up over cost — is increasing in the world price. Thus, as p^* falls, so, too, does the domestic price and a marginal increase in domestic sales is less profitable. Consequently, this result applies whether the government is a welfare-maximiser or simply serves the interests of the domestic producer. Furthermore, one would anticipate that, even in a model of lobbying by domestic firms, this result would still prevail, as the incentive to lobby for assistance falls with the world price.[17]

5. Demand rotations

We now consider policy aimed at compactifying the support of the distribution from which consumers' idiosyncratic valuations are drawn. As explained in the Introduction, we consider this case to be useful in capturing the provision of real information to consumers, in JM's terms, rather than simply "hyping" the domestic product. As there is a great deal of ambiguity in the results here, our coverage here is rather summary; an expanded discussion is provided in the online Appendix.

a. *Autarky*

Consider again the case of autarky where the market is covered. In this setting, the effect on welfare of increasing dispersion in the δs is indeterminate: so long as the market is covered, higher ε induces a lower price, which will reduce the firm's profits — an effect that is more than offset by the consequent increased consumer surplus — but reduces aggregate consumer welfare directly. Where the market is uncovered, then only if the marginal consumer has an idiosyncratic valuation that is greater than the population average are domestic profits in autarky increasing in ε. Regarding a spread in the distribution of δ_i, the effect on welfare is indeterminate in sign, but it is certainly negative at low ε when the market is not covered (bearing in mind that the firm will choose to cover the market for sufficiently low ε).

All up, while profits are declining in ε, overall welfare is non-monotonic until the firm switches to incomplete market coverage at which point welfare decreases in ε. Figure 6 illustrates a numerical

---

[17] We are grateful to an anonymous referee for suggesting this discussion.

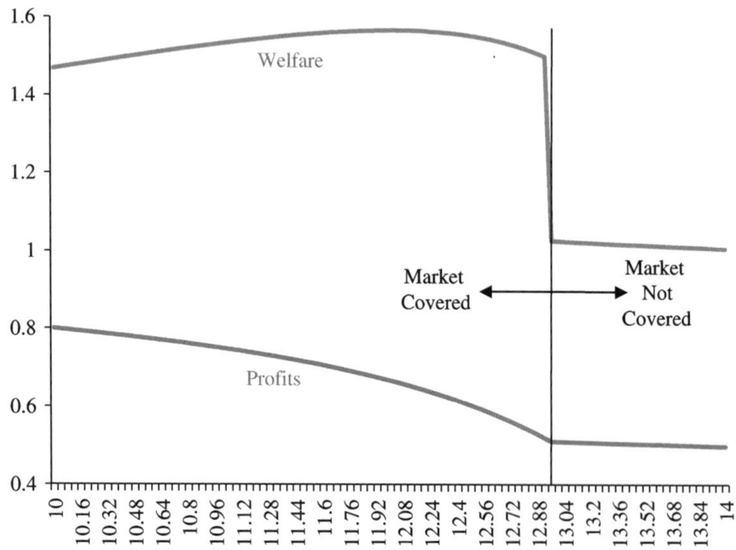

Fig. 6. Autarky changes in ε.

simulation of a typical case looking at changes in ε.[18] At lower values of ε, the market is covered completely, but a discrete fall in welfare occurs when ε is sufficiently high that the firm chooses to drop some consumers, as this involves a discrete change in market coverage.

Ignoring the costs associated with any campaign to reduce ε, note again that welfare is always highest where the market is completely covered. Consequently, a welfare-maximising government would wish to either reduce ε or leave it unchanged, depending on where the laissez-faire value ε^0 lies. This would (weakly) raise firm profits and so would also be undertaken by a government biased towards producer interests. The latter sort of government, however, would pursue more extreme policies in this case too — a lower ε than a welfare-maximising government.

[18]Details of the simulations are available on request. This example sets β to 15 and c to 1 and plots profit and welfare over a range of ε from 10 to 14. For low values of ε, we have complete market coverage, but the firm switches to covering only about 75 per cent of the market at around $\varepsilon = 13$ or so.

b. *Trade*

Turning to trade, the effect on domestic welfare of a change in ε cannot be signed in general, but we can consider a couple of special cases. At the upper limit of c, the expression is unambiguously positive: welfare is increasing in ε when costs are very high. One might argue that this is a relevant case in the context of "green" consumers: when the local good is relatively expensive to produce, providing finer information to consumers (lower ε) can be welfare-reducing as the resulting lower price reduces the home firm's profits and is not enough to offset the direct effects of lower valuations for low value consumers, who shift to the import good. At the other extreme, at the lowest feasible value of c we can show that $dW/d\varepsilon < 0$ so, when home production costs are low, a reduction in ε is welfare-improving.

c. *Trade liberalisation*

Now how might a policymaker respond to falling trade costs (or export subsidies from trading partners)? Again, suppose there is some cost associated with an informational policy intervention: the government starts from some initial endowment (β^0, ε^0) and an information campaign is costly with the costs, as before, increasing and convex in the fineness of information — that is, decreasing in ε — and we suppose that the cost to the government, $C_\varepsilon(\varepsilon^0 - \varepsilon)$, is such that $C'_\varepsilon(\cdot) \geq 0, C_\varepsilon(0) = C'_\varepsilon(0) = 0$ and $C''_{\hat{\varepsilon}} > 0$.[19]

For a campaign with regard to ε, while we can generate no clear analytical results, Figure 7 displays a numerical simulation[20] in which, at high world prices, the marginal welfare effect of raising ε is negative, suggesting an interventionist campaign to reduce is ε

[19]It is worth noting that we do not permit the government to misinform consumers in terms of raising ε (as we did not consider it choosing to discourage consumers by reducing β). One might, for example, consider a set-up in which the government could vary ε away from ε^0 symmetrically, incurring increasing costs either way (for example, $C_\varepsilon(\varepsilon) = (\varepsilon - \varepsilon^0)^2$) which would allow the government to widen the support of the δ distribution. We do not consider this, so a feature of our analysis is that the optimal level of ε may be unattainable: if ε^0 is less than the optimal value of ε, then there is nothing that the government can do to improve welfare with this sort of campaign.

[20]Note that the graph has been rotated to make the marginal impact of changes in p^* on the welfare effects of changes in ε more clear, and p^* is falling as we go from the front to the back.

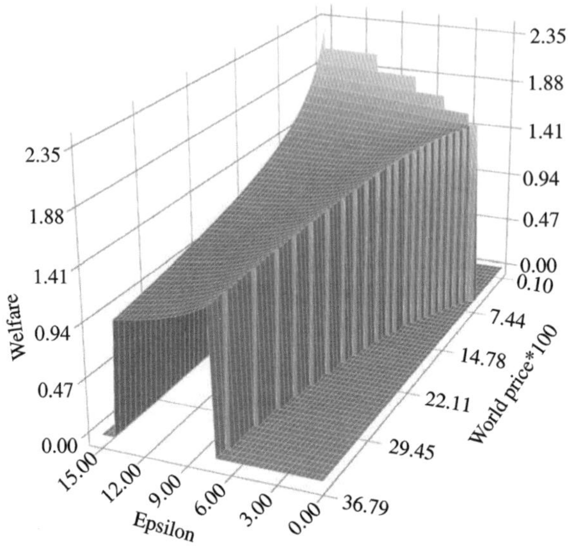

Fig. 7. Welfare in trade over ε and p^*.

is likely, but, at low world prices quite the reverse obtains: welfare is increasing in ε.[21]

6. Concluding remarks

This paper has made a first step in analysing the effects of and incentives for governments to fund information campaigns about domestic goods designed either to simply persuade consumers to buy more of a local good or to better inform consumers about inherent characteristics of domestic versus foreign goods. In the former case, a campaign shifts out the demand curve for the local good; in the latter, it will rotate it anticlockwise.

We show that, in autarky, a welfare or profit-maximising government will want the market to be covered but that the former will typically not wish to shift out or flatten the demand curve without

[21]The same qualitative effects hold for profits: at high p^*, profits are declining in ε but at low p^*, they are increasing. So a profit-maximising government would have the same qualitative incentives as does a welfare-maximiser.

limit, in contrast to a profit-maximising government. With trade, however, welfare is monotonically increasing as the demand for the domestic good shifts out, until imports are squeezed out altogether: complete market coverage by the domestic firm. The welfare effects of a mean-preserving spread in the distribution of valuations are analytically unclear, but simulations suggest that such a spread is desirable when demand is low but, if domestic valuations are uniformly high, a reduction in the spread of such valuations becomes attractive.

A key policy implication of our analysis comes from the finding that the government of a foreign exporter would respond aggressively to a domestic buy local campaign. Furthermore, we show that such a campaign is less attractive to a local government following reduced trade costs, for example through trade liberalisation. Thus, the notion that a buy local campaign can simply recreate border barriers postliberalisation is not supported by our analysis.

Supporting information

Formal calculations and derivations may be found in the online technical appendix of this article:
Appendix S1. Technical Supplement.

References

Bagwell, K. (2007). The Economic Analysis of Advertising. In M. Armstrong and R. Porter (eds.), *Handbook of Industrial Organization*, Vol. 3, pp. 1701–844. Amsterdam: North-Holland.

Chiou, J.-R., J.-L. Hu and Y.-S. Lin (2003). "Buy domestic" campaigns and optimal tariffs. *Journal of Economics*, 80(2), 143–60.

Desrochers, P. and H. Shimuzu (2008). Yes, We Have No Bananas: A Critique of the "Food Miles" Perspective. Policy Primer No. 8, Mercatus Policy Series. Arlington VA: Mercatus Center, George Mason University.

Dinopoulos, E., G. Livanis and C. West (2010). Country of origin labeling (C.O.O.L.): How cool is it? *International Review of Economics and Finance*, 19(4), 575–89.

Dixit, A. and V. Norman (1978). Advertising and welfare. *The Bell Journal of Economics*, 9(1), 1–17.

Johnson, P. and D. Myatt (2006). On the simple economics of advertising, marketing, and product design. *American Economic Review*, 96(3), 756–84.

Kotchen, M. J. (2006). Green markets and private provision of public goods. *Journal of Political Economy*, 114(4), 816–34.

Mason, C. (2006). *On the Use of Consumer Information to Address Externalities: The Economics of eco-Labelling.* Mimeo Laramie WY: Department of Economics and Finance, University of Wyoming.

McCracken, S. (2012). *Informative Advertising Under Duopoly.* Mimeo (Canberra: Research School of Economics, CBE, ANU).

Podhorsky, A. (2008). *Environmental Labelling.* Toronto, Mimeo: York University.

Robertson, P. (2007). Global resources and eco-labels: A neutrality result. *Review of International Economics*, 15(4), 735–43.

Saunders, C. and P. Hayes (2007). Air Freight Transport of Fresh Fruit and Vegetables. Research Report 299 (Lincoln, Lincoln University).

Wilson, T. (2007). IPA. Review July 2007. Institute of Public Affairs, Australia. Available at: http:// www.ipa.org.au/library/59_2_WILSON_ FoodMiles.pdf (accessed 13 January 2016).

Index